FOUNTAINHEAD OF JIHAD

Drawing upon a wealth of previously unresearched primary sources in many languages, the authors shed new light on a group frequently described as the most lethal actor in the current Afghan insurgency. For decades the Haqqani network has been at the centre of a nexus of transnational Islamist militancy fostering the development of jihadi organizations from Southeast Asia to East Africa. Bringing to light abundant new evidence documenting the Haqqani network's pivotal role in the birth and evolution of the global jihadi movement, the book also advances our knowledge of the history of Al-Qaeda, and fundamentally alters the picture painted by existing literature on the subject.

*

Vahid Brown is a specialist in the history of Islamist militancy and the author of *Cracks in the Foundation: Leadership Schisms in al-Qa'ida, 1989-2006.*

Don Rassler is an instructor in the Department of Social Sciences and director of the Harmony Research Program at the Combating Terrorism Center at the United States Military Academy at West Point.

Praise for *Fountainhead of Jihad*

'[This book] is a tremendous compendium of information on local, regional and global dimensions and designs of the HQN known to date.' – *Outlook India*

'Compelling… *Fountainhead of Jihad* suggests we will have to rethink our understanding of the Haqqani network, its motivation and its worldview at a crucial time, just as international forces withdraw and pressure for peace talks intensifies… In placing the Haqqani network not so much at the centre of the extremist nexus but at its origin, this book makes an important contribution to our understanding of Afghan and Pakistani militant groups.' – Rob Crilly, *Daily Telegraph*

'The conventional wisdom is that the Haqqanis simply host Al-Qaeda, but the authors paint a much more intimate picture to illustrate that the group has served, and continues to serve, as a platform from which Al-Qaeda wages its global jihad… This book should be required reading for anyone working on security issues in South Asia or the evolution of the jihadist movement globally.' – Stephen Tankel, *Foreign Policy*, author of *Storming the World Stage: The Story of Lashkar-e-Taiba*

VAHID BROWN
DON RASSLER

Fountainhead of Jihad

The Haqqani Nexus

hachette
INDIA

First published in the United Kingdom in 2013 by
C. Hurst & Co. (Publishers) Ltd.
41 Great Russell Street, London, WC1B3PL

First published in India in 2013 by Hachette India
(Registered name: Hachette Book Publishing India Pvt. Ltd)
An Hachette UK company
www.hachetteindia.com

This edition published in 2016

SRD

ISBN 978-93-5195-099-8

Hachette Book Publishing India Pvt. Ltd
4th & 5th Floors, Corporate Centre,
Plot No. 94, Sector 44,
Gurgaon 122003, India

Printed and bound in India by
Manipal Technologies Limited, Manipal

CONTENTS

Authors' Acknowledgements vii
List of Illustrations ix

Introduction 1

PART I

ESTABLISHMENT AND HISTORICAL EVOLUTION OF THE HAQQANI NEXUS

1. Situating the Haqqanis: Origins, Political Culture, Regional Contexts 21
2. Birth of the Nexus: the Haqqani Network, Foreign Fighters, and the Origins of al-Qa'ida 59
3. The Fountainhead: The Haqqani Network, The Taliban, and the Rise of Global Jihad 83

PART II

CONTINUITY, VALUE, CHANGE, AND THE HAQQANI NEXUS POST-2001

4. Local: Pakistani Taliban Factions and Other Local Insurgent Units 129
5. Regional: The Pakistani State and its Inter-Services Intelligence Directorate 151
6. Global: al-Qa'ida and Other Global Jihadist Groups 183

7. Entanglements and Management of the Haqqanis' Nexus Position 219
Conclusion 235

Notes 245
Bibliography 295
Index 307

AUTHORS' ACKNOWLEDGEMENTS

This book would not have been possible without the assistance provided by many people over several years, and in the course of writing it we have incurred a number of debts.

First, we owe a special thanks to Thomas Hegghammer.

Our partner Ahmed was responsible for all Pashto and Urdu translations found within the text and without his talent and assistance this book would have lacked important nuance and the presentation of these primary sources. It is our hope that he will build upon this work in his future endeavors and give voice to additional Pashto and Urdu materials and the contributions of Afghans to other facets of history.

A similar thank you needs to be extended to the staff at the Afghanistan Center at Kabul University and to Atifa Rawan at the University of Arizona for facilitating access to some of the primary sources we used. The National Endowment for Humanities should also be commended for their wisdom in supporting efforts to preserve these and other rare documents found within Afghanistan.

This book was much improved by the helpful feedback and criticism that we received from the four anonymous reviewers of our manuscript. We also appreciate the comments and suggestions provided by Thomas Hegghammer, Thomas Ruttig, Nelly Lahoud, Gretchen Peters, and Robert Nickelsberg, who all reviewed an earlier version of our work.

Jere Van Dyk, Pir Zubayr Shah, Anand Gopal, Morten Skoldager, and others who cannot be named provided critical insights and firsthand perspectives on a range of topics.

Our gratitude also goes to the Combating Terrorism Center at West Point for supporting our initial research into the Haqqani network and for publishing an earlier report of our work.

For his excellent work on our graphics and maps we are thankful for the skill of Rami Moghadam.

Rassler appreciated the support provided by a number of mentors, friends, and colleagues, especially Liam Collins, Rob Greenway, David Asher, Mike Pease, Christopher O'Leary and Jenna Watson for their efforts to facilitate opportunities and help him make a broader impact. He is also extremely grateful for the leadership and support provided by Mike Meese, Cindy Jebb, John Abizaid, Vinnie Viola, and Bill Ostlund, and for the assistance provided by his Harmony comrades. The friendship and advice of Assaf Moghadam and Alex Gallo, have been equally as valuable. His biggest thank you, however, goes to G and his family, as without them and their sacrifices and patience none of this would have been possible.

Brown would like to extend his gratitude to Kevin Bell, David Bikman, Will McCants, and Brian Fishman for all the helpful conversations and editorial insights. Thanks to Cyrus Schayegh and Şükrü Hanioğlu for their comments on early versions of two of the chapters. To all the friends and family in Portland, Tacoma, and Princeton: this wouldn't have been possible without your support.

Finally, we would like to thank Michael Dwyer and the rest of the team at Hurst for supporting this project.

Vahid Brown
Princeton, NJ

Don Rassler
New York, NY

LIST OF ILLUSTRATIONS

(after Introduction)

Fig. 1: Haqqani fighter using an anti-aircraft gun during the anti-Soviet jihad period.

Fig. 2: Entrance to the Zhawara base.

Fig. 3: Abdullah Azzam.

Fig. 4: Jalaluddin Haqqani recovering from injuries sustained during a Soviet and Afghan assault on his Zhawara base in 1987.

Fig. 5: *Nusrat al-Jihad* cover with Jalaluddin Haqqani and Zia ul-Haq.

Fig. 6: Jalaluddin Haqqani and Sami ul-Haq in a General Gathering of the Jamiat-e-Ulama-e-Islam in Lahore, Pakistan, April 1991.

Fig. 7: Jalaluddin Haqqani with Gulf Sheikhs.

Fig. 8: The Manba' 'Ulum madrassa, in North Waziristan, Pakistan circa 1989.

Fig. 9: Jalaluddin Haqqani (back seated row, third from right), Ahmed Shah Massoud (to his right), Abdul Haq (in white with Afghan pakool) and leaders at the National Commanders Shura, May 1990.

Fig. 10: Ibrahim Haqqani after the capture of Khost garrison in 1991.

Fig. 11: Uighur fighters cleaning guns in Khost, 1990.

Fig. 12: Ibrahim Haqqani being interviewed by Rahimullah Yusufzai and Lyse Doucet after the capture of Khost in 1991.

Fig. 13: Burhanuddin Rabbani with Jalaluddin Haqqani in the weapons room at the Zhawara base.
Fig. 14: Poster of Osama bin Laden captured at the Zhawara base after the U.S. invasion of Afghanistan in October 2001.
Fig. 15: Screen grab from a Haqqani network video of President Barack Obama giving the commencement address at the U.S. Military Academy at West Point, 22 May 2010.
Fig. 16: Screen grab of the emir of the Pakistani Taliban, Hakimullah Mehsud, sitting with Jordanian suicide bomber, Humam Khalil Abu-Mulal al-Balawi (Abu Dujanah al-Khorasani) before his attack against Forward Operating Base Chapman in December 2009.

KAZAKHSTAN
KYRGYZSTAN
UZBEKISTAN
TAJIKISTAN
CHINA
TURKMENISTAN
Mazar-e-Sharif
Jalalabad
KASHMIR
Peshawar
Herat
Kabul
AFGHANISTAN
Islamabad
Khost
Miran Shah
Lahore
Kandahar
Quetta
PAKISTAN
IRAN
INDIA
Karachi
ARABIAN SEA
N
200 mi
500 km

Map 1

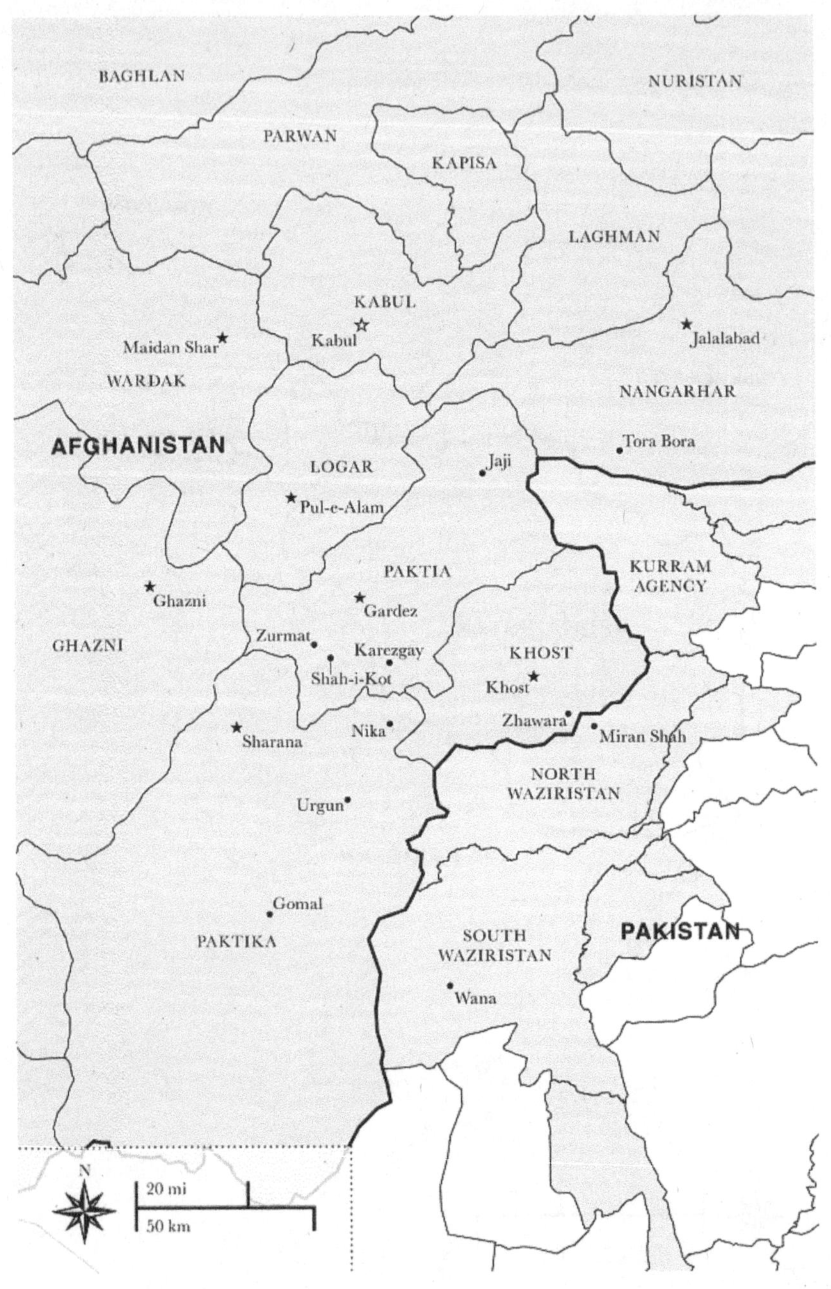
BAGHLAN
NURISTAN
PARWAN
KAPISA
LAGHMAN
KABUL
Kabul
Maidan Shar
WARDAK
Jalalabad
NANGARHAR
AFGHANISTAN
Tora Bora
Jaji
LOGAR
Pul-e-Alam
KURRAM
AGENCY
PAKTIA
Ghazni
Gardez
GHAZNI
Zurmat
Karezgay
KHOST
Shah-i-Kot
Khost
Zhawara
Miran Shah
Nika
Sharana
NORTH
WAZIRISTAN
Urgun
Gomal
PAKTIKA
SOUTH
WAZIRISTAN
PAKISTAN
Wana
N
20 mi
50 km

Map 2

NANGARHAR
Landi Kotal
KHYBER AGENCY
Parachinar
PAKTIA
Kalaya
KURRAM AGENCY
ORAKZAI AGENCY
AFGHANISTAN
KOHAT
HANGU
KHOST
FR BANNU
KARAK
Danday Darpakhel
Miran Shah
Mir Ali
Data Khel
BANNU
NORTH WAZIRISTAN
Razmak
MIANWALI
FR LAKKI MARWAT
LAKKI MARWAT
FEDERALLY ADMINISTERED TRIBAL AREAS
FR TANK
SOUTH WAZIRISTAN
TANK
PAKISTAN
Wana
DERA ISMAIL KHAN
BHAKKAR
SHEERANI
FR DERA ISMAIL KHAN
ZHOB
N
15 mi
40 km
LAYYAH

Map 3

INTRODUCTION

As we prepared this book for press it seemed that the Haqqani network scarcely needed any introduction. The network began consistently making international headlines with a July 2008 suicide attack on the Indian Embassy in Kabul, followed by a years-long campaign of high-profile attacks in the Afghan capital that shows no signs of abating. On 13 September 2011 the Haqqanis staged the longest and most audacious attack in the capital since the beginning of the war, raining a twenty-hour barrage of rockets and gunfire from the unfinished upper floors of a high-rise building upon the embassies of Kabul's diplomatic neighborhood.[1] At the end of the following week, the outgoing chairman of the Joint Chiefs of Staff Admiral Mike Mullen set off a storm of international controversy by declaring in US Senate testimony that the Haqqani network acts as "a veritable arm" of the ISI, Pakistan's powerful intelligence agency.[2] These comments and the ensuing media frenzy made public what many policy insiders had long known: that the Haqqani network is one of the most powerful forces in the Afghan insurgency, and among the most important points of conflict in the troubled relationship between the United States and Pakistan.

Yet if barely a week goes by these days without the Haqqani network making the front page, when we began our research over three years ago it was still an obscure group to most people, including many involved in regional policy. The Haqqani network was not even known as such in the West until 2006. The appellation first appears in a diplomatic cable sent to Washington on 18 January of that year from Richard Norland, then chief of mission at the US Embassy in Kabul. Discussing a recent series of bomb attacks in the city of Khost, the cable notes that "Khost Governor [Merajuddin] Pathan is convinced that the bombings were the work of the Haqqani Network, operating out of Miram Shah in Pakistan's North Waziristan."[3] Only one other 2006 usage of the term appears in the diplomatic cable traffic leaked by the WikiLeaks organization, a 2 July 2006 cable in which, again, the term is used in a passage summarizing statements made by an Afghan official.[4] Beginning in 2007, however, the phrase is used with increasing frequency in cable traffic, reflecting its entry by that time into wider usage in the Western press, following its appearance in Senate testimony delivered by Rear Admiral Robert Moeller in March 2006.[5]

A sense of how the Haqqanis were understood in these early references to the newfound "network" is perhaps best summarized by Admiral Moeller's testimony:

> The Haqqani Tribal Network, which has ties to the Taliban, operates primarily in eastern Afghanistan and the FATA region of Pakistan. Haqqani goals are limited primarily to obtaining autonomy in eastern Afghanistan and the FATA region. Although the most tactically proficient of the enemy we face in Afghanistan, they present a limited strategic threat.[6]

This has been the standard view of the Haqqani network ever since, and it is generally accurate as far as it goes. But we felt from our previous research on the history of al-Qa'ida and regional conflict that there was a larger story being missed here, a larger significance to the organization not reflected in the assessment of the Haqqani network by those that first named it so in 2006, nor in the secondary or historiographic literature. So we assembled and studied a unique archive consisting of thousands of pages of Haqqani-relevant primary sources that others before us had not. What we found, ultimately, is the *Fountainhead of Jihad*.

The title of our book was the name of a series of magazines published by the Haqqanis in the 1980s and 1990s, as well as a media "studio" that has been producing and distributing Haqqani propaganda videos in more recent years. It is, in other words, the Haqqanis' brand. This is not a metaphor, as the Haqqani network quite literally had something to sell, and the nature of their product is directly advertised in the brand itself. Since the late 1970s the Haqqani network has provided a variety of state sponsors, private donors, and entrepreneur revolutionaries with a particularly valuable resource in the global economy of conflict: a platform for the delivery of violence. The Haqqanis' provision of this service has reaped for them a great deal of wealth and local power, and has given them a hitherto unrecognized influence in violent conflicts far beyond the border hinterlands where they reside. This book, through the lens of the primary sources, explores the Haqqani network's rise to this position of power in the conflict economy. Understanding that rise requires an unpacking of the three key terms used in our title, which also serve as the central themes of the chapters that follow: fountainhead, jihad, and nexus.

Fountainhead

The Haqqani network magazines and video production studio are called, in Arabic, *Manba' al-Jihad*. A *manba'* is a wellspring, platform, or source, a site from which something originates or flows forth. But what did it mean for the Haqqanis to offer a platform of jihad, which we will gloss for now simply as violence, in a series of magazines that provided bank account routing numbers for potential customers right on the covers? What kind of production site were they advertising, and how did they come to be in a position to put it on the market in the first place?

One very simple way in which this Haqqani network value proposition has been understood is in terms of safe haven. Indeed, in recent years the Haqqanis have used their influence in North Waziristan to provide shelter to a disparate group of international malcontents all seeking to deliver violence against various states. Uighurs opposing China's rule of its Muslim-majority northwest; Uzbeks at war with the government of Uzbekistan; Pakistanis at war with India, Pakistan, and in some cases both; and the polyglot group of al-Qa'ida supporters fighting to undermine an American-dominated international system—all have taken refuge with the Haqqanis on Pakistan's highland frontier. But understanding the Haqqanis' offer of a fountainhead of violence in these terms alone ignores the much broader support the Haqqani network provided to these groups for many years prior to 9/11. More importantly, it obscures the relationship between the Haqqanis' capacity to provide such support to these relatively marginal groups on the one hand, and the Haqqani network's earlier dealings with much larger and wealthier clients on the other. It was the latter—and in particular Pakistan and the United States—that enabled the Haqqanis to establish the fountainhead, to consolidate their territorial dominance, and to become primary producers of violence in their own right in the decades-long Afghan conflict. Direct American support for the Haqqani network ended in the early 1990s; the Pakistani state relationship continues to this day.

The Haqqani network's area of operation, the place of the fountainhead, straddles the Durand Line, which is more of a geopolitical fault line than an international border dividing Afghanistan from Pakistan. The Haqqani network's early members all hailed from southeastern Afghanistan and studied in the late 1960s at the Haqqaniyya seminary in northwestern Pakistan. Rooted in both countries, the Haqqanis proved particularly well suited to facilitating a conflict between the two states, one centering initially on the ultimate status of the Pashtun homelands bisected by the Durand Line. For reasons explored in greater depth in Chapter 1, the Haqqanis sided with Pakistan in this dispute, and because of this alliance their area of operation in Afghanistan developed into the single richest pipeline for war materiel servicing the anti-Soviet conflict during the 1980s.

Pakistan's military support for the Haqqanis began in the 1970s when Pakistan looked to Afghan Islamists opposed to a Moscow-leaning Afghan government to serve as its agents in a tit-for-tat Pak-Afghan proxy war. Pakistan's most famous Afghan partners in this conflict were urban Islamist elites who had fled Kabul for the Pakistani border city of Peshawar. Most of these men had no roots in the highland tribal areas on the Afghan side of the Durand Line, nor any infrastructure there with which to mobilize resources for a sustained campaign of anti-regime violence. The Haqqani network did. More importantly, the southeastern region where the Haqqanis originated and where they began their 1970s jihad against the

Afghan government was singularly blessed in terms of strategic space. Mountainous and peopled by tribes who had long maintained a significant degree of autonomy from the state center, the region known as Loya Paktia was easily defended—especially as the heights overlooking the areas along the border lie on the Pakistani side. It was also relatively close to Kabul and even closer to Jalalabad, and so could pose a real threat to two cities that were strategically vital to the regime, including the capital. Long-standing ties of tribal solidarity and cooperation in shared struggles against state intervention meant that the Haqqanis and their Afghan tribal allies would have no trouble finding refuge and support from just over the border, and from the mid-1970s the Haqqanis were based just as much in Pakistan's North Waziristan Tribal Agency as they were in the Afghan southeast.

After the Soviet Union invaded Afghanistan in 1979, the Haqqanis' advantageous strategic location and well-developed capacity for mobilizing the tribes for war made them among the most favored recipients of the massive amounts of military and financial aid that the United States, Saudi Arabia, and several other states poured into Pakistan to counter the Soviet advance. With money from the CIA and Pakistan's Inter-Services Intelligence Directorate (ISI), and using Saudi contractors, a sprawling base and supply depot was built at Zhawara in the province of Khost and put under the Haqqanis' command. Flying in the face of guerrilla warfare doctrine, the Pakistani military decided that this base would be a fortified fixed position and principal node for distributing war materiel to the Afghan resistance from within the country. When attacked by Soviet and Afghan forces, the ISI and Pakistani army twice deployed forces to defend the base, the only instances of this kind of direct cross-border incursion by Pakistan in the entire conflict.

With control of this strategic asset, the Haqqanis' position was further consolidated throughout the 1980s by hundreds of millions of dollars worth of military aid provided directly by the ISI and CIA. According to the CIA official in charge of the provision of American assistance to the Afghan mujahidin, 60,000 tons of materiel were shipped across the border from Pakistan every year.[7] The ISI official responsible for the distribution of this massive resource supply to the various resistance parties has written that 20 percent of these supplies were routed directly to the Haqqanis at Zhawara.[8] This would mean that, by their own estimates, the ISI and CIA supplied the Haqqanis with at least 12,000 tons of war materiel every year during the 1980s conflict with the Soviet Union in Afghanistan. The Haqqani network thus served as a fountainhead of violence without parallel during that conflict.

From Zhawara the Haqqanis supplied resistance groups throughout the south and east of Afghanistan, and in that sense alone it is clear that the Haqqanis were more than local actors, concerned only with regional autonomy. Moreover, their very local autonomy was predicated upon the unrivalled access to resources afforded them by their ISI and CIA relationships. But from the mid-1980s the Haqqanis' fountainhead began to service conflicts much further afield as well. Pakistan's military dictator Zia ul-Haq is reported to have said in 1980 that "the biggest share of the international arms and American financial assistance" would be given to "whoever trains our boys from Kashmir."[9] The areas surrounding the Haqqanis' Zhawara base became the central facility for this training initiative in Afghanistan, and the Haqqani network continued to host and support these camps, with direct ISI involvement, until September 2001. And it was not just holy warriors bound for Kashmir who benefited from the Haqqanis' Zhawara training complex. Al-Qa'ida established its first major camps in the Zhawara Valley, and it was from these camps that it declared war on the United States in the late 1990s. The Uighurs, Uzbeks, and other Asian and Arab militant groups that shelter today with the Haqqani network in North Waziristan also trained in the Zhawara camps. As these groups continue to wage their various revolutionary struggles from the Haqqani network's strongholds on the Pakistani frontier, the Haqqanis remain to this day intertwined in cycles of violence that extend throughout the world.

Jihad

The Haqqani network's clients, be they states or anti-state revolutionaries, have not sought the Haqqanis' services for the delivery of violence in some abstract sense. The Haqqanis' brand indicates a fountainhead of "jihad," of violence specifically sanctioned by Islam. The way this term is understood and deployed by so-called jihadi groups taking recourse to political violence is of relatively recent origins however, and was the product of a profound transformation in the theory and practice of jihad wrought during the last quarter of the twentieth century. The Haqqanis played a key role in this transformation, though this fact has not previously been recognized.

The term jihad, which literally means struggle, has been employed for multiple purposes during the past century. From the political activism of the Muslim Brotherhood in Egypt to the international missionary work of the Tablighi Jama'at, the appropriation of this term by different actors in the contemporary world has not always referred to organized violence. Even in the case of the latter there are many variations and ambiguities, from irredentist liberation struggles to revolutionary political violence against repressive regimes. There is no question, however, that the concept of jihad as a category of action around which large numbers of people mobilized for collective struggle underwent a profound transformation in the context of the Afghan–Soviet war of the 1980s. One critical site of that transformation was the Haqqanis' fountainhead of jihad.

In the sense used by al-Qa'ida, jihad has come to mean universal, privatized, volunteer militarism in asymmetrical conflict with a globally distributed enemy. This phenomenon—also known as global jihadism—arose in large part due to the initiative of two famous Arab supporters of the anti-Soviet mujahidin: 'Abdullah 'Azzam and Osama bin Laden. 'Azzam has long been credited with issuing the foundational Islamic legal decisions declaring the Afghan jihad a universally and individually binding duty borne by all Muslims worldwide. As documented in Chapter 2, however, Jalaluddin Haqqani preceded 'Azzam in this innovation by several years, and was the first Afghan Islamist known to have actively recruited Arab foreign fighters into his ranks. The Haqqanis also figured prominently in the propaganda through which 'Azzam first popularized this notion of global jihadism throughout the Arab world. As for Bin Laden, his most important contribution to global jihadism was in establishing al-Qa'ida, the earliest form of which was a training camp that, as one early eyewitness put it, was "advertised as forming the nucleus of an Islamic army capable of fighting jihad anywhere in the world."[10] That camp was established just north of the Zhawara base, using construction equipment from that base, and employing Arab trainers that had fought for years alongside the Haqqanis in the southeast. The founder of al-Qa'ida, its first two military leaders, and the man credited with crafting its anti-American strategy, all began their careers in jihad as volunteer fighters at Haqqani network fronts. Al-Qa'ida and the Haqqani network, in other words, evolved together, and they have remained intertwined throughout their history. They remain so to this day.

Al-Qa'ida's particular brand of sacralized global violence was not the only form of militant Islamism to emerge from the Haqqani network's fountainhead of jihad. Veterans of Haqqani battlefields and alumni of the Zhawara camps figure prominently in a bewildering variety of contemporary jihadisms. From North Africa to the North Caucasus, the Persian Gulf to the Philippines, a truly global coterie of militant groups has been actively supported by the Haqqani network through training, fundraising, and propaganda services. Though the Haqqanis established this network of relationships during the 1980s and 1990s, they did not cease with the American invasion of Afghanistan in 2001. As discussed throughout Part II of this book, the Haqqanis continue to provide valuable services to a diverse group of regional and transnational militants from their haven in North Waziristan.

Nexus

In light of the fact that North Waziristan falls nominally under the sovereignty of a "frontline partner" in the US-led global war on non-state terrorism, one naturally wonders how the Haqqani network is able to maintain these connections to transnational jihadism. A similar question could be raised about the Haqqanis' support for jihadi groups in the 1990s. As discussed in Chapter 3, the Taliban regime was under intense international pressure to crack down on non-Afghan militants operating from within their borders, and the

Taliban leadership took a number of measures in the last years of their rule to do just that. The Haqqani network, however, remained effectively outside Taliban control, and Taliban restrictions on al-Qa'ida and other jihadis were easily circumvented in Haqqani-controlled Khost. Why was this so? How, in other words, was the Haqqani network able to maintain their autonomy from state control and keep the fountainhead of jihad in business during all these years?

The answer lies in a complicated set of relations to local, regional, and global allies, clients and resource providers, whose various interests and goals have often been in direct contradiction with each other. The Haqqani network has survived for nearly forty years in an extremely volatile region of the world, and it has done so primarily through a careful balancing act that has kept it at the center of a nexus of violence. The dynamics of this nexus are explored at length in Part II, but its contours can be grasped by briefly considering the Haqqanis' triangle of relations with the Pakistani Taliban, the Pakistani military, and al-Qa'ida.

Respectively representing the local, regional, and global dimensions of the Haqqani nexus, these are not three groups that one would expect to find sharing a single partner. Al-Qa'ida and large segments of the Pakistani Taliban—in particular the Tehrik-e Taliban Pakistan (TTP)—are at war with the Pakistani state, and despite their differences, Pakistan does aid the United States in the latter's drone war on al-Qa'ida and the TTP. Yet all three of these groups rely on the Haqqanis as a platform for the delivery of violence that serves their various interests, and in ways that mutually reinforce the Haqqani network's position of power in North Waziristan and Loya Paktia.

All three of these groups rely on the Haqqanis for the latter's unparalleled capacity to deliver anti-regime and anti-Coalition violence in Afghanistan—a capacity that, again, is itself built partly on the Haqqanis' relations with these groups. Pakistan is determined to limit the influence of its archrival India in Afghanistan, and the Haqqanis have proven willing to direct their violence toward this end. The 2008 Indian Embassy bombing in Kabul is perhaps the most notable example. The Afghan government's defense ministry, moreover, is led largely by former leaders of the pre-2001 Northern Alliance, an anti-Taliban coalition that was supported by India. Pakistan continues to view these men as pro-India and thus hostile to Pakistan's interests. All of the Haqqani network's anti-regime violence is therefore viewed by the Pakistani military establishment as weakening India's position in Afghanistan. No other segment of the Afghan insurgency can offer the Pakistani military the same level of capability in delivering destabilizing violence to the Afghan capital. So long as Pakistan's army remains committed to unilaterally shaping the post-American future of Afghanistan in its perceived interests, the Haqqani network will continue to be a valuable asset of the military.

In addition to the provision of safe havens, al-Qa'ida relies on the Haqqanis to provide access to a symbolically important front against the "Zionist-Crusader" occupiers of Afghanistan. For years al-Qa'ida has been sending its fighters with Haqqani commanders carrying out attacks in the southeast, though the most important weapon al-Qa'ida has brought to these fights is a video camera. Dozens of videos have been produced in this way, allowing al-Qa'ida to capitalize on this Haqqani-assisted access in the form of recruitment and fundraising productions. Al-Qa'ida's media efforts attract further resources for violence in North Waziristan, though how much this directly benefits the Haqqani network is not entirely clear. The Uighur Turkestan Islamic Party and the Uzbek-dominated Islamic Jihad Union have adopted the same symbiotic practices, repackaging their Haqqani-facilitated involvement in the fight in the southeast as resource-generating propaganda videos.

Since 2007 the various Pakistani Taliban militias have directed much of their violence against Islamabad, though initially the raison d'être of these groups was supporting the Afghan fight against foreign invaders. The Mehsud tribes that dominate the TTP today do not occupy territory contiguous with Afghanistan, and they rely on the Haqqanis to facilitate access to the Afghan battlefields and provide in-country military leadership for their fighters. The TTP has a material interest at stake here: if they cannot send men to the fight, they cannot raise men or money for the fight. In this sense their business model relies heavily on the Haqqani network's fountainhead services.

All three of these groups also rely on the Haqqanis for the latter's diplomatic "good offices." The Pakistani state has repeatedly turned to the Haqqanis to negotiate on its behalf with the TTP and other Pakistani militants based in the tribal areas, negotiations that have resulted in a number of infamous peace accords that have effectively ceded sovereignty in parts of the tribal areas to the Haqqanis and their allies and have included in some cases the release of TTP leaders from Pakistani prisons. According to one source, Iran even turned to the Haqqani network when one of its diplomats was kidnapped in Peshawar, and the Haqqanis allegedly secured the release of the hostage in return for the release of a number of prominent al-Qa'ida members from Iranian custody.[11] The Haqqanis were recently called upon to assist in settling a long-running sectarian war between Sunni and Shi'i tribes in Kurram Agency. Its ability to intervene effectively in these instances and to help regulate levels of intra-Pakistani violence underscores the ways in which the Haqqani network's status as a proxy of the Pakistani state is not limited to the latter's interests in Afghanistan.

For its part, the Haqqani network derives clear benefits from this triangle of relations. Its value as a "strategic asset" to Pakistan has proven so great that the latter has not taken any significant measures to restrict the Haqqani network's activities or curtail its power, despite unrelenting pressure from the United States to do so. There seems little doubt that the Pakistani military establishment is the Haqqanis' most valuable partner, for without the effective impunity afforded them by the state they would be unable to provide services to or derive benefit from their local and transnational militant allies. The Haqqanis' relationship with the Pakistani Taliban provides them with tens of thousands of reserve foot soldiers. The Pakistani Taliban's reliance on the Haqqani network for access to Afghanistan gives the Haqqanis a certain degree of influence over the TTP's direction of violence, a card that considerably strengthens their hand with the Pakistani state. Al-Qa'ida continues to provide the Haqqanis with a global media platform and a highly visible profile within its constituency of potential donors and supporters. More tangibly, the Haqqani network has made extremely lethal use of al-Qa'ida's innovative tactics and technologies of violence, introducing suicide attacks into Afghanistan and reportedly importing IED technologies developed by al-Qa'ida in Iraq.[12]

Unresolved Tensions

Despite the various ways in which the Haqqanis clearly benefit from their alliance with al-Qa'ida, a good argument could be made that the relationship is actually more of a liability than an asset for the Haqqani network. From the cruise missile strikes on its camps in 1998 to the current wave of drone attacks on its stronghold in North Waziristan, the Haqqani network's ties to al-Qa'ida have made it the target of a United States willing to go to extraordinary lengths in its war on global jihadism's vanguard. The al-Qa'ida alliance would also seem to complicate the Haqqani network's relationship with the Pakistani military. For it is one thing for Pakistan to be seen as hedging its bets toward an uncertain future in post-American Afghanistan, and quite another for Pakistan to be perceived as facilitating, even indirectly, al-Qa'ida's war on the United States. For an organization that has proven itself in so many other respects an extremely pragmatic actor, why do the Haqqanis remain so invested in al-Qa'ida's quixotic global jihad?

This question points to certain unresolved tensions that have emerged in the four-decades long career of the Haqqani network, not least being its ideological definition. No other organization or group has had as long, as close, and as enduring a relationship with al-Qa'ida as the Haqqani network. This relationship has always entailed significant risks and has complicated the Haqqani network's relations with much more powerful partners, including the Taliban and the Pakistani military. One is tempted therefore to put this down to ideological extremism and to read the Haqqani network as committed on principle to al-Qa'ida's jihadi project. The evidence for this, however, is ambiguous. As discussed in Part I, the Haqqanis did anticipate al-Qa'ida's anti-American turn in their own publications in the early 1990s, but this hardly set them apart from other Afghan mujahidin groups or indeed from the main currents of Islamism worldwide, which were largely united in condemning the American military involvement in the first Gulf War. The

Haqqanis also proved adept at talking out of both sides of their mouths in these publications, sometimes making mutually contradictory statements in different magazines to suit the perceived preferences of those magazines' different audiences. Public rhetoric aside, what did set the Haqqani network apart was that its ideological pronouncements were being backed by significant investment in and support for al-Qa'ida's training camp infrastructure in Loya Paktia throughout the 1990s. In that sense the Haqqani network was decisively less moderate than the Taliban, as it was not simply ideologically sympathetic to al-Qa'ida's cause but was actively helping the group to operationalize its vision.

However, the picture of the Haqqani network's ideological commitments that emerges from its publications is markedly different from that of so-called Salafi jihadism, bearing a much greater resemblance to mainstream Pakistani Deobandi Islamism. These publications bear little if any trace of the Salafism of many of al-Qa'ida's leaders, do not cite the standard traditional authorities or proof-texts of Salafi jihadism, and show no signs of the hyper-monotheistic rigidity associated with Salafi or Wahhabi movements. As noted in Chapter 3, the Haqqanis took exception to the Taliban's repressive interpretations of Islamic orthodoxy and did not allow certain Taliban restrictions on women and popular customs to be applied in Khost. Unlike their "fundamentalist" counterparts in the anti-Soviet war, the Haqqanis did not subscribe to the tenets or adopt the organizational models of revolutionary Islamism; they never sought to seize state power for themselves, did not employ hierarchical cadre structures, and there is no evidence that they ever expressed the least displeasure with popular forms of Islamic ritual practice. On the contrary, Saudi trainees headed for the Haqqani camps at Khost were warned to bite their tongues at the "heresies" that they would there see on display.[13] In their attitudes toward Islam and tribal political culture, the Haqqanis appear in most respects as conservatives, not radicals.

Again, this is a tension that the Haqqani network—or at least our study of its history—has been unable to resolve completely. Many writers have argued that Sirajuddin Haqqani, the current military leader of the network, seems to have presided over a shift toward a more radical ideological position than that held by his father Jalaluddin. But a further tension remains, one whose resolution only the future can determine. Throughout its history the Haqqani network has literally and figuratively straddled the Pak-Afghan border, always with one foot in two nations. Yet its relations with the Pakistani state, while long-standing, have had their ups and downs. The ISI's single-minded favoritism for Gulbuddin Hekmatyar during the post-Soviet Afghan civil war was not lost on the Haqqani network, which largely charted its own course during those years and made common cause with many Afghan mujahidin leaders that the ISI considered bitter enemies. The Haqqanis first took up arms in defense of highland Pashtun autonomy in Afghanistan's southeast, and their acceptance of Pakistan's military assistance has been predicated from the beginning on furthering that aim. Pakistan's interests in Afghanistan are not limited to Loya Paktia, however, and it remains to be seen to what extent the Haqqani network will continue to hitch its fate to the Pakistani military's perilous regional strategies.

A Note on Sources

This study of the Haqqani network is the first of its kind in that it is based almost entirely on primary documentary sources. We conducted the first known review of near-complete sets of three magazines produced by the Haqqani network from 1989 to 1993, in all comprising well over 1000 pages: *Manba' al-Jihad* (one version in Pashto and another in Arabic) and *Nusrat al-Jihad* ("Support for Jihad," in Urdu). We were able to obtain and study a number of book-length publications by the Haqqanis dating to this period, books which have likewise been hitherto unknown to scholarship, as well as a series of digital videos produced by the group since 2001. We also make extensive use of materials stored in the US Defense Department's "Harmony" database, including a review of several thousand pages of letters written to and from Haqqani commanders during the 1980s and 1990s. While this latter material is extremely rich and illuminating, readers should be aware of the limitations that surround the use of these documents. Items in the Harmony database were collected on the battlefield in an ad hoc manner. There is no way to know how representative the documents captured by US forces are of a potentially much larger body of texts produced by the Haqqani network, al-Qa'ida, or other groups active in Afghanistan.

Our study is also informed by a review of over two dozen volumes of memoirs and first-person narratives, as well as hundreds of pages of private correspondence, by Arab supporters of the Haqqani network, al-Qa'ida members, and other members of the Afghan Arab community (non-Afghan Muslim volunteers who travelled to Pakistan and Afghanistan to aid the Afghan mujahidin). As with the Haqqani network publications, many of these texts have never been studied before, and the material made available here for the first time sheds much new light on the history of the Afghan Arabs, al-Qa'ida, and the origins of global jihadism.

We also conducted interviews with a number of historians, journalists, and policy practitioners who have either personally encountered or have had firsthand knowledge of the Haqqani network at specific points in its history. In addition to those that asked not to be named here, we benefited from communicating with Anand Gopal, Antonio Giustozzi, Bob Nickelsberg, Thomas Ruttig, Pir Zubayr Shah, and Jere Van Dyk.

As for secondary sources and materials in Western languages, we made every effort to be comprehensive, including in our research all references to the Haqqanis in the English-language press, in the foreign press translated by the Foreign Broadcast Information Service (FBIS), in the documents released by WikiLeaks, and in the considerable body of secondary literature on Afghanistan and Pakistan. Whenever possible, however, our emphasis in this book is placed squarely on the primary sources, and we have not attempted to provide an analytical survey of the secondary literature here. Particularly valuable secondary sources are cited in the text and listed in the bibliography.

Caveats

In giving primacy to what the Haqqanis and their various allies have written about themselves, we are in a certain sense privileging their version of events. Many of our sources were originally intended as propaganda, presenting the Haqqani network in a particular light in order to attract support. This book does not simply mediate the Haqqanis' self-representation, however. As already noted, our archive consists just as much of private, internal communication as it does of texts meant for public consumption. Moreover, we have sought to contextualize the sources within the broader history of regional conflict and to corroborate statements by, wherever possible, presenting multiple sources on specific points of fact. In some instances, however, we have had to rely on single sources, sources whose version of events may be challenged or contradicted by the emergence of further evidence. We decided to include such details to provide a baseline primary source history of events about which many questions still remain.

It also bears pointing out what *Fountainhead of Jihad* isn't. We do not attempt to provide here a comprehensive history of the Haqqani network. As its subtitle indicates, our book is as much concerned with the larger context of the development of transnational Islamist militancy (the nexus) as it is with the Haqqanis themselves. In being the first monograph centered on the Haqqani network we of course hope to have gone some way to filling this significant gap in the literature, though much remains to be done. However valuable our primary sources are for understanding the history of the Haqqanis and their relationships, studies based on fieldwork—such as those of Thomas Ruttig—or interviews with the principal actors—such as the work of Anand Gopal—are still indispensable. We hope our book will have supplemented, but certainly not replaced, the work of such scholars.

Finally, the authors decided at the beginning of our research that we would leave the policy debates surrounding the Haqqani network aside and instead focus on the available primary sources. Our sole aim has been to advance public knowledge and understanding of one of the most complicated set of actors in a long-running and ongoing conflict, and not to advocate for or against any particular policy option by any particular state involved in this conflict. To the extent that our findings bear upon the Haqqani network's potential futures as we near the 2014 drawdown of US and NATO forces in Afghanistan, such questions are addressed in the Conclusion.

Layout of the Book

At every stage of the research, this project has been a shared and collaborative process, though we have divided the writing neatly down the middle. Part I, including this Introduction, was written by Vahid Brown. Part II, including the Conclusion, was written by Don Rassler. We have arrived at our interpretations and conclusions in conversation with one another, though the respective authors are solely responsible for whatever is written in their segments of the text.

Part I is primarily historical, providing a narrative of the origins of the Haqqani network and of the course of its development up to 11 September 2001. Chapter 1 seeks to situate the Haqqani network's origins within their regional, cultural, and political contexts. Part of what has made the Haqqanis distinctive in Afghanistan's recent violent history is their relationship to highland Pashtun tribal politics, a relationship that has left an indelible imprint on the forms of Islamism and popular mobilization they have deployed. This chapter explores this relationship and identifies the Haqqanis' place in Pak-Afghan interstate conflict, a position that first attracted the resources enabling them to establish the fountainhead of their future jihadi enterprises. Chapter 2 centers on the Afghan–Soviet war and the Haqqani network's pivotal role in facilitating the militant evolution of the Afghan Arab movement, a process that included the birth of al-Qa'ida as among its most fateful consequences. Chapter 3 charts the course of the Haqqani network's further development in the aftermath of the Soviet withdrawal, including its relations with the Taliban movement and the expansion of its support for a wide variety of transnational jihadi organizations.

Though partially offset with a wealth of audiovisual materials, documentary sources for the period covered in Part II are relatively few. The second part of the book therefore shifts from the primarily historiographic register of the first half to a more analytic effort to explore and explain the organizational dynamics of the Haqqani network and its various relations. Beginning with a separate introduction, Part II explores these relationships during the post-2001 period through the lens of the group's value proposition to its local, regional, and global partners. The first three chapters of Part II are organized around this framework, with Chapter 4 providing an assessment of the local Afghan and Pakistani components of the Haqqani network and how and in which functional areas the Haqqanis' operations are integrated with and provide value to its local partners (i.e., various factions of the Pakistani Taliban). Chapter 5 broadens this view to a regional aperture and explores the dynamics of the Haqqani network's relationship with the Pakistani state and its military and intelligence agencies. Chapter 6 documents the nature of the Haqqani network's ties with al-Qa'ida and other global jihadist actors, such as the Islamic Jihad Union, across functional and operational realms since 9/11. Chapter 7 provides an overview of how the Haqqani network has been able to manage and maintain its nexus position over time, and an assessment of the entanglements and organizational tension associated with the group's nexus position. The text concludes with an overview of our major findings and what they potentially tell us about the future of US–Pakistan ties, the Haqqani network, and al-Qa'ida.

PART I

ESTABLISHMENT AND HISTORICAL EVOLUTION OF THE HAQQANI NEXUS

1

SITUATING THE HAQQANIS

ORIGINS, POLITICAL CULTURE, REGIONAL CONTEXTS

The Haqqani network has been an enduring feature of the violent political landscape of Afghanistan and Pakistan for the past four decades, a period that has not been kind to either country. Seemingly endless coups and foreign military interventions; regimes that have oscillated between authoritarianism and ineptitude; unprecedented levels of displaced civilians, suicide terrorism, and heroin production; devastating ecological disasters; and pervasive social and economic instability have bedeviled the region during these turbulent years. Afghanistan, the last battleground of the Cold War and the first of the global War on Terror, has not known peace since the Soviet invasion of 1979. Pakistan, which entered this period with the loss of half its territory in Bangladesh's war of independence, has been locked in a nuclear stalemate with India punctuated by varying levels of cross-border war-by-proxy, and is currently fighting Baluch and Pashtun insurgencies all along its western frontier. Against this background of unrelenting chaos, how has the Haqqani network managed not only to survive but to maintain the sanctuary for the jihadi groups whose global campaigns of violence have done so much to define the course of the still young twenty-first century?

There is no single, simple answer to this question. Rather, the factors that explain the rise and remarkable longevity of the Haqqani network are as complex and messy as the history of the region itself. This chapter seeks to locate the Haqqani network in the first decade of its existence within the cultural, political, and physical geography of the area from which it emerged. The particular history and characteristics of this region—eastern Afghanistan and the mountainous tribal areas of Pakistan's western frontier—have not only shaped the Haqqanis' evolution and strategic behavior over time; they have also provided the Haqqanis with assets critical to their success in eking out an enduring position of power and far-reaching influence over four decades of regional conflict and globalized political violence.

The Highland Pashtun "Shatter Zone"

The Haqqanis' primary areas of operation since the early 1970s have been the southeastern Afghan provinces of Khost, Paktia, and Paktika—known collectively as Loya Paktia or "greater Paktia"—and North Waziristan, one of the seven Tribal Agencies that make up Pakistan's Federally Administered Tribal Areas (FATA). This area lies at the southern end of the highland Pashtun region, which stretches from Paktika, Afghanistan, and South Waziristan, Pakistan, in the south, to Kunar, Afghanistan, and Bajaur, Pakistan, in the north. This mountainous and agriculturally unproductive region straddles the Durand Line, the (disputed) international boundary between Afghanistan and Pakistan, and is home to the Karlanri Pashtun confederacy, a group of tribes that share, in addition to a single quasi-legendary ancestor, a distinct political culture that is very different from the lowland Pashtuns of the two countries.[1]

The Pashtuns themselves mark this distinction in terms of the binary pair *nang* (honor-bound) and *qalang* (rent-paying), as in the Pashtun proverb "taxes ate the valleys, honor ate the hills."[2] Anthropologist David Edwards succinctly summarizes this binary in the following terms:

> Nang Pakhtuns generally inhabit the mountainous fringe of the Pakhtun universe where the land is poor and life is harsh; nang societies are acepha-

lous and segmentary in structure, and codes of conduct are bound by traditional codes of honor. Qalang Pakhtuns, on the other hand, are hierarchical; they inhabit tracts of fertile land that produce large marketable surpluses; their patterns of social interaction are asymmetrical and structured less by Pakhtunwali (the Pakhtun code of honor) than by the economics of patron–client relations.[3]

Given the poor agricultural resources and fiercely defended independence of the *nang* highland tribes, it is not altogether surprising that neither Afghanistan nor Pakistan—nor, indeed, any of a long list of invading empires that ruled the wider region in centuries past—has ever been successful in completely integrating the highland Pashtun region into their respective polities. Instead, Afghanistan and Pakistan (and the British Raj before 1947) traditionally adopted what Thomas Barfield has called a "Swiss cheese model" of governance, whereby "regimes expected their writs to run completely only in the most populated and economically prosperous parts of the country. The people in the poorer high mountains ... were left to fend for themselves as long as they did not challenge state authority. If they did, the state resorted to a range of weapons well short of direct rule to get them to cease."[4] Though thus marginal to the central political cultures of the two states, the Pashtun highlands were also the source of "most acts of antistate violence over the preceding hundred years or so," to such an extent that "the Pakhtuns of the frontier were the kingmakers and breakers"[5] within Afghanistan and were similarly troublesome to British rule in the late nineteenth and early twentieth centuries—to say nothing of Islamabad since 2007.

A consistent feature of these highland Pashtun mobilizations of violence against the two political centers on their flanks that has particular bearing for our understanding of the Haqqani network is that they were largely led and organized under the auspices of clerical rather than tribal leadership. Indeed, the general political significance of clerical authority in the Pashtun highlands has existed in marked contrast to the role of mullahs in the political economies of lowland Pashtuns, where their status is often defined as marginal.[6] It is because of this perceived marginality that the rise of the Taliban in southern Afghanistan in the mid-1990s appeared as a revolutionary and unprecedented assertion of religious authority over Afghanistan's political destiny.[7] However valid this insight may be with regard to the Taliban, which arose among lowland Pashtuns of the Kandahar region, the history of the Haqqani network's clerically based leadership is to a much greater extent in continuity with the last century and a half of highland Pashtun political history.[8]

While that history cannot be traced in full here, some of its features bear mentioning as they shed direct light on the form of organization taken by the Haqqanis and their various regional allies over the past forty years.[9] Although there are numerous individual antecedents earlier in the nineteenth century, the existence of a broad-based "clerical network" throughout the highland Pashtun zone that mobilized both resistance to Kabul and a series of uprisings against the British in India dates to the charismatic Sufi leader Mullah Najmuddin (d. 1903), known as the Hadda Mullah, and his network of disciples throughout the frontier.[10] As the Haqqanis would do decades later, this network established centers of religious education that doubled as spaces for the articulation and deployment of a political discourse that went beyond those of individual clans. This helped lay the groundwork for collective state-evasive action that the atomized and acephalous form of *nang* Pashtun political culture could not of itself sustain. Again, to quote Edwards:

> Hadda Sahib was connected to an extensive network of support and identification through the *tariqat* [Sufi organization] system, which provided him with an organizational structure that was unique in the area. As we have seen, tribes represent the dominant form of social organization in the region and one that has a particular resiliency in the face of state encroachment, but tribes also tend to be insular in orientation and provide neither the idioms of relationship that would allow for more far-reaching alliances nor the resources to support a widespread and sustained mobilization of manpower.[11]

The generation of leaders of this network following in the wake of the Hadda Mullah's death—centered in particular on one Haji Sahib Turangzai—became increasingly influenced by the teachings of the revivalist and anti-colonial Deobandi school of South Asian Sunni Islam, whose influence was rapidly spreading throughout the region during this same period.[12] Thus the network of charismatic Sufi preachers (*pirs*) and their disciples (*murids*) that spearheaded collective political action among the frontier Pashtuns in the late nineteenth century gave way during the twentieth century to a network of Deobandi madrassa-based clerics (*mawlanas*, 'ulama) and their students (*talibs*) who carried on in the same political tradition. These networks created supratribal solidarities among their members and new institutions for political mobilization: the Deobandi madrassa networks. The latter, in turn, afforded the clerical leaders a base of manpower capable of sustaining *talib* militias, periodically fielded by these clerical leaders to either resist the encroachment of state power or to enforce social–moral control, which "accorded *mullas* a military power that they could use in pursuit of personal or ideological objectives, becoming a coercive influence within the tribal set-up."[13]

The highland Pashtun region throughout this period bears many of the hallmarks of what James C. Scott has recently termed "shatter zones" or "regions of refuge."[14] Geographically and ecologically remote spaces on the margins of empires and states—most typically mountainous regions—shatter zones have throughout human history been magnets for diverse human groups seeking refuge from the predations and disadvantages of emerging state-forms, such as taxation, forced conscription, corvée labor, warfare, monocrop-induced famines, and epidemics. In their social, political, and economic life-ways, shatter zone populations have developed patterns of organization that appear, in Scott's analysis, "designed to thwart state appropriation."[15] As opposed to the intensive agriculture of lowland state space, highland shatter zones have tended toward nomadic pastoralism, swiddening, mixed cropping, and forest collecting. In terms of social and political organization, the inhabitants of regions of refuge formed "escape social structures ... designed to aid dispersal and autonomy and to ward off political subordination."[16] The central feature of such social structures is their radical egalitarianism, the absence of clear or durable hierarchies. All of this has been characteristic of the highland Pashtuns and is precisely what distinguishes them from their lowland cousins, dividing the *nang* from the *qalang*.

Significantly, Scott's analyses found that when the fissiparous peoples of shatter zones needed to mobilize in collective defense of their hard-won autonomy from the violent encroachments of states, it has been religion that most commonly "provide[d] the social cohesion necessary for collective action."[17] Scott's primary example is drawn from a predominantly Buddhist context—the upland massif of Southeast Asia—and his numerous cross-cultural examples demonstrate that there is nothing unique to Islam per se in the mobilizations of this particular type of collective violence.[18] Indeed, a noteworthy comparison to a Western European highland tribal context was made by Howard Hensman, an eyewitness to the second Anglo-Afghan War in 1879: "The fiery cross, which was sped from end to end of the Scottish Highlands, in the old days, when the call to the arms was made, was no more powerful than is the Koran now carried from village to village by the moolah of Afghanistan."[19]

A defining feature of shatter zones in Scott's model is a high degree of ethnic and linguistic variation. He identifies "relative geographical inaccessibility and ... enormous diversity of tongues and cultures" as the two "diagnostic characteristics of shatter zones."[20] In this connection, the Pashtun highlands, in that they appear to share a common Pashto culture and language, do not fit Scott's ideal type, as he himself points out.[21] The Muslim-majority region that best fits Scott's model is the North Caucasus, one of the most ethno-linguistically diverse and geographically inaccessible regions on the planet, where in the nineteenth and early twentieth centuries Sufi organizations provided the glue binding the veritable Babel of North Caucasus groups in resisting attempts at state encapsulation by tsarist and communist Russia.[22] Yet Scott's exclusion of the Pashtun highlands on grounds of cultural unity is, on closer inspection, perhaps somewhat misplaced.

As noted above, the tribes that predominate in much of the Pashtun highlands form part of the Karlanri confederacy, one of the four maximal descent groups through which all of the Pashtun tribes trace their lineage and claim, ultimately, to be interrelated. The three other supertribal Pashtun confederacies—the Durrani (also known as Abdali), the Ghilzai, and the Ghurghusht—all trace their descent to one of the three sons of Qais, an Arab contemporary of the Prophet Muhammad and the putative ancestor of all of the Pashtuns (except the Karlanri; see below). The genealogies of these tribes and confederacies, however, are hugely diverse and inconsistent, and in the case of the Karlanri the apical ancestor is sometimes considered an adopted son of Qais, and in other cases a son of that adopted son. As Thomas Barfield notes, there is no historical documentation of the Pashtuns as a single distinct group going back further than 1500 CE, and there is evidence in the genealogical texts that call into question the notion of their always having constituted a single group. To quote him at some length:

> [S]triking anomalies in the basic genealogies themselves hint at a more complex origin. In a society where all descent is patrilineal, only the senior line (Abdali in the west and Yusefzai in the east)[23] and the Ghurghusht claim an unbroken patrilineal descent from the founder. By contrast, the Ghilzai genealogies trace their line to a Pashtun ancestress who married a Ghorid prince after having a child with him out of wedlock (the founding male ancestor of the Ghilzais). The Karlanri tribes, which constitute the most important groups in today's NWFP,[24] have no genealogical link at all (male or female) to the sons of Qais, the Pashtun's apical ancestor. They are the descendents of an adopted child of uncertain origins raised by Pashtuns. ... The Ghilzais appear to have intermarried and absorbed different groups, particularly the Turks, who passed through eastern Afghanistan. The bulk of the Karlanri, by contrast, appear to be the indigenous inhabitants of the mountains of the NWFP who mixed little with outsiders, but who became Pashtuns (or more precisely Pakhtuns) by adopting their language and culture.[25]

The various highland groups that trace their lineages in such a way as to be designated as Karlanri are each quite distinct from one another—they have distinctive "tribal" regalia and clothing, linguistic variation, territorial settlements, and even religious practices.[26] To cite one recent example, a May 2009 diplomatic cable from the US Embassy in Kabul leaked by the WikiLeaks organization describes a meeting that month between Afghan officials and Zadran tribespeople in the Gayan district of Paktika, which borders North Waziristan in the Pakistani tribal areas and lies within the Haqqani network's area of operation.[27] The cable describes appeals to the Zadrans by Paktika Governor Katawazay to resolve an ongoing dispute with the Waziri tribe, a minority population in Gayan district and, like the Zadran, part of the Karlanri confederacy.[28] In response, "the Zadran elders energetically denied that the Waziris belong to Gayan district, saying they belong to neighboring Bermel district, where nearly all Paktika's Waziris reside. They insisted that the Waziris differ fundamentally from the Zadran in language, custom, and culture and cannot be trusted because they are more Pakistani than Afghan."

Issues of highland Pashtun cultural unity aside, the shatter zone status of the Haqqani network's area of control since the late 1970s is, in light of their multiethnic jihadi guests, much less ambiguous. As detailed in the following two chapters, "Haqqani country" has become a true region of refuge for an astonishing variety of polyglot revolutionaries and Islamist militants, hailing from nearly every region of the world. From Algeria to Indonesia, California to Germany, would-be holy warriors from around the globe have sought and continue to seek an anti-state base of operations in the state-evading safe haven maintained by the Haqqani network throughout these decades. As these diverse refuge seekers have used the Haqqanis' non-state space as both a hideout and a platform from which to attack the states that hunt them, this region has truly become a shatter zone—and one that shatters back.

Jalaluddin Haqqani—His Life in Regional Context

Jalaluddin Haqqani, the founder and leader of the Haqqani network, was born in 1939 in the tiny village of Karezgay in the Wazi Zadran district of Paktia Province.[29] This area now falls within the unofficial Paktian district of Gerda Serai, as yet unrecognized by the Afghan government and notorious to US and coalition forces in the current conflict as a Haqqani network stronghold.[30] As a teenager Jalaluddin moved with his family to a larger village in the same district, and locals in the area now identify Sultankhel as the "hometown" of the Haqqani family.[31] Jalaluddin and his family belong to the Sultankhel clan of the Zadran tribe.[32] His father, Khwaja Muhammad Khan, was a relatively wealthy landowner with trading interests in both Afghanistan and Pakistan, prosperous enough to send his sons in later years to Pakistan for advanced religious education.[33] Jalaluddin was the first of at least four sons born to Khwaja Muhammad Khan, and his three younger brothers—Muhammad Isma'il (d. 1990), Ibrahim, and Khalil—all went on to play leading roles in the family's jihadi enterprises, as did Jalaluddin's brother-in-law Ghazi Khan.[34]

In the years surrounding Jalaluddin's birth the southern end of the Pashtun highland region continued to be the center of numerous uprisings and violent resistance movements against both the Afghan state and British colonial India, with the Zadran and their Karlanri cousins often playing a leading role. During the latter half of the 1920s the Afghan king, Amanullah, hoping to modernize his country along the lines of Turkey's Atatürk, pursued a widely unpopular reformist agenda that in the end proved his undoing. Amanullah's decrees attempting to end the practice of *purdah*—the veiling and seclusion of women—and instituting coeducational schools were met with fierce resistance by Afghanistan's conservative religious leaders. He also departed from long-standing policies by which Afghanistan's leaders had sought to contract the nominal loyalty of the southeastern highland tribes, reducing allowances to the tribes and extending penal codes and conscription rules to a frontier that had long been accustomed to exemptions from such intrusions of the state. For nine months in 1924 and 1925 the Zadran and Mangal rose up in a rebellion against these policies, led by a Kharoti cleric known as Mullah-i Lang ("the Lame Mullah").[35]

Though the Khost Rebellion, as this uprising came to be known, was eventually put down through a mixture of negotiations and military assaults, the eastern tribes' resentment of Amanullah did not cease. After the latter's return from a European tour in 1928, the Zadran joined the Shinwari, Jaji, and Khugiani tribes in an open revolt against the king that swept the east, forcing Amanullah to flee Kabul and opening the way for the brief takeover of Afghanistan by its first Tajik ruler, the ill-fated and illiterate Bacha Saqqao (Habibullah Kalakani).[36] Seen as an outsider usurping the time-honored Pashtun right of rule, he proved no more popular to the eastern tribes than did his predecessor. The Hazrat of Shor Bazaar, a member of the Mujaddidi family, then the most powerful religious family in Afghanistan and later the leaders of one of the main anti-Soviet mujahidin parties, led the highland Pashtuns in an assault on Kabul that put a violent end to the nine-month reign of Bacha Saqqao. Pashtun rule was reinstated in the person of King Nadir Shah (r. 1929–33), who promptly reestablished strict rules of *purdah* and rewarded the eastern highlanders who had brought him to power by reinstating their traditional exemptions from taxation and army conscription.[37] Memory of these events has retained its power years later in the southeast. In 1995 the Taliban prevailed upon the Haqqanis, to whom they had likewise granted regional autonomy in exchange for support, to send some of their men to aid the Taliban's offensive against Tajik-led opponents in the north. Jalaluddin gathered a force of some 2000 fighters, "raised and dispatched to Kabul with suitable exhortations over the patriotic role of the border tribes in ousting Tajik usurpers [Bacha Saqqao] from the capital in 1929."[38]

The brief reign of Nadir Shah was a period of relative peace in Afghanistan's highland southeast, though there was a short-lived Zadran uprising against him during the twilight of his reign in 1933.[39] His successor to the throne, Zahir Shah, also saw a period of respite throughout most of the 1930s and 1940s from highland Pashtun insurgency.[40] On the other side of the Durand Line, however, North Waziristan emerged in this period as the center of an anti-British jihad that engulfed the frontier and was sustained virtually without interruption from 1930 until the British quit the subcontinent in 1947.

Sparked when police fired upon a peaceful demonstration in Peshawar in early 1930, the wave of anti-British mobilization by the frontier Pashtuns during that year was the largest since the Anglo-Afghan war of 1919.[41] The movement was organized by activists from the Jamiat Ulema-e-Sarhad (JUS), the frontier branch of the Jamiat Ulema-e-Hind, the Deobandi political organization of Indian Muslims that worked, often alongside Gandhi's Congress party, for Indian independence from British colonial rule. The JUS was a forerunner of the Jamiat Ulema-e-Islam (JUI), the Deobandi Islamist party in Pakistan with which the Haqqani network has long been—and remains—closely associated. The uprisings were led by clerics from the aforementioned Hadda Mullah network, including Haji Turangzai in the northern tribal areas and the famous Faqir of Iqi (Mirza 'Ali Khan) in North Waziristan. The Waziristan forces were strengthened by thousands of well-armed and battle-seasoned Waziri tribesmen returning from the successful campaign to oust Bacha Saqqao from Kabul, a battle to which many of the highland Pashtuns from east of the Durand Line had rallied. The Faqir of Ipi, a member of the Uthmanzai Wazir tribe, continued to lead anti-British insurgencies from North Waziristan until Partition in 1947.[42] His direct descendent, Gul Bahadur, currently leads the North Waziristan Taliban and is a close ally of the Haqqani network.[43]

The world into which Jalaluddin Haqqani was born was thus a maelstrom of similar types of borderland violence that he would find himself at the center of later in adulthood. Armed defense of highland Pashtun territorial independence; violent resistance to state meddling with tribal or Islamic customs; and large-scale mobilizations against foreign invasion—these are not new to the highland frontier, but rather have periodically characterized its history since long before Haqqani's birth. Haqqani, his siblings, and fellow Paktians have long been familiar with these modes of political life among the highland Pashtuns, a familiarity that would stand them in good stead as emerging resistance leaders in the turbulent years after the Soviet invasion.

After Partition: Pashtunistan, Marxism, and the first Daoud Regime

In one sense the emergence of the Haqqani network is a tragic legacy of the partition of India. The Haqqani network was not one of "midnight's children" in the literal sense—a full quarter century separates that bloody summer of 1947 from Jalaluddin Haqqani's first declaration of jihad in the summer of 1973. But the events and personalities that led Haqqani to make that fateful declaration are bound up with Partition, and in particular with the adversarial relationship between Afghanistan and newly born Pakistan that it set in motion.

Kashmir was not the only territorial dispute left over from the division of the subcontinent into the two states of India and West and East Pakistan (now Bangladesh), nor has the Kashmir dispute been the only central determinant of Pakistan's often bloody relations with its neighbors. Even before the partition was finalized, Afghanistan began lobbying aggressively for the annulment of the Durand Line, which it viewed as an illegal boundary imposed by Britain in 1893 by force. Afghanistan appealed to the British Parliament in early June 1947 for the inclusion of two additional options to the upcoming plebiscite in the Northwest Frontier: union with Afghanistan and the formation of an independent Pashtun nation, or "Pashtunistan." Parliament rebuffed the request and the plebiscite went ahead, limiting the Pashtuns of the frontier to the choice of joining Pakistan or India.[44] The highland Pashtuns of the tribal areas, of course, were not allowed to vote in the plebiscite, living as they did beyond the administrative zone of British India proper in a semi-autonomous legal limbo that Britain had established at the turn of the century and which was largely carried over by the newly emergent Pakistan.[45] Not surprisingly, the NWFP plebiscite overwhelmingly favored union with Pakistan.

These events immediately soured relations between Afghanistan and its new neighbor and shaped the two nations' policies toward one another for decades. Afghanistan voted against Pakistan's entry into the United Nations, and conflict on the "Pashtunistan question" led to frequent cessations of diplomatic and economic relations between the two states.[46] Afghanistan vigorously supported Pakistani Pashtun movements for Pashtunistan independence, led in the NWFP and the tribal areas by both Pashtun nationalists and traditional tribal religious leaders. The former were initially represented by the Khudai Khidmatgar ("Servants of God," also known as the Red Shirts), led by the nonviolent Gandhian activist Abdul Ghaffar Khan, while the latter found a leader in North Waziristan's Faqir of Ipi, whose "Free Pashtunistan" movement battled the Pakistani state well into the 1950s. Pakistan viewed these movements as threats to its territorial sovereignty and sought to counteract Kabul-supported ethno-nationalism with appeals to Islamic solidarity, the only ideological glue holding the multiethnic Pakistani state together. Pakistan's "Islam over tribe" approach became a pillar of its policies on the frontier and has characterized its deep involvement in Afghanistan's conflicts over the last thirty years, including its support for the Haqqani network.

Pakistan's first opportunity to manipulate these alternative solidarities emerged immediately after Partition. The NWFP was not immune to the intercommunal violence that erupted over the massive population transfers attending the hasty division of the subcontinent into Muslim and Hindu homelands, and a wave of anti-Sikh and anti-Hindu mob violence swept the Pashtun frontier in September of 1947. In the following month Pakistan capitalized on these impassioned sentiments by mobilizing highland Pashtuns from the tribal areas for an incursion into Kashmir, the first of many attempts by Pakistan to wrest Kashmir from India via irregular Muslim militias.[47] In the 1980s and 1990s, Pakistan would turn to the Haqqani network to train such militias for the Kashmir jihad (see below, Chapter 2). While no doubt motivated by its conviction that Kashmir rightfully belonged with Pakistan, Arnold Fletcher notes that, in part, the October 1947 operation "was intended at once to arouse Moslem enthusiasm, block Pushtoon separatism, bring discredit to the Khudai Khidmatgaran, and hinder action by Afghanistan."[48] The Afghan government sought to prevent highland tribesmen from joining the Kashmir incursion, and an Afghan clerical group issued a fatwa (Islamic legal decision) declaring that the war in Kashmir was not a true jihad.[49] Afghanistan also stepped up its efforts over the following years on behalf of Pakistani Pashtun independence.

The most aggressive Afghan champion of Pashtunistan was King Zahir Shah's cousin Muhammad Daoud Khan, the target of the Haqqanis' first jihad in 1973. Defense minister under Zahir Shah's first prime minister, and prime minister himself from 1953 to 1963, Daoud's open support for the irredentist claims of the Pashtuns east of the Durand Line made him the nemesis of a series of Pakistani leaders. At the same time, his fostering of increasingly close ties with Moscow and his revival of the Amanullah-era reforms won him many enemies within Afghanistan's conservative clerical establishment and among the highland Pashtuns. The specter of creeping communist influence began to haunt Daoud's relations with the frontier tribes on both sides of the Durand Line, eventually tipping the balance in favor of Pakistan in the Pak-Afghan contest between Islamocentrism and ethnocentrism for control of the borderlands.[50] The communist stain on Daoud's pro-Pashtunistan stance became indelible in 1955. The Pakistani government abolished the provincial status of the NWFP as part of the "One Unit" scheme, which in 1955 amalgamated West Pakistan's provinces into one in order to redress power-sharing imbalances between East and West Pakistan. Daoud openly denounced this move as a direct attack on Pashtun independence, and in April protestors in Kabul nearly destroyed the Pakistani Embassy, hoisting the Pashtunistan flag over the badly damaged building. In response, Pakistan closed all diplomatic offices in Afghanistan and suspended transit trade, isolating its landlocked neighbor. At the end of the year, Soviet leader Nikita Khrushchev arrived in Kabul bearing a generous assistance package, including substantial military aid, and directly entered the fray by demanding "an impartial plebiscite in the Pashtun areas of Pakistan."[51] The United States had by this time made Pakistan a central pillar of its Soviet containment strategy in the region and had lavished it with generous military aid packages, and the United States backed Pakistan in the Pashtunistan squabble. Washington viewed Afghan aggression against Pakistan as more likely than an outright Soviet takeover of Afghanistan, and it refused several requests from Daoud for military aid.[52] Afghanistan had no choice but to tilt ever closer into the Soviet sphere of influence.

The Soviet relationship only added fuel to the fires of highland Pashtun resistance to Daoud's reform efforts. In 1959 Daoud brought the Afghan state into a direct conflict with the tribes of Paktia in a series of events that were both reminiscent of the rebellions of the 1920s and a sign of things to come. Since 1957 Daoud had sought to force a departure from the Afghan practice of *purdah,* staging high-profile appearances of unveiled female members of his family and issuing a series of decrees affecting gender restrictions that raised the ire of many of the traditional clerics. At the same time he rescinded the exemptions granted by former rulers to the frontier tribes, and embarked on an ambitious public works project to run roads through Loya Paktia. In September 1959 the Afghan army was sent into Paktia to put an end to a violent dispute over timber rights between the Zadran and Mangal tribes, a military intervention that proved to be the last straw, inciting an anti-government uprising in the southeast. There had already been riots in Kandahar earlier in the year over Daoud's anti-*purdah* measures, but the Paktian revolt proved both more complex and more consequential. Tribesmen fleeing across the Durand Line received support from Pakistan, where the conflict was cast in the national press in such a way as to highlight the triple grievances of Daoud's affront to Islam, communist influence, and infringement upon highland Pashtun autonomy. In one press release the following statements were attributed to a Mangal khan speaking in Peshawar:

> The exodus of about 4,000 Mangals from their homeland, in whose liberation from the Bacha Saqqao rule they had played a prominent part, is a matter which deserves serious consideration by all those who believe in fundamental human rights. My countrymen in Afghanistan as well as our co-religionists in Pakistan probably know that the late king, King Mohammad Nadir Shah, had through a royal proclamation granted us certain concessions, which the present regime in Kabul has decided to withdraw for no fault of ours. The crux of the matter is that the Afghan Government has taken strong exception to our objection of the growing Russian influence in Afghanistan which has brought the country into the iron grip of communists, who are preaching their atheistic creed under one garb or another. As true Muslims, we cannot silently watch the spread of communist ideology in the land.[53]

The final sentiment expressed in this statement was coming to be shared by a growing segment of Kabul's ruling elite. In the summer of 1960 Daoud sent Afghan troops across the Durand Line to support the khan of Bajaur in a local dispute. Once again all diplomatic relations between Afghanistan and Pakistan were suspended and the border was closed to transit trade, interrupting the limited development aid that the United States had begun to provide in an effort to balance Soviet influence in the country.[54] The blockade remained in place into the early 1960s, making Afghanistan almost totally dependent on Soviet trade and economic assistance. Daoud's mania for Pashtunistan had by 1963 brought Afghanistan to the brink of ruin, a fact not lost on King Zahir Shah and other members of the royal household. Taking the reins of government for the first time since ascending the throne in 1933, Zahir Shah accepted Daoud's "resignation" from the position of prime minister and reversed the course of Afghan policy, patching up relations with Pakistan, strengthening ties to the United States, and embarking on an unprecedented period of political liberalization that was to last until his own removal from power in a bloodless coup staged by Daoud in 1973.

The Constitutional Period (1963–73): Urban and Highland Islamic Organization

Zahir Shah's efforts to create a more open political atmosphere in Afghanistan did not resolve the underlying tensions roiling Afghan society, which now found opportunity for open expression. The king commissioned a new and more liberal constitution in 1964 and introduced unprecedented freedoms of press and political organization. Legislation that would legalize the formation of political parties was passed by both houses of parliament in 1968. Though the king ultimately declined to sign the bill into law, Afghanistan in this period saw an explosion of informal political parties, often forming around the sudden profusion of journals and magazines representing every shade of the political spectrum. On the left, the Marxist–Leninist People's Democratic Party of Afghanistan (PDPA) emerged in 1965, organized into the two factions of Parcham ("Banner") and Khalq ("Masses"), named after two communist magazines. On the Islamic right, a group of professors from the Faculty of Shari'a at Kabul University inspired a network of student activists that formed the Jawanan-i-Musulman ("Muslim Youth") in 1969.[55] As in much of the rest of the world in the turbulent 1960s, the primary ideological—and increasingly physical—battleground of radical politics in Afghanistan was the urban campuses of universities and technical colleges. All of these developments were concentrated in Kabul and their protagonists were literate, highly politicized, and hailed predominantly from the middle and upper classes of Afghan society. In contrast, an alternative form of organized Islamic opposition to the state emerged during the same period in the Pashtun highlands. Economically depressed and having the lowest literacy rates in the entire region, the border tribes' mobilizations against Zahir Shah's reforms had less to do with the radical milieu of private presses and campus activism than with the age-old struggle for regional autonomy. It is to the latter context that the ideological and organizational origins of the Haqqani network can be traced.

The Kabul Islamist scene coalesced around the leadership of Professor Ghulam Muhammad Niazi, who became dean of the Shari'a Faculty at Kabul University after completing advanced studies in 1957 at al-Azhar in Cairo, the most prestigious center of Sunni learning in the world.[56] Kabul's university-centered Islamist movement was ideologically rooted in the radical wing of the Egyptian Muslim Brotherhood, as exemplified by the writings of Sayyid Qutb, whose works the Kabul Islamists translated and studied, and in the writings of Abu'l-'Ala Maududi, the ideological architect of Pakistan's Jamaat-i Islami (JI).[57] Their confrontational campus activism was in direct response to the growth of radical Marxist and Maoist groups at the university, and they even studied Marxist texts in order to develop counterpropaganda. This often-violent "conversation" with Marxist organizers left an indelible imprint on the Kabul Islamist circle—whose leading members included the future leaders of the so-called "fundamentalist" mujahidin parties: Gulbuddin Hekmatyar, 'Abd al-Rabb Rasul Sayyaf, Burhanuddin Rabbani, and Ahmad Shah Massoud—and led them in modernist ideological and organizational directions that were ultimately very similar to those of their leftist opponents.[58]

By 1970 the Kabul Islamists had developed close organizational ties to their nearest ideological cousins in Pakistan, the JI.[59] Founded in 1941 by Maududi—himself a major influence on Sayyid Qutb—the JI had a great deal in common with the Kabul Islamists and their 1980s-era mujahidin parties.[60] Both were largely urban and modern university-based in the origins of their leaders and cadres; both were organizationally centralized and highly bureaucratic; and both were revolutionary in that they sought the eventual seizure of state power in order to usher in "a new sociopolitical order based on varying interpretations of Islamic tenets."[61] Again reflecting their common "enemy in the mirror," both the Kabul Islamists and the JI adopted Leninist-style cadre structures, cultivating a vanguard of Islamist elites that would, in theory, capture the state at the propitious revolutionary moment.[62] The étatism of the Kabul Islamists was signaled from the very beginning, declaring in a *shabnama* ("night letter") shortly after the formation of the PDPA in 1965 that they would launch a jihad to establish an Islamic state in Afghanistan.[63] When the Kabul Islamists finally formed a party in 1972, they further underlined their closeness to Pakistan's JI by naming the party Jamiat-i Islami Afghanistan (JIA).[64]

Jalaluddin Haqqani also began his Islamic activism in a campus environment during these years, but one far removed both in space and political temper from that of Kabul University. Beginning in 1964 Jalaluddin embarked on a program of advanced religious studies at the Dar al-'Ulum Haqqaniyya madrassa in the NWFP, Pakistan, graduating in 1970 with the equivalent of a doctoral degree and qualified to be addressed as a *mawlawi*.[65] This Deobandi seminary was the birthplace of a distinctively Pashtun Islamism, embodied in an alumni social network of religious and political elites that has had tremendous political success and far-reaching social influence in both Afghanistan and Pakistan. It was also the birthplace of the Haqqani network, and the institution from which the Haqqanis take their name.[66]

The Dar al-'Ulum Haqqaniyya was established in 1947 in the village of Akora Khattak, 30 miles southeast of Peshawar, by Abdul Haq Akorwi, a graduate of the Dar al-'Ulum Deoband in northern India, from which the Deobandi movement originated in the late nineteenth century.[67] The site of the Dar al-'Ulum Haqqaniyya school is significant, as it was in the same location in 1826 that the famous nineteenth-century anti-colonial activist-cum-mujahid Sayyid Ahmad Shahid won the first major battle of his jihad against the British-backed Sikhs of the frontier.[68] The school has always been closely affiliated with the Jamiat Ulema-e-Islam (JUI), one of the two large Pakistani Sunni Islamist political parties—the other being the JI. The current leaders of the two main factions of the JUI—Mawlana Fazl ur Rahman (head of JUI-F) and Mawlana Sami-ul Haq (head of JUI-S), both members of Pakistan's National Assembly—are graduates of Haqqaniyya. Mawlana Sami-ul Haq, the son of Abdul Haq Akorwi, has been the chancellor of the madrassa for many years. By the 1960s the Dar al-'Ulum Haqqaniyya had become the "main institution for the production of graduates of the Deobandis" in Pakistan, and between 1966 and 1985 roughly a third of all Deobandi clerics in Pakistan graduated from Haqqaniyya.[69] It is thus not surprising that so many of the most prominent figures in Pakistan's Deobandi political party, the JUI, are Haqqaniyya graduates. Most of these graduates hailed from the highland Pashtun regions of Pakistan and Afghanistan, with the largest number of students originating from North Waziristan and Bannu, and the second largest group coming from eastern Afghanistan—especially Paktia.[70] A number of Jalaluddin's fellow classmates at Haqqaniyya from greater Paktia would go on to join him in anti-government uprisings in Afghanistan in the 1970s and serve as Haqqani network field commanders during the 1980s, including Mawlawi Nizamuddin Haqqani, Fathullah Haqqani, Hanif Shah, and Mawlawi 'Aziz Khan.[71]

Despite the ideological and social distance separating the Kabul Islamist scene from the more traditional Pak-Afghan activist current centered at Haqqaniyya, the two groups did have some overlap during the late 1960s. Two older Haqqaniyya alumni in particular bridged the two movements: Yunis Khalis and Muhammad Nabi Muhammadi. Khalis (d. 2006), a Khugiani Pashtun from Nangarhar Province in eastern Afghanistan, was one of the few traditional Afghan 'ulama who supported the Islamist student movement at Kabul University in the 1960s.[72] He helped to introduce the thought of Sayyid Qutb in Afghanistan, publishing a Dari translation of one of the latter's early works in 1960.[73] Khalis was also a frequent contributor to one of the earliest Islamist newspapers of the liberal period, *Gahez* ("Dawn"), established in 1968 by Minhajuddin Gahez.[74] Khalis was just as alarmed as the Kabul Islamists by the growing Marxist influence in Afghanistan but he did not share their statist revolutionary ideals. In one of his *Gahez* articles he warned that the "acquisition of [state] power by capital or by the sword is forbidden in Islam."[75] In an interview with David Edwards in 1984, Khalis stated that the "Muslim Youth wanted to do demonstrations and talk about the government, but we wanted to work deeply and bring about a theological revolution. ... The Muslim Youth would make up slogans just like the communists."[76]

Similar ideals motivated the Haqqaniyya graduate Nabi Muhammadi, who emerged in the 1960s as one of the leading clerical anti-communist activists in Afghanistan. Elected to parliament in 1965 from Logar Province, where he taught at a large madrassa, Muhammadi became nationally famous for his role in a parliamentary debate on Marxism that was broadcast over national radio. To the assertions of the leftist parliamentarian Babrak Karmal, the future communist president of Afghanistan, that there was no contradiction between religion and Marxism, Muhammadi countered with "detailed passages from Marx, Engels, Lenin and Stalin to demonstrate the opposition of Marxist ideologies to religious belief."[77] He toured the country with other 'ulama preaching against the menace of communism, and organized a protest demonstration in 1972 in Kabul composed of clerics and madrassa students opposing the activities of communist groups.[78] Like Khalis, Muhammadi's anti-communist activism was waged in defense of Afghanistan's traditional religious culture, and not in pursuit of a revolutionary étatist agenda.

During the anti-Soviet years, Yunis Khalis and Muhammad Nabi Muhammadi would establish, respectively, the two traditional highland Pashtun mujahidin parties: Hizb-i Islami-Khalis (HIK) and Harakat-i Inqilab-i Islami (hereinafter "Harakat"). These two party leaders and their senior battlefield commanders—foremost of them being Jalaluddin Haqqani, who was affiliated during the war with Khalis' HIK—formed, along with the Pakistani Pashtun Islamist politicians of the JUI, what could be called the "Haqqaniyya network," an intertwined group of Haqqaniyya graduates who deployed distinctive practices of Islamist mobilization in the highland tribal regions of Afghanistan and Pakistan during the 1970s and 1980s and from which some of the Taliban leadership emerged in the 1990s. The ideological tensions between the Haqqaniyya-educated leaders and the Kabul Islamists may have been relatively muted during the late 1960s and early 1970s, but they would emerge as major fault lines splitting the mujahidin parties during the anti-Soviet conflict and in the subsequent civil war.[79]

In contrast to what is often termed the fundamentalism of the Kabul Islamists and their JI allies, the "Haqqaniyya network" of highland Pashtun Afghan mujahidin and Pakistani clerical politicians could better be described as traditionalist, in the sense that their political activities were "defined in terms of the defense of traditional Islamic culture" against strong central states, colonial or imperial powers, or Marxist reforms.[80] This is not to say that the JUI and the Haqqanis did not wish to see some form of Islamic government in Islamabad and Kabul: they did and still do, but they have remained committed to decentralized, grassroots, and predominantly rural forms of mobilization that emphasize continuity with tribal political culture and (highland) Pashtun regional autonomy.[81] In contrast to the fundamentally anti-leftist orientation of the Pak-Afghan urban Islamists, the JUI has often made common cause with the political left in Pakistan, seeing the socialist populism of the PPP as "basically in resonance with the populism and anti-imperialism of the pre-Partition Jamiat Ulema movements."[82] From these two distinct traditions of Islamism emerged two regional blocs of Islamist mobilization, with the JI aligned with the mujahidin parties of the Kabuli Islamists, headquartered during the anti-Soviet war at Peshawar, and the JUI aligned with the Haqqanis and the two Haqqaniyya network mujahidin parties of HIK and Harakat.[83]

These two strands of Pak-Afghan Sunni Islamism—the revolutionary and the traditionalist, or put differently, the urban statist and the highland state-evading—developed along separate but interrelated trajectories over the course of the ensuing four decades of regional conflict. Over time the two regional blocs forged their own alliances with different segments of the Pakistani state and international aid donors; with various Pakistani sectarian and Kashmir-focused militant groups; and eventually with a variety of transnational jihadi organizations. Across these developments, the unique regional and sociopolitical location of the Haqqanis would give them an ever more valuable advantage, an advantage they were able to capitalize on by making the territory which they controlled the center at which all of these lines of development converged.

The Islamist Blocs in Anti-Daoud Resistance

In 1970, after completing his studies at Dar al-'Ulum Haqqaniyya, Jalaluddin Haqqani campaigned in northwestern Pakistan for Mawlawi Abdul Haq, founder of the Haqqaniyya madrassa, in the latter's (successful) bid for a seat in Pakistan's National Assembly as a JUI candidate in the general elections that year.[84] Jalaluddin spent the following year teaching at the Haqqaniyya madrassa, made the pilgrimage to Mecca, and then decided to return to Afghanistan and establish a madrassa of his own—the Rahimiyya madrassa in the town of Nika in Paktika Province.[85] He gives the following account of this period himself in an interview published by one of the Haqqani network's magazines in 1990:

> I had planned to stay in the Haqqaniyya madrassa for at least four or five years, until a strong, organized and informed group could be formed from among the Afghan *taliban* (students) there, whom I could then take into Afghanistan. But due to persistent emphasis by certain friends, I went to Afghanistan instead and began teaching there. There [in Nika, Paktika], I laid the foundation of a large madrassa and began cementing my contacts with the 'ulama. We began our campaign of inviting people to our Islamic movement, and commenced our "cold" struggle against the communists.[86]

Jalaluddin might have gone on to a successful and nonviolent career in Pak-Afghan Islamist politics were it not for the eruption of a fresh round of profound turmoil on both sides of the Durand Line in 1973, throwing him together with the Kabul Islamists in a guerrilla campaign of anti-communist resistance in Afghanistan that would dominate his life through the 1980s. These events also drew the Pakistani state more directly into the conflict in Afghanistan and marked the beginning of the long and still ongoing ties between the Haqqanis and the Pakistani military establishment.

After the catastrophic 1971 war in East Pakistan that ended with the creation of Bangladesh and, among other losses, the holding of 90,000 of (West) Pakistan's troops as prisoners of war in India, Zulfikar Ali Bhutto became president and chief martial law administrator and oversaw the reorganization of a much-reduced Pakistan into its current four provincial governments. The earlier general elections handed Bhutto's PPP party significant majorities in Sindh and Punjab, but a coalition of the National Awami Party (NAP) and JUI parties in the NWFP and Baluchistan won enough seats from their respective provinces to form the provincial governments there. Despite a great deal of bad blood between them, in March of 1972 Bhutto's government signed tripartite agreements with the NAP–JUI coalitions in these two provinces that recognized their provincial rule of the Northwest Frontier and Baluchistan. The JUI's Mufti Mahmood headed the NWFP government, while the Baluch nationalist Sardar Ataullah Mengal was elected chief minister of Baluchistan by its provincial assembly. This rule of Pakistan's frontier provinces by an ethno-nationalist coalition, however, did not last a year. Bhutto's government grew increasingly alarmed at the assertive calls for autonomy by the Baluchistan provincial government. It was also under pressure from the shah of Iran to curtail a rising Baluch nationalism that threatened to spill over into Iranian Baluchistan. In February of 1973 Bhutto dismissed the Baluchistan provincial government, followed immediately by the resignation-in-protest of the NAP–JUI coalition government in the NWFP. Across the border, after ten years in the political wilderness, former Prime Minister Daoud returned to power in Kabul in July in a palace coup, ousting Zahir Shah and returning immediately to his prior agitation on behalf of "Pashtunistan." On the day of the coup itself, Daoud issued a radio broadcast announcing that relations with Pakistan would be predicated upon a "peaceful and honorable solution to this problem [Pashtunistan] in accordance with the hopes and aspirations of the Pashtun and Baluch people and their leaders."[87] Leaders of the NAP from Baluchistan and the NWFP fled to Kabul where they received support from Daoud's government in leading nationalist resistance to the Bhutto regime along the Pakistani frontier. Bhutto sent the army into Baluchistan and launched a war against the Baluch uprising that would last until his ouster from power in 1977.

In the aftermath of the 1973 developments, Daoud and Bhutto initiated covert campaigns of symmetrical cross-border support for destabilizing insurgencies against one another's regimes. Daoud's government provided ammunition and arms to Baluch and Pashtun nationalists that Pakistan regarded as "secessionist forces."[88]

Bhutto, meanwhile, tasked then-Brigadier Naseerullah Babar, inspector general of Pakistan's Frontier Corps, with arming and training Afghan Islamists in their anti-Daoud efforts. Among the thousands of recipients of the Pakistani training, provided at camps established throughout the tribal areas, were prominent members of the Kabul Islamist circles including Hekmatyar, Massoud, and Rabbani, who had fled crackdowns on Islamist activism in Kabul by Daoud upon his return to power. The ISI drew up a list of 1,331 Afghan resistance activists who were to receive monthly payments through the Frontier Corps, while guerrilla warfare training was provided to "at least 5,000 Islamists" in 1973 and 1974.[89] The American diplomat Peter Tomsen was told by Pakistani officials of ISI payments delivered to Hekmatyar while the latter was still in Kabul, and after the Kabulis fled to Peshawar Hekmatyar was selected by the ISI and Babar as their liaison to the group.[90]

Babar, who would go on to serve as a primary link between the ISI and the Taliban as Benazir Bhutto's interior minister during the mid-1990s, claimed that American aid was also directed to the Afghan anti-Daoud activists at this time. He told the *New York Times* in 1989 that when the Kabul Islamists fled to Pakistan, "We took them under our cover because we knew that some day there would be trouble in Afghanistan. We wanted to build up a leadership to influence events." He is then reported to have said that "the United States had also been financing such potential leaders since 1973 and had taken Mr. Hekmatyar 'under its umbrella' months before the Soviet invasion."[91] Though this claim is not to my knowledge corroborated by other sources, neither is it entirely implausible. In March 1973 the Nixon administration relaxed restrictions on military aid to Pakistan, releasing $24 million worth of military equipment to Bhutto's government. In September President Nixon received Prime Minister Bhutto on a state visit at the White House, announcing on that occasion that "the independence and integrity of Pakistan is a cornerstone of American foreign policy."[92] Given that one of the most active threats to Pakistan's integrity in 1973—as the Pakistani government saw it—was Daoud's support for the Baluch insurgency, and that Pakistan's policy in response was to aid the Afghan Islamist resistance, Babar's claim of American involvement in the latter effort would concord with Nixon's statement about America's policy priorities. Jalaluddin Haqqani and his Haqqaniyya allies became direct beneficiaries of the Pakistani support initiative by the end of 1973. Babar's claim, then, raises the possibility that the Haqqanis benefited from US government aid much earlier than has previously been thought, and in the earliest phase of their militant activities.

According to Haqqani sources, Jalaluddin and his nascent network of anti-communist 'ulama began their war on the Daoud regime several months before the establishment of the Pakistani training initiative. In 1989 the Pashto-language Haqqani magazine *Manba' al-Jihad* ("Fountainhead of Jihad") published a historical account of the Haqqanis' jihadi beginnings that dates their first calls for jihad to July 1973, immediately after Daoud's coup. The account was written by Mawlawi Aziz Khan, who fought in some of the earliest battles in the 1970s, spent the first half of the 1980s living in the Gulf to mobilize support for the Haqqani network's anti-Soviet struggle, and went on to become the first dean of the Haqqanis' Manba' al-'Ulum madrassa on the outskirts of Miranshah, North Waziristan. After recounting the history of Islamist groups in Afghanistan and their efforts to counter communist influence in the country, Aziz Khan writes:

> As soon as Daoud declared the establishment of the Republic through the national radio [on 17 July 1973], Mawlawi Sahib Jalaluddin Haqqani declared jihad in the village of Nika, Zadran, and raised the flag of jihad there.[93] He announced the commencement of jihad by loudspeakers throughout the region, and some 'ulama and taliban [madrassa students] joined him. But the government interfered and prevented the spread of this movement by appealing to the tribes, who in turn did not let Haqqani Sahib continue his jihad. Having no choice, Haqqani Sahib began a secret jihad. At that time, I joined him. It was night when I left my village, Gomal, and went to Zadran to meet with Haqqani Sahib.[94] There I was introduced to him and Mawlawi Ahmad Gul, who was later killed. They told me all about their preparations. They also informed me that another group of 'ulama and youth, led by Hekmatyar Sahib, was forming, which also wanted to work toward the establishment of a true Islamic state in Afghanistan. Haqqani Sahib then instructed me, Mawlawi Ahmad Gul, Mawlawi Fathullah and Mawlawi Sher Muhammad, under the leadership

of Mutiullah Khan,[95] to go to Peshawar to meet with Hekmatyar Sahib. After we met with Hekmatyar in Peshawar, he instructed Mutiullah Khan to take the group back to Afghanistan to start jihad against the regime and its communist backers in Urgun.[96] We also met with Qazi Muhammad Amin Waqad[97] to start making the preliminary preparations for the jihad.[98]

Aziz Khan's claim that Jalaluddin called for jihad in 1973 is repeated in numerous other articles in the Haqqani magazines, though no details are provided about any specific actions taken against the regime beyond issuing calls for popular uprisings. Aziz Khan's account also does not specify how long Jalaluddin and his comrades engaged in "secret jihad" in greater Paktia, though his and other accounts do establish that the Haqqani resistance established links with the Kabul Islamists in Peshawar at some point between 1973 and 1975, at which time Jalaluddin Haqqani shifted his base of operations to North Waziristan. During this period the Kabul Islamists and the highland Pashtun cleric activists forged closer ties with each other, received training and support from Pakistan via the Frontier Corps, and argued over strategy. Hekmatyar, representing the radical youth wing of the movement, wanted to embark immediately with widespread armed struggle, but Burhanuddin Rabbani, a professor at Kabul University, did not think that the Afghan resistance-in-exile had sufficient resources or local support to sustain a violent campaign.

It is well known that in the summer of 1975 the assembled Afghan Islamists in Peshawar launched a series of uprisings against the Daoud regime throughout Afghanistan, though no previous account has ever noted the involvement of the Haqqanis in these largely failed efforts.[99] The decision to launch the revolts, which were meant to coincide with an ill-planned coup to be carried out by sympathizers within the military in Kabul, was taken by Hekmatyar—with Pakistani support—while Rabbani was visiting Saudi Arabia. In the account quoted above, Aziz Khan ends by describing how the party of Haqqani activists sent by Jalaluddin to liaise with Hekmatyar's group in Peshawar was sent back by Hekmatyar to Paktika to "start jihad ... in Urgun." Another Pashto article in *Manba' al-Jihad* describes the resultant efforts in Urgun and dates them to the late summer of 1975. It would thus appear that this Haqqani uprising in Paktika was clearly meant to coincide with the other uprisings called for by Hekmatyar and that it was planned in concert with the Kabul Islamists and Frontier Corps officers in Peshawar.

As the Urgun uprising is the first battle by the Haqqani network for which we have details, and as it claims to draw upon Jalaluddin Haqqani's personal diary, I quote from the article at some length:

It was a night in August 1975. The local communists who had infiltrated the local government organizations in Urgun District were continually bothering people, particularly the religious scholars, by beating them and jailing them for no reason. Eventually, the local people became very upset with the situation and decided to do something about it. The people got the backing of the *'ulama* and found weapons. One day, when the Urgun District Chief and his friends were supervising a project, the mujahidin attacked them. They were a group of twenty-five fighters, led by Mawlawi Jalaluddin Haqqani. The battle continued for a few hours. The District Chief was wounded, but he fled and lived. The District Police Commander and nine of his men were killed.

Soon the news spread in the area. The government began searching for those who had perpetrated this attack. The first person was Haqqani, whose house was surrounded by government troops. The government warned that the local people must surrender Mawlawi Haqqani alive to the government. ... Let's hear the story from Mawlawi Jalaluddin Haqqani himself:

"When government forces surrounded my house, some of the elders wanted to give me up to the enemy. But Haji Amanullah and some other elders decided against it. Haji Amanullah told me: 'We will all fight with you. Even if they kill my brothers and destroy my house, I will not let them take you alive.' I decided that I would not surrender myself, and we all decided to fight the government ... There were a few problems, though. First, some elders were opposed to our plan; and second, we did not have enough ammunition ... The elders asked the government forces to let the women and children get out of the house, and then I would speak with them and would go with them ... The forces allowed the women and children to leave and, taking advantage of this, I took the Qur'an in one hand and the gun in the other, and fled the house, reciting a verse from the Qur'an."

Some of Mawalwi Haqqani's madrassa pupils had set an ambush in Ziruk so that if Haqqani was taken by the government they could ambush the forces and set him free.[100] But when they received the news that Haqqani had fled the house and gotten to the mountains safely, they, too, went to the mountains and joined Haqqani. The total number of fighters was then thirty men. Besides Mawlawi Haqqani, his younger brother, Haji Ibrahim, who is now commander of the 'Umar-e-Faruq Division, was also there.[101] They spent a month and a half there. When their presence became known, the government, with the assistance of people from Zadran and other districts (those people were in appearance on the government's side, but their hearts were with the mujahidin) attacked the mujahidin many times, but did not succeed in pushing the mujahidin out of the area. Finally, the government blocked all the roads leading to the area in an effort to flush the mujahidin out.

The local people, who were with the mujahidin, consulted Mawlawi Haqqani and reported to the government that the mujahidin had evacuated the area and gone toward Katawaz.[102] When the government forces left for Katawaz, the mujahidin came out of their hideouts and went toward Pakistan. In this caravan, Mutiullah, whose real name was Gulbaz and had taken part in multiple operations, and Mawlawi Mansoor, who had fled from Zurmat, joined Mawlawi Haqqani.[103] When these soldiers of God set their journey off to Pakistan, the [Afghan] government arrested several of Mawlawi Haqqani's friends—Mawlawi Ahmad Gul, Sahib Qari Shah and Mawlawi Mahmud—and put them in dark jail cells. But after spending some time in jail, they were released. In consultation with Mawlawi Haqqani, Mawlawi Aziz Khan and Mawlawi Ahmad Gul remained in the area in order to keep the flames of jihad burning and to maintain the flow of weapons and ideas into the area.[104]

This early effort by the Haqqanis at inciting a popular struggle against the government was a failure, ending with most of its leaders either fleeing to Pakistan or in jail. A similar pattern marked the efforts by Islamists elsewhere in the country that summer, though many of the activists were not as lucky as Jalaluddin and his group. The Muslim Youth networks in Kabul were decimated and many of Afghanistan's leading Islamists were executed. Hekmatyar's precipitous action, combined with the fact that he had remained in Peshawar during the uprisings, earned him a lasting reputation for rash and autocratic leadership. Rabbani was furious and split with Hekmatyar upon his return from Saudi Arabia. Jalaluddin Haqqani and other highland Pashtun leaders joined the Kabul Islamist leaders in Peshawar in late 1975 and an attempt was made to heal the rift and overcome the centrifugal tendencies and ethnic divisions of these often-divisive leaders. With Qazi Amin Waqad named its first amir, the Hizb-i Islami Afghanistan party was formed in May of 1976, merging all of the factions of anti-Daoud Sunni Islamist activism into one organization. The executive committee of the new party included, in addition to the aforementioned Kabuli leaders, Jalaluddin Haqqani, Nasrullah Mansur, and Haji Din Muhammad, another Haqqaniyya network cleric who would work closely with Haqqani during the 1980s.[105] Though the alliance ultimately failed, this would not be the last time that Jalaluddin played a prominent role in efforts at uniting the ranks of the fractious Kabuli elites, an endeavor that would come to characterize his relationship to these groups during and after the anti-Soviet war.

After the short-lived 1975 Islamist revolts, Pakistan's support for the Afghan dissidents waned, and Hizb-i Islami lost any hope of having the necessary resources or influence to inspire a broad-based rebellion. Instead, the group focused on assassinations and political violence in the capital and turned increasingly to the Arab world for support (discussed further in Chapter 2). Qazi Amin and Hekmatyar both told David Edwards in interviews that the party dispatched several hit squads to Kabul during these years, with their only prominent success being the assassination of Parcham ideologue Mir Akbar Khyber in 1978.[106] Hekmatyar told Edwards in 1983 that the killing "was the doing of Hizbi guerrillas." As Edwards notes, the murder was widely believed at the time to have been Daoud's doing. Yet in a profile of Jalaluddin Haqqani in the English-language magazine *Arabia*, Haqqani sources claimed that the killer was an early Haqqani network member. According to this article, after the Muslim Youth leadership issued a call for jihad against the regime and "initiated a national guerrilla campaign against the ruling oppressors," "Maulana Jalaluddin was an enthusiastic worker of the jihad movement and one of his men was responsible for killing Mir Akbar."[107] The article further claims that the unnamed assassin had earlier participated in a 1977 attempt by Haqqani's men to dig an underground tunnel to the Deh Mazang prison in Kabul and free Islamist activists imprisoned there by Daoud. The plot was discovered and all of the Islamist prisoners were later executed at Pul-e-Charkhi prison, a grisly event that has been amply documented elsewhere.[108]

As far as Pakistan was concerned, continued support to the Afghan Islamists was now no longer necessary nor justified. Bhutto's 1975 gambit had paid off: the credible threat of a widespread Pakistan-supported Islamist insurgency in Afghanistan proved sufficient to get Daoud to back down on "Pashtunistan" and cross-border relations began to improve dramatically. Bhutto and Daoud exchanged state visits in 1976 and Iran and the United States joined in urging closer Pak-Afghan ties—and a lessening of Afghan–Soviet ties. Daoud had already grown suspicious of Soviet involvement in his administration and had begun a purge of PDPA members from prominent government and military positions.[109] During a visit to Moscow in April 1977, Daoud alarmed his hosts with an angry display of defiant independence that may have sealed his own fate. When pressed by General Secretary Brezhnev to curtail the number of Western aid personnel in Afghanistan, Daoud retorted that the USSR could "not dictate to us how to run our country and whom to employ in Afghanistan" and then abruptly walked out of the meeting.[110] A year later Daoud was dead, killed in a coup by the PDPA that brought Nur Muhammad Taraki to power as Afghanistan's first communist president.

Taraki, Zia, and the Mujahidin Parties

By the time of the coup against Daoud in April 1978, the united Hizb-i Islami Afghanistan had fallen apart and the senior Kabuli Islamist leaders had begun to establish their own parties.[111] Hekmatyar led the Hizb-i Islami-Gulbuddin (HIG), the most ideologically radical and organizationally centralized of all the parties, while Rabbani went on to form the Jamiat-i Islami Afghanistan (JIA), whose most capable commanders were Ahmad Shah Massoud in the north and Isma'il Khan in Herat in western Afghanistan. Though both were multiethnic in makeup, Pashtuns predominated in HIG while JIA emerged as the premiere representative of the Tajik resistance. Haqqani joined the Hizb-i Islami-Khalis (HIK) of fellow Haqqaniyya alumnus Yunis Khalis, while Nasrullah Mansur joined the other Haqqaniyya party, Nabi Muhammadi's Harakat.[112] Sayyaf, imprisoned in Kabul during this period, was later released and formed the Ittihad party in 1980. The different political cultures of the Kabuli Islamists and the highland Pashtun clerical leaders not surprisingly led to very different types of organization among these various parties.

In the years prior to the massive influx of foreign aid and the manipulative patronage practices of the ISI and CIA, Haqqani and the other Haqqaniyya network parties already enjoyed certain advantages over the Kabuli-Peshawar parties in terms of organizational effectiveness and advantageous geographical position. As the war against the communist regime in Kabul was staged from Pakistan, the first and most vital fronts, and the essential supply lines to all areas of resistance in the country, were all located in the highland Pashtun regions. The route through the southern end of this region—Miranshah to Khost—was especially important, and was the single most vital and abundant line of communication during the whole of the conflict. On either side of the Durand Line, in these areas the Haqqanis were respected locals, with deep familiarity with and a strong attachment to the highland Pashtun traditions of political mobilization.

The Haqqani fronts were organized on tribal lines, distributing power, local decision-making and rights to materiel between the front commander and a tribal council, the latter composed of elders selected by the tribes themselves.[113] The Haqqani leaders were not likely to forget the successes of the Daoud government in manipulating tribal loyalties against their earliest efforts, and when Taraki and later Babrak Karmal attempted to pursue similar strategies, the Haqqanis prioritized good relations with the tribal councils and vigorous counterpropaganda against Kabul's outreach campaigns.[114] In January of 1980 Faiz Muhammad, a former interior minister under Daoud, was appointed minister of frontier and tribal affairs—the same position that Jalaluddin Haqqani would later hold under the Taliban—and dispatched from Kabul to the Zadran areas in the southeast in an effort to "win over rebel or neutral ethnic groups in eastern Afghanistan and to take advantage of rivalries."[115] In response the Haqqanis distributed a leaflet signed by

Jalaluddin Haqqani, "General Amir of the Paktia Jihadi Fronts," calling on the people to "reject the perfidy of the professional turncoat and spy, this Parchami traitor element, Faiz Muhammad. Discard him and obliterate him."[116] In September of the same year, after distributing $28,000 in cash to a meeting of Zadran elders in a village near Khost, the minister was killed by locals.[117] Even at this early stage in the conflict, the Haqqanis were clearly able to mobilize popular support against the regime in the face of determined campaigns to undermine them.

The Kabuli Islamist parties, on the other hand, were exiles rather than locals on Pakistan's highland frontier, and they had much less success in establishing a predominant presence along the Pak-Afghan border. Rabbani's JIA had almost no presence in the Pashtun areas, and was strongest in the Tajik north and the Persian-speaking west.[118] Hekmatyar's HIG, though present throughout the Pashtun east, never established a predominant presence in any of these areas and was subject to the logistical control of resources given by the ISI to the Haqqanis in the southeast.[119] The HIG also remained inflexibly unaccommodating of Pashtun tribal practices, and "insisted that all disputes and criminal proceedings be handled according to Islamic law under the supervision of party leaders."[120] These strictures alienated the HIG from local people in the border regions and created tensions with the Haqqaniyya parties of HIK and Harakat. As Edwards notes, the HIG had a "long list of complaints against Khales, Nabi, and other members of the ulema, beginning with their condoning of popular religious practices that had no basis in Islamic scripture." Among the list of ritual practices that Hekmatyar and his followers found objectionable was a custom whereby "travelers embarking on a journey customarily passed under a copy of the Qur'an to ensure their safe return."[121] The American writer Jere Van Dyk, who visited the Haqqanis in Paktia in 1981, witnessed Jalaluddin presiding over an instance of this very practice with a group of fighters about to set off for an attack on an Afghan army base:

> The men gathered in a circle like players do around their coach before a game. It was *Azon*, the call for *jihad*. Jaluladin [*sic*] prayed and each man bowed, then raised his hands to the sky, palms upward, to receive the

blessings of Allah. For a moment it was silent; then each man, single file, passed underneath an unwound turban held by two men over the path. A Koran lay wrapped in the cloth. They shouted, raised their rifles.[122]

Participation in such popular religious practices by the leaders of the Haqqani network not only set them apart ideologically from the "fundamentalist" parties like HIG; they also granted their leadership a popular legitimacy that the radical parties never managed to attain.

Issues of popular legitimacy aside, HIG and the other Peshawar-based Kabuli mujahidin parties received an unexpected boon in 1977 when General Zia ul-Haq ousted—and then executed—Zulfikar Ali Bhutto in a coup, ending democratic rule in Pakistan for the next decade and eventually restoring Pakistani aid to the Afghan resistance. Zia had long been a supporter of the JI, and while serving as army chief of staff under Bhutto he had proposed making the writings of Abu'l-'Ala Mawdudi, the founder of the JI, part of the examinations for military promotion.[123] When he came to power Zia succeeded in co-opting the JI and bringing them into his regime, favoring them as bolsterers of his claims to Islamic legitimacy and as bulwarks against the Pakistani left. The JUI, on the other hand, remained in opposition to Zia's military dictatorship and joined the Movement for the Restoration of Democracy (MRD), a coalition of political parties that included the leftist PPP.[124]

With the hundreds of millions of dollars in military aid that began pouring from the United States and other countries into Pakistan after the Soviet invasion of Afghanistan, Zia and the ISI, Pakistan's sprawling intelligence agency, had tremendous resources at their disposal with which to manipulate the direction of the Afghan insurgency. The welter of parties and resistance groups that had sprung up in Peshawar were reduced to seven—all Sunni—and only commanders fighting for one of these parties would receive weapons or other forms of aid.[125] Zia directed the ISI to prioritize the JI-linked Afghan mujahidin parties, first and foremost Hekmatyar's HIG, but also Sayyaf's Ittihad party and, to a lesser extent, Rabbani's JIA as favored recipients of aid. This favoritism meant that HIG was nearly always flush with resources and able to buy access to more fronts than its unpopular organizational style may have otherwise allowed for. But the ISI also distributed aid on the basis of battlefield effectiveness and rewarded parties for actions taken—thus in reward for bringing down one Afghan or Soviet plane with a Stinger missile, the ISI would supply the same front with two more.[126] Because of his unrivalled capacity as a guerrilla leader in the all-important southeast, Jalaluddin Haqqani and his fronts were thus not disadvantaged by Zia's alliance with the JI-HIG, and he was instead given tremendous latitude and power as the overall coordinator of logistical support in that region.[127]

Despite their opposition to his regime and the presence of their JI rivals in Zia's cabinet, the JUI and their Afghan mujahidin partners would benefit enormously from another aspect of Zia's rule: the Islamization campaign, and in particular the Zakat Ordinance. This law, enacted under Zia in 1980, instituted a deduction at source withdrawal on the first day of every Ramadan of 2.5 percent from all savings accounts in Pakistan above a certain exemption limit, the funds to be distributed to "the needy."[128] One of the primary beneficiaries of this massive new source of state revenue were the madrassas, as in providing room and board to indigent students they were deemed legitimate agents of distribution of aid to the needy. The JUI, already much more madrassa-based than the JI and operating before the Zakat Ordinance a much larger network of schools, saw an immediate and rapid "mushroom-growth" in the construction of new schools, many of them on the highland frontier, throughout the 1980s.[129] As is now well known, this boom in the jihad-era madrassa business, often catering to Afghan war refugees along the border and operating with the express intent to prepare and deploy young mujahidin to the theaters of conflict, wreaked profound and still-unfolding havoc on the fabric of Pashtun society. As Joshua White notes, the fallout of these developments in the tribal areas included "the proliferation of small arms and the development of the so-called 'Kalashnikov culture;' the entrenchment of sectarian movements and their ideologies-of-difference; and, perhaps most dangerously, the creation of a vast cadre of both ideological and opportunistic veteran *jihadis* beholden in only the most tenuous fashion to the state system."[130] For the Haqqanis, however, these were precisely the elements of the JUI madrassa boom that gave them a critical resource mobilization advantage that none of the other Afghan parties could match.

The Haqqanis were not simply beneficiaries of the growth in the madrassa networks: they were also contributors. As already noted, Jalaluddin Haqqani began the work of establishing his own seminaries in eastern Afghanistan in the early 1970s, beginning with the Rahimiyya madrassa in Nika, Paktika—the same village from which he had issued his first call for jihad against Daoud in 1973. With the influx of Zakat funds after 1980 his cross-border archipelago of religious schools grew to include no less than eighty madrassas.[131] The crown jewel was the Manba' al-'Ulum ("Fountainhead of Knowledge") in Danday Darpakhel, near Miranshah, North Waziristan, a highly ornate building for which construction began in 1980. Its Deobandi curriculum modeled after that of Dar al-'Ulum Haqqaniyya, Manba' al-'Ulum's faculty consisted mainly of Haqqaniyya graduates.[132] As the Haqqani magazines later described it:

> The location of the institute of *Manba' al-'Ulum* was chosen to be only a few kilometers away from the borders of the province of Paktia, and overlooks the gates of Khost where the battles have never ceased since the beginning [of the jihad]. The location was chosen so that the students of the *shari'a* sciences can be raised on the same soil where the battles are waged or at least at a nearby location. It was necessary for the scholars who established the institute to take into consideration the location because such a thing definitely has an influence over the spirits as it could establish a living bond between the students and the jihad. Often times the walls of the institute were shaken by the explosions in Khost.[133]

Zia's Zakat Ordinance thus helped the Haqqanis broaden their social base as the most prominent religious leaders and providers of religious education in their region, allowing them to build an extensive local infrastructure for mobilization, recruitment, and training. But Zia's and the ISI's manipulation of the ideological direction of the resistance also strengthened the Haqqanis' position in local tribal politics, marginalizing one of the most powerful Zadran families. In accordance with Kabul's "Swiss cheese" approach to governing the Pashtun highlands, the Afghan state had long negotiated local allegiances on the frontier through the patronage of prominent landowning families, and throughout the twentieth century the most important such family among the Zadran tribes was the Babrakzais. Babrak Khan, the eponymous patriarch of the family, had served Abdur Rahman in the nineteenth century and was killed in 1924 while aiding King Amanullah's crackdown on the Khost Rebellion.[134] His grandson Muhammad Umar Babrakzai, a French-educated former Afghan Supreme Court justice and the most prominent Babrakzai Zadran leader at the time of the Soviet invasion, organized a Loya Jirga ("Supreme Council") in Peshawar, which led to the creation of the Islami Milli Inqilabi Jirga ("National Islamic Revolutionary Council") in early 1980.[135] This jirga sought to become an umbrella organization for all of the resistance groups and it invited the Islamist leaders to join, but the latter refused, calling the jirga an "enemy of the sacred Islamic revolution" on account of its secular orientation.[136] Zia's government withheld any support for the jirga and refused permission for it to convene an assembly in Quetta, seeing the jirga as in direct conflict with the government's program of Islamization and a potential vehicle for the reemergence of a Pashtun independence movement.[137] The jirga quickly faded into irrelevance, and the Haqqanis were thus rid of a potential rival for control of the resistance among the Zadran tribes.[138]

Conclusion

This chapter has sought to situate the origins and earliest activities of the Haqqani network within several contexts, and with an eye toward understanding its remarkable endurance in a place and time characterized by constant change and violent upheaval. In terms of its immediate local context, the Haqqani network emerged from within a long-standing tradition of cleric-led highland Pashtun resistance to state attacks on the political and cultural autonomy of the tribes. Unlike the more radical Pashtun Islamists of the HIG party, the Haqqanis utilized existing social structures and patterns of mobilization that had been adapted by previous generations to resist state appropriation. In building a network of activist seminaries and harnessing religious authority to the cause of intertribal defense against perceived threats to the social order, the Haqqanis followed in the footsteps of the Hadda Mullah and his early twentieth-century disciples. This continuity with aspects of local political culture helps to explain the measure of popular support that the Haqqanis managed to win for their struggle. But it does not explain the Haqqanis' access to the resources needed to develop the infrastructure that this support was predicated on in the first place. For that we examined the Haqqanis in terms of broader contexts, namely the rise of Islamism and Pak-Afghan interstate conflicts.

The first generation of Haqqani network leaders was almost entirely composed of seminary students who attended the Haqqaniyya madrassa during a decade in which radical Islamist political movements were gaining a foothold in Kabul. The Haqqaniyya students shared the anti-Marxist grievances of the Kabul Islamists and had personal links to the latter movement through older alumni like Yunis Khalis and Muhammad Nabi Muhammadi. Their years at the madrassa also allowed the Haqqani leaders to forge ties with a segment of Pakistan's Islamist political establishment—the JUI—which greatly broadened their access to resources, especially after Zia's Islamization campaign. These ideological links made the Haqqanis enemies of the Afghan state, but they also made them extremely useful to Pakistan. Feeling threatened by Kabul's support for irredentist Pashtun nationalism, a succession of governments in Pakistan saw Afghan Islamists—especially Pashtun Islamists—as an ideal counterweight, and poured ever-increasing amounts of resources into supporting them. For ideological and political reasons, Pakistan's most favored representative of this Pashtun Islamist antidote was Hekmetyar's HIG, and this would remain the case until the rise of the Taliban in 1994. But the Haqqanis were much savvier than the HIG at tribal politics, which, combined with their foothold in the strategically critical southeast, assured them a significant share of the Pakistani largesse.

Already by the late 1970s, then, the Haqqani network had amassed many of the assets that would prove critical to their endurance across the ensuing decades of conflict. Direct support from the Pakistani military establishment, a nationwide network of political sympathizers in Pakistan's JUI, safe haven in North Waziristan, and deep roots in the social infrastructure of greater Paktia—the same elements that make the Haqqanis such formidable opponents of the Western and Afghan armies today—were all well in place by 1979. But the Haqqanis could not yet claim to represent the "fountainhead of jihad" announced by their magazines of later years. In order to achieve that distinction, the Afghan jihad—and the Haqqanis' place within it—would have to be significantly globalized, a process that forms the central concern of the next two chapters.

2

BIRTH OF THE NEXUS

THE HAQQANI NETWORK, FOREIGN FIGHTERS, AND THE ORIGINS OF AL-QA'IDA

The Soviet invasion of Afghanistan in December of 1979 dramatically altered the shape and scale of the Afghan resistance in ways that the Kabuli exiles in Peshawar could not have imagined just a year before. Afghanistan became the focal point for the final battle of the global Cold War, and staggering quantities of resources poured into Pakistan from all over the world to aid the mujahidin. The United States, Saudi Arabia, China, and other partner states contributed upwards of 12 billion dollars worth of direct aid to Pakistan in the 1980s to support the insurgency, and according to some estimates more small arms were shipped into Afghanistan than to any other country in the world during that period.[1] According to the CIA official in charge of the agency's aid program, the CIA alone was providing 60,000 tons of weapons and supplies to mujahidin field commanders every year by the mid-1980s.[2] In the spring of 1978, however, none among the Afghan Islamist resistance could have foreseen this turn of events, and the picture at that time looked much more bleak. Despite the renewed interest in their struggle shown by General Zia, Taraki's communist coup in April of 1978 found the Afghan Islamists resource-poor and disunited, and it reignited the strategy debates that had divided the Islamist leaders in 1975. Some wanted to return to Afghanistan and attempt another broad uprising, while others, citing lack of weaponry and cash, argued that appeals must first be made to the oil-wealthy Arab states for aid.[3]

The Haqqanis pursued both tracks simultaneously, but they also introduced an innovation in their appeals to the Arab world that would have fateful consequences in years to come. Unlike any of the other parties, the Haqqanis made direct calls for foreign fighter volunteers, and the Haqqanis would remain throughout the 1980s the only group consistently willing to welcome large numbers of non-Afghan volunteer fighters into their ranks. This innovation transformed the nature of the jihad in Afghanistan, linking it to broader struggles and giving birth in the following decade to what would come to be known as global jihadism. It was in this context and as a result of the Haqqanis' strategic decision regarding foreign fighters that Osama bin Laden and his supporters established the al-Qa'ida organization in the last years of the 1980s. It was also in this connection that the Pakistani military would turn to the Haqqanis to train Kashmiri militants, establishing the Haqqanis as a "strategic asset" in Pakistan's policies of war-by-proxy.[4] Historians have largely neglected the central role played by the Haqqanis in these historic processes, and this chapter seeks to redress this by introducing previously unstudied primary sources that firmly establish the Haqqanis at the center of these world-changing events.

The Haqqani Network and the Rise of the Afghan Arabs

Though certainly the most famous, Osama bin Laden was by no means the first or only "Afghan Arab" to have begun his military engagement in the Afghan jihad with the Haqqanis.[5] The first movers of direct battlefield participation on the part of Arab volunteers were in fact recruited by the Haqqanis in the Gulf several months before the Soviet invasion. Before 1986 the vast majority of the Afghan Arabs were humanitarian aid workers providing services out of offices set up in Peshawar by (mostly Saudi-supported) Islamic non-governmental organizations.[6] These early volunteers hailed from Islamist activist networks with long-standing ideological and personal links with the JI and the JI-associated Kabuli Islamist parties. Bin Laden, for example, made his first visit to Pakistan shortly after the Soviet invasion in order to meet with Mian Muhammad Tufail, the second leader of the JI, to whom he presented money collected from members of his family for the cause of the Afghan mujahidin.[7] Early volunteers who came wishing to fight alongside the Afghans had extremely few opportunities for doing so, and those who succeeded before 1986 appear to have numbered in the dozens at most.[8] Of these, the largest number fought with the Haqqanis, who were the first of the Afghan mujahidin to directly appeal to the Arab world for volunteer fighters.

Indeed, the Haqqani fronts were distinctive throughout the war for their willingness to accept Afghan Arabs seeking battlefield participation, and Haqqani-dominated Paktia was the single most common destination for the Afghan Arabs who went beyond Peshawar. Yet most accounts of the origins of the Afghan Arab phenomenon ignore Haqqani and emphasize the part played by the Palestinian scholar-activist 'Abdullah 'Azzam and his Maktab al-Khidamat (Afghan Services Bureau, hereinafter MAK), established in Peshawar in 1984, in initiating the movement, and point to Hekmatyar and Sayyaf as the primary Afghan patrons of the foreign fighters.[9] There is no question that 'Azzam played a significant role in mobilizing volunteers in the late 1980s and that some of these men ended up fighting with Sayyaf or Hekmatyar. However, Jalaluddin Haqqani's mobilizations of Arab fighters preceded those of 'Azzam by five years. And while Sayyaf and Hekmatyar later allowed Arabs onto their battlefields, it was the Haqqanis more than any other Afghan mujahidin group who shaped the militant evolution of the Afghan Arab phenomenon in the first place, transforming *muhajirun* into *mujahidun*, emigrants into holy warriors.

Much of 'Azzam's fame rests on what has long been regarded as his revolutionary innovation in the doctrine of jihad, declaring in a fatwa published in a booklet in 1984 that supporting the Afghan jihad was an individual duty (*fard 'ayn*) borne by all able-bodied Muslims worldwide, and thus not contingent upon one's parents' or government's permission to come and offer aid.[10] Yet in a lengthy interview with the Abu Dhabi-based newspaper *al-Ittihad* in the summer of 1980, Jalaluddin Haqqani, introduced as a "member of the supreme council of the Islamic Alliance for the Liberation of Afghanistan and a top official in the alliance's military committee,"[11] declared:

Even though the revolutionary fighters are great in number, this does not mean that the revolution should close its doors to those who wish to participate in the jihad. Scores of volunteers from various parts of the world are coming to us to join the ranks of the mujahidin. They are doing so of their own volition. If the Islamic world truly wants to support and help us, let it permit its men and young men to join our ranks. There is a tendency in most of the Islamic countries which wish to help us to present aid and food as a kind of jihad. Some even think that this is the best kind of jihad. This, however, does not absolve the Muslim of the duty to offer himself for the jihad.[12]

This declaration was made years before 'Abdullah 'Azzam would issue his "revolutionary" fatwa on the individually obligatory (*fard 'ayn*) nature of supporting the Afghan jihad. Clearly Haqqani, and not 'Azzam, was the innovator in this regard, and it is even possible that Jalaluddin's views on this issue influenced those of 'Azzam, as the two were very close—'Azzam wrote his own will and testament in Haqqani's home.[13] In the same year in which 'Azzam published *The Defense of Muslim Territories* he also published another celebrated work—*The Signs of the Merciful in the Jihad in Afghanistan*—portions of which were published in 1983 in the Muslim Brotherhood magazine *al-Mujtama*. Based on accounts of divine miracles experienced by the Afghan mujahidin, the book begins by introducing four men from whom 'Azzam gathered the miracle accounts, the first of which is Jalaluddin Haqqani. He writes of Haqqani with lavish praise, introducing him with these words:

Who among us does not know the learned scholar Jalaluddin Haqqani, unquestionably the most famous Afghan mujahid? Firm in faith, he has lived inside the war since the first day, and to this day remains on the field of battle. Ask any Afghan about him and they will not hesitate for a moment to heap upon him all manner of praise and laudation.[14]

While Haqqani's 1980 appeal did not take the same technical jurisprudential form as 'Azzam's 1984 fatwa, it was nevertheless innovative in all of the ways claimed for 'Azzam's ruling.[15] Haqqani stated that it was the individual duty of Muslims living outside Afghanistan to "offer themselves" to the jihad, a duty that could not be absolved by providing other forms of aid. Haqqani further stated that the "scores" of foreign fighters that had joined his ranks had done so of their own volition—that is, by no one's permission. The notion of "universal private military participation" was thus advocated by Haqqani several years before 'Azzam, and, unlike 'Azzam, Haqqani had the means and the wherewithal to facilitate that participation directly.[16]

The 1980 interview was not the first time that Jalaluddin Haqqani had appealed for support from the Arab world. He had already by this time made numerous personal visits to Saudi Arabia, the UAE, and Iran.[17] More than a year before the Soviet invasion of Afghanistan Jalaluddin sent several of his followers to establish offices throughout the Gulf to raise money and awareness of the threat posed by Taraki's communist coup in Kabul.[18] In 1978, Mawlawi Hanif Shah, a junior classmate of Jalaluddin's at the Haqqaniyya madrassa and an early supporter in the mid-1970s uprisings in Paktika, was sent for a two-year stint for this purpose in Saudi Arabia.[19] Mawlawi 'Aziz Khan, later the director of the Manba' al-'Ulum madrassa in Miranshah, was also sent around this time "along with a few other brothers ... to the Gulf to promote the cause of the Afghan jihad there. Spending five years in the Gulf, I had many material and moral achievements for the jihad. Then other brothers were appointed for that job."[20] That their efforts to procure financial support were successful is indicated by the existence as early as 1980 of an assistance program for Gulf-based donors to aid the families of Afghans "martyred" on Haqqani fronts. A letter from Fathullah Haqqani to other senior Haqqani commanders in the summer of 1980 asks that the numbers of the family members of martyrs be recorded, as "we must send those numbers to the [United Arab] Emirates and other Arab countries so they can decide what type of assistance they would give to the families."[21]

The Recruitment of Abu'l-Walid and the First Afghan Arabs

These efforts also succeeded in recruiting the first of the Afghan Arab war volunteers, a full five years before 'Azzam established the MAK and several months prior to the Soviet invasion. In the spring of 1979, a group of Paktian 'ulama was sent by the Haqqanis to tour mosques in the Gulf in search of support. At a mosque in Abu Dhabi, the Egyptian journalist Mustafa Hamid (better known by his *nom de guerre* Abu'l-Walid al-Masri)[22] encountered this delegation and, after being shown photos from the war and letters in Arabic by Jalaluddin seeking support, he and two Egyptian friends decided to make their way to the Haqqani fronts.[23] Travelling to Peshawar that summer, they were escorted to Miranshah by Haji Din Muhammad[24] before joining up with Jalaluddin in Paktia in June.[25] This was a month before President Carter authorized a $500,000 covert aid program to the mujahidin.[26]

Abu'l-Walid al-Masri fought with the Haqqanis for the next twelve years and began working closely with al-Qa'ida in the early 1990s, becoming the amir of al-Qa'ida's al-Faruq training camp, located at the Haqqani base at Zhawara.[27] He was later credited by al-Qa'ida's senior leadership with having convinced Bin Laden in the early 1990s to reorient the organization around a global confrontation with the imperial hegemony of the United States.[28] This "first mover" of Afghan Arab participation at the Haqqani fronts would prove consequential for the Haqqanis in a number of ways, not least of them in the media realm. Having already worked for several years as a journalist for a magazine in the Gulf before coming to Afghanistan, he soon got a job with the Abu Dhabi-based *al-Ittihad* newspaper and was most likely responsible for arranging the above-quoted 1980 interview with Jalaluddin. As noted by 'Isam Diraz, another well-known Arab journalist who spent years in Afghanistan chronicling the Arab involvement in the Afghan jihad, there were no Arab or Muslim television reporters covering the Afghan conflict up through the first half of the 1980s, nor did any of the Arab newspapers maintain offices in the region—with the exception of *al-Ittihad*, whose chief correspondent was Abu'l-Walid, "one of the first Arab journalists to cover the Afghan cause from the beginning."[29] Abu'l-Walid was thus instrumental in presenting the Haqqanis and their struggle before an international Arabophone audience, a fact that no doubt played a role in the primacy of the Haqqani fronts as the destination of choice for the earliest of the Afghan Arab war volunteers. Abu'l-Walid later contributed a number of articles to the Arabic-language version of the Haqqani network's monthly publication, *Manba' al-Jihad*.[30]

Prior to the 1984 establishment of the MAK in Peshawar, the majority of the Arab war volunteers who came to Afghanistan ended up like Abu'l-Walid, fighting for the Haqqanis in Loya Paktia, and all early visitors to the Haqqani fronts noted the presence of foreign fighters.[31] The American writer Jere Van Dyk, for instance, who was briefly hosted by Jalaluddin at a Haqqani base camp in Shah-i Kot in 1981, encountered there a former major in the Egyptian Army named "Rachid Rochman" (Rashid 'Abd al-Rahman) who had been working for Jalaluddin since the previous year.[32] Another early arrival was 'Abdullah 'Abd al-Rahman, who arrived at Peshawar in July of 1981, stayed at the single guesthouse operated by Sayyaf, and then "left from there with Shaykh Jalaluddin Haqqani and Mawlawi Arsalan ... The Arabs at that time were very few, and some of the Syrian and Iraqi brothers went for jihad, participating in the battles with Shaykh Jalaluddin."[33]

In late 1983 another Egyptian, 'Abd al-Rahman al-Masri, came to join the Haqqanis, bought a home in Miranshah, married an Afghan refugee, and fought on the Haqqani fronts until his death at Khost in 1988.[34] Soon after his arrival, 'Abd al-Rahman al-Masri would make a fateful introduction for another early Afghan Arab to the Haqqani scene: Abu Hafs al-Masri (Muhammad Atif), who later became the first lieutenant and then head of al-Qa'ida's military committee. Abu Hafs was in Peshawar at the time, and recalls that the condition among the Arabs was extremely somber, as fighting had broken out inside Afghanistan between forces loyal to Hekmatyar and Sayyaf, respectively, resulting in the deaths of hundreds of Afghan mujahidin. At this time he encountered 'Abd al-Rahman:

> 'Abd al-Rahman had preceded me [in coming to the jihad] by some months, and informed me about the fronts of Shaykh Jalaluddin Haqqani and his treatment of the Arabs, which I discovered was truly different than the treatment [in Peshawar]. Professor Sayyaf's group made you feel like you

were just a guest ... so when I heard from 'Abd al-Rahman about Shaykh Jalaluddin and his relations with the Arabs, and the involvement of the latter in training and operations, I said "God willing I will return with you."[35]

Abu Hafs accompanied 'Abd al-Rahman down to Zhawara, where he met Abu'l-Walid al-Masri, Abu 'Ubayda al-'Iraqi, and Abu 'Ubayda al-Banshiri (Ali Amin al-Rashidi)—the last-named later becoming the first military leader of al-Qa'ida. Of the growing group of Arabs working with the Haqqanis at this point, Abu Hafs recalls that "we continued during the following years to work in a variety of ways at the fronts of Shaykh Jalaluddin, far from the vortex of Peshawar and the problems of the Arab presence there."[36]

Most accounts of the origins of the Afghan Arabs have neglected these sources and instead refer to an oft-cited memoir of 'Abdullah Anas, an Algerian Afghan Arab who came to Peshawar at the end of 1983. According to Anas, when he arrived at Peshawar with two other Arab volunteers, he was told by Sayyaf that "up to now the Afghan cause has had but twelve Arabs; with you three it comes to fifteen."[37] Yet as Anas' memoir makes clear, these "first" twelve Arabs referred to by Sayyaf were simply the first group of Arabs that were then attending the inaugural session at the recently opened Camp Badr, a separate training area for Arabs that Sayyaf had agreed to establish in early 1984 at his base in Pabbi, a suburb of Peshawar. This number does not take into account the various Syrians, Iraqis, and Egyptians whose presence at the Haqqani fronts prior to the establishment of the Badr camp are attested by the primary sources cited above. Moreover, of the Badr trainees themselves, one source enumerates nine of the participants in February of 1984 and notes that "they went on to participate in the first operation at Khost after having trained for fifteen days at Badr."[38]

The Zhawara Base: Resourcing the Jihad

Soon after Abu'l-Walid joined them and during the same period as the establishment of the Manba' al-'Ulum madrassa outside Miranshah, the Haqqanis began to erect a network of training facilities in Loya Paktia that would soon make the region the unrivalled center for guerrilla training in all of Afghanistan, and the only region within the country where large numbers of non-Afghan fighters could come for training. In July 1980 Jalaluddin Haqqani dispatched two trainers to the front near Khost to set up a camp for machine gun and mortar training.[39] Much more ambitious projects, however, soon became possible with the fast-growing resources available from the international support for the jihad, and in 1981 the Haqqanis completed plans for a vast military base in the Zhawara Valley, just 4 kilometers inside Khost from North Waziristan, which was partially constructed by the following year but continually expanded throughout the 1980s.[40] According to the brigadier general of the ISI responsible for directing the supply chain to the mujahidin during the first half of the 1980s, "up to 60 percent of our supplies" were routed through Khost and Paktia, a full third of this directly through Haqqani's headquarters and supply base at Zhawara.[41] Much of the remaining materiel was distributed in Peshawar to the leaders of the mujahidin parties, who had to maintain their own supply lines to fronts within Afghanistan where men loyal to them were fighting. In contrast, Jalaluddin Haqqani had the unusual position of being in overall tactical command of all the fighting groups in his area of responsibility—sometimes defined as "eastern Afghanistan," sometimes more narrowly as greater Paktia—regardless of their party affiliation, and of "coordinating logistical support" to each of these groups.[42]

The Zhawara base was the first major training center inside the borders of Afghanistan, and it grew over the first half of the 1980s to include a hospital, a hotel for visitors,[43] a machine workshop, a garage, a mosque, numerous caves for storing arms, and the *Voice of Afghanistan*, the first Afghan mujahidin radio station, which from 1984 on issued three daily hour-and-a-half broadcasts in Pastho, Dari, Uzbek, and Russian. As a headquarters of al-Qa'ida and other foreign jihadi groups during the 1990s, the complex was further expanded in the post-war period to include more than sixty aboveground structures and an underground network of more than fifty caves.[44] The single most important transshipment point for war materiel, the Zhawara base was the target of three major assaults by Soviet and Afghan army forces between 1985 and 1987, the last of which—Operation Magistral—was the single largest communist offensive of the entire war.[45] Despite the scale of these assaults, the ISI leadership had determined early on that should Zhawara or its sister facility north of Jaji, Paktia, be attacked, "they would be defended, we would not withdraw into Pakistan, but attempt to hold our own and fight a conventional defensive battle. This was against the normal principles of guerrilla war ... [But] with up to 60 percent of our supplies passing through these two forward base areas we just could not afford to lose them. They were essential jump-off points for the entire campaign."[46] No other fixed position in Afghanistan was defended by the Pakistani military in this way during the entire war.

According to a Defense Intelligence Agency assessment, the Zhawara base "was built by Pakistani contractors, funded by Pakistan's Inter-Services Intelligence (ISI) Directorate and protected under the patronage of a local and influential Jadran tribal leader, Jalaluddin Haqqani. However, the real host in that facility was the Pakistani ISI."[47] While the ISI did coordinate the funding for the Zhawara project, much of the money was contributed by Saudi sources, and construction and mining equipment for blasting the tunnels was imported by Osama bin Laden, who spent much of his time in the latter half of the 1980s fortifying the Haqqanis' infrastructure at Zhawara and other sites in Paktia.[48]

The Haqqanis' strategically important position and growing reputation for effectiveness also brought them to the attention of American and Saudi officials in charge of coordinating the massive aid effort from Pakistan. Jalaluddin deeply impressed Congressman Charlie Wilson, an instrumental figure in the covert program of US support who once called Haqqani "goodness personified."[49] According to Steve Coll, Jalaluddin was "seen by CIA officers in Islamabad and others as perhaps the most impressive Pashtun battlefield commander in the war."[50] These impressions translated into direct financial and military support as well. At Pakistan's insistence, US and Saudi funding for the Afghan mujahidin was all to be funneled through the ISI, not given directly to any mujahidin leaders, but both the US and Saudi intelligence agencies made a small number of exceptions during the war. Jalaluddin Haqqani was one such exception, and in addition to the ISI-directed aid and extensive private funding sources established in the Gulf, by the mid-1980s he had secured a personal pipeline of Saudi aid through the Saudi ambassador to Pakistan, Yousef Mottakbani, and had gained "unilateral asset" status with the CIA, making frequent trips to Peshawar where he regularly received "tens of thousands of dollars in cash directly from CIA officers working undercover in Pakistan, without the mediation of Pakistani intelligence."[51] This independent source of money and materiel gave the Haqqanis a tremendous amount of influence within Afghanistan's mujahidin community and underpinned their capacity for assembling coalitions of commanders from various parties.[52] They were able to broker arms deals with other field commanders independent of the ISI's own metrics, and their willingness to equip Arab volunteers was no doubt a factor in their unique relationship with foreign fighters during the early years of the conflict.[53]

At the Nexus of the Kashmiri Jihad

At around the same time as the graduating class of Arabs from Sayyaf's Camp Badr was making its way to the Haqqani fronts at Khost, the Pakistani military leadership was looking to the Afghan jihad as a preliminary staging ground for the furtherance of its strategy of proxy war with India over control of Kashmir, another development in which the Haqqanis would play a central role. Early on in the war, Zia and the ISI had decided on a plan to increase the pressure on India in Kashmir through the use of cross-border attacks by Pakistani jihadi proxies, and Afghanistan presented the ideal place to establish training camps in pursuit of this end. Such camps could easily be camouflaged as being in support of the Afghan conflict, as could the diversion of some of the international military aid in funding and equipping the camps. The obvious location for this enterprise was Zhawara, the most hardened and well-resourced facility in all of Afghanistan and located just 4 kilometers over the Pak-Afghan border.

Given Zia's above-noted alliance with the JI, Pakistan gave priority to the JI-associated Hizb ul-Mujahidin in the effort to prepare for the Kashmiri mobilization.[54] As already noted, the mujahidin party closest to the JI was Hekmatyar's HIG, and the latter maintained a base protecting the southeastern approach to the Zhawara facility known as Jihadwal.[55] Here, beginning in 1985, a vast training complex for Hizb ul-Mujahidin cadres known as Badr I and Badr II was established, and over the next decade thousands of Hizb activists were trained there, all at camps resourced by the Haqqanis' Zhawara facility.[56]

Not to be outdone, the JUI also sought to position itself for the coming conflict in Kashmir—which erupted almost immediately upon the withdrawal of the Soviet Union from Afghanistan in 1989—and in the early 1980s several Kashmir-focused jihadi groups arose out of the JUI madrassa networks. As with Hizb, these groups established camps in and around Zhawara to train their cadres, with the direct participation of the Haqqanis.

In mid-May of 1989, Abu'l-Walid recorded a series of notes taken during his travels through Khost with Jalaluddin Haqqani's deputy commander Nizamuddin Haqqani.[57] Arriving at Bori, located just northeast of the Zhawara base, they came upon a large group of Pakistani mujahidin encamped there, from two different organizations: Harakat-ul Jihad al-Islami al-'Alami (HuJI) and Harakat al-Mujahidin (HuM).[58] Abu'l-Walid was informed by his Haqqani companion that the former group operated in Paktika under Nasrullah Mansur, the long-time comrade of Jalaluddin, while the latter group operated in the areas directly under Haqqani's control.[59] According to Nizamuddin, both groups had become heavily involved in the fighting in Loya Paktia beginning in 1984.[60] Volunteer fighters from Bangladesh also established a camp at Zhawara, and it was from this group that the Bengali branch of Harakut-ul Jihad al-Islami (HuJI-B) was formed.[61] The leader of the HuJI camp, Fazlur Rahman Khalil, was later a signatory to Osama bin Laden's "World Front," announced in 1997 at a press conference held at one of the Zhawara camps.

The 1986 Zhawara Battle and the Birth of al-Qa'ida

By the middle of the 1980s the Haqqani fronts had already emerged as the center of the growing nexus of the diverse strands of transnational militancy then converging in Afghanistan. The makings of what would become the global jihadi movement were all present: robust resource mobilization networks spanning the globe, training camps for foreign fighters of many nationalities, and open fronts for the transformation of international *muhajirin*—emigrants, or in Abu Hafs' phrase, "guests"—into fighting mujahidin. Out of this mix the self-proclaimed vanguard of that movement—al-Qa'ida—would be born, and in a form that was and remains to this day inextricably bound up with the Haqqani network.

The catalyst for that birth was the Battle of Zhawara in the spring of 1986, the first battle of the Afghan jihad in which significant numbers of Afghan Arabs participated as a group.[62] The Zhawara battle and the much larger Operation Magistral the following year were the last major offenses of a Soviet military then seeking to craft an exit strategy from Afghanistan. Moscow had announced in January 1986 that it would embark on a policy of "national reconciliation," and in February Mikhail Gorbachev gave his famous speech to the Twenty-Seventh Party Congress calling the war in Afghanistan a "bleeding wound." The drawdown began with the removal of six battalions that year, though the final Soviet withdrawal would come three years later. The Afghan leader installed at the end of 1986 to pursue the Soviet reconciliation policy, President Najibullah, appealed to the mujahidin leaders, including Jalaluddin Haqqani, to enter into negotiations with the regime. Hoping to tip the military balance in favor of Kabul and give it a stronger bargaining position down the road, the Soviets singled out the strategically critical Haqqani positions in the southeast for a series of massive assaults. The base was deemed a critical asset by the ISI, which directly facilitated its defense. Twenty-five years later, facing the same time horizon as the Soviet Union in 1986, the United States in 2011 would pursue an almost identical Afghanistan exit strategy of "fight, talk, build," pushing for reconciliation while at the same time focusing the endgame brunt of its military might on the ISI-supported Haqqanis in the southeast.[63]

The Battle of Zhawara began at the end of March 1986, as the Afghan army, with Soviet aerial support, launched an attack on the Haqqani base that would last more than a month. Jalaluddin Haqqani was in Miranshah when the siege began, but Nizamuddin Haqqani spotted transport helicopters flying over the area and radioed in an alert, which was also relayed to Peshawar.[64] Logistical coordination for defense of the base was overseen out of Miranshah by Brigadier Mohammad Yousaf, in charge of the ISI's activities in Afghanistan between 1983 and 1987, and Pakistani armed forces became directly involved in the defense of the base.[65] Hekmatyar was also present in this engagement, defending his position at Jihadwal, at the southeastern approach to the Zhawara complex. Under Haqqani's leadership, the Afghan mujahidin were able to repel the attack for several weeks, but briefly lost the mountainous facility to the Afghan army on 19 April 1986. By the evening of that day, however, the mujahidin pushed the Soviet-backed forces out and recaptured Zhawara; the Afghan army held the base for only five hours, and was thus unable to destroy the base or its fortifications.

At the beginning of the siege, Jalaluddin Haqqani had issued an emergency appeal for support to Peshawar and other commanders in the region, and a group of Arabs training at the MAK camps in Pakistan rushed down to Miranshah. The group of Arabs already working directly with Haqqani—including Abu'l-Walid al-Masri, Abu Hafs al-Masri, Abu 'Ubayda Banshiri, Abu Jihad al-Masri, and Abu 'Ubayda al-'Iraqi—all entered Zhawara early and took part in the battle from the second week of April on.[66] The base was under intense and constant aerial bombardment, and on 6 April a direct hit caused the collapse of the cave in which Jalaluddin Haqqani was taking shelter. Many in the cave with Haqqani were killed, and he was badly wounded and unconscious when he was evacuated. Assisting in his rescue was another survivor of the cave collapse: Wa'il Julaydan, also known as Abu'l-Hasan al-Madani, then the director of the Saudi Red Crescent and later a founding member of al-Qa'ida.[67] On 17 April, a team of Pakistani officers dispatched by Brigadier Yousaf to fire Blowpipe anti-aircraft missiles from the heights surrounding the base came under heavy fire, and Abu Hafs al-Masri and Abu 'Ubayda al-Banshiri went to help them at their firing positions. Both of the Egyptians were soon wounded, as were several of the Pakistani officers, and they were transported together in the same vehicle to the Zhawara hospital.[68]

The contingent of MAK-affiliated Arabs from Peshawar, including 'Azzam and Osama bin Laden, arrived at Miranshah on Sunday 20 April, the day after the brief loss of the facility and the beginning of the withdrawal of the communist forces. They gathered at the home of Jalaluddin, where 'Azzam wrote out his will and testament, eager to join a battle that he thought could very well cost him his life.[69] In a eulogy delivered after 'Azzam's assassination in 1989, discovered after 9/11 on a tape in the cassette library that had belonged to Bin Laden in Kandahar, one of his followers confirmed that 'Azzam had first formed the desire for martyrdom at Jalaluddin's house that day in 1986.[70] According to a recent jihadi biography of 'Azzam:

> The first opportunity for battle arrived, and the Ansar [the MAK leaders] went as a group to the Battle of Zhawara. Shaykh 'Abdallah 'Azzam and Usama bin Ladin traveled to Miranshah and stopped at the home of the mujahid Jalaluddin Haqqani—who never turned back, unlike Sayyaf, Rabbani or [Ahmad] Shah Massoud. Allegiance was pledged to 'Azzam as the amir of the Ansar fighting in that battle, which was the first such opportunity to participate on the front.[71]

Haqqani told 'Azzam and his men on 20 April that it was too dangerous to cross the border, but the primary sources offer differing accounts as to what happened next. According to one account, when the group learned that Hekmatyar's base at Jihadwal was under heavy attack, they gave their *bay'a* (pledge of allegiance) to 'Azzam as the amir of their party, which dubbed itself the "Brigade of Strangers,"[72] and proceeded to make their way across the border towards Hekmatyar's positions. They arrived, however, after the Jihadwal battle had concluded and were sent back, where they were ordered to deposit their weapons at Haqqani's guesthouse in Miranshah.[73] The MAK Arabs returned to Peshawar, and one of their number—Abu Hajar al-'Iraqi (Mamduh Mahmud Salim, a co-founder of al-Qa'ida)—quipped that, having been repeatedly restrained from exposing themselves to the dangers of battle, they should call themselves the "Brigade of Dandies."[74]

According to other accounts, however, a significant number of Arabs were able to enter the area of Zhawara after the base was recaptured by the Haqqanis and assisted in beating back the remaining communist forces.[75] Abu'l-Walid wrote that 'Azzam asked him on 21 April to take some of the MAK volunteers under the wing of the "Khost Group," as the Haqqani-affiliated Afghan Arabs had become known, to stage an attack on the Khost airport, in two separate groups under the leadership of Abu 'Ubayda al-'Iraqi and 'Abd al-Rahman al-Masri.[76] According to 'Isam Diraz:

> Shaykh Jalaluddin Haqqani told me of the role of the Arab mujahidin and said that they significantly raised the level the Afghan mujahidin's morale. He claimed that the Arabs' presence was militarily beneficial.[77]

After the battle, Abu'l-Walid noted in his diaries that the MAK began at that time to send groups of newly arrived Arabs to the Zhawara area. During the month of Ramadan after the battle (May 1986), Jalaluddin Haqqani directed these men to Abu'l-Walid to "entertain" them, and Abu'l-Walid wrote of the first group to arrive, "this was the largest group of Saudi youth I had ever seen inside Afghanistan."[78]

However significant the Arab involvement in the battle, one thing is certain—the experience had taught Bin Laden that there were definite advantages to being based close to the Haqqanis' fronts. Having helped 'Azzam establish the MAK in October 1984, Bin Laden was well aware that the ever-increasing number of new recruits were eager for more than target practice at Sayyaf's camps on the Pakistan border or soccer matches in Peshawar. The group of Arabs with Abu'l-Walid had demonstrated that working directly with the Haqqanis meant access to the battles, and this is what the growing number of would-be Afghan Arabs languishing in Peshawar had come for. After the battle Bin Laden invested heavily in repairing and fortifying the damaged base at Zhawara, and, according to Abu Ibrahim al-Logari, a Yemeni Afghan Arab who was present in Paktia during this period:

> Jalaluddin Haqqani gave him [Bin Laden] three caves at the side of the [Zhawara] base near the central Afghan kitchen. Abu 'Abdullah [Bin Laden] built within these caves until they became like a beautiful home, walled in the interior with red brick and divided into many rooms, including a library, mosque, and several bathrooms. Another cave, extending a little over 150 meters, was used as a weapons and ammo depot.[79]

In October of 1986 Bin Laden went on to use his construction equipment to build a fortified training area at Jaji in northern Paktia, on the supply line between Zhawara and Ali Khel. His decision to establish an independent camp for Arabs within Afghanistan led to a split with 'Azzam, who saw Bin Laden's projects as a misuse of resources and a challenge to the MAK's mission of being at the service of the Afghan mujahidin parties. Bin Laden dubbed his camp "Ma'sadat al-Ansar" (the Lion's Den of the Supporters), though it quickly became known among the Afghan Arab community as *al-qa'ida al-'askariyya,* or the military base. It was from this appellation that the name of the al-Qa'ida organization was later taken,[80] and indeed the training camp represented an early stage in al-Qa'ida's development. According to the memoirs of Abu Ja'far al-Qandahari, an Egyptian Afghan Arab who arrived at Peshawar in the summer of 1988:

> It was customary for new arrivals to go to the Sada training camp run by the Maktab al-Khidamat, but I preferred to go to a new training camp that had been announced at that time to any and all who sought to carry out jihad, a training camp in which the course of training would be of a higher and more strenuous level than that at Sada.[81] It was a center which would winnow out those suitable to be admitted into "al-Qa'ida al-'Askariyya," an organization that had been advertised as forming the nucleus of an Islamic army capable of fighting jihad anywhere in the world.[82]

Though the area in Jaji where the Ma'sada camp was built was under the supervision of Sayyaf's party, Ma'sada was structurally integrated with Haqqani operations at Zhawara, and Sayyaf's front there was logistically integrated and often dependent on the Haqqanis' supply base at Zhawara.[83] Abu Ja'far relates that before proceeding to the advanced training at Bin Laden's "military base," he and a group of other Arabs bound for Ma'sada had to proceed first to Zhawara via Miranshah and there undergo ten days of preliminary training alongside the Haqqanis' Afghan trainees.[84] To join the nascent al-Qa'ida, in other words, meant first training with the Haqqani network.

Bin Laden also managed to win over Abu Hafs al-Masri and Abu 'Ubayda al-Banshiri to his project, thus benefiting from their years of experience in mountain guerrilla warfare with the

Haqqani network and their prior experiences in the Egyptian military. The camp project required people with military training, and Bin Laden reached out to Abu 'Ubayda first, who agreed to visit the site and offer advice on its suitability. During the visit Bin Laden urged him to stay and be the military leader of the project. Abu 'Ubayda recalled later that "Abu 'Abdullah [Bin Laden] desired to entrust me with the administration of the site, but on account of my involvement with my brothers in other operations in Khost, I agreed only to stay for ten days."[85] Bin Laden ultimately convinced him to stay on after seeing through the preparation of the camp, and Abu 'Ubayda inaugurated the first general training program as amir of what would become known as al-Qa'ida on 17 February 1987.[86] Abu Hafs was initially uninterested in Bin Laden's venture and remained fighting with the Haqqanis at Khost, though after Abu 'Ubayda began training operations Abu Hafs was finally convinced to join the effort.[87] Abu'l-Walid al-Masri notes that in this sense Zhawara was a kind of "military academy" for the two Egyptians that would go on to lead al-Qa'ida's military committee, and that in the famous "Battle of Ramadan" at Jaji in the spring of 1987 it was Abu Hafs' and Abu 'Ubayda's expertise that made all the difference.[88]

The Ramadan battle at Jaji was a watershed moment for al-Qa'ida and for the Afghan Arab movement in general, leading to an exponential increase in the number of war volunteers pouring into Pakistan and Afghanistan from throughout the Muslim world. As the Afghan army and Soviet forces moved south through Paktia for Operation Magistral—the largest and last major communist offensive of the entire war—they encountered Bin Laden's forces in the area of Ma'sada, the latter putting up a successful defense of their position and killing a number of Soviet special forces in the process.[89] Touted as a major "victory," it was the first of its kind for an independent Arab unit in Afghanistan. More important, however, was the media impact of the battle. Following Abu'-Walid's example, who had for years been filing regular reports from the front lines of the Haqqanis' battles for *al-Ittihad*, Bin Laden had invited Arab journalists from the Gulf to observe his men at Jaji.[90] He even commissioned a film crew to record their exploits—again, an area in which the Haqqanis had been earlier innovators.[91] The resulting growth in volunteers was immediate and dramatic. As Hegghammer notes, "mid-1987 seems to have represented a tipping point of the mobilization, after which recruitment transcended personal social networks ..."[92] Abu'l-Walid al-Masri made a similar assessment, calling 1987 the "year of the Arabs in Afghanistan."[93]

Though in the midst of a split with Bin Laden's *al-Qa'idat al-'askariyya*, 'Azzam's MAK also benefited from the media-driven recruitment boom. The Haqqanis' contribution to and representation within this proliferating media was extremely significant. The MAK aggressively publicized the activities of the Arabs fighting in Paktia, and were now able to present to their Muslim audiences around the world a clear path to becoming a mujahid, even a martyr, uncomplicated by the ever-shifting ground of the fractious Afghan parties in Peshawar. The openness of the Haqqani fronts became a key selling point in this propaganda; as 'Azzam himself states in one of his publications, regarding the MAK's lead fund-raiser and recruiter Tamim al-'Adnani:

> When Shaykh Tamim became connected to the Afghan jihad he began to inform the youth of the Arabian Peninsula about the Afghan cause and to relate to them the miracles and activities of the mujahidin. He began to come to Afghanistan, and the first time he came he was told that there were centers close to Shaykh Jalaluddin. ... So the first time he went for jihad his connection was with Shaykh Jalaluddin Haqqani. There was a commander of Haqqani's named Muhammad Hasan and Tamim would relate stories about him and his bravery ...[94]

The MAK's flagship propaganda organ, the *al-Jihad* magazine, beginning in its first year of publication, printed more than a dozen stories about and interviews with Jalaluddin Haqqani and several of his senior commanders.[95] In a notable contrast, *al-Jihad* made infrequent mention of Osama bin Laden by his *nom de guerre* Abu 'Abdullah, and often only in passing. In one of his earliest appearances in the magazine, for instance, he is quoted in a story about a recent martyr which ends, "and Abu 'Abdullah said, 'We offer our condolences on the loss of our brother Abu'l-Walid al-Sa'udi.'"[96] Thereafter Bin Laden is mentioned in several issues, but much less frequently than the Haqqani leadership.[97]

By facilitating access to the fronts, the Haqqanis performed a dual service to the growing transnational jihadi movement. First, while other mujahidin parties were loath to involve Arabs in the fighting, viewing the foreigners as either suicidal madmen or religiously intolerant bigots, the Haqqanis gave such men the opportunity to fulfill what they viewed as a sacred duty (*fard 'ayn*) to jihad.[98] Second, such access allowed the Arab jihadis to capture their experiences and repackage them as media products—something the Haqqanis had been doing themselves since the beginning of the 1980s—which served to vastly expand the Arab jihadis' international resource mobilization capabilities.

The Haqqanis were not immune to the problems posed by the religious extremism or martyrdom-seeking tendencies of some of the Arab volunteers. The Haqqani correspondence contained in the Harmony database reveals that they sometimes had to manage the consequences of having overzealous and underprepared foreigners on their battlefields. In a letter written sometime in the first half of the 1980s to Fathullah Haqqani, Jalaluddin writes of reports he'd received of an Arab wasting ammunition in ineffective use of his weapon. Asking that the Arab be sent back from the front "with an excuse," he requests that Fathullah communicate the issue to the field commander "so that in a wise manner the Arabs will be placed with the right personnel."[99] Abu'l-Walid al-Masri relates that a young Egyptian named Abu Dujana al-Masri, who worked with a group of Haqqani's men on the outskirts of Gardez in the mid-1980s, was disliked by the Afghan mujahidin for his rigorous practice of "forbidding evil" (*nahi 'an al-munkar*), insisting that the Afghans desist from what Abu Dujana regarded as lapses in their adherence to Islamic law. He was notorious for seizing Afghan mujahidin's dipping tobacco (*naswar*), on one occasion grabbing a local commander's snuff box and stomping it underfoot, about which Abu'l-Walid remarked, "If he had not been the guest of Jalaluddin Haqqani, they would have killed him instantly."[100]

In a recent biography of Yunis Khalis, Haji Din Muhammad provides an account of a clash between Khalis and an unnamed Arab at Jalaluddin Haqqani's home in Miranshah during the 1986 Battle of Zhawara. The assembled Afghans and Arabs were listening to the radio for news reports from the front, and when the program began playing music after one such update had concluded, one of the Arabs rose and turned it off, shouting "Hey Shaykh! Haram (forbidden)! Haram!" Khalis asked the man to explain himself with reference to Islamic law, and in response to the Arab's feeble attempts to provide a justification Khalis scolded him by saying, "Provide some documented reasons, and if you do not have them with you, well then do not make commands out of place." According to Haji Din Muhammad, at these words "the Arab became quiet and no one dared to silence the radio in that meeting."[101]

The Egyptian mujahid Abu Ja'far al-Qandahari relates that while going through his preliminary training at Zhawara before proceeding to the early al-Qa'ida camp he "witnessed a distressing sight":

> In one area two groups had formed for prayer, one Arab and the other Afghan. When I asked why this was so, I was told that they [the Afghans] pray with haste and are tardy in performing the 'asr prayer.[102] It hardly seemed to me that this was sufficient cause. The Afghans were followers of Yunis Khalis, who had amply demonstrated his affection for and amity with the Arabs, so why allow such divisions? How could we fight together if we couldn't pray together?[103]

With the arrival of large numbers of new recruits after 1987, the areas under Haqqani control witnessed an explosion of training camps serving an extremely eclectic spectrum of ideological interests and militant causes, and these would continue to proliferate throughout the 1990s. In 1988 al-Qa'ida officially established itself as a clandestine, hierarchical organization, and it began to erect its first training camps: al-Faruq at Zhawara, and the Jihadwal and Siddiq camps in Hekmatyar's region at Zhawara's southeastern approach.[104] These would remain core elements of al-Qa'ida's infrastructure until 9/11, and agents of all of al-Qa'ida's major attacks during the 1990s would be trained in these camps.[105] According to Jalaluddin Haqqani, the main Haqqani base at Zhawara was itself renamed in 1989 to the 'Umar al-Faruq Base, and the main al-Qa'ida camp in the valley was in turn given the name "al-Faruq."[106] Bin Laden's former bodyguard "Abu Jandal" Nasir al-Bahri says of the early days of al-Faruq:

> It was established on the basis of a clear military methodology, a military college where cadets passed through a number of stages and levels until

they finally graduated at the command level, as military commanders capable of leading any jihadist action anywhere. The idea of establishing that military college was a global idea. Thus, if the jihad in Afghanistan ends, graduates of the college can go anywhere in the world and capably command battles there. Those objectives have actually been achieved through the success accomplished by the young men who had moved to many fronts outside Afghanistan, in Bosnia-Herzegovina, Chechnya, the Philippines, Eritrea, Somalia, Burma, and elsewhere.[107]

Not to be outdone, the MAK established the Khaldan camp in Khost as well, though the first amir of the camp—Abu Binan al-Jaza'iri—who was in charge for its first four years, was seldom present as he was frequently fighting at the Haqqani fronts; he fought at Khost in 1990 and 1991 and was killed fighting at Gardez in October 1991.[108] The Khaldan camp was noted for the extreme Salafi bent of its ideological curriculum.[109] In contrast, the Yemeni Abu Ibrahim al-Logari, along with two Saudi Afghan Arabs, established Camp Mubarak at Lezi in the later 1980s, which was characterized by its non-Salafi—even anti-Salafi—tone and its non-affiliation with any of the Arab jihadi organizations.[110] Another Arab training camp in Paktia close to the South Waziristan border and supplied from Azam Warsak was dedicated to training Tajik Islamists involved in the short-lived Tajikistan civil war.[111] There was eventually an Arab mujahidin shura council at Khost responsible for coordinating the activities of the growing variety of Arab groups centered in the region.[112]

Other camps are attested in the sources as well, but the al-Qa'ida camps around Zhawara appear to have been the destination of choice for the majority of the new arrivals, and in the Afghan Arab memoir literature from this period al-Faruq stands out as the most frequently attended camp. 'Abdullah Muhammad Fazul, who came to Peshawar in 1991 and became the leader of al-Qa'ida operations in East Africa until his death in 2011, described in his memoirs the massive influx of people into Peshawar during this period and the proliferation of guesthouses and jihadi organizations. "For training, though," he writes, "most went to the al-Qa'ida camps at Jihadwal and Zhawara [sc. al-Faruq] in Khost."[113] A similar observation about the relative predominance of al-Qa'ida during this period was made in the first ever account of al-Qa'ida in the Western press, a May 1991 magazine article on the Afghan Arabs. After noting that there was a "multitude of amorphous secret groups" operated by Arabs in the border areas, the article states that "Qaada [*sic*], the most powerful and numerically the largest Arab group, operates several camps on both sides of the Pakistani–Afghanistan border."[114]

The large concentration of foreign fighters and training camps in Loya Paktia towards the end of the Afghan jihad facilitated the first large-scale involvement of Afghan Arabs in major battles[115]—the battles of Jalalabad (1989), Khost (1990–1), and Gardez (1991).[116] The latter two were fought under the general command of Jalaluddin Haqqani and witnessed the most extensive integration of foreign fighters into the order of battle of the entire anti-communist conflict in Afghanistan. As for the Battle of Jalalabad, the Arabs were initially frustrated by the refusal of several party commanders to take them into their ranks. The lead commander for Sayyaf's forces in that ultimately disastrous engagement, Commander Saznur, "totally refused any cooperation with Arab mujahidin at that battle, because he said that the Arabs were disorganized and were seeking nothing but martyrdom."[117] Instead, the Arabs fought there under one of Jalaluddin Haqqani's HIK colleagues—Haji Khalid (Ruzaddin Shinwari)—though ultimately the ill-planned attack on the city was a fiasco and resulted in large losses among both the Afghan and the Arab mujahidin.[118] Jalaluddin sent 300 of his men to take part in the fight, which came as a surprise to Abu'l-Walid al-Masri, learning of this while serving as Jalaluddin's driver during a visit to the Gulf soon after the battle. Abu'l-Walid was an outspoken critic of the Jalalabad siege both before and after it took place, and clashed with the al-Qa'ida leadership at the time over their push to involve the Arabs.[119] According to Abu'l-Walid, when he expressed his criticisms of the debacle to Jalaluddin in the UAE, the latter agreed entirely.[120] In an interview in *Manba' al-Jihad* shortly after the battle, Ma'afi Khan, the commander of the Haqqani forces at Jalalabad, noted that "the lack of a unified, structured command created a huge obstacle on our way to success."[121]

The Battle of Jalalabad was the first major engagement between mujahidin and communist forces after the Soviet withdrawal, though foreign fighter volunteerism did not diminish with the removal of the "foreign occupiers." In fact, 1989–91 saw the largest numbers of Arabs and other foreign fighters arriving in Afghanistan, hailing from more than forty countries.[122] This proved a boon for the Haqqanis, who welcomed hundreds—if not thousands—of these men into their orders of battle at Khost, conquered by Haqqani-led forces in the spring of 1991. Khost was the first major city to fall to the mujahidin, followed soon after by Gardez, losses that were instrumental in the fall of the communist government of Najibullah in Kabul in 1992. Participation in the Battle of Khost subsequently became a badge of honor for Afghan Arab veterans of the war, and the foreign fighter involvement represented a cross-section of transnational jihadism at the time. Noman Benotman, a Khost veteran and the former leader of the Libyan Islamic Fighting Group, stated that "there were Saudis, Kuwaitis, Jordanians, Palestinians, Algerians, Tunisians, Syrians, Libyans and other nationalities in our ranks."[123] The Arabic-language Haqqani network magazine ran a story after the battle on the Arab martyrs of Khost, which gives obituaries of a Yemeni, a Saudi, a Qatari, an Algerian, and two Tunisians.[124] For the first time, Arabs fighting in this battle were led by Arab commanders who were integrated into the Haqqanis' chain of command; these included a Yemeni front led out of Camp Mubarak at Lezi, as well as a Jordanian front under the command of Abu'l-Harith al-Urduni.[125] Al-Qa'ida's military leadership also participated in the battle, as did cadres of the Egyptian al-Jama'a al-Islamiyya (EIG).[126] Many of the leaders of the militant Islamist organizations established in the 1990s, from North Africa to Southeast Asia, got their first taste of jihad under Haqqani's command in this fight. It was not just al-Qa'ida, then, that the Haqqani network had helped foster into being during the anti-Soviet jihad, but rather a broad spectrum of late twentieth-century transnational jihadism.

3

THE FOUNTAINHEAD

THE HAQQANI NETWORK, THE TALIBAN, AND THE RISE OF GLOBAL JIHAD

The decade following the Soviet withdrawal witnessed a devastating civil war in Afghanistan; eruptions of jihadi violence in Kashmir, northwestern China, and the former Soviet Central Asian states; the rise of the Taliban; and the initiation by al-Qa'ida of a global campaign of political violence against the United States. The Haqqani network figures prominently in each of these contexts, though in ways that have up to now been largely unexplored. The triangle of relations between the Haqqani network, the Taliban, and al-Qa'ida lie at the heart of this story, one in which the Haqqani network fulfilled its ambitions to become the "fountainhead of jihad."

During the period between the Soviet withdrawal and the rise of the Taliban, the activities of the Haqqani network present something of a paradox. The Haqqanis initially spearheaded efforts at building a coalition of Afghan mujahidin commanders that sought to establish an inclusive and broad-based government, one that would accord significant autonomy to Afghanistan's distinct regions. When these efforts failed and the mujahidin parties fell into civil war, the Haqqanis distinguished themselves by not making a power play for control of Kabul, and instead led a reconciliation effort that brokered a number of short-lived ceasefires between Hekmatyar's and Massoud's opposing forces in the capital. In this sense, the Haqqanis appeared as relatively politically moderate in terms of the mujahidin parties during the early 1990s, and their stated goals regarding the shape of a post-communist Afghan state were in some ways similar to those expressed by the US State Department at the time. Yet the Haqqanis also extended their control of the southeast during this period, and offered this relatively secure space as a region of refuge for a growing number of militant Islamist movements from throughout the world. Most famously, this included the main camps of al-Qa'ida, which during this period trained the men who would initiate al-Qa'ida's campaign of globalized violence against the United States. As a key player in Afghan politics, then, the Haqqanis focused on stabilizing the country and protecting their regional autonomy, but this autonomy in turn was put to the service of an emerging global jihadi milieu. These two trends would continue to characterize the Haqqani network's relationship with the Taliban after 1995, with enormous consequences, as it was their very autonomy from the Taliban that allowed the Haqqanis to shelter al-Qa'ida as it prepared to carry out the 9/11 attacks.

The Haqqani Network and the National Commanders Shura

At the beginning of 1989, with the last of the Soviet troops making their way north out of the country, Pakistan, the United States, and Saudi Arabia pressured the mujahidin leaders to form the basis of a transitional government to replace Najibullah's regime, which was believed to be too weakened by the Soviet withdrawal to hold on to power for long. In February 1989, a shura of all the mujahidin parties was convened for this purpose in Rawalpindi, and the ISI put Jalaluddin Haqqani in charge of the council.[1] The shura was hampered from the beginning by disunity among the mujahidin parties and differences of interest in the foreign powers supporting them. Saudi Arabia heavily favored Sayyaf, the ISI favored Hekmatyar, and the United States was comfortable with neither, favoring a negotiated settlement that would prioritize Afghan "self-determination" and the "sidelining of extremists" like Sayyaf and Hekmatyar.[2] Frustrated with the squabbling of the party leaders at the shura, Jalaluddin sequestered them in his home toward the end of February and at one point is said to have extracted an agreement to a balloting procedure from Hekmatyar at gunpoint.[3] The shura led to the creation of the Afghan Interim Government (AIG), a venture doomed from the start by the competing ambitions of the Peshawar leaders and their international backers.[4] Jalaluddin Haqqani quickly became disillusioned with the AIG, and was quoted in the *New York Times* in April 1991 after the capture of Khost saying that "there is no possibility of the AIG to come to Khost. We did not free it for the AIG."[5] In the Haqqani network magazines he expressed his dismissal of the interim government and instead promoted a new national leadership structure that would bypass the fractious Peshawar-based parties.[6]

On 7–9 May 1990, Jalaluddin convened a gathering of twenty-seven major mujahidin field commanders at the Zhawara base to discuss post-Soviet military strategy.[7] The result was the formation of the National Commanders Shura (NCS), led by Jalaluddin Haqqani.[8] The most prominent leaders of the NCS at first were Haqqani and his two HIK colleagues, Mullah Malang and Abdul Haq.[9] Though initially composed primarily of Pashtun commanders, it eventually grew to include the famous Tajik commander Ahmad Shah Massoud, Shi'a commanders, and northern military leaders after a further meeting in October in Kunar Province.[10] Hekmatyar and Sayyaf boycotted the meetings and refused to join the shura—Sayyaf declaring it a CIA attempt to "sabotage their jihad."[11] After the October meeting the United States reportedly began to offer support to the NCS, seeing in it an alternative military and political solution independent of the ISI and Hekmatyar, and equipped the NCS leaders with, among other things, sophisticated radio equipment that would enable them to communicate in Afghanistan and bypass Pakistan's control of logistics.[12] In an interview published in *Manba' al-Jihad*, however, Haqqani criticized the American support and said it would hurt rather than help their efforts.[13]

The platform of the NCS provides a good insight into the Haqqanis' political preferences for a post-communist Afghanistan. While Haqqani insisted that the NCS would pursue a national government based on shari'a law, it would not be a centralized (or Pashtun-centric) emirate of the type that the Taliban would attempt to impose in the latter half of the decade, but would instead comprise nine regional administrative divisions whose administrations would be drawn from the mujahidin commanders—not the Peshawar party leaders—as well as religious and civic or tribal leaders from the local areas.[14] Though at this time Jalaluddin rejected the notion of the direct election of state leaders by universal suffrage as contrary to Islamic law, he did envision the possibility of indirect election by 3000–5000 delegates "chosen from the people."[15]

Haqqani began to establish the rudiments of such an administrative system in his own region after the capture of Khost, arranging for the establishment of a Khost shura.[16] According to Jalaluddin:

> In an attempt to establish order and commence reconstruction, a joint administration has been established in Khost. In it, various departments such as health, agriculture, reconstruction, education and others have been organized. To this end, we brought together the commanders, 'ulama and tribal elders in a grand meeting. Through this, we created a unified provincial council out of the various tribal factional councils that existed. A commission was chosen from among the provincial council, and was confirmed by the entire council. Then from among the appointment commission, a delegation was given responsibility for implementation and appointing people to the various posts. As such, all the directors and their deputies have been appointed, and the commission has been given the task of completing all the appointments throughout the various offices of the administration. The appointments have been endorsed by all the factions.[17]

After Haqqani-led NCS forces captured Gardez, the capital of Paktia, in 1991, a similar system was put in place there, with Haqqani described as leader of the Gardez shura.[18] Another governing shura was established in Jalalabad and led by Jalaluddin's HIK ally Haji 'Abd al-Qadir. Together these institutions maintained a relative degree of order in eastern Afghanistan, while much of the rest of the country became subject to the predations of warlords and Kabul increasingly became an urban battleground between Hekmatyar and Massoud.

As they had done during the anti-Soviet war, the Haqqanis continued to integrate highland Pashtun tribal modalities of power sharing and conflict resolution into the post-Soviet system that they established in the southeast. In 1993, when the Jalalabad governor Shamali Khan was killed and blame fell on Haji 'Abd al-Qadir of the Jalalabad shura, a vengeance claim (*badal*) was made by the slain governor's Ahmadzai tribe. Forces loyal to Hekmatyar joined the conflict on the side of the Ahmadzai, while Massoud sent forces from the north to dislodge the pro-Hekmatyar party.[19] Jalaluddin Haqqani, "to prevent further bloodshed," claims to have stepped in and convened a peace jirga that brokered a cessation of hostilities and a commitment from all parties to abide by the terms of an eight-point resolution.[20]

The Haqqanis also involved the Arabs in these local political activities, as evidenced by the Arab mujahidin shura of Khost that was established after the capture of that city. Around that time the Yemeni Afghan Arab Abu Ibrahim al-Logari and Shirin Jamal al-Qurashi, leaders of the Mubarak camp in Lezi, attended a shura meeting at Bori "as representatives of the Lezi area." Abu Ibrahim says there were more than thirty commanders and over twenty local tribal shaykhs present at the meeting presided over by Jalaluddin Haqqani, and which was described by Abu Ibrahim as "representing the central leadership of Paktia Province."[21] Abu Ibrahim was bored at the lack of discussion of military issues, but notes that the council spent hours discussing the distribution of the spoils of war and administrative committees to be established from among the parties and tribes.[22]

The Haqqani Network and the Emergence of Global Jihadism

The first years of the 1990s proved to be fateful in several ways both for the trajectory of the Haqqani network and for the transnational militant Islamist movement. On the international level, the Gulf War radically polarized the already conflict-prone Peshawar scene, and led to the departure of Bin Laden and much of the al-Qa'ida leadership to Sudan, where it focused its early efforts on the Arabian Peninsula.[23] The Haqqanis and al-Qa'ida continued to pursue intertwined lines of development during this period. The Gulf War proved a critical catalyst for the emergence of global jihadism, and the Haqqani network again was involved in that redirection of Islamist violence.

The invasion of Kuwait by Saddam Hussein's forces in the summer of 1990 and the subsequent involvement of American military forces were met with vastly divergent reactions by the Afghan mujahidin leadership.[24] The AIG, under Mujaddidi's presidency, offered its support to Saudi Arabia, while Hekmatyar emerged as the most outspoken supporter of Saddam. Sayyaf was critical of the Saudi response to the invasion of Kuwait, a position which severely damaged his relationship with the Saudi regime. The Haqqanis' response was somewhat more measured, denouncing both the Iraqi invasion and the American bombing of Iraq. Jalaluddin Haqqani criticized "some Muslims here who have been demonstrating in support of Saddam, giving him inappropriate titles like 'mujahid.' Before making such declarations, Muslims need to observe caution and await Islamic rulings on this matter."[25] Though the Haqqani leaders refrained from directly criticizing the Saudi government, the latter closed the offices of both Hekmatyar's HIG and the Haqqani network in the kingdom. According to Abu Ibrahim al-Logari, along with the tightened control over Saudi aid groups at this time, these closures "cut off 90% of what was coming to the Afghan jihad from Saudi Arabia."[26]

Osama bin Laden made an offer to the Saudi government during this period to dispatch 12,000 of his own trained mujahidin to defend the kingdom, which it declined. At the same time the AIG made a similar if less extravagant offer, one that the Saudis accepted.[27] "Several hundred" Afghan mujahidin were sent to Saudi Arabia in February, while "a second batch of guerrillas would leave for Riyadh soon. These guerrillas will operate under Saudi command."[28] Haqqani ally and HIK representative Haji Din Muhammad was asked by the AIG to detail HIK fighters for the effort, but he demurred, saying that the issue had not been discussed by the AIG cabinet.[29] It is extremely unlikely that any Haqqani fighters were involved in this mobilization. Hekmatyar, meanwhile, reportedly went to Baghdad and offered to send HIG soldiers to fight alongside Saddam's army.[30]

After his offer was rejected, Bin Laden set up the Advice and Reform Committee in London, through which he issued criticisms of the Saudi royal family's involvement of "infidel" troops in the affairs of the kingdom, though as the name of this organization indicates, Bin Laden was seeking reform at this stage, not revolution.[31] Nor did Bin Laden reorient the fundamental orientation of the al-Qa'ida organization at this time, which remained focused on three interrelated goals: continuing the training operations in Khost, establishing a presence in the region of the Arabian Peninsula (principally Yemen and Somalia), and offering support and training to revolutionary Islamist groups that had emerged in the aftermath of the Afghan jihad. The Haqqanis, while continuing their involvement in al-Qa'ida's pursuits during this period, also began to become increasingly global in their jihadi orientation, and in ways that some evidence suggests decisively influenced the direction of al-Qa'ida strategy.

One area of cooperation between the two groups was in efforts at averting the disastrous civil war into which Afghanistan plunged after the fall of the Najibullah regime. In the spring of 1992, as Hekmatyar was amassing his forces to the south of Kabul and Massoud worked to secure the capital, Jalaluddin Haqqani assembled a reconciliation committee consisting of 300 Afghan commanders and clerics in an attempt to bring the two opposing factions into negotiations. Obtaining authorization letters from Mujaddidi, the president of the by-then-defunct AIG, as well as Rabbani, president of the UN-brokered transitional government, Haqqani won the approval of both Hekmatyar and Massoud to come to Kabul and pursue a peaceful settlement.[32] Haqqani would lead the peace commission through 1994, after which the emergence of the Taliban fundamentally altered the balance of power and Haqqani returned to Khost.[33]

Bin Laden lent his support to Haqqani's reconciliation initiatives during the same period that he was relocating most of his followers to Khartoum. According to Rabiah Hutchinson, an Australian Afghan Arab who was briefly married to Abu'l-Walid al-Masri, Bin Laden returned briefly to Peshawar in 1992 and arranged a telephone conference between Hekmatyar and Massoud.[34] The

Palestinian journalist Jamal Ismail describes a much more significant effort on Bin Laden's part:

> In 1991 and 1992 I interviewed him [Bin Laden] more than once. … At that time … he was head of a reconciliation committee between the Afghan factions that were at war in some states. He was chosen by the factions as a neutral party that is supportive of the Afghan jihad in general. … After 1992, when the Afghan mujahedin entered the Afghan capital, and were at war with each other, which stunned all observers, Osama bin Laden—along with a number of Islamic activists who were in Peshawar and other Arab countries—exerted intensive mediation efforts between Hekmatyar, Masood, and Rabbani, but all these efforts failed.[35]

While Bin Laden supported the Haqqanis' peace initiatives in Afghanistan during this period, the Haqqanis lent their aid to al-Qa'ida's earliest efforts in Africa. In the same month that Bin Laden and much of the senior leadership of al-Qa'ida were settling into Khartoum, the Haqqanis published a lengthy communiqué and request for assistance by the Eritrean Islamic Jihad Movement (EIJM) in the Arabic-language *Manba' al-Jihad*. This was the first of such communications by a non-Afghan organization published in the *Manba'* magazines.[36] Leaders of the EIJM were also then enjoying Sudan's hospitality, and al-Qa'ida reportedly extended financial aid and training to the Eritrean Islamic Jihad at this time.[37] The EIJM liaison to al-Qa'ida was reportedly close to Abu 'Ubayda al-Banshiri, and the leader of the "militant Salafi faction" of the EIJM—Muhammad Ahmad Salih (Abu Suhayl)—is said to have previously fought in Afghanistan.[38] Given this information and the fact that the EIJM communiqué appeared in *Manba'*, it seems likely that the EIJM veterans of the Afghan jihad had fought or trained at Haqqani fronts.

The Haqqanis also issued declarations of support during 1991 for the "jihad" being waged by al-Qa'ida's new hosts in Khartoum, the revolutionary Islamist regime of Hassan al-Turabi, against the southern Sudanese forces of John Garang. In 2002 Bosnian authorities raided the offices of the Benevolence International Foundation (BIF) in Sarajevo being run by Enaam Arnaout (Abu Mahmud al-Suri), a co-founder of al-Qa'ida and a veteran of the Haqqani fronts during the anti-Soviet war. On Arnaout's computer police found scanned images of statements written by both Jalaluddin Haqqani and Yunis Khalis issued in 1991, calling for support of the Sudanese jihad.[39] Jalaluddin's letter, written in his own hand under the letterhead of "Hezb-e-Islam Afghanistan, Shk Jalaludin Haqani Office," reads:

> To the Muslims of East and West ... From the land of jihad in the path of God, the Muslim land of Afghanistan, victorious by the permission of God against the union of infidels, unto my Muslim brothers in general: I give you glad tidings that the banner of jihad—which remains a duty until the Day of Resurrection—has been raised from the heart of Africa in Muslim Sudan. The enemies of God loathe that the Muslims should return to their religion and to their lord, so the Crusaders, the apostates and infidels have united in supporting one another in fighting the Muslims [of Sudan], who are now waiting expectantly for your help and support through your raising the call, money and your pens, in hope of divine rewards and the intercession of the noble Prophet.[40]

The correspondence discovered on the BIF computers also documents the extensive al-Qa'ida infrastructure in and around Zhawara at this time, referring to "centers which belong to al-Qa'ida" at Zhawara, Bori, Jihadwal, and Manikandaw, noting that the Khost-area operations of al-Qa'ida are "in the hands of Abu Hafs."[41] The files also included numerous receipts and records of transactions between al-Qa'ida members, including Arnaout, and HIK, for vehicles, weapons, and ammunition, making frequent reference to the al-Qa'ida training camps in Paktia.[42]

These areas of cooperation demonstrate that the Haqqani–al-Qa'ida relationship did not cease with Bin Laden's move to Africa, but rather expanded and was considerably internationalized. But whereas Bin Laden focused his efforts on the Arabian Peninsula, the rhetoric and activities of the Haqqani network became markedly global during this period. In a series of conferences in Pakistan convened by the JUI and its jihadist offshoots in 1991–2, Jalaluddin Haqqani began to identify the United States as the next main enemy of the Muslim world following the disintegration of the Soviet Union, a turn which was also reflected in the publications of the Haqqani network in the first years of the 1990s.

Already in 1988 the Haqqanis began declaring their support for a range of jihadi causes beyond Afghanistan. Speaking at a conference held by Harakat-ul Jihad al-Islami (HuJI) in Gujrat City, Pakistan in 1988, Jalaluddin Haqqani stated:

Brothers: Know that we will not lay down our arms once Afghanistan becomes free. We will fight with and help Muslims in India and Kashmir to get their freedom from the Hindus; we will help rescue the Palestinians from the cruelties of the Jews; we hope that God, through us, helps free the Muslims of Balkh, Bukhara, Tashkent and Samarqand from the yoke of the Russians. We ask that God will help us keep our arms until the defenseless Muslims of the world are rescued and freed.[43]

This rhetoric is remarkably similar to that of al-Qa'ida in 1988. According to Enaam Arnaout (Abu Mahmud al-Suri):

The al Qaeda idea ran through Osama's mind for the first time in 1988, namely after the establishment of al-Masadah and after young Arabs began to join the jihad in large numbers with the emergence of the signs of victory in Afghanistan. Osama believed he could set up an army of young men responding to the jihad call. When he presented the idea to us he did not speak of jihad against Arab regimes, but of helping Muslims against the infidel government oppressing them, as was the case in Palestine, the Philippines, and Kashmir, especially Central Asia, which was under the Soviet rule then and no one dreamed that two years later it would be independent.[44]

In the same year, the Haqqanis published what appears to be their first jihadi magazine, issued a year before they began producing the *Manba' al-Jihad* and *Nusrat al-Jihad* journals in Arabic, Pashto, and Urdu respectively.[45] The Haqqanis' decision to produce their own media products and send Jalaluddin on speaking tours at this time may have been meant to compensate for the loss of resources that came with the reduction of direct CIA support beginning in 1988.[46] Provocatively entitled *The Voice of Global Jihad* (*Sawt al-Jihad al-'Alami*), their first magazine only appeared in one issue, printed out of Peshawar in June of 1988, and carried, in addition to articles about developments in Afghanistan, a statement by the "Blind Shaykh" 'Umar 'Abd al-Rahman calling for revolutionary jihad against the Egyptian regime. According to Ahmad Zaydan, who notes that the magazine was backed by the Haqqanis, *The Voice of Global Jihad* "was financed and supervised by Egyptians who were opposed to the Egyptian regime. This might be the first indication against the Egyptian regime in Peshawar. Otherwise, before that the Arab volunteers were restricting their activities to the Afghan jihad."[47] In 1991, Jalaluddin gave an interview to *al-Murabitun*, the Peshawar-based magazine of the Egyptian Jama'a al-Islamiyya (the Egyptian Islamic Group), in which he said regarding the Arabs in Afghanistan: "I believe that even if a small group of them go back to their countries and start jihad there, all of their problems would be solved, just like jihad has solved our problems. And our Arab brothers are doing well in terms of finances, so that should help too."[48]

Through a variety of media, then, by 1988 the Haqqanis were promoting far-flung defensive jihads against non-Muslim invaders as well as revolutionary jihadi movements in the Arab world. Beginning in 1991 they began to promote anti-American militant activism as well. Speaking at a conference convened by the NCS in 1991, Jalaluddin Haqqani declared:

Jihad continues to be a sacred duty until the infidels are defeated throughout the world. ... God will not bless us for our past jihad. To win His blessings, we have to continue jihad until the end ... In the past, we had one enemy, Russia. But now, our enemies are numerous and stronger because now America, Britain, China and all non-Muslim countries have backed the Russians in an attempt to weaken the Muslim community ... The premise that made jihad a sacred duty of all Muslims in the past still holds and backing the jihad and helping in its path is a duty of all Muslims.[49]

The following year at a conference in Karachi dedicated to the Haqqanis and celebrating their contributions to the Afghan and Kashmiri struggles, Fazl ur-Rehman, the head of the JUI-F, said in a speech:

The Afghan jihad, which was spearheaded by Mawlawi Haqqani and other truthful leaders, defeated the Soviet empire. But now there is another enemy to this jihad. That is America and its conspiratorial policies that are intended to bring ruin to Afghanistan, the center of jihad, under American attacks. But we are absolutely certain that people like Mawlawi Haqqani will give the Americans the same answer they gave to the Russians. And we are sure that people like Haqqani will fuel the flames of jihad worldwide.[50]

The anti-American tone of Haqqani pronouncements was not limited to the perception of American "conspiratorial policies" in

Afghanistan, but was also linked in several Haqqani publications to the view that US involvement in the Gulf since 1990 was part of a broader American–Israeli strategy to exercise an oppressive and anti-Islamic hegemony throughout the Muslim world.[51]

The Haqqanis' statements during this period were being backed up by investment in the training and mobilization of Islamist militants from Pakistan, Kashmir, Bangladesh, northwestern China, Tajikistan, Uzbekistan, Southeast Asia, and a variety of Arab countries.[52] Though none of our sources document direct ISI material support to these initiatives, the ISI leadership was making unequivocal statements of ideological support for just such a regional expansion of jihad at this time.[53] At a meeting of the NCS in Rawalpindi in October 1990, Mirza Aslam Beg, Pakistani chief of army staff, presented a vision of Afghanistan and Pakistan uniting "to foster Islamic revolutions in the Muslim world," with special reference to the former Soviet states and Kashmir.[54] Brig. Yousaf, by then retired from the ISI, described an identical vision in an article published in a Pakistani daily the following month.[55] In the summer of 1991 several new training camps were established at Zhawara in partnership with the JUI-linked and ISI-supported Kashmiri jihadi organizations Harakat ul-Mujahidin (also known as Harakat al-Ansar) and HuJI.[56] One of the Haqqani camps serving this population was the Salman al-Farsi camp, established at Zhawara and described in *Manba' al-Jihad* as the main military training camp for students of the Manba' al-'Ulum madrassa near Miranshah.[57] At the Salman al-Farsi camp "Pakistanis, Kashmiris, Filippinos, Bosnian Muslims, Uighurs from Xinjiang etc. were being trained."[58] When photojournalist Bob Nickelsberg visited the Zhawara base in 1990 and 1991 he was surprised by the large number of Kashmiri and Uighurs engaging in training, and Jalaluddin boasted to him about their presence but declined Nickelsberg's request to interview some of the trainees.[59] One Uighur separatist in Chinese custody later claimed to a Chinese journalist that the camps at which the Uighurs trained were financed by Osama bin Laden.[60]

The Furqan Project

The Haqqanis also realized their ambition to support jihad in the former Soviet CIS states, and in this initiative they worked directly with al-Qa'ida. Between 1992 and 1995 the al-Qa'ida camps in and around Zhawara were partially dedicated to the "Furqan Project," a training program spearheaded by Abu'l-Walid al-Masri and providing training and arms to Tajik, Uzbek, Chechen, and other Central Asian jihadis in support of anti-regime and irredentist Islamist movements in their respective countries of origin. Unlike in the early days of the al-Qa'ida camp at Jaji, when recruits first went through training at Haqqani camps before proceeding to al-Qa'ida's facilities, in this case training was provided in one location and in a joint fashion, with al-Qa'ida and Haqqani personnel training the international classes together.

In a book detailing the history of this project, Abu Walid al-Masri writes that it began with a visit to Peshawar in 1992 by Haq Nazar, a member of the Shura Council of the Nahda Party of Tajikistan. Haq Nazar came seeking support from the Afghan Arabs for the Nahda's revolutionary efforts in Tajikistan, and over a series of meetings Abu'l-Walid agreed to set up a training program for Nahda cadres at al-Faruq in Zhawara. The al-Qa'ida camps were being run by skeleton crews at this time, most of the organization having moved to Sudan and Somalia, but Abu'l-Walid met with Sayf al-'Adl at al-Faruq and secured al-Qa'ida support for the project.[61] Al-Qa'ida donated its remaining stores of weapons in Afghanistan to be used in the training and then shipped north to the Nahda fighters in Tajikistan. Abu 'Ata al-Sharqi (Zayd al-Tunisi) and the remaining al-Qa'ida personnel at the Jihadwal camp offered training support, as did two members of the Egyptian Islamic Jihad (EIJ).[62] Abu'l-Walid was also able to hire several trainers who had been working at camps around Peshawar and who had fled to Afghanistan after Prime Minister Nawaz Sharif cracked down on the Peshawar Arabs and ordered their offices in Pakistan closed. While these Arabs would provide the operational training to the Central Asians, mullahs from the Haqqani network gave ideological and religious instruction. Abu'l-Walid writes of the Tajik trainees, of which the first group numbered 150 young men:

They were from a country long controlled by communism and knew little of Islam. Many learned to pray and read the Qur'an for the first time in their lives. I was determined to keep the influences of Salafism from them, as they came from a people who were historically Hanafi and of whom many were Sufis. Thus we agreed with some of the 'ulama among my neighbors at the Zhawara base from the Haqqani group (*jama'a Haqqani*) to teach them Islam and the rules of shari'a according to the Hanafi school. We explained to our brother trainers from al-Qa'ida that we were teaching them the Islamic jurisprudence that prevailed among them in their own country so that they would not find themselves further isolated in their own communities. We convinced them [the al-Qa'ida trainers] with difficulty, but our actions were welcomed by the Nahda party.[63]

The overall training program, according to Abu'l-Walid, was designed on the model of the Haqqani network and sought to impart to the Central Asian jihadis the best practices of coordinated command and centralized force that the Haqqanis had refined during the anti-Soviet struggle.

In 1994 Abu Walid escorted the first batch of Tajik graduates and their al-Qa'ida-donated military supplies north to the Afghan province of Taloqan, which borders Tajikistan. To get there at that time meant crossing several lines of opposing mujahidin groups engaged in civil war. As one of the few senior mujahidin leaders attempting to mediate rather than join that conflict, Jalaluddin Haqqani was in an ideal position to help Abu'l-Walid negotiate the dangerous passage north, and according to the latter Jalaluddin intervened for him on numerous occasions during the trip.[64] Crossing into the no-man's-land between the opposing front lines of Hekmatyar and Ahmad Shah Massoud south of Kabul, Abu'l-Walid discovered that the commander in charge of that gray zone was a man despised by the Arab foreign fighter community for allegedly capturing Arab fighters and handing them over to Pakistan. He was also, however, an old friend of Ibrahim Haqqani, one of Jalaluddin's younger brothers, and with a letter from Ibrahim requesting safe passage Abu'l-Walid sailed through the danger zone unmolested with the men and weapons in his charge.[65]

There were other mishaps along the way, but finally Abu'l-Walid and the Tajiks reached Taloqan and delivered the arms to the Nahda leadership. While there, Abu'l-Walid met one Tahir Yuldashev, an Uzbek then on the Nahda Shura Council. Abu'l-Walid and Yuldashev discussed the latter's ambitions for jihadist action in Uzbekistan, and after Abu'l-Walid returned to the al-Qa'ida-Haqqani camps at Zhawara Yuldashev began sending groups of Uzbeks down to him for training. Four years later Yuldashev announced the formation of the Islamic Movement of Uzbekistan (IMU), which has been fighting ever since in Central Asia's Ferghana Valley. After 9/11 many of the IMU's activists in Afghanistan fled with al-Qa'ida into North and South Waziristan, where they are now estimated to number several thousand.

After beginning the training session for the Uzbeks, Abu'l-Walid went to Peshawar to meet with a delegation of Chechen mujahidin that had come seeking support for their struggle against Russia. Chechen rebel leader Shamil Basayev was among the delegation, and Abu'l-Walid met with Shamil and discussed the Khost training operations. Shamil sent six Chechen mujahidin back with Abu'l-Walid to train at al-Faruq, and Abu'l-Walid writes that in their physical fitness and military skills they were superior to anyone he had trained before. After their graduation Abu'l-Walid learned that they all filled prominent leadership positions in the jihadi movement in Chechnya, and that five of them were eventually killed fighting the Russians.[66] He writes of this period in 1994, when al-Faruq was filled with new recruits from Tajikistan, thirty-five Uzbek cadres sent by Yuldashev, and Basayev's six Chechen "giants," as the high point of al-Faruq's history, characterized by extremely high morale and enthusiastic involvement by the Haqqani 'ulama and other local Afghans.

Abu'l-Walid: Architect of Global Jihad

Recently, two senior al-Qa'ida leaders have made claims that suggest that the Haqqani network played an oblique role in the anti-American turn on the part of al-Qa'ida at this time. In 2009, 'Abdullah Muhammad Fazul, the late leader of al-Qa'ida operations in East Africa and al-Qa'ida's "confidential secretary" (*amin sirr al-qa'ida*), published online a two-volume autobiography which narrates the whole course of his two-decade long career within the al-Qa'ida organization. In it, Fazul claims that the "architect of the strategy" of al-Qa'ida's anti-American jihad was Abu'l-Walid al-Masri, "whose great merit it was to have convinced the al-Qa'ida leadership to confront the United States of America."[67] Killed in Mogadishu in June 2011, Fazul's stature within the al-Qa'ida organization requires that his testimony be given significant weight. Already by the early 1990s Fazul had risen to a senior position in the organization, and during the later 1990s he worked directly under Abu Hafs al-Masri as the latter's lieutenant in an al-Qa'ida military committee.[68] Bin Laden's former bodyguard Nasir al-Bahri notes that while in Afghanistan in the late 1990s Fazul "offered special and ultra-secret training to certain members of the organization,"[69] which Fazul himself reveals to have centered on al-Qa'ida's quest to develop chemical, biological, and nuclear weapons.[70] During the later stages of the preparation of the 9/11 plot, Fazul worked in Kandahar as Khalid Shaykh Muhammad's personal assistant and was thus—according to him—the only person in the al-Qa'ida organization privy to the details of that plot beyond Bin Laden, Abu Hafs al-Masri, and Khalid Shaykh Muhammad himself.[71]

More recently, al-Qa'ida's senior military official Sayf al-'Adl addressed a series of letters to Abu'l-Walid that the latter posted on his website, and in which Sayf also describes Abu'l-Walid as having been famous in Afghanistan for promoting a strategic focus on a hegemonic United States. Sayf wrote that Abu'l-Walid, using the metaphor of pack mules and the mule driver, explained that the American–Israeli imperial project distributes the burden of subjugation among various internally conflicting interests, making revolutionary jihadism against "apostate regimes" the like of a pack mule bearing a load that furthers the interests of empire. He also refers to Abu'l-Walid's involvement in the development of al-Qa'ida's strategy when he asks:

Was it not the strategy of al-Qa'ida, which you participated in developing, to work to weaken the present world order and thus weaken the underlying political establishment so that our people in Arab and Muslim countries could seize the opportunity and free themselves from the idols weighing on their chests, both rulers and agents? And today you write that the solution will be in the hands of the people. Is not what you are writing about a success of al-Qa'ida's strategy which, I repeat, was a strategy you yourself took part in crafting, and which was a constant point of contention between al-Qa'ida and other organizations and brought al-Qa'ida severe criticism because it chose to strike the far enemy rather than the near enemy?[72]

A series of letters contained in the Harmony database written by Abu'l-Walid al-Masri from the Zhawara base in 1993 and 1994 to the al-Qa'ida leadership in Sudan lends support to Fazul's and Sayf's claims. In these letters—the "Five Letters to the Africa Corps"—Abu'l-Walid writes at length of al-Qa'ida's lack of strategic focus and Bin Laden's obsession with the Arab heartlands—that is, the Arabian Peninsula.[73] He bemoans the transition of al-Qa'ida's main focus from Afghanistan to the Gulf region, noting that "before you abandoned the Asian position under the slogan that you were going to work in the heartland region—the Arab region—you had totally rejected the concept of movement on the flanks, claiming that the battle would be decided in the heartland" and that the route of approach would be to support anti-communist Islamist movements in Yemen and Somalia.[74] Yet after committing to this strategy and without warning, American forces had appeared in Somalia, presenting a golden opportunity to al-Qa'ida to strike a blow at "the Crusaders":

When you entered Somalia, the Somali arena was barren and futile. The situation changed, however, after the intervention by America and the Knights of the Cross. You most resembled a hunter aiming his rifle at the dead branch of a tree, with no leaves or birds on it. Suddenly, a bald eagle lands on the branch of the tree, directly in line with the rifle. Shouldn't the hunter pull the trigger to kill the eagle or at least bloody it? The American bald eagle has landed within range of our rifles. You can kill it or leave it permanently disfigured. If you do that, you will have saved Sudan, Yemen, Bab al-Mandab, the Red Sea, the Arabian Gulf, and the waters of the Nile. Could you want more magnificent objectives of war than these?[75]

According to Fazul, it was after this that al-Qa'ida shifted from solely focusing on training the Somali Islamist militia known as al-Ittihad al-Islami (the forerunner of al-Shabab) to working on confronting the American presence in Somalia. By his account, al-Qa'ida was directly involved in the "Black Hawk Down" incident in Mogadishu that took place a month after Abu'l-Walid's letter was written and in which nineteen American soldiers were killed.[76] Fazul writes:

Somalia was for al-Qa'ida the birthplace of its confrontation with the sole superpower, and was a single arena in which we were able to apply all that we had learned in Afghanistan. And don't forget that this confrontation would be between the great powers of the "New World Order," under the leadership of the Zionist Americans, and the [Muslim] youth, who have nothing but their souls, submitted to God. It was Abu'l-Walid al-Masri who hit the mark when he persuaded the al-Qa'ida leadership to focus on the United States, as it is the chief instigator of the chaos erupting in the Muslim world.[77]

Bin Laden had stated in a number of places that the withdrawal of American forces after the "Black Hawk Down" incident emboldened al-Qa'ida and spurred the organization to plot further attacks, culminating in the bombings of the US embassies in Kenya and Tanzania in 1998.[78] Again, the perpetrators of these attacks underwent their training at the Zhawara-based training camps in Khost prior to being dispatched to Africa.[79]

Neither Fazul nor Sayf relate this claim regarding Abu'l-Walid's influence directly to the Haqqani network. However, if their statements are accurate, the strategic shift in al-Qa'ida's target selection and ideology after 1993 would have to be understood as growing, to a certain extent, out of the long-standing relationship between the Haqqanis and the al-Qa'ida leadership. Abu'l-Walid, after all, had a much deeper history with the Haqqanis than he did with al-Qa'ida—which he claims to have never formally joined, though he admits to his tenure as amir of the al-Faruq camp during the first half of the 1990s.[80] Abu'l-Walid was still working directly with the Haqqanis during this period, and had contributed to the *Manba' al-Jihad* magazine over the previous three years. He had been based since arriving in Afghanistan in 1979 at Haqqani headquarters, and it was from the al-Qa'ida camp established at these headquarters that he wrote his letters urging al-Qa'ida to confront American forces in Somalia. He has more recently emerged as a rather staunch critic of the al-Qa'ida leadership, though he remains a Haqqani loyalist. For its part, the Haqqani network went on record beginning in 1988 in support of global jihad, and maintained a consistent ideological position of enmity for the United States from 1991 on, and in this the Haqqanis preceded al-Qa'ida by several years. As will be seen, the Haqqanis' role in helping to shape al-Qa'ida's war on the West was far from over, and after the rise of the Taliban it would continue to deepen.

The Haqqani Network, al-Qa'ida, and the Taliban: 1994–2001

In 1994, the direction of the Afghan civil war was irrevocably altered with the rise of a new and obscure party to the conflict: the Taliban. Centered on the figure of Mullah Muhammad Omar, a minor player during the anti-Soviet jihad who had, along with his earliest supporters, fought with the Haqqaniyya-linked parties of HIK and Harakat, the Taliban was a lowland Pashtun movement composed mostly of Kandaharis. In this it hailed from a very different political culture than that of the highland mujahidin groups like the Haqqanis, as evidenced first and foremost in the Taliban's nationalist ideology and ambitions for national dominance.[81] In its rise to power and eventual consolidation of control over Kabul the Taliban was assisted by both the Haqqanis and al-Qa'ida—and in that order—but this support was by no means a foregone conclusion. In fact, the relations between the Haqqanis and al-Qa'ida on the one hand and the Taliban on the other were marked by mutual suspicion and conflict from the beginning, and remained turbulent throughout the period of the Taliban regime. They arguably remain just as turbulent, if not more so, today.[82]

The fact that many of the early leaders of the Taliban had been educated at the Haqqaniyya madrassa in Akora Khattak has often been noted, but this did not necessarily make them natural allies of the Haqqanis.[83] On the contrary, many of the commanders of what I have termed the "Haqqaniyya network," with which the Haqqanis had worked most closely during the anti-Soviet jihad, emerged in the mid-1990s as some of the most prominent opponents of the Taliban. As already noted, the core leadership of the Haqqani-led NCS was initially provided by Jalaluddin and the two senior HIK commanders Mullah Malang and Abdul Haq. Mullah Malang, the HIK's most capable Kandahar-based commander during the anti-

Soviet jihad, opposed the Taliban from the beginning, went into exile in Pakistan, and later joined Hamid Karzai and other leaders in Quetta to organize anti-Taliban opposition within Afghanistan.[84] Abdul Haq, who fought under Haqqani at Khost before leading HIK fighters around Kabul in the 1980s, followed a similar path to Mullah Malang and went back into Afghanistan after 9/11 to rally anti-Taliban support, only to be killed by the Taliban in October of 2001.[85] Haji 'Abd al-Qadir, the leader of the Jalalabad shura, tried to maintain its independence from the Taliban but other members of the shura favored an alliance, so he fled to Pakistan on the eve of the arrival of Taliban forces in Jalalabad in September 1996, just four months after Bin Laden's arrival as his guest.[86] Another close Haqqani ally was Qari Baba, whom Jalaluddin Haqqani singled out in an interview after Operation Magistral in 1987 as one of three commanders who had shown solidarity with the Haqqanis in aiding their defense of the Zhawara base—the other two being Mullah Malang and the Taliban's chief rival Ahmad Shah Massoud.[87] Qari Baba refused Taliban demands to disarm, and the Taliban's forceful extraction of his eventual capitulation was the watershed moment leading to the Taliban's capture of Ghazni at the end of 1994.[88]

The capture of Ghazni was a turning point for the Taliban in the southeast and forced the Haqqanis to come to terms with the rise of this new power now on their very doorstep. Jalaluddin had remained focused up to that point on the peace commission that he led out of Jalalabad, still hoping for a political resolution to the civil war. The ISI was providing military support to Hekmatyar up through late 1993, though when Benazir Bhutto replaced Nawaz Sharif in the October elections Pakistan grew increasingly frustrated with Hekmatyar and began to shift its support to the Taliban in the south. Hekmatyar's forces in Khost were second only to the Haqqanis' there, and the shifting political winds heightened the already tense relations between HIG and the Haqqanis, leading to a confrontation between them over resources on the eve of the Taliban's arrival.

The Haqqanis had a long history of troubled relations with Hekmatyar. In the 1986 Battle of Zhawara, discussed in Chapter 2, Hekmatyar released a statement after the communist forces were repelled from the base claiming responsibility for the victory. As Abu'l-Walid put it, "this put yet another black mark on the record of a relationship that had hardly any white space remaining."[89] Similar conflicts arose after the capture of Khost in 1991, when Hekmatyar's forces, having played a relatively minor role in the fighting, were enabled by the ISI to claim the victory, seizing the radio station and most of the garrison's heavy weapons. This was in violation of pre-campaign agreements, and the ISI refused to recover any of the war spoils for Haqqani. Hekmatyar then hosted General Durrani of the ISI and Qazi Hussein Ahmed, amir of the Pakistani JI, on a triumphant and well-publicized visit to the city, all of which was met with angry rejoinders in the Haqqani publications at the time.[90]

As the Taliban moved north and east out of Kandahar, its fiercest opposition came from the HIG. As Taliban forces approached Khost, however, the HIG commander there—Fayez Muhammad, amir of the Jihadwal base—decided to flee with HIG's weapons stores and vehicles. Al-Qa'ida had been renting its training camp at Jihadwal from the HIG, and Fayez Muhammad moved to seize al-Qa'ida's weapons and demanded from Abu 'Ata al-Sharqi that he turn over a tractor and other vehicles, saying they were all needed for the HIG's fight against Massoud in Kabul. The al-Qa'ida leaders refused, and when Fayez Muhammad moved to seize their equipment the Haqqani network stepped in and threatened to destroy his base and expel the HIG from Khost.[91] In September Abu 'Ata reported on these developments to al-Qa'ida in Sudan, noting that the situation was much improved on account of the fact that "the governor of Khost, who is from the Haqqani organization (*tanzim Haqqani*), told Fayez Muhammad: 'By God, if you fire a single shot we will destroy the Matun citadel'—which belongs to the Hizb [HIG] in Khost—'and we will kick you out of Khost' ... These incidents made me feel much more at ease, as Fayiz Muhammad has begun to face many problems and is daily losing power, and I don't think he would dare try repeating what he did to us before."[92] He also reports that al-Qa'ida representatives had communicated their outrage to both the HIG offices in Kabul and the vice president of the JI at a meeting at the Badr camp.[93] Fayez Muhammad fled to

North Waziristan, where according to Abu'l-Walid he sold off all of the HIG supplies on the local weapons market.[94]

With the HIG out of the picture, the Haqqanis were the sole major mujahidin power remaining in Khost, and the provinces surrounding them had all fallen, surrendered, or thrown in their support to the Taliban. The Mansur family, a long-time Haqqani ally and one of the strongest mujahidin groups in Paktika, joined the Taliban in February 1995, and the Taliban began to move from there into Khost during the third week of same month. According to Haji Din Muhammad, the deputy leader of HIK and a long-time associate of Jalaluddin Haqqani, the latter came to Jalalabad at this time to consult with Yunis Khalis about how to respond to the Taliban's encroachment. In his recent biography of Khalis, Muhammad writes:

> It happened that they [the Taliban] went to Paktika, Khost and Paktia. Mawlawi Jalaluddin Haqqani, who had a very large military power in Khost and Paktia, dreaded this kind of development of the Taliban. This was at a time when the Taliban also did not have an understanding with the forces of the mujahidin. The Taliban were already in Paktia when Mawlawi Jalaluddin Haqqani came to Nangarhar and met with Mawlawi Khalis. Mawlawi Khalis said to him: do not fight with them; yourself, try to understand their words, and they also will understand—in order that there be no blood spilled amongst us.[95]

Following a pattern established in a series of earlier encounters with local mujahidin leaders, a Taliban force surrounded Ibrahim Haqqani's house and, holding aloft copies of the Qur'an, demanded that the Haqqanis "surrender" the area to Taliban control. Ibrahim came out and convinced the Taliban that he would get his brother Jalaluddin to speak with them, and Ibrahim and his brother Khalil Haqqani then oversaw a series of negotiations between the Taliban leadership and the Haqqanis that set the terms of their relationship. High on the list of priorities was protecting Jalaluddin's booming business ventures, especially the scrap metal "export" business using the Haqqani-controlled Khost airstrip, repaired in 1993 by their Arab allies, from which the Haqqanis were making millions in the resale of metals scavenged in some cases from Iraqi heavy weaponry shipped to the Haqqanis by the CIA in 1991.[96] The

Haqqanis explicitly demanded regional autonomy in return for recognizing the Taliban, and stressed that the southeastern tribal culture and local political processes be left alone. They also specifically required that there be no effort to enforce Kandahari dictates on the highland tribes.[97]

Haqqani insiders later told Western writers that the Haqqani leadership was initially hostile to the Taliban and considered confronting them militarily when they moved into Khost.[98] Some have suggested that the ISI pressured the Haqqanis against this and encouraged them to lend what proved to be indispensable military support during a critical moment, as the Taliban struggled to wrest Kabul from Massoud's control.[99] Whatever the case, following a series of defeats against Massoud around Kabul in early 1995, the Taliban were joined there during the summer of 1995 by Jalaluddin Haqqani and a group of 2,000 fighters from Khost, recruited with "suitable exhortations over the patriotic role of the border tribes in ousting Tajik usurpers [Bacha-e Saqqao] in 1929."[100] In other words, Haqqani's men were appealed to on the basis of an identity rooted in a history of fiercely defended highland autonomy, not in terms of the Taliban's nationalist agenda. It was only after the Haqqanis joined the battle in the north that the Taliban succeeded in capturing Kabul, and Jalaluddin was then tasked with confronting Massoud's forces on the Shomali plain north of the city.

Despite this provision of military aid, relations between the Haqqanis and the Taliban continued to be strained. In an interview with Ahmed Rashid two years after the capture of Kabul Jalaluddin related that when he arrived with his men in 1995, "he was powerless to make military decisions[,] and the fact that they were led by Kandahari officers at the front led to mass desertions. Within two months Haqqani had only 300 of his new recruits left."[101] Rashid writes that Haqqani "remained extremely bitter" over being "kept out of the decision-making process that took place in Kandahar under Omar, rather than in Kabul."[102]

The early relations between the Taliban and al-Qa'ida were even worse. When Bin Laden arrived in Nangarhar Province in 1996 he was given hospitality and the freedom to move his family into primitive dwellings in the Tora Bora Mountains above Jalalabad by the Jalalabad shura. The shura's leader, Haji 'Abd al-Qadir, opposed the Taliban and soon after Bin Laden's arrival fled to Pakistan. Another of Bin Laden's protectors, Commander Saznur, who had been a celebrated commander under Sayyaf during the 1980s, was killed soon after Jalalabad fell to the Taliban, leaving Bin Laden without a protector and leading to much anxiety among the Bin Laden clan.[103] The suspicion was mutual. When asked by State Department officials in 1997 about the Taliban's relationship with Bin Laden, Mullah Rabbani, Mullah Omar's deputy, responded that "Bin Ladin came to Afghanistan when Haji Qadir controlled Nangarhar Province. The Taliban did not control that area then." The Taliban Foreign Minister Mullah Abdul Jalil "who also attended the meeting with Rabbani, interjected that Bin Ladin had lived in caves south of Jalalabad in Tora Bora and the Taliban had become suspicious. They told him to move out, to live in an ordinary house."[104]

Bin Laden's former bodyguard Nasir al-Bahri also describes the mutual distrust between Bin Laden and the Taliban in these days, and says that when the Taliban sent representatives to find out where Bin Laden stood, the latter refused to meet them personally. He says that Bin Laden also refused to allow his followers, who were still actively engaged in training at the various al-Qa'ida camps around Zhawara, to fight for the Taliban, and refers in this connection to the negative impression of the Taliban among many of the Arabs and the circulation of rumors about there being former communists among their ranks.[105] Another "Afghan Arab," Rabiah Hutchinson, also reflects on the presence of suspicions about the Taliban among the Afghan Arabs even at the end of the 1990s: "I didn't support the Taliban at all. I had heard a lot of negative things ..."[106]

In August of 1996, Bin Laden issued from Jalalabad his communiqué entitled "Expel the Polytheists from the Arabian Peninsula," the first public indication of the anti-American turn in al-Qa'ida's strategy.[107] Though falling far short of the sweeping declaration of global jihad against the United States that al-Qa'ida would issue two years later, it did call on Muslims to boycott American-made goods and to wage jihad against "Zionist-Crusader" interests in

Saudi Arabia. In the following month the Taliban captured Jalalabad, and Bin Laden's provocative statements against Western interests and the meetings with journalists that he arranged in Afghanistan to promote them would become an immediate bone of contention between him and the Taliban movement.

In the month after the Taliban's conquest of Jalalabad, al-Qa'ida finally offered some support to the Taliban, but this appears to have been a second-order effect of its alliance with the Haqqanis. In October of 1996, in response to an urgent appeal for reinforcements to hold Kabul against a massive counterattack by Massoud, Jalaluddin led 4,000 of his own men north to support the Taliban.[108] It was only at this time that Bin Laden "modified his position regarding the participation of al-Qa'ida in the ranks of the Taliban against the Northern Alliance."[109] Nasir al-Bahri and eight other al-Qa'ida fighters, including Abu'l-Faraj al-Libi and Abu Hafs al-Masri, went north to join the fight, "though at that time there was still no coordination between the Taliban command and al-Qa'ida, which led to much chaos."[110]

In early March 1997 Bin Laden invited journalist Peter Bergen of CNN to visit him in Tora Bora and film an interview. His rhetoric in this interview went much further than that in "Expel the Polytheists"—and came much closer to the language and ideological tone of the early-1990s statements of the Haqqanis as well as the writings of Abu'l-Walid al-Masri. In the course of the interview Bin Laden refers to the "New World Order" and calls in a less restrictive fashion than in earlier statements for "jihad against the U.S. government."[111] A CNN interview was a much more public pronouncement than the distribution of his 1996 fatwa, and drew the immediate ire of the Taliban. At the end of March Mullah Omar, citing concerns for Bin Laden's security, ordered him and his family to pack up and relocate to Kandahar, "where the situation is more secure."[112]

The Taliban suffered a major setback that summer at Mazar-i-Sharif, and again the Haqqanis were called in for military aid. As in the deployment to Kabul in 1996, al-Qa'ida and the Haqqanis worked together in the siege of Mazar-i-Sharif. Bin Laden reportedly told Mullah Omar that "we cannot participate further in your battles. Your commanders are immature. They cannot read the situation correctly." Instead, Bin Laden offered to detail Abu Hafs al-Masri as a field commander for the battle, on the condition that Abu Hafs work under Jalaluddin Haqqani rather than with regular Taliban forces.[113] Among the highland Pashtun fighters mobilized by Haqqani for this engagement was Baitullah Mehsud, who would later become the leader of the Tehrik-e Taliban Pakistan (TTP).[114]

The Mazar-i-Sharif battle seems to be the last major offensive in which the Taliban turned to the Haqqanis for aid, and after the capture of the city Jalaluddin was awarded the sinecure position of Taliban minister of borders and tribes. As had characterized his relationship with the Hizb-i Islami Khalis during the anti-Soviet war, Haqqani was only nominally a Taliban figure, and the southern end of the highland Pashtun region remained largely autonomous from Taliban control. This autonomy was obvious to the Arab jihadi community inside Afghanistan; in a late-1998 tract written in defense of the Taliban, Abu Mus'ab al-Suri's refers to Jalaluddin Haqqani and Yunis Khalis as "non-Taliban *'ulama*."[115] The autonomy of the Haqqanis' "region of refuge" would also prove immensely important to al-Qa'ida, as we will see.

The differences for the lives of ordinary people were striking as well, and numerous diplomats and aid workers noted the contrast between Loya Paktia and the rest of Afghanistan as far as the application of Taliban law was concerned. In January 1997, US State Department officials noted that "Haqqani's tribe, the Zadrans, are considered more liberal in their treatment of women than the tribes in the Kandahar area."[116] Between 1995 and 1997 CARE International built thirty coeducational schools in Khost, "believed to be unique in Afghanistan" at the time, all built "thanks to a well-known local mujaheddin [*sic*] commander, Jalaluddin Haqqani, who has close ties to some Persian Gulf sheiks."[117] According to several former Haqqani network commanders interviewed in 2009, "Jalaluddin Haqqani was opposed to some Taliban measures such as banning music, enforcing beard length, and limiting women's access to education."[118] The Haqqanis had distinguished themselves from other mujahidin groups in this way during the 1980s as well, as evidenced by the letter in the Harmony database of Haqqani correspondence with a female administrator of Médecins Sans

Frontières (Doctors Without Borders) invited by Haqqani to extend MSF medical aid at Haqqani clinics.[119]

In another indication of the Haqqanis' autonomy from the Taliban, the latter were unable to provide any assistance to Pakistan—upon whose support the Taliban were dependent—in response to numerous requests from the Pakistani civilian government for the extradition of wanted Pakistani fugitives known to be training in Haqqani-run camps. In 1996, the Badr camps at Jihadwal were removed from Hekmatyar's and the JI's control, and reportedly closed.[120] Pakistani journalist Rahimullah Yusufzai reported from Khost in 1997 that these camps had been transferred to Jalaluddin Haqqani's control, who reallocated them to al-Qa'ida and the JUI-linked Harakat ul-Ansar (a merger of Harakat ul-Mujahidin and Harakat-ul Jihad ul-Islami).[121] These, in addition to the already established camps at Zhawara, were hosting many of Pakistan's most-wanted jihadis, charged in a broad variety of international terrorism incidents, political assassinations, and sectarian murders.

The Pakistani government had been under increasing international pressure since 1995 to move against the Haqqani camps and the terrorist groups training in them. In 1995, six Western tourists were kidnapped by jihadis in Kashmir, and one of the captives was beheaded. Blame fell on HUA, which was subsequently listed by the US State Department as a terrorist group. According to Husain Haqqani (no relation to the Haqqani network), the former Pakistani ambassador to the United States, Prime Minister Benazir Bhutto responded to American pressure by ordering the arrest of HUA's leadership. When she turned to Pakistan's powerful intelligence agency, however, "the ISI told Bhutto that it had no contact or connection with the organization and failed to arrest anyone. A few days later, most of Harakut-ul-Ansar's known leaders surfaced as leaders of a new formation, Harakat-ul-mujahideen."[122] Two years later the civilian government changed hands again, with Nawaz Sharif once again becoming prime minister. Sharif inherited Bhutto's problems with the HUA and ISI's jihadi connections, but they were made much worse in 1998. After al-Qa'ida bombed two American embassies in East Africa, the United States responded with scores of cruise missiles that pounded the camps in Zhawara, which, it was subsequently discovered, included not just al-Qa'ida camps but also those being run by HUA—by then calling itself Harakat-ul-Mujahidin (HUM). Pakistani journalists who rushed to the scene of the latter camps reported that the dead included a number of ISI agents.[123]

US pressure on Pakistan in the wake of these events was unrelenting, but the Americans had little leverage. President Clinton had earlier slapped sanctions on Pakistan for its nuclear program and Pakistan's military establishment felt betrayed and estranged from its erstwhile ally. Sharif was similarly at odds with the army over his back-channel efforts on a peace process with India over Kashmir. By 1999 the international pressure on Sharif over the camps in Haqqani country was compounded by domestic chaos. Anti-Shi'a terrorist groups, spin-offs of the HUJI/HUA/HUM, initiated a campaign of sectarian murder that killed dozens of Pakistani Shi'a—a campaign that is now being repeated by the same groups in Baluchistan. Sharif's government sent a letter to the Taliban in Kandahar asking for assistance with the cross-border sectarian violence. Written in Pashto, this document was discovered in Afghanistan after the American invasion in 2001. It names nine of the most-wanted leaders of Pakistan's anti-Shi'a groups, including Riaz Basra and Akram Lahori, both identified as having been last seen at the HUA camp in Zhawara.[124] It also says that these men were last seen or known to be training at certain camps, among which the document lists the following:

Harakat-ul Ansar: This camp (*mu'askar 'Umar Faruq*) is located in uluswali [administrative district] Zhawara Gharbuz near Khost. The camp was established in June, 1991. Maulvi Abdul Jabbar is its director. Presently there are 300–500 persons under training. The camp is politically affiliated with JUI-F. It has the backing of Jalaluddin Haqqani.

Jamiat-ul Mujahidin: The camp was established in 1991 in Zhawara and is headed by Akhtar Hussein Muavia. At present, 30–40 students from AK/IHK[125] are receiving training. This camp also has the backing of Haqqani.

Harakat-ul Jihad al-Islami (Liza): This camp is located in Zhawara and is sponsored by Maulvi Fazlur Rahman Khalil. Presently, Qari Saifullah Akhtar is in charge of training. 150–200 students are receiving training currently. Mawlana Jalaluddin Haqqani is providing local support to it.[126]

The Taliban denied any involvement. In the first week of October 1999, Sharif sent a special emissary to meet with Mullah Omar to press for cooperation on the sectarians taking refuge with the Haqqanis, specifically discussing Riaz Basra and Saifullah Akhtar. The Pakistani press reported that "Mullah Umar assured the Pakistani envoy that he would continue to raise [his] voice against terrorism while also taking practical measures to stamp out the menace."[127] On 11 October Prime Minister Sharif made a one-day visit to the UAE in order to meet with President Sheikh Zayed bin Sultan al-Nahyan in Abu Dhabi. The UAE was one of only three countries to recognize the Taliban, but it was also the Haqqani network's main base of operations in the Arab world. Shaikh Zayed had accorded Jalaluddin Haqqani a personal state reception in 1991—the only Afghan mujahidin leader to be given this honor, and the only such state visit ever made by Jalaluddin (who did not, contrary to some recent reporting, visit President Reagan at the White House).[128] The Pakistani press reported on the following morning that Sharif had gone to meet with the UAE leadership in order to "urge it to use its influence for asking Taliban to close down these camps."[129] By that evening the news cycle was dominated by events of much greater consequence. Pervez Musharraf had seized power from Sharif in a bloodless coup and declared himself chief martial law administrator. The Haqqani camps remained open, and neither the Taliban nor the Musharraf regime had any success in curtailing their activities before 9/11.

The Birth of the Turkistan Islamic Party (TIP)

This period also saw the reconstitution at Khost of the former East Turkestan Islamic Movement (ETIM) in its current form as the Turkistan Islamic Party (TIP). Since at least the beginning of the 1990s the Haqqanis had been hosting Uighur separatists from northwestern China at its training camps, and as already noted Jalaluddin made numerous references at that time to Haqqani support for both the Kashmiri and Uighur "jihads." In a statement published in 1991 in the Haqqanis' Urdu-language magazine, Jalaluddin declared that the "Afghan jihad has inspired Muslims all over the world. The jihad in Kashmir is a result of the Afghans' struggle, and the uprisings of the Muslims of China are inspired by the Afghans."[130] By the "uprisings" in China Jalaluddin is most likely referring to the brief Uighur Muslim rebellion centered on Baren Township in Xinjiang, which took place in April 1990.[131] After this rebellion much of the leadership of the ETIM was imprisoned and the group collapsed in 1993. One of its leaders—"Abu Muhammad" Hasan Makhdum[132]—was imprisoned in Xinjiang until 1996, and in 1997 travelled to the Gulf and thence to Khost where he reestablished the group as the Turkistan Islamic Party.[133]

Hasan Makhdum was killed in an encounter with Pakistani soldiers in Angor Adda, South Waziristan, in 2003, but a series of interviews with his successor, 'Abd al-Haqq al-Turkistani, in the TIP's Arabic-language magazine details the reorganization of the group at the Haqqanis' Khost training camps in 1997. After a brief term in prison in Urumqi, Xinjiang, 'Abd al-Haqq, a former student of Hasan Makhdum, was able to leave China and settle in Islamabad, where he attended classes at the Islamic University and made contacts with the Uighur separatist diaspora through the Kashgar Ribat, a guesthouse in Islamabad.[134] Through the latter 'Abd al-Haqq was directed to Miranshah, North Waziristan, where he was taken across the border to the burgeoning Haqqani training complex at Khost, where he discovered his old teacher and numerous other Uighurs training at Haqqani and al-Qa'ida camps. Eventually the TIP established its own training camps in Khost and in other regions of Afghanistan, though it apparently continued to send its members to the camp complex at Zhawara throughout the late 1990s. 'Abd al-Haqq even mentions a TIP member that was killed in the US cruise missile strikes on the Zhawara facilities in response to the American embassy bombings in Africa in 1998.[135]

As with al-Qa'ida, the TIP also sent its trainees to fight on the Taliban front lines in the north of Afghanistan, and again the Haqqani network was the initial conduit for their participation in these battles. 'Abd al-Haqq states that in the summer of 1999 about twenty Uighur fighters went to support the efforts against Ahmad Shah Massoud's forces north of Kabul, in a group led by long-time Haqqani ally Saifurrahman Mansur, son of Jalaluddin's Haqqaniyya colleague Nasrullah Mansur.[136] After 9/11, Saifurrahman "led the embittered resistance of over a thousand fighters, including his own men, those from the Haqqani network, Arabs, Uzbeks, Tajiks and Chechens, against" the US Operation Anaconda.[137] To this list can be added Uighurs, as 'Abd al-Haqq also describes the involvement of the TIP membership in these battles and the eventual retreat of the Uighurs, along with the other regional and global jihadis, to South and North Waziristan. According to the recent testimony of a French jihadi arrested in connection with the Bryant Neal Vinas case and who trained in the tribal areas in 2007 and 2008, the Uighurs were the largest single group of transnational jihadis taking refuge with the Haqqanis in North Waziristan.[138]

The TIP's literature further illustrates the interconnected nature of the training infrastructure around the Zhawara base in the late 1990s, in which local, regional, and global jihadi organizations all shared resources and facilities. The provision and maintenance of the autonomous space for these diverse groups to interact and mutually influence one another is among the Haqqani network's most important contributions to the evolution of jihadism during the 1990s in Khost and more recently in North Waziristan. In a remarkable obituary for Bilal, the first deputy amir of the TIP who was killed at Mazar-i-Sharif in November of 2001, the TIP magazine lists what amounts to a jihadi academic transcript, describing Bilal's course of study at the Khost camps. According to the article Bilal studied politics and Islamic law with Abu Mus'ab al-Suri; creed and jurisprudence with Abu 'Abdallah al-Muhajir; a famous Wahhabi text on *tawhid* (divine unity) with Abu 'Amr 'Abd al-Hakim Hasan (better known as Shaykh 'Isa); the book *Fiqh al-Sunna* with Abu Hamza al-Muhajir, "the war minister in the Islamic State of Iraq"; and *Fath al-Bari* and several hadith texts with Abu'l-Walid al-Ansari.[139] With the exception of Suri, who was independent of al-Qa'ida during this period, all of these trainers are well-known figures in al-Qa'ida's senior leadership.[140]

The Launch of the Global Jihad

Following Bin Laden's forced relocation to Kandahar after his CNN interview, al-Qa'ida increasingly came to rely on the Haqqanis' autonomy from the Taliban in Paktia as a launching pad for its declarations of war on the West, activities that had been expressly forbidden by Mullah Omar.[141] Al-Qa'ida established its operational headquarters at a camp constructed near the Kandahar airport and began to provide training to new recruits at this and other camps in Taliban-controlled Afghanistan, but the Khost camps remained active up until the American response to the 9/11 attacks. According to Nasir al-Bahri, who accompanied him on trips to the southeast, Bin Laden frequently visited these camps after the move to Kandahar and would regularly call on "his friend Jalaluddin Haqqani" in Khost.[142]

In April of 1998, Bin Laden and several leaders from other jihadi organizations operating in Khost convened a press conference at the al-Siddiq camp in the Zhawara Valley to announce the formation of the "World Islamic Front for Jihad against the Jews and Crusaders."[143] This was the most sweeping declaration of global jihad ever issued by al-Qa'ida, and it called on Muslims worldwide to "kill the Americans wherever you find them." Representatives of the international press were invited ahead of time to attend, and were escorted across the border into Khost from North Waziristan by members of Harakat-ul-Ansar, the Kashmir-focused jihadi organization whose training operations were integrated with the al-Qa'ida camps at Zhawara.[144] Additional high-profile interviews were arranged with American, British, Canadian, Pakistani, and Chinese journalists under a similar arrangement at the al-Faruq camp at Zhawara in May.[145]

Carried out in direct contravention of Taliban restrictions, these media events enraged the Taliban leadership and led to severely strained relations between the Taliban and the Arab jihadis residing in Afghanistan.[146] After a 26 May press conference, Mullah Omar angrily phoned Rahimullah Yusufzai, a Pakistani journalist present at that event, to ask how the latter had entered Afghanistan without a Taliban-approved visa. After Yusufzai explained his presence, Mullah Omar shouted "How dare he [Bin Laden] give a press conference without my permission! There will be one ruler in Afghanistan, either I or Osama bin Laden ... I will see to it."[147] According to the journalist Ahmad Zaydan, who was also present during these events, the Arabs in Afghanistan clearly understood that al-Qa'ida was using its alliance with the Haqqanis to get around Taliban attempts to restrict their activities:

I learned later from Afghan Arab sources who were there that Usama had sought to sidestep the Taliban pressure on him by meeting the press in areas far away from the Taliban city of Kandahar, such as Jalalabad, where Hizb-i Islami leader Mawlawi Yunis Khalis enjoyed power and good relations with Usama since the days of the Afghan jihad, or in Paktia, where Shaykh Jalaluddin Haqqani, the Taliban Minister of Borders and Tribes, had strong ties with Bin Ladin as well. Haqqani was considered a king in his region, particularly since he descended from the famous Zadran tribe of Khost, which had struck terror into a succession of Afghan governments. He is also known to have established good relations with Pakistani Islamist groups and the security agencies in Pakistan since the days of Afghan jihad. This might explain why the declaration of the World Islamic Front for Jihad Against the Jews and Crusaders in May of 1998 by Bin Ladin, Zawahiri, and Pakistani figures, was issued in Khost, not Kandahar, or other areas where the Taliban and Mullah Muhammad Omar enjoyed significant influence.[148]

The Taliban, the Foreign Jihadis, and the Haqqanis: Increasing Tensions

On 7 August 1998, al-Qa'ida operatives, some of whom had trained in camps in Khost, carried out near-simultaneous bombings of two American embassies in Tanzania and Kenya. Thirteen days later the United States responded with cruise missile strikes on the jihadi training camps around Zhawara. According to Abu'l-Walid, the embassy bombings and retaliatory American strikes led to an immediate and rapid influx of new Arab volunteers into Afghanistan, which only exacerbated the fractious tendencies of the many Arab jihadi groups that had established bases in the country.[149] Long-running doctrinal disputes took on new urgency as the foreign jihadist groups competed for a share of the freshly mobilized human resources, and new training camps were hastily built in various parts of the country.[150] "A number of the Arab jihadi leaders rose in opposition to Bin Laden at this time," writes Abu'l-Walid, "all of them affirming the primacy of the domestic fronts against the

Arab regimes, convinced that a shift to a 'global confrontation' against the United States was ill conceived."[151] Those opposing Bin Laden and his "global jihad" had patrons within the Taliban movement and sought to sideline al-Qa'ida and undermine Bin Laden's unique status among the Arab jihadis, leading to the emergence of pro- and anti-al-Qa'ida factions within the Taliban leadership.[152]

After the American missile strikes on Zhawara and until the fall of the Taliban regime following 9/11, al-Qa'ida's relations with the Taliban remained tenuous, oscillating between angry fall-outs and calculated rapprochements, and the Haqqanis' relations with the Taliban began to be increasingly marked by open conflict. The pro-al-Qa'ida faction of the Taliban, backed by Pakistani religious authorities whom Bin Laden lobbied for intercession on his behalf, convinced Mullah Omar to reject any consideration of extraditing Bin Laden to the United States.[153] In November of 1998, Bin Laden was persuaded by Abu'l-Walid to give Mullah Omar a pledge of allegiance (*bay'a*) to smooth the tensions, but he agreed to do so only by proxy, which did little to improve the situation.[154] The following month Bin Laden broke the media silence he had maintained since the embassy bombings, giving a series of interviews in a remote, mountainous location on 21 and 22 December in which he reiterated al-Qa'ida's bellicose rhetoric against the United States.[155] According to Bin Laden's bodyguard at the time, these interviews enraged the Taliban leader, who summoned Bin Laden personally in Kandahar and ordered that he, his family, and followers immediately quit the country.[156] Bin Laden reportedly acquiesced but pleaded for time to prepare for the move, in the meantime working to gather more support from Pakistani clerics for his position and persuading Mullah Jalil, the most prominent pro-al-Qa'ida Taliban leader, to buy al-Qa'ida time from Mullah Omar. Ultimately, it was a failed assassination attempt on Mullah Omar in Kandahar in 1999 that served to reduce the tension and win Bin Laden a reprieve from the deportation order. Al-Qa'ida helped the Taliban leadership investigate the bombing of Mullah Omar's compound, rebuilt the latter with improved fortifications, and provided the Taliban leader with a specially trained bodyguard detail, all steps that helped to patch up the rocky relationship between the two groups and allow the 9/11 plot to run its course.[157] The latter, according to a number of insider sources, was kept entirely secret from the Taliban leadership.[158]

The source of tensions, however, was never removed, and in many ways the last three years before the 9/11 attacks marked the lowest point in the relations between the Taliban on the one hand and the foreign jihadis and the Haqqanis on the other. The Haqqani-controlled region, as already noted, had maintained relative autonomy from Taliban law during the mid-1990s and Jalaluddin Haqqani had personally supported local initiatives such as schools for girls that directly contravened Kandahar's policies. According to former Taliban minister Wahid Muzhda, Jalaluddin Haqqani's son Siraj, currently the operational leader of the Haqqani network, "used to complain to me [in the 1990s] about how heavy-handed and dogmatic the Taliban were in their interpretation of Islam."[159] Yet from the end of the 1990s the Taliban appear to have sought to impose greater control on the Haqqanis' traditional areas of influence, with predictable results: the highland tribes in the southeast rebelled.

Numerous indications of this increased conflict between the Haqqanis and the Taliban emerged beginning in January 1999, when Taliban crackdowns on a traditional egg-throwing game in Khost—declared "un-Islamic" by the Taliban—led to an uprising by locals who attacked Taliban officials.[160] The practice of appointing Kandahari officials to Taliban posts in the Haqqanis' areas of control—a practice that had led to mass desertions of Haqqani's men from the northern lines during the mid-1990s—continued to fuel local anti-Taliban sentiments, and in January of 2000 an anti-Taliban uprising broke out in Khost and Paktia.[161] According to Iranian press reports, after seizing the local administration the local rebels demanded that the Taliban either abandon the region or provide official recognition of local autonomy, including the removal of all Kandahar-appointed officials.[162] *Agence France-Presse* reported that locals protested Taliban land appropriation, resource extraction for the benefit of other regions, and forced conscription, all elements of a centralizing government policy that the highland Pashtuns had been violently resisting for generations.[163] Ultimately the Taliban were forced to relent and replaced the unpopular local governor with another official.[164]

As for the Arabs, the Taliban also sought to exert greater control of the foreign jihadi community after the US embassy bombings in Africa, and between 1998 and 1999 most of the jihadi camps in Taliban-controlled Afghanistan were ordered closed.[165] Some of the Arabs in Afghanistan directly rebuked Bin Laden for disobeying Taliban orders and thus causing trouble for the entire foreign fighter community, and fears circulated, both at al-Qa'ida camps and among the other Arab jihadi groups, that the Taliban could order them all out of the country.[166] A number of prominent Afghan mujahidin leaders opposed to the Taliban convened in 1999 in Takhar Province in northern Afghanistan—then under the control of Ahmad Shah Massoud—and issued a fatwa calling for Bin Laden to be executed.[167] When Bin Laden convened a meeting in the summer of 2000 of Arab jihadi leaders from various groups in Afghanistan and issued a further appeal for a united jihadi front against the United States, he was met with sharp refusals. The Libyan contingent angrily demanded a pledge from the al-Qa'ida leadership that it would cease provoking the United States.[168] The Haqqanis were a significant exception to this trend of increasing isolation and opposition to al-Qa'ida during this period. In April of 2001, Jalaluddin Haqqani personally delivered a letter from Osama bin Laden to Mullah Omar, in which the al-Qa'ida leader denounced the restrictions imposed upon him by the Taliban. "It is surprising," Bin Laden wrote, "that the United States is free to do whatever it feels like and I have been placed under restrictions. History will record this fact."[169]

Apart from the Haqqanis, then, the years between 1999 and 2001 saw growing opposition to al-Qa'ida from every side within Afghanistan, and the various non-al-Qa'ida Arab jihadi groups, bearing the brunt of increasing Taliban restrictions, were particularly resentful. They had good reason to be: towards the end of 1999 the Taliban issued a thirteen-point decree that imposed extremely stringent limitations on all foreign jihadis, amounting to a nationwide house arrest of these individuals.[170] Aside from numerous references in the Arab jihadi memoir literature to these restrictions, to my knowledge no primary source reflecting this policy from the Taliban has previously been published. I therefore provide below a complete summary of the "thirteen points."

The decree stipulated that all "foreign guests" were to have their personal information collected by the Taliban administration and would be issued identity papers; any foreign jihadis resident in Kabul or at Taliban military centers were to leave immediately and seek private residence in the provinces and away from provincial centers, "in order to safeguard the Emirate from becoming a target of foreign states' accusations and to prevent disturbances to the Afghan people." The foreigners' housing and food were to be provided by the organizations that they were associated with, the latter to maintain liaison relations with the Taliban government. No foreign jihadi was to be allowed access to fax, phone, "or any similar means of communication," it being "necessary to break off all foreigners' relations with other states." None were to speak to foreign journalists or hold press conferences, and they are specifically forbidden to release any statement to the Pakistani press. Any foreigner wanted for murder in another country—as we have seen, already an issue for the Taliban vis-à-vis the Haqqanis' camps for Pakistani jihadis—"shall not be allowed in the Islamic Emirate," and "people who shelter such criminals shall be expelled and punished." "Foreign guests" may only participate in jihad "after we have found a suitable arena," and such "guests" are admonished not to "act in a selfishly nationalistic manner or manipulate jihad according to their own views and desires." Jihad, point ten of the statement continues, "has to be conducted only to advance the word of God, to help victimized Muslims, and to defend ourselves." All decrees issued by the Taliban leadership are declared binding on the foreign jihadi community, and the latter are banned from establishing offices or representatives outside of the areas allotted to them for the purpose of residence. Finally, all issues between the Taliban and the foreign jihadis are to be addressed to Mullah 'Abd al-Razzaq, the Taliban interior minister, appointed in the decree as a "special liaison for foreign guests."[171]

Al-Qa'ida's anti-American jihad, launched from Haqqani headquarters, had thus made operating outside of Haqqani-controlled territory in Afghanistan an increasingly prohibitive exercise for the foreign jihadis prior to 9/11. This, along with the deep history between the Haqqani network and the other regional and international militant groups operating in Afghanistan, helps to explain why it was to the Haqqanis' refuge in Waziristan, and not the Taliban's in Baluchistan, that these groups turned for safe haven after the American invasion of Afghanistan following the 9/11 attacks in 2001. The nexus of local, regional, and global jihadism that the Haqqanis had fostered into being over the previous two decades may have been forced to flee its Haqqani-controlled sanctuary of southeastern Afghanistan, but it did not have far to go to reestablish itself. In fact, the American-led invasion of Afghanistan that had succeeded in toppling the Taliban so quickly only managed to force this nexus a few dozen kilometers east, into North Waziristan, where it has remained ever since, serving as a nerve center of international jihadism without parallel in any other part of the world.

PART II

CONTINUITY, VALUE, CHANGE, AND THE HAQQANI NEXUS POST-2001

Introduction

During the decade following the 9/11 attacks, the Haqqani network would further consolidate its nexus position and act in a manner similar to prior decades, proving central to the Taliban, Afghanistan's internal conflicts, and Pakistan's efforts to hedge its position and cultivate influence on both sides of the Durand Line. Assisted by the ISI, and leveraging its key characteristics and nexus position, the Haqqani network quickly emerged as a primary and lethal driver of anti-Coalition activity inside Afghanistan. The 9/11 attacks and the US response did not cause the Haqqani network to disassociate itself from al-Qa'ida and its global jihad, but rather have arguably brought the Haqqanis and al-Qa'ida members even closer together. The Haqqani network has fostered this closeness by maintaining its open fronts and by providing protection and a base from which al-Qa'ida and others could conduct attacks inside Afghanistan and plan acts of international terrorism. Today, as Part II illustrates, the activities of the two groups remain deeply integrated across operational and functional lines in Loya Paktia and North Waziristan. The close bonds between al-Qa'ida and the Haqqani fighters during the post-2001 period indicate that the ties between the two groups are not just historic, but are also now multigenerational, a fact that is likely to contribute to al-Qa'ida's longevity and future development in the region. It is because of these dynamics that the Haqqani network has emerged as a key pivot issue between Pakistan and the United States. The irony here is that the group simultaneously functions as both a strategic asset—through which Pakistan can shape and secure its interests along the Durand Line—and a central obstacle—hindering the US ability to achieve its core objectives in Afghanistan.

Early attempts were made by the United States, the Afghan government, and members of the Haqqani network to reach a political settlement immediately after 9/11 and in the subsequent years to follow, but for reasons that remain poorly understood all of these efforts failed.[1] One of the first attempts took place in mid-October 2001, when Jalaluddin Haqqani was brought to Islamabad for a series of meetings with Pakistani and US officials.[2] The one insider account available about this episode paints a bleak picture that helps to situate potential missed opportunities and the actions of the United States and the Haqqani network in the challenging decade that followed. It also suggests that Jalaluddin Haqqani's partnership with al-Qa'ida was not without its limits. As recounted by Joby Warrick in October 2001:

> Jalaluddin Haqqani had been sanguine about the Taliban's defeat and was prepared to switch loyalties, as he had done so often in the past. Pakistani officials who had dealt with him for decades strongly urged the Americans to accommodate him and perhaps even give him a token role in the new Afghan government. But in Washington, Bush officials in the Defense Department were not in a mood to bargain. Haqqani had abetted the escape of Usama bin Laden and might still know his whereabouts. Two rounds of secret talks were held with Haqqani's emissaries, in Islamabad and then in the United Arab Emirates, according to a senior US official intimately familiar with the events. But at both meetings, the official said, the US side offered the same terms: unconditional surrender, including Haqqani's personal acquiescence to donning an orange jumpsuit and joining the other detainees at the newly opened US prison camps at Guantanamo Bay. After a reasonable interval—presumably after Haqqani told military interrogators everything he knew about Bin Laden—he would be allowed to return home. Haqqani's refusal to accept such an offer was a given, the former intelligence official

said. "I personally believe that Haqqani was someone we could have worked with," the official said. "But at the time, no one was looking over the horizon, to where we might be in five years. For the policy folks, it was just 'screw those little brown people.'"[3]

Whether Jalaluddin would have been willing to reconcile if the appropriate offer had been made, or if his disengagement from al-Qa'ida and the Taliban would have lasted (or been meaningful), all remain open, and at this point unanswerable, questions. The role played by the director general of Pakistan's ISI during this period, Mahmud Ahmed, also remains somewhat ambiguous. According to Kathy Gannon, before Jalaluddin met with US officials Ahmed urged him to hold firm and not to give up the al-Qa'ida network.[4] He also reportedly promised Haqqani ISI aid from the Pakistan side of the border.[5] US airstrikes in Afghanistan soon followed, and on 8 October Ahmed was sacked by Pakistani President Pervez Musharraf and replaced by Ehsan ul Haq. Any hopes that Pakistani mediation would bring Jalaluddin to a political settlement evaporated at the end of his meeting with US representatives when he gave an interview with a Pakistani journalist and vowed to fight on; "We will retreat to the mountains and begin a long guerrilla war to reclaim our pure land from infidels and free our country like we did against the Soviets."[6] It is similarly not known whether Jalaluddin would have supported an Afghan effort, led around the same time by his former Hizb-e-Islami (Khalis) colleague Abdul Haq, which aimed to replace the Taliban, or co-opt some of its members, in support of a new government.[7]

Other early outreach efforts involving Jalaluddin's brother, Ibrahim, between 2001 and 2003 appear to have only deepened the mistrust between all parties, as Ibrahim was "held" for a certain period by Afghan authorities and later the US military after he reportedly "surrendered to the Kabul government."[8] According to some sources, Ibrahim had been sent to explore reconciliation opportunities with US and Afghan officials, but was detained based on the urging of Badshah Khan Zadran, a local Haqqani family rival.[9] The animosity deepened after several members of Jalaluddin's family were killed in airstrikes and Hamid Karzai (with US support) attempted to sideline the Haqqanis by elevating Badshah

Khan Zadran to the governship in Paktia—an attempt which disastrously failed.[10]

Initiatives involving Sirajuddin Haqqani and Karzai administration officials in 2007 and 2010 and a meeting between US officials and Ibrahim Haqqani in 2011 (brokered by Pakistan) in Qatar also fell flat, leaving little hope that a political solution involving the Haqqanis is currently attainable.[11] Unless, that is, one of the major parties to the negotiations—the Haqqani network, the United States, Pakistan, or the Afghan government—is willing to recalibrate its red lines. Given what is at stake for all parties, this seems unlikely, especially since the US government formally designated the group as a Foreign Terrorist Organization in early September 2012.[12]

The decade following the US invasion of Afghanistan was also characterized by change and other challenges, especially in the kinetic dimensions of the war. The US efforts to consolidate its initial gains against the Taliban and al-Qa'ida were hampered by its military intervention in Iraq—with Afghanistan being seen as less of a priority for several critical years. By the time the United States had turned its attention and resources back to Afghanistan the conflict in the country had evolved into a full-blown insurgency. Similar to the past, during the post-2001 period the Haqqani network has proven central to the development of the Taliban's campaign of violence and the extension of the latter's writ across Loya Paktia and regions further afield. Even more challenging (and perhaps more critical to the Taliban's long-term strategy) has been a relatively new development: the Haqqani network's role as spoiler, a position the group has been able to occupy given its early embrace of suicide attacks and its deadly and consistent use of the tactic to conduct attacks in Kabul, which usually generate international news headlines.

Despite significant setbacks and multiyear operational efforts to degrade the Haqqani network's capabilities, the group has proven itself to be resilient. "Haqqani is the most resilient enemy network out there," noted the commander of the US military brigade in Khost in May 2011.[13] Every spring, at the beginning of each fighting season, the group arrives back in force—having replenished its ranks during the winter lull. It would be a mistake to view the Haqqani network as anything but capable and determined, but the group's regenerative capacity cannot be separated from the value provided by Pakistan's nearby border, a central asset which the group has leveraged for decades to limit its own rate of attrition and protect its strategic infrastructure, including its leaders.

Another central change has been the transition of the Haqqani network leadership from father Jalaluddin to son Sirajuddin. While this transition represents a change in personalities, surprisingly little has changed in terms of the Haqqani network's relations, strategy, and outlook during the post-2001 period. As in the past, the core goal of the group today remains local control and autonomy in the Loya Paktia/Waziristan corridor. The group also still wants to see an "Islamic" government in power in Kabul that is guided by sharia. Extremely little is known about what the group wants beyond that. Up to this point Sirajuddin has proven himself to be quite restrained, preferring—like his father—not to seek public office and to defer to the Taliban rather than challenge the group and its authority, at least publicly. Whether the young leader is more ambitious or will remain as deferential to the Taliban in the future, especially in a post-Mullah Omar world, still remains an open question, however.

The post-2001 period has also seen a considerable amount of change in terms of Pakistan's militant landscape, a dynamic which has also affected the Haqqani network. These changes have primarily been driven by complications associated with Pakistan's alliance with the United States, Islamabad's policy of selectively differentiating between "good" and "bad" jihadis, the blowback from its military operations in the FATA and Khyber Pakhtunkhwa Province (KPP, formerly called the Northwest Frontier Province), and the escalation of the US drone campaign. When viewed in aggregate, these changes in Pakistan's militant landscape are characterized by two main trends. The first is ideological hybridization, whereby an increased number of locally oriented, Pakistan-based militant groups have either been inspired by or now describe their fight in terms ideologically similar to those defined by al-Qa'ida.[14] This change is best typified by the post-2001 operational activity of

Jaish-e-Mohammad, the emergence of the Tehrik-e-Taliban (TTP) in 2007 and the development of the jihad against Islamabad. Numerous sources, as the following chapters reveal, suggest that some Haqqani network leaders and lower-level fighters have been considerably influenced by al-Qa'ida's rhetoric as well.

The second major observable trend is the further blurring of organizational boundaries between Pakistan-based militant groups, a change which has in part been facilitated by the co-location of militant groups in the FATA and the pressure Pakistan has placed on some groups, but not others. This dynamic has enhanced the Haqqani network's importance and value to the Pakistani state since Islamabad increasingly has fewer militant actors it can rely on and trust. Yet these conditions have also created new challenges for the Haqqani network. For example, due to its close ties with Pakistan's ISI and the primary actors—al-Qa'ida and the TTP—who are waging war on Islamabad, the group must now more carefully balance the tensions inherent in its nexus position. The Haqqani network has proven itself adept at hedging its position and managing conflicting ties in the past, but the atmosphere in the FATA now appears to be more ideologically fractured, making one wonder whether the group is tired of sitting in the middle and could be pushed to choose sides and take a more hard and open ideological stance.

The endurance of the Haqqani network as a nexus actor has always been intimately tied to its trustworthiness and ability to remain relevant to a diverse mix of actors over time.[15] Indeed, when the Haqqani network is no longer seen as reliable and/or relevant to the ISI and its interests Pakistan may have less of an incentive to continue its relationship with the group. The Haqqani network's relations with al-Qa'ida and the TTP are guided by similar principles. Other factors, such as pragmatic considerations (e.g., the local alliances that are needed to ensure the movement of fighters from North Waziristan to Khost), deep personal ties, and the limited partnering options that some of these actors have, also play important roles in this calculus. Therefore, to ensure its continued relevance and maintain its nexus position, the Haqqani network must provide services or other items of value that suit the interests and needs of its local, regional, and global partners. To that end, Part II provides an assessment of the Haqqani network's value proposition to these three—local, regional, and global—group actor categories during the post-2001 period.[16] The breakout of the section's four chapters reflects these distinctions (the last chapter explores management challenges and the tension inherent to the Haqqani network's nexus position). Attention is specifically given to identifying what the Haqqani network provides to and receives from each group category, and how these various parties benefit. By using this analytical framework we are able to shed light on the nature and depth of Haqqani network relations and the incentives driving the Haqqani network and its partners. Such an exploration also reveals insights into the identity of the Haqqani network and how it has been able to enhance its local effectiveness as well as serving as a fountainhead for jihad elsewhere simultaneously.

It is the local dimension which we evaluate first.

4

LOCAL

PAKISTANI TALIBAN FACTIONS AND OTHER LOCAL INSURGENT UNITS

The Haqqani network is best understood as being both an Afghan and Pakistani organization as its history is intimately and equally tied to both countries. Jalaluddin Haqqani himself best puts the cross-border nature of his organization into context: "I am also the [Taliban] minister for border regions. Our tribes are settled on both sides of the Durand line since ages. Our houses are divided on both sides of the border. Both sides are my home. Pakistan is my home. And besides, my migration hasn't ended."[1] Afghanistan remains central to the identity of the Haqqani network, its trajectory as a battle-tested militant entity and jihadist facilitator, and rise as the strongest militant entity in Loya Paktia.[2] Yet, at the same time, over the past thirty years Pakistan's North Waziristan has been as important as Loya Paktia to the development and evolution of the Haqqani network as an insurgent fighting force and local institution of power. As established in Part I, Jalaluddin settled in North Waziristan before initiating jihad against the Daoud regime in 1973 and he and his compatriots later retreated there after this jihad had officially commenced.[3] From that point until today, North Waziristan has functioned as the Haqqanis' sanctuary and rear resource mobilization base.[4] The mountainous geography of the local terrain and the shelter provided by the international border has proved invaluable, allowing the Haqqani network to limit its own rate of attrition when under attack. It is the combination of these factors—the Afghan and Pakistani components of the organization—that have led to the Haqqani network's resilience and enduring success over time. Understanding how the two faces of the organization intersect, and how the Haqqani network's operations are integrated with and provide value to other local actors on both sides of the Durand Line is the focus of this chapter, as it is essential to understanding some of the local dynamics upon which the Haqqanis' enterprise rests.

At the local level, the Haqqani network functions as a power broker and the primary facilitator of a regional, cross-border system of violence that is based in the Waziristan region and deployed across the border inside Afghanistan.[5] The Haqqani network's value to local militant actors on both sides of the border occurs across various levels, and it is firmly rooted in the centers for religious and military instruction in Loya Paktia and North Waziristan that the Haqqani family have historically operated there. These centers of learning, all of which are now believed to be based in the FATA, are useful to entities like the Afghan and Pakistani Talibans because they help to inculcate an ideological worldview that embraces violent jihad. This, in turn, makes them ideal places for local militant factions to recruit new members and to replenish their ranks. Of equal importance and local value is the Haqqanis' broad control of a platform—a network—through which these students and other recruits can operationalize and apply their knowledge on the battlefields of Loya Paktia and Afghanistan more broadly. The Haqqani network similarly functions as a primary partner for TTP elements from South and North Waziristan to gain entry to the Afghan jihad and to develop the operational capabilities of their fighters. The Haqqani network provides additional value to the TTP by acting as a trusted "office" to mediate disputes and manage violence between local tribal entities and militant factions, and for entities like the Mehsud faction of the TTP to negotiate with state representatives in Islamabad and Rawalpindi.

Across the border in Afghanistan, the Haqqani network provides value to the Quetta Shura Taliban in two main areas. First, both before and after 9/11 the Haqqani network has acted as an important regional platform that the Taliban can leverage to project power and influence in southeastern Afghanistan. In doing so, the Haqqani network helps the Taliban to extend its brand and project itself as a cohesive, national (i.e., more than a Kandahari) movement. Second, given its record for operational effectiveness the Haqqani network functions as a force multiplier for the Taliban, strengthening the latter's campaigns in Loya Paktia and elsewhere.[6]

Centers for Religious Instruction and Military Training in Loya Paktia and NWA

Since the mid-1970s the Haqqani network has worked to develop religious and military infrastructure on both sides of the Durand Line in the Loya Paktia/Waziristan corridor. According to one estimate provided by Shuhrat Nangyal—the former editor of the Pashto-language version of *Manba' al-Jihad*—the Haqqani network is affiliated with over eighty madrassas in the tribal areas of Afghanistan and Pakistan.[7] This infrastructure has historically functioned as a mechanism for the Haqqanis to cultivate influence and provide services and religious instruction to local communities in the tribal areas who derive value from these offerings.[8] The Haqqanis' network of madrassas has also been a tool through which the organization can propagate its worldview and prepare young, ideologically motivated recruits to wage jihad in Afghanistan and other theaters. In that sense the Haqqani network's religious and military infrastructure serves as a synergistic source of social and military power that supplies recruits, and helps to sustain the Afghan Taliban's operational prowess over time.

The Haqqani network's credentials and deep ties to the Dar al-'Ulum Haqqaniyya madrassa in Akora Khattak lend credibility, and arguably even prestige, to the religious training that the Haqqani family provides.[9] In addition to filling educational voids left by the Pakistani government, local community members also likely find value in Haqqani religious instruction in that, similar to most madrassas in Pakistan, students at Manba' 'Ulum do not have to pay for tuition, accommodation, food, or access to basic medical care.[10] Haqqani-sponsored religious and educational opportunities also provide a number of other important benefits, such as teachers and trained imams, for local communities. For some, studying at Manba' 'Ulum is also an entry-point to study at a larger and more prestigious madrassa, such as Dar al-'Ulum Haqqaniyya or Jamia Farooqia, located outside of Pakistan's tribal areas.[11] The depth and continued importance of Haqqani network/Dar al-'Ulum Haqqaniyya ties is reflected by Nasiruddin and Khalil Haqqani's presence at a recent Haqqania graduation ceremony in Akora Khattak in 2010.[12] It is believed that another, younger member of the Haqqani family was one of the graduates.[13]

The two central pillars of the Haqqani network's curriculum, as the organization itself defines it, are ideological preparation for jihad and military instruction, subjects that are viewed as being mutually reinforcing.[14] An article about the establishment of Manba' 'Ulum puts the practical and synergistic nature of these two subjects into context:

> it was not enough for our scholars and students who study in this institute [Manba' 'Ulum] to only hear the sounds of explosions in the battles that are fought in the nearby region, and it was not enough for them as well to only see the vehicles transferring the dead and the injured who have fallen on the borders by the bullets of the communists, but many of the students did participate in those battles. In tough times, all the students who are capable of bearing arms will be called upon to take part and no one would be left but the minors, and the institute will be almost completely empty, so what an institute of Sharia sciences is it?![15]

The combination of ideological and military training is valuable to the Haqqani network and the Taliban on two levels. First, it provides students with an opportunity to prepare themselves religiously for jihad and their participation in, and potential death from, violent military conflict. Second, it provides local militant organizations with a supply of committed fighters familiar with basic military equipment and tactics. For, according to Aziz Khan—the first administrator of Manba' 'Ulum—"by the time they graduate, every *talib* [student] will be armed with a good base of Islamic knowledge, as well as excellent training in military tactics."[16] It would be problematic to assume that all graduates from Manba' 'Ulum engaged in violent jihad in Afghanistan and/or Pakistan, but the number of students studying at Manba' 'Ulum in 1989 (830) illustrates the utility and surge capacity these students can provide.[17] During the 1990s Dar al-'Ulum Haqqaniyya engaged in a similar practice, with Sami ul Haq at times closing the madrassa's doors and sending its students to fight with the Taliban against the Northern Alliance in Afghanistan.[18]

Cohesiveness of the Afghan Taliban and Extension of its Brand

The Haqqani network has a rich history with the Afghan Taliban and its precursor organizations, but as Thomas Ruttig points out, "Loya Paktia was never a stronghold of the Taliban movement, neither during their Islamic Emirate (1996–2001) nor in the phase of its new incarnation, the post 2001 neo-Taliban insurgency."[19] Upon entering the territory the Taliban struggled "to impose their orders on the Tribes of Loya Paktia as they did in the rest of the country."[20] Therefore, ever since Jalaluddin Haqqani first partnered with the Taliban in 1996 the Haqqani network has functioned as an important regional platform for the Taliban to project power and influence in southeastern Afghanistan. The Taliban affords the Haqqani network significant organizational autonomy in this area due to the Haqqani family's prestige, their control over important logistics routes, and its proven ability to act as a trusted and capable partner. The relationship between the two parties is also structured in this way out of necessity as there are important differences between the lowland tribes of Loya Kandahar, where the majority of the Taliban's leadership is from, and the mountain tribes of Loya Paktia. As some scholars have noted, the Kandahari/Paktiawal split represents one of the major fault lines of the Afghan insurgency.[21] These differences came to the fore on numerous occasions during Taliban rule when the "Loya Paktia tribes openly resisted what was perceived of Kandahari dominance."[22] Both the Taliban and Haqqani network are cognizant of these differences, and the need to manage them. As Thomas Ruttig notes, the Haqqanis':

symbiotic relationship with the "Kandahari" Taleban holds because it is mutually beneficial. It gives ... [the Haqqani network] access to the label of the Taleban, as the most popular insurgent organization, while the Taleban are enabled to project presence in regions that have never been their strongholds and to present themselves as more than a purely Kandahri movement.[23]

The Haqqani network therefore essentially acts as a regional bridge through which the Taliban can localize its representation and adapt its strategy to the political, social, and tribal landscapes of Loya Paktia. Due to its local tribal connections and its history in the region, the Haqqani network is more credible than the Taliban in these areas and is thus more capable of navigating local issues successfully. This leaves the Taliban reliant upon the Haqqani network to function as its local representative.

In return, the Haqqani network is given more freedom to operate autonomously in its control zones. Again, as Thomas Ruttig notes:

The Haqqani and Mansur networks, the Tora Bora front practically operate under their own command and strategy. They are also not subjected to the Taleban practice of rotating "provincial governors" and commanders. Internally, this makes them much more static than the mainstream "Kandahari" Taleban. At the same time, their pre-Taleban background gives them organisational autonomy, making them "Taleban-associated networks" and their leaders a sort of semi-independent warlords.[24]

The relationship between the Haqqani network and the Taliban works because it is pragmatic and is guided by a common set of goals (i.e., to expel foreign invaders, capture Kabul, and install sharia). It also works because the Haqqani network publicly defers to the Taliban. Time and again, the Haqqani network has identified Mullah Omar as its leader and has deferred—at least in public—to his guidance. The Haqqani network has even gone so far as to publicly reject the "Haqqani network" label, preferring instead the title "Taliban."[25] On a practical level, the Haqqani network is also willing to allow the Taliban to take credit for its operations—or at least those operations where Haqqani network commanders approved the operation, logistically supported it, and served as the main command and control element. For example, several hours after the January 2008 attack against the Serena hotel in Kabul it was not the

Haqqani network but the Taliban's main spokesperson Zabihullah Mujahid who claimed responsibility for the incident.[26] Yet, in an interview six months later, Sirajuddin said that he organized this attack and the assassination attempt on Afghan President Hamid Karzai, which was also initially claimed by the Taliban.[27]

The Haqqani network's public deferment to the Taliban can also be seen in digital videos produced by Manba' al-Jihad, a Haqqani media production company that operates as a regional component of the Taliban's media syndicate. During their introduction Manba' al-Jihad videos are branded as products of the "Islamic Emirate of Afghanistan," but for their duration these videos carry the Manba' al-Jihad logo and are focused on highlighting attacks in Loya Paktia and local fighters from Haqqani control zones.[28] By branding its videos in this way and not directly referencing the Haqqani organization, the Haqqani network reinforces the perception that the Afghan Taliban is pervasive and strong, and that they are a loyal partner. Yet the Haqqani network's decision to brand these videos as "Manba' al-Jihad," which is a historic media brand associated with the pre-Taliban Haqqani network, indicates that the group seeks to maintain an organizational identity that is both identifiable and at least partially distinct from the Quetta Shura Taliban. Haqqani deference to the Taliban is beneficial because it diminishes the likelihood of intragroup competition, which has historically plagued the Afghan mujahidin. That this issue is a concern to the Quetta Shura Taliban is arguably reflected in an interview Sirajuddin conducted with *Reuters* after the attack against the US embassy and ISAF headquarters in September 2011. After being asked whether his fighters were behind the attack, Sirajuddin responded: "For some reasons, I would not like to claim that fighters of our group had carried out the recent attack on U.S. embassy and NATO headquarters. Our central [Taliban] leadership, particularly senior members of the shura, suggested I should keep quiet in future if the US and its allies suffer in future."[29]

Portraying the Haqqani–Quetta Shura Taliban relationship along such simple lines is useful from a strategic communications and branding perspective, especially since it obscures areas of tension between the groups, but it does little to elucidate the complex nature of the Haqqani–Taliban relationship. For example, it does not adequately account for the Haqqani network's level of operational autonomy and areas where the group exhibits distinct organizational characteristics (i.e., through media, maintaining its own logistics/supply lines, independent and transnational funding streams, etc.). This is not to suggest that the Haqqani network is an entirely separate entity—it isn't. But conflating the two groups as Taliban, while useful in some regards, glosses over differences between the two regional factions and significant areas where the Haqqani network and the Taliban have historically not seen eye-to-eye. Three issues that are worth noting include the Haqqani network's relationships with actors like al-Qa'ida, discussed in Part I, the Haqqanis more recent use of violent tactics, and the ties each group has historically had with the ISI. The actual relationship between the two groups is nuanced and is guided more by Haqqani respect or trust and public deference to (the younger) Mullah Omar, but not outright obedience or subordination.[30] In that sense, the relationship functions as a political alliance built upon similar histories, ideological connections, and a common vision of the future that accommodates each group's regional preferences.

Military Effectiveness and a Trusted Partner to Enhance the Taliban's Operational Impact and Reach

Another way in which the Haqqani network provides value to the Afghan Taliban is through its military effectiveness and ability to strengthen the Taliban's campaigns in regions outside Loya Paktia, especially in Kabul.[31] Such value is not new as since at least 1996 the Taliban has drawn from the assistance of Jalaluddin Haqqani and other members of the Haqqani network to deepen its ranks and enhance its fighting capabilities. It is also telling that it was Jalaluddin Haqqani who the Taliban appointed as its military commander during the US invasion of Afghanistan in October 2001.[32] Since that time the Haqqani network has been essential to the rise—and geographic spread—of the neo-Taliban insurgency inside Afghanistan. The value of the Haqqani network's contributions to the Taliban has been acknowledged by senior Taliban leaders, such as Mullah Dadullah, who—before being killed in 2007—confirmed Jalaluddin's important role: "There is no doubt that Shaykh Haqqani and his son lead the battles and draw up military plans."[33] The Haqqani network's leadership of the Miranshah Shura, and its representation on the Rahbari Shura (the Taliban's central coordinating body), similarly highlights the organization's strategic value to the Taliban as a trusted military partner.

Over the last several years many analysts have noted an expansion of the Haqqani network beyond its traditional area of influence in Loya Paktia into Kabul and Wardak and Logar provinces. Although it is challenging to separate the two actors in Afghanistan's north, in 2009 Haqqani network operatives provided some support to help the Taliban deepen its insurgency in the region, which some interpreted as an attempt by Mullah Omar's group to strategically "encircle" Kabul and fracture the NATO Coalition.[34] While the geographic expansion of the Haqqani network is extremely useful to the Taliban, the presence of Haqqani commanders in these areas is not entirely a new development.[35] Indeed, "Six days after the Saur Coup [in 1978], ... [Jalaluddin] Haqqani sent in secret orders that armed operations must commence in the Shamal, Logar, and Kabul vicinities."[36] Jalaluddin Haqqani's support for attacks in Kabul in 1980 has also been documented.[37] Moreover, during the anti-Soviet jihad one of Jalaluddin's most important commanders—Fathullah Haqqani—led fighting units in Logar, Ghazni, Paktia, and Nangarhar.[38] The Haqqani network's early and broad geographic reach was matched by the group's inclusion of Afghan fighters from regions as far as Herat and Kabul, and from minority ethnic groups such as the Hazaras.[39]

What appears to have recently changed is the strength of the Haqqani network in these areas and the frequency of the group's attacks outside Loya Paktia, especially in Kabul, since the rise of the neo-Taliban insurgency. The intensification of Haqqani network activity beyond Loya Paktia illustrates the group's ability to enhance its operational presence in regions further afield, and to do so in a way that is acceptable to other local fighting elements.[40] This feat was likely achieved by leveraging old Hizb-e-Islami (Khalis), Taliban, and other networks and forging a series of tactical alliances with local commanders active in Logar, Wardak, Kabul, and northern Afghanistan.[41] To avoid competition and conflict in Logar Province, for example, the Taliban and Haqqani network established a commission to select a governor that was acceptable to both parties.[42] The kidnapping case of *New York Times* journalist David Rohde illustrates Haqqani and Taliban integration in Logar Province as Rohde and his two Afghan colleagues were driving through the province to interview Taliban commander Abu Tayeb (aka Najibullah Naeem) when they were kidnapped, transported to North Waziristan, and handed over to Badruddin Haqqani (killed in August 2012) by Tayeb himself.[43] In 2008, Sirajuddin Haqqani is believed to have played a role in mediating conflict between two rival Taliban commanders in Logar—Mir Ahmad Gul and Mullah Abdullah (also known as Mullah Toor)—both of whom were later dismissed by the Taliban.[44] These arrangements, as well as the Haqqani network's pragmatism and willingness to subordinate itself to the Taliban politically, reduce potential friction between the two parties and help to ensure that these tactical alliances hold.

Local Partnering and Operational Development of Local Pakistani Taliban Elements

On the other side of the border, the Haqqani network functions as one of the most important partners in facilitating the operational integration of Pakistani Taliban fighters from North and South Waziristan into fighting units in Afghanistan.[45] As established in Part I, during times of crisis and foreign invasion fighters from different tribal confederacies in Loya Paktia and North Waziristan have historically cooperated with one another to combat a common enemy and achieve common aims.[46] For example, Zadran and other tribal groups from Loya Paktia helped Pashtuns living east of the Durand Line in 1915 and later, in the 1930s and 1940s, the Faqir of Ipi (Mirza Ali Khan) to fight against the Indian Army (and by extension British colonialists) in North Waziristan.[47] The Faqir of Ipi's journey to Khost in 1933 as a part of a lashkar "to join a revolt against the Afghan King ..." illustrates that the movement of Afghan and Pakistani tribal fighters in this region has historically been multidirectional.[48] The Haqqani network's ability to draw upon these other tribal networks is born out of this history and sense of intertribal solidarity. Over a thirty-year period this "combination of tribal and ideological loyalties" has, at least in part, contributed to the Haqqani network's coherence, effectiveness, and endurance.[49] It is not hard to find examples of the Haqqanis integrating Pakistani tribal fighters to augment their ranks. Prior to the Soviet invasion of Afghanistan in 1979, the Haqqani and Mansur networks had "extensive links" with Pakistan's tribal communities in North and South Waziristan and they were thus well prepared to tap into and make use of fighters from these areas.[50] This dynamic is best documented by the Urdu-language version of the Haqqani network's magazine—*Nusrat ul-Jihad*—sections of which catalogue and pay tribute to fighters from Waziristan who died fighting under Jalaluddin and his lieutenants during and after the anti-Soviet jihad.[51]

This trend continued during the Taliban period, and since the US invasion of Afghanistan in October 2001 the Haqqani and Mansur networks have served as the primary partners for Pakistani Taliban factions from North and South Waziristan to conduct operations in Loya Paktia.[52] The list of Pakistani fighters who were first exposed to battle under Haqqani commanders and have gone on to form and assume leadership positions in the TTP is noteworthy.[53] Baitullah Mehsud was a close ally of key Haqqani commanders and fought with the Taliban (likely under Jalaluddin in the Shomali Plains north of Kabul), and both Baitullah and his successor Hakimullah Mehsud helped the Afghan Taliban to regroup after the US invasion.[54] Until his death in January 2008 Haqqani commander Darim Sedgai reportedly served as a liaison between the two groups.[55] Jalaluddin Haqqani's brother-in-law, Haji Mali Khan, a senior commander who was detained by Coalition forces in Paktia province in October 2011, is believed to have played a similar role.[56] In short biographical notes allegedly written by Hakimullah Mehsud, the TTP commander emphasized that he, Baitullah Mehsud, and Abdullah Mehsud (killed in 2007) fought together with Mullah Sangeen, a key Haqqani network commander, in Khost province.[57] The more recent TTP-sponsored suicide attack by Jordanian operative Abu Dujanah al-Khorasani, which killed seven CIA operatives at a strategic outpost in Khost, was likely conducted with some form of Haqqani assistance and/or approval.[58]

This attack, and other supporting evidence, only reinforces the close personal and operational ties between the Haqqani network and those who created and continue to develop the TTP. To facilitate the integration of fighters from Waziristan, senior Haqqani leaders are known to vouch for TTP members who want to gain access to the fight.[59] According to Pir Zubayr Shah, "when fighters under [Mullah] Nazir or [Hafiz] Gul Bahadur [the TTP commander in North Waziristan] go in [to Afghanistan], they operate under the Haqqani network and need them to allow access."[60] The Haqqani network is able to play such a role because their geographic centrality and reputation for military effectiveness "gives them influence over North Waziristan militants who lack their own networks across the border" in Afghanistan.[61] Other sources confirm that Mullah Nazir is close to Sirajuddin and that Gul Bahadur "coordinates closely with the Haqqani network on both strategy and operations in Afghanistan."[62] The death of Nazir's deputy, Maulana Iqbal, and a mix of other Pakistani fighters in Paktika by Coalition forces on 11 May 2008 lends additional credence to these claims.[63]

This is not to suggest that the Haqqani network's relations with the various components of the TTP are always smooth. The reality is undoubtedly more complicated, as divisions are known to exist within and external to the TTP over a number of issues including the group's violent tactics, killing of Muslim civilians, and its reliance on kidnapping to secure funds.[64]

That being said, the operational ties between the Haqqanis and TTP are likely driven just as much by their historical relationship as out of pragmatic necessity given the local geopolitical landscape, specifically Gul Bahadur's control of territory in North Waziristan that abuts the Afghan border in Khost. Ground-level coordination is facilitated by specific individuals, as it was in the past by the now deceased Haqqani commander Qari Amil who was charged with integrating Pakistani fighters into Haqqani operations in Loya Paktia.[65] The upward integration of Pakistani Taliban fighters into the leadership of the Haqqani network, or the Taliban's regional coordinating bodies, is less clear, however. Some scholars have suggested that TTP personnel are members of the Miranshah Shura, although evidence for this remains slim.[66] Perhaps more likely is an informal or parallel structure, where key Afghan and Pakistani commanders meet to coordinate their activity along the lines of the meeting that is believed to have been held in Khost between Sirajuddin, Hakimullah, Bahadur, and Nazir in September 2009.[67]

By serving as a platform for operational development and force projection, the Haqqani network functions as a military incubator for lethal segments of TTP. This is yet another example of how the Haqqani network functions—at least indirectly—as a fountainhead (*Manba'*) of jihad. In fact, one can argue that the TTP and its jihad against the Pakistani state are an outgrowth, or at least a partial result, of the operational intermingling between local and global actors in Loya Paktia.[68] Even though the Haqqani network does not actively, or publicly, support attacks against the Pakistani state, they have helped to create and sustain the conditions and relationships that facilitate and drive the jihad against Islamabad. It is true that the Quetta Shura Taliban and the Haqqani network have tried, on numerous occasions, to reorient the TTP's jihad away from Islamabad towards Afghanistan. The Haqqani network has also put systems in place to minimize its public association with and participation in the Pakistan jihad (explored in more detail in the "Management" chapter). But just as the Afghanistan and Pakistan jihads are distinct and have separate command chains, the infrastructure and economy of violence that they create are integrated and mutually reinforcing, ultimately enhancing the resiliency and longevity of each jihad. For example, the deployment of Pakistani Taliban manpower (i.e., suicide bombers and actual fighters) to Loya Paktia operationally benefits the Haqqani network, and thus also the Quetta Shura. Yet the benefits of this integration are not unidirectional and limited to the jihad in Afghanistan alone. They are bidirectional and the TTP can also leverage Haqqani network expertise and resources—either through training or personal contacts—and incorporate the knowledge and combat experience gained in Afghanistan to strengthen its campaign against Pakistan.

Trusted "Office" to Mediate Local Disputes and Negotiate Issues with the State

The Haqqani network also functions as a trusted "office" to mediate local disputes between militants and tribal entities and for these factions to negotiate issues with Islamabad.[69] As discussed in Part I, Jalaluddin had played central roles in mediating political and tribal conflict on both the national and regional levels since the 1980s. After his infamous capture of Khost garrison in 1991, Jalaluddin led numerous shuras to ensure stability between groups and to aid the political transition.[70] The influence and reputation of Jalaluddin Haqqani as a trusted and fair actor can also be seen in the geographic reach of his mediation activities. For example, after Sibghatullah Mujaddidi and Gulbuddin Hekmatyar failed to solve a dispute between the Ahmadzai Wazir and the Nangarhar Shura during the early 1990s, Jalaluddin Haqqani and one of his commanders stepped in to reconcile the two sides.[71] Jalaluddin set up a commission "to study the situation in detail, hear grievances, and pave the way for the resolution of all the problems between the two sides." The elder Haqqani also made both parties sign a written agreement which outlined a set of principles that would guide their interaction and prevent further loss of life.

Sirajuddin and some of his closest advisors have assumed this role and have similarly been central to a number of recent agreements that have aimed to reduce tension in Pakistan's tribal areas. According to local reports, Sirajuddin helped to mediate the 2005 Sararogha peace deal between Baitullah Mehsud and the Pakistani government.[72] In 2006 and 2007, Sirajuddin Haqqani, Mawlawi Bakhta Jan (deceased), and Afghan commander Mullah Dadullah established a variety of jirgas to mitigate violence in South Waziristan between Uzbek militants, backed by Baitullah Mehsud, and Pakistani Taliban commander Mullah Nazir.[73] Tribal sources described Sirajuddin's presence and role as being essential to the eventual agreement between the parties.[74] Bakhta Jan and Sirajuddin played a similar role in 2008 when they helped Pakistan to negotiate a short-lived peace with Baitullah Mehsud and several tribal leaders in South Waziristan.[75]

The mediating hand of the Haqqani network can also been seen in the establishment of the Shura Ittihad-ul-Mujahidin (SIM) and the Shura-e-Murakeba, two umbrella groups of Afghan and Pakistani militant leaders, including Baitullah Mehsud, Gul Bahadur, and Mullah Nazir, that were respectively created in February 2009 and December 2011.[76] Both were established to unify local militant groups and to avoid the conflicts that had plagued them in the past. Several months after the creation of the SIM, Sirajuddin "showed his sway when the Pakistani Taliban ... were on the verge of a bloody struggle following the death of its leader [Baitullah Mehsud] in a US airstrike ... He called the major factions to North Waziristan to settle the dispute, telling them they must 'follow the path of a great leader ... You should save your bullets for your true enemies,' said a tribal elder who attended the meeting."[77] Similar to the past, the influence and geographic reach of the group's mediating activities extends today as far as Pakistan's Kurram Agency where two brothers of Jalaluddin—Khalil and Ibrahim—reportedly helped to bring an end (at least temporarily) to hostilities between Sunni and Shi'a tribal groups there.[78] These examples illustrate how the Haqqani network's value to local militants and tribal leaders in Pakistan is a lot broader than their role as a military force.

Haqqani Network Incentives and Benefits to Maintain their Local Value Proposition

The Haqqani network receives numerous benefits in exchange for the value it provides to local militant groups like the Afghan and Pakistani Taliban. When viewed from a strategic perspective, the Haqqanis' ability to maintain good relations with tribal and militant actors in North and South Waziristan is valuable in that it contributes to the Haqqanis' local survivability and endurance. It also helps to ensure that the illicit dimensions of the political economy of the Loya Paktia and North Waziristan region continues to function with less obstacles. Not only do the Haqqanis receive added manpower and expertise from various local TTP factions, but they can also use their relationship with the TTP as a point of leverage against Pakistan. Partnering with the Afghan Taliban allows the Haqqani network to enhance the perception of their role in Afghanistan's jihad and maintain their relevancy as a leading militant actor. The Haqqanis' partnership with the Afghan Taliban also gives Sirajuddin and his cohort nominal control and oversight of the geographically central terrain in Loya Paktia, an area to which the organization's history is intimately tied.

Strengthening its Local Position and Ensuring its Long-Term Survival

Cooperating with and providing value to the TTP allows the Haqqani network to be looked upon as a local partner rather than an obstacle or unfriendly foe. Given the Haqqani network's large support base in North Waziristan and the movement of its fighters across the border, it needs to maintain good relations, or at least mutually beneficial alliances, with other powerful militant actors and tribal leaders in North and South Waziristan. In fact, as a cross-border insurgent movement, the Haqqani network's ability to sustain its violent enterprise is predicated on its ability to be seen as a legitimate and trustworthy local partner—even if this involves maintaining close relationships with tribal militant groups that are actively waging war against the Pakistani state. For example, the Haqqanis and Gul Bahadur need each other in order to ensure the smooth travel of fighters across the Loya Paktia/North Waziristan corridor, and their cooperation is likely governed by a standing agreement that facilitates such movement. One could even go so far as to state that TTP–Haqqani relations are just as essential, if not more so, to the long-term survival and endurance of the Haqqani network as Pakistani state protection.

Maintaining its Financial Position and Role in the Region's Local Political Economy

Maintaining these alliances is also beneficial because they help the Haqqani network to sustain the local conflict economy, preserve their important role in it, and to facilitate kickbacks to their group and allies. Loya Paktia has very little arable land, due to the high altitudes and mountainous environment in the area. Unlike southern Afghanistan the region does not produce much opium and locals must rely on other natural resources and enterprises to make a living. "Smuggling and cross border business in and around Khost is huge ... and is crucial to everyday existence and general welfare of the Zadrans and Karlanri tribal infrastructure," notes veteran journalist Robert Nickelsberg. "This [activity] keeps the merchant-class happy and complicit." It also helps to enrich and reinforce the position of local power brokers: "Smuggling out natural resources, chromium, for example, from Ghazni province all travels through and out of Haqqani territory enriching Ghazni provincial and district governors."[79] Such facilitation arguably comes at a price and it provides the Taliban, the Haqqani network, and other insurgents with opportunities to gain political capital and favors from other local power brokers.[80]

The Haqqani network financially benefits from these illicit markets: "You name it, Haqqani smuggles it."[81] For example, the Haqqani network "taxes commodities moving through its control zones, with a particular focus on timber operations, stone and marble quarries and weapons smuggling ... Trucks coming from the southeast towards Kabul carrying timber and stone for construction purposes are typically taxed 10–20 percent of their carriage, with fees negotiable."[82] Sources interviewed by Gretchen Peters also say that "the Haqqanis receive substantial funds in the form of Hawala transfers from the Gulf, which are often termed 'donations,' but which in some cases could be better described as 'security investments' by Afghan traders who live in the United Arab Emirates (UAE) and who want to ensure that the militants do not interfere with or destroy their businesses or properties back home."[83] In that sense the Haqqani network function like the mob—protecting others while also deepening their own pockets and consolidating their power. High levels of corruption and the inability of the NATO Coalition and the Afghan government to provide security in large swaths of southeastern Afghanistan have only helped to further institutionalize these problems.

Manpower and Expertise from the TTP and Access to Additional Infrastructure

The Haqqani network receives added manpower and expertise from the North and South Waziristan factions of the TTP. For example, as Thomas Ruttig notes, "Since the spring of 2008 in particular, the Haqqanis' fighters had been reinforced by a large number of Pakistani Taliban from the Wazir, Dawar and Mehsud tribes. Some sources speak of up to 4,000 of them, mainly based in the Zadran Arc [in Afghanistan]."[84] There are also indications that the TTP assists the Haqqanis with suicide bomber training.[85] As noted by Pakistani journalist Imtiaz Gul, "In May 2008, Noor Ahmed Wazir told me in Peshawar that three of his cousins from Miranshah, in North Waziristan, had already been through suicide attack training at a camp near Shawal, run jointly by TTP's Qari Hussain [killed in October 2010] and Sirajuddin Haqqani."[86] Collaboration in this realm is believed to extend to Mullah Nazir who supplies suicide bombers and Gul Bahadur's deputy—Sadiq Noor—who reportedly assists the Haqqani network with car bombs.[87] Those deployed by the Haqqani network as suicide attackers in Afghanistan are a mix of fighters—local Afghans, Afghans raised in Pakistan, Pakistanis, and foreigners—but the case of captured suicide bomber Rafiqullah illustrates the deployment of Pakistani youth from Waziristan across the border to Khost.[88] The story of "Ahmad," another captured suicide bomber, shows how closely the TTP and the Haqqanis cooperate in this realm.[89] After Ahmad finished his religious schooling in Pakistan's Punjab Province he travelled to Waziristan, where:

> His friend took him to a Pakistani Taliban camp, where his hosts welcomed him and gave him lodging. At first he wanted to leave, but his hosts asked him to stay for a short while and "learn about Islam." …
>
> The camp belonged to Maulavi Nazeer [Mullah Nazir], a powerful Pakistani Taliban commander. According to Ahmad, many of the fighters trained under Mr. Nazeer and then went to Afghanistan to fight with the Haqqanis. Ahmad's destiny was not to become a fighter, however: He told his hosts that he would like to become a "martyr," a suicide bomber.

Nearly seven months passed, then one day Nazeer came to Ahmad and told him that he had a job for him.

Some of Nazeer's men drove Ahmad to the Afghan border. On the other side, he was met by Haqqani representatives, who led him to a car full of explosives and a suicide vest. "They told me to drive down a particular road for a short while, after which I would find some foreign soldiers who had killed many Muslims," he recalls.

When Ahmad reached the checkpoint, he realized that he was about to attack Afghan security forces and not foreigners, and instead of detonating his charge he turned himself in to local authorities. Ahmad's story illustrates the Haqqani network's use of Pakistani youth trained and radicalized through TTP channels to enhance its campaign in Afghanistan. The kidnapping and captivity of David Rohde similarly highlights the overlap of Haqqani and TTP resources in Pakistan's tribal areas, as the Haqqanis used a facility associated with Baitullah Mehsud in South Waziristan to hide the captured *New York Times* journalist.[90]

TTP as Tool to Gain Leverage over Pakistan

Maintaining close ties with TTP elements and functioning as a conduit/liaison between those elements and the Pakistani state reinforces the Haqqani network's value to Islamabad. Yet, at the same time, "Sirajuddin Haqqani is using the TTP as leverage against Pakistan. Sirajuddin is playing a double game, and the military in Pakistan believes this very much."[91] A 2007 prisoner swap between the Pakistani government and Baitullah Mehsud's faction of the TTP highlights this dynamic, and how the Haqqani network is able to use their intermediary position to extract benefits from Pakistan. According to Haqqani commander Mullah Sangin, in exchange for more than 200 Pakistani security personnel captured by men loyal to Baitullah, the Pakistani government released forty-three local Taliban, including three Haqqani family members—Jalaluddin's brother Khalil Ahmad, son-in-law Ghazi Khan, and Dr Fazl-e-Haqqani.[92] One can imagine how the release of these Haqqani family members was a condition likely extracted by the Haqqani network—or by Baitullah himself—for helping to facilitate the release of an entire company of Pakistani soldiers. This case reinforces Pakistan's dependence upon the Haqqani network, as well as the group's awareness of and ability to manipulate that dependence.

Conclusion

All of these benefits help to enhance the Haqqani network's centrality and its position of power in Loya Paktia and North Waziristan, two areas which have long been beyond the writ of effective, central state control. The Haqqani network's legitimacy and effectiveness in these areas is derived by the value it provides to local militant groups and tribal power brokers, and its ability to cultivate an image that it is acting in their interest. The Haqqani network primarily does this by providing local schools, being a good and capable military partner, and by allowing Pakistani militants to leverage its networks and infrastructure in Afghanistan. A series of tactical and strategic alliances guide cooperation between these actors and help to ensure the smooth movement of logistics and fighters across the Afghanistan–Pakistan border. Some of the actions of the Haqqani network, such as its diplomatic activity in the FATA and Loya Paktia, also exhibit state-like characteristics, indicating that the group is not only deeply interwoven into the fabric of each place, but that its removal from power would create turmoil for those (i.e., Islamabad) that rely on the Haqqanis to manage local hostilities. It is thus reflective that journalist Pir Zubayr Shah, a Waziristan native, viewed the Haqqani network's primary local role as being "to make peace with the tribes."[93]

This chapter highlights the Haqqani network's ties to the TTP, the Afghan Taliban, and other actors, and in doing so it illustrates that militancy in Loya Paktia is directly associated with multiple systems of violence, including the violence affecting the Pakistani state. For the Haqqani network, maintaining good relations with local militant groups and tribal partners appears to take precedence over its relation to the Pakistani state. In terms of the Haqqani network's long-term survival it makes sense that positive local relations would matter most. Statements made by North Waziristan TTP commander Hafiz Gul Bahadur echo similar themes. They also demonstrate Gul Bahadur's frustration, and his wearing patience with Pakistan, given Islamabad's partnership with the United States, and his willingness to walk away from talks with the government.[94]

US counterterrorism efforts in North Waziristan—orchestrated primarily through its use of armed drones—are also challenged by the collective action logic that has increasingly been at play in the FATA. Take, for example, the calls made in March 2011 by local North Waziristan tribal leaders to wage jihad against the United States after a drone killed forty elders who were meeting to discuss chromite prices in the agency earlier that month.[95] This response illustrates that while drones have been a central tool to target and degrade al-Qa'ida's and the TTP's leaders, their use has enhanced local resentment of the United States and broadened the organizational pool of militant actors who now seek revenge, problems which will likely endure and need to be managed.

5

REGIONAL

THE PAKISTANI STATE AND ITS INTER-SERVICES INTELLIGENCE DIRECTORATE

During the early morning of Monday, 7 July 2008, Hamza Shahkoor, a twenty-two-year-old Pakistani, rammed his explosive-laden vehicle into the front gate of the Indian Embassy in Kabul.[1] The damage was catastrophic, with the scene being described as one of "utter devastation."[2] The two Indian diplomatic vehicles that he was following were immediately destroyed. The 100 kilogram bomb, which was heard miles away, also blew the gates of the embassy off, damaged several buildings, and destroyed nearby cars.[3] The bodies of Afghan guards, "innocent civilians and shopkeepers, women and children" and several people waiting in line for an Indian visa also littered the street.[4] Fifty-eight people were killed by the blast, and more than a hundred were injured.

Hamza had been successful though, at least in the eyes of those who planned his mission, because—in addition to all the civilians—Hamza killed Brigadier Ravi Datt Mehta, India's defense attaché in Afghanistan. The message that Hamza's bomb was meant to send had been delivered: Islamabad viewed India's increasing influence inside Afghanistan as a threat. Its strong role in the country would not be tolerated. Strategic stakes and regional geopolitics were at play. It thus was not a surprise when details later emerged that the young Pakistani bomber had been trained by Laskhar-e-Taiba, and that the organization trusted with carrying out this mission was the Haqqani network.[5]

This is because the Haqqani network has historically functioned as a proxy through which elements of the Pakistani state have pursued their strategic interests and sought military and political influence inside the FATA and Afghanistan. The relationship between the two parties works because it is built on the basis of a shared history and overlapping interests; and it has been sustained by necessity and codependence. The Haqqani network has proved useful to the Pakistani state for three decades by functioning as a reliable partner which can provide strategic depth (in case of total war with India) and added military capacity in the tribal areas of Afghanistan and Pakistan, and do so with a measure of plausible deniability. The Haqqanis have also been valuable by serving as a diplomatic liaison, a mechanism through which Islamabad can shape the local environment in the tribal areas and manage hostilities in ways that suit Pakistan's interest. Since the rise of the neo-Taliban insurgency Pakistan has distanced itself from openly expressing its support for the Haqqani network. This is for good reason, given the important and lethal role the group plays in Afghanistan and the causalities they inflict on US, Afghan, and Coalition troops.

Statements made by senior Pakistani officials, as well as recent actions taken by the Pakistani government, demonstrate, however, that the Haqqani network remains a strategic, state asset.[6] Consider, for example, Pakistan's claims that it can deliver the Haqqani network and reconcile it with President Hamid Karzai's Afghan government.[7] The fact that Pakistan offered up the Haqqanis as a solution to the Afghan conflict at a time when the United States is preparing for its withdrawal and is pressuring Islamabad to take action against the group in North Waziristan indicates that they are a strategic asset. The timing of Pakistan's offer seems all too convenient, and it reveals that Pakistan has continually refused to move against the Haqqani network precisely because the organization is immensely valuable. In order to better understand how and why this is the case, the focus of this chapter is on assessing the Haqqani network's value proposition to the Pakistani state.

During the anti-Soviet jihad Jalaluddin Haqqani was a key recipient of aid from Pakistan and a variety of other donors, including the United States and several Arab nations. It was during this period that the Haqqani network solidified its value as a reliable, committed, and effective partner which was highly capable of achieving military results in Loya Paktia. Jalaluddin's facilities in Peshawar, Miranshah, and Loya Paktia were important hubs of activity. They were key meeting places where a mix of actors—Afghan fighters, Arab volunteers, and Pakistanis from various backgrounds—could get weapons and food, as well as prepare for attacks across the border.[8] With his openness and effectiveness, Jalaluddin quickly rose to be one of the ISI's most favored field commanders and the access he provided would have a significant impact upon Pakistan's security establishment in the years to follow. ISI officers frequently visited his headquarters and advised him during key battles, such as the one that took place in Zhawara in 1987, where Haqqani and his men defended their headquarters.[9]

Jalaluddin also facilitated fighting opportunities for ordinary Pakistani army officers who sought action inside Afghanistan during this period. A personnel letter addressed to Jalaluddin and Nizamuddin Haqqani typifies how these interactions transpired and how Pakistan deliberately masked their role. In the letter, an aide to Jalaluddin specifically points out that the three military officers, two of them from Lahore, "have asked us to introduce them as mujahideen, and deploy them."[10] Jalaluddin's connections to Pakistan's military, however, extended far beyond the ordinary rank and file. In an interview in 2009 former ISI chief Hamid Gul characterized Jalaluddin Haqqani as a "personal friend" and when Gul sent his two sons to Afghanistan to wage jihad against the Soviets he made sure that "they fought alongside Jalaluddin Haqqani's men."[11] The intimacy of Jalaluddin's relations to various spheres of Pakistan's military establishment, and the assistance he provided Pakistan's army and intelligence service during the 1980s, serve as the foundation to best understand the Haqqani network's value to Pakistan, as well as Islamabad's reluctance to move against the group.

As established in Part I, after the withdrawal of Soviet forces Jalaluddin Haqqani continued to provide Pakistani organizations access to local fighting fronts and centers for their mobilization. It was the elder Haqqani whose capture of Khost city set the conditions for the mujahidin to eventually take power in Kabul, a feat which only gave Pakistan more power and influence west of the Durand Line. By providing Pakistani fighters with training facilities and continued access to the battlefield, Jalaluddin Haqqani also played a pivotal role in facilitating the early development and military sophistication of many anti-Kashmir groups. Many of the Pakistanis who fought with Haqqani would soon shift their attention and employ the fighting skills and training they had acquired in Loya Paktia against Indian forces in Kashmir. Some would even go on to create their own jihadist organizations and become legendary commanders, a dynamic which is best exemplified by individuals such as Maulana Fazlur Rahman Khalil and Zakiur Rahman Lakhvi, who were respectively central to the formation of Harakat ul-Mujahidin (HuM) and Lashkar-e-Taiba (LeT).[12] These proxies provided Pakistan with strategic depth and formed the basis of a covert army that Rawalpindi deployed—and in some cases continues to deploy—in order to wage asymmetric war against India in the contested region of Kashmir.

Jalaluddin Haqqani was not bashful about his influence or impact upon the Kashmir jihad, and his assistance would pay dividends to the Pakistani state.[13] During a meeting in Karachi attended by some of Pakistan's religious elite, including the general secretary of Jamaat-e-Ulema-e-Islam, Haqqani boasted that "We have trained thousands of Kashmiri mujahideen, and have made them ready for jihad."[14] The audience's respect for Haqqani was reflected by Farooq Kashmiri, the deputy head of HuM, who told students at the madrassa to spend their summer in Afghanistan so they could train under Jalaluddin.[15] These and other Pakistani madrassa students likely formed the rank and file at a number of HuM–Harakat-ul-Ansar (HUA) training camps throughout the 1990s, all of which were based in Loya Paktia and supported by the ISI.[16] The Haqqani network's direct support for various Kashmiri training camps is revealed in a 1998 communication from the Pakistani government to the Taliban.[17]

Although Jalaluddin Haqqani initially wanted to confront the Taliban, and there were some skirmishes between the two groups, his decision to join and assist the Taliban was critical to the Taliban's consolidation of power inside Afghanistan.[18] Jalaluddin brought a depth of military expertise to the Taliban, and it is likely that the Taliban's capture of Kabul would not have been possible without securing an alliance with the man with the most military influence in Afghanistan's southeast. Although likely not his intent, Haqqani's membership in the Taliban also functioned as another mechanism through which the ISI could diversify their influence over Mullah Omar and his movement, something which still holds true today.[19] The ability of Jalaluddin and his lieutenants to train and raise fighters similarly proved important to the Taliban in a number of battles in Afghanistan's north against the Northern Alliance, a force backed by India and other countries.[20]

Before exploring additional aspects of this history and what can be discerned about the Haqqani network's ties to Pakistan's security establishment today, it is important to note that "the exact role of the Pakistani government in the [Afghan] insurgency is not easy to pin down."[21] Pakistan's role is complex and is best understood as being driven by various actors who are guided by a spectrum of evolving interests and loyalties. Interestingly, it is the veteran jihadist ideologue Abu Musab al-Suri (captured in Pakistan in 2004) who, in a lengthy book about the region, most clearly breaks down the landscape of major actors. "In Pakistan there are political blocs, the Army bloc, and the Military Intelligence bloc, and it is this triumvirate that rules Pakistan and trades or divides up centers of power." Explaining the varied interests of these parties further, al-Suri adds: that "the American master can still find in it those who will faithfully serve [America], those who are dedicated to the interests of Pakistani national security, and those who are completely sympathetic to the Taliban, the Arab terrorists, and the various Islamic movements."[22]

Adding to these challenges is the fact that Pakistan's primary (but not only) interface with militant entities—the ISI—is a military intelligence organization that operates covertly, sometimes through (or in partnership with) intermediaries or proxies, such as retired military personnel, local Afghans, private companies, and religio-political parties.[23] The ISI and its mission is also fairly broad, with different offices responsible for different issues, such as external operations or domestic security.[24] Thus while some of the contours of the Haqqani–ISI relationship are observable, other dynamics remain obscured. Details about the nature of their interaction often prove elusive. Accounts about the precise role of the ISI are also challenging to verify. It is also worth keeping in mind that while there are areas of cooperation between the two parties, some sources from the post-2001 period suggest that there is also some distrust between them—and that Haqqani and Taliban fighters resent the ISI's influence over them and that they fear ISI harassment.[25] Some of the insurgents' ire appears to be driven by the methods employed by the ISI, and particularly actions such as the ISI's detention of Afghan insurgent leaders (and in some cases their family members), which are seen as attempts to coerce those individuals or manipulate the behavior of the groups they represent. Frustration also appears to exist over the ISI's efforts to play militant groups off of one another—to either shape their trajectories or make them more compliant, a tactic which has long been used by the ISI in Kashmir. Yet even if the Haqqani–ISI relationship is not always smooth, both parties still need each other. The pages that follow explore this issue by providing insight into the value that each actor provides to the other. Attention is specifically placed on the areas where Haqqani–ISI cooperation can be established, or is strongly suggested.

Spoiler and Kinetic Signaling Tool

Two of the main ways in which the Haqqani network provides value to the Pakistani state today is by acting as a proxy mechanism through which the ISI can: (1) kinetically counter Indian activity and influence in Afghanistan, especially in Kabul, and (2) ramp up pressure against the United States and the NATO Coalition. Indian influence in Afghanistan has been of particular concern to Pakistan since the removal of the Taliban regime in 2001.[26] After the Taliban's ouster, India moved swiftly and developed a "strong relationship with Afghanistan, building and managing infrastructure projects in what analysts say is a concerted effort to minimize Pakistani influence in the country."[27] Given its regional trade and security interests, India has spent US$1.3 billion in Afghanistan on reconstruction projects since 2001 and as of mid-2010 there were about 4,000 Indian specialists and security personnel in Afghanistan helping to facilitate and protect these initiatives.[28]

While much of India's activity could be considered beneficial to Afghanistan's development, it still must be viewed through the historical lens of India–Pakistan interstate rivalry and competition, especially as both countries prepare for a post-NATO Afghanistan. To Pakistan, India's increased activity and presence in Afghanistan is a direct affront to its security interests. Pakistan's main worry is that India is actively attempting to strengthen its influence and economic and military posture along Islamabad's long western front (in areas like Baluchistan) and to reduce Islamabad's strategic depth. It is in this context that the Haqqani network's value to the Pakistani state as an instrument to attack and subvert Indian interests in Afghanistan covertly is best situated and understood.

The two major suicide attacks conducted against the Indian Embassy in Kabul, the first on 7 July 2008 and the second a little more than a year later on 8 October 2009, illustrate the Haqqani network's role in facilitating important signaling effects vis-à-vis India and its regional posture.[29] As noted in the introduction, during the first attack on the Indian Embassy, the most deadly in Afghanistan at the time, a suicide car bomber killed fifty-eight people, including India's defense attaché. This attack is believed to have been a joint operation executed by a Lashkar-e-Taiba-trained suicide bomber who was facilitated locally by the Haqqani network.[30] After the attack American intelligence officials claimed that they had intercepted communications between Haqqani fighters and members of the ISI, indicating that the latter had helped to plan and direct the attack.[31] In a BBC documentary about Pakistan a former aide to US Vice President Dick Cheney noted that "Through information [likely the intercepted communications mentioned above] and a series of events it became pretty clear the Pakistanis were behind the Haqqani network, which was behind the bombing."[32] Statements made by other members of the attack network, who were captured after the event, led Afghanistan's domestic intelligence agency—the National Directorate of Security—to the same conclusion.[33] Evidence presented to the Bush administration indicated that the attack had been approved by senior members of Pakistan's military and was probably conducted to send a strong signal to India to limit its role and influences inside Afghanistan.[34]

Similarly brazen Haqqani attacks directed at Afghan and international targets in Kabul over the last several years have formed part of a broader Taliban strategy to embarrass the Karzai government and make the US/NATO occupation costly.[35] These lethal attacks aim to instill psychological fear, generate international media attention, destabilize the Afghan regime, and accelerate the withdrawal of US and NATO forces from Afghanistan. The connections between several recent Haqqani network attacks in the capital, such as those against the Intercontinental Hotel (June 2011) and the US Embassy and ISAF headquarters (September 2011), and elements of the ISI strongly suggests that the early withdrawal of US forces is an objective that both the ISI and Haqqani network share. A little over a week after the September attack the chairman of the Joint Chiefs of Staff, Admiral Mike Mullen, publicly accused Pakistan of supporting the incident. "With ISI support, Haqqani operatives planned and conducted ... the assault on our embassy. We also have credible intelligence that they were behind the June 28 attack on the Intercontinental Hotel in Kabul and a host of other smaller but effective operations."[36] News accounts of the September attack also reveal that the cell phones recovered from the deceased gunman had been used to call "Pakistani intelligence operatives before and during the assault."[37]

Communication intercepts taken during the Intercontental Hotel attack, which were leaked by Afghan authorities to the press and broadcast by *al-Jazeera,* illustrate a similar pattern and support Mullen's claims. During the recorded conversations Badruddin Haqqani—using a Pakistan-based number—can be heard encouraging and providing live instructions to the gunmen.[38] The Haqqani network's targeted strategy of attrition and focus on Kabul follows a similar pattern of behavior used by ISI-linked proxies in Indian-occupied Kashmir.

Diplomatic "Office" to Shape Militancy and Influence Local Commanders

The Haqqani network also provides value to the Pakistani state by acting as a diplomatic liaison, an "office" through which it can achieve three main functions: manage hostilities, gain access to TTP leaders, and try to shape the direction and priorities of militant groups in the FATA, especially those waging jihad against Islamabad. As noted earlier, on numerous occasions Jalaluddin, Sirajuddin, and Haqqani confidante Mawlawi Bakhta Jan (now deceased) have helped to manage hostilities by mediating a number of cease fire agreements and peace deals in North and South Waziristan between the Pakistani state and Pakistani Taliban commanders.[39] The Haqqanis played a significant role in brokering the September 2006 North Waziristan Peace Accord between the Pakistani government and Hafiz Gul Bahadur (the two parties had been fighting one another for almost two years).[40] Bakhta Jan also reportedly played a similar role in 2008 when he helped Pakistan negotiate a short-lived peace with the late emir of the TTP, Baitullah Mehsud.[41]

Given its influence and ties with a wide range of militants in the tribal areas, the Haqqani network functions as an important conduit for Pakistan to gain access to other insurgent leaders and enemies of the state. Today, this dynamic is best illustrated by the case of Tariq Azizuddin, Pakistan's former ambassador to Afghanistan, who was kidnapped by TTP militants in 2008 while traveling from Peshawar to Kabul via the Khyber Pass.[42] In an interview with *Der Spiegel* in 2009 former Pakistani President Pervez Musharraf described the Haqqani network's value in this regard: "He [Sirajuddin Haqqani] is the man who has influence over Baitullah Mehsud, a dangerous terrorist, the fiercest commander in South Waziristan and the murderer of Benazir Bhutto as we know today. Mehsud kidnapped our ambassador in Kabul and our intelligence used Haqqani's influence to get him released. Now, that does not mean that Haqqani is supported by us. The intelligence service is using certain enemies against other enemies. And it is better to tackle them one by one than making them all enemies."[43] Musharraf's statement illustrates that members of Pakistan's intelligence services, or individuals associated with those services, have access to individuals close to Sirajuddin, if not Sirajuddin himself, and that the commander has been strategically valuable to the Pakistani state as a "diplomatic" liaison to the TTP's leadership.[44] Musharraf's comments provide insights into Pakistan's rationale and the practical, but very problematic, distinction Islamabad makes between "good" and "bad" Taliban.[45]

What Musharraf failed to mention during the interview is that in exchange for Tariq Azizuddin's freedom Pakistan reportedly paid a $2.5 million ransom to Baitullah Mehsud and released a number of TTP militants, as well as Mullah Obaidullah Akhund and Mansur Dadullah, two high-ranking members of the Afghan Taliban.[46] At the time of his release Mullah Obaidullah Akhund was a member of the Quetta Shura and third in command behind Mullah Omar and his deputy. He was also the most senior Afghan Taliban figure to have been captured by Pakistani authorities since 2001.[47]

Even more noteworthy and revealing is how the Pakistani state uses the access the Haqqani network provides to shape the priorities and interests of other insurgent actors. Over the last several years Haqqani network leaders have been intimately involved in numerous efforts to reorient militants conducting jihad against the Pakistani state to fight against the United States and its allies across the border in Afghanistan. In June 2006, Sirajuddin Haqqani issued a circular in South Waziristan "informing militants that while the 'jihad' against the United States and the Karzai government would continue 'till the last drop of blood,' fighting Pakistan did not conform with the Taliban policy." The circular went on to add that "those who do not agree and (continue to wage) an undeclared war against Pakistan are neither our friends nor shall we allow them in our ranks."[48] Members of the Haqqani network issued similar appeals after the 2006 North Waziristan Peace Accord.[49]

Then, over two and half years later (in February 2009), Sirajuddin and Bakhta Jan helped to forge the Shura Ittihad-ul-Mujahidin (SIM), an umbrella group comprised of Afghan and Pakistani militants, including Baitullah Mehsud, Gul Bahadur, and Mullah Nazir.[50] The announcement of the new alliance came at the end of the week during which President Obama announced a surge of 17,000 additional American troops into Afghanistan.[51] In its first official statement the SIM declared that, under the leadership of Mullah Omar and Osama bin Laden, the alliance would fight the "infidels" led by presidents Barack Obama, Hamid Karzai, and Asif Zardari.[52] Mullah Omar publicly welcomed the emergence of the new alliance but reiterated his instructions for fighters to focus on Afghanistan and not attack Pakistan, emphasizing the need for a unified front to oppose the US troop surge.[53] Several months later, during an interview with *The News* in April 2009, Sirajuddin affirmed that "he had always been pleading with his Pakistani brothers to focus attention on Afghanistan instead of their fighting against their own security forces."[54] As the likely beneficiary of added TTP manpower, the Haqqani network probably had its own interests in mind, yet many believe that the group undertook these initiatives on behalf of the ISI or based upon its urging.[55] Regardless of the Haqqani network's motives, the uptick in TTP attacks in Pakistan throughout 2009 indicates that the SIM and other reorientation efforts fostered by Sirajuddin were short-lived and failed to achieve their primary objective.[56]

It still remains unclear whether the Shura-e-Murakeba, an alliance between Afghan and Pakistani militant groups that was brokered by Sirajuddin Haqqani in late December 2011 to unify groups, will maintain a similar fighting focus on Afghanistan and cease attacks against the Pakistani state, and whether it will hold or prove more productive than the SIM.[57]

Platform to Shape Afghanistan's Political Landscape

Across the border the Haqqani network functions as a venue for Pakistan to shape Afghanistan's political landscape and ensure that its interests will be adequately represented in the future. Statements made by Tariq Fatemi, Pakistan's former ambassador to the United States, elucidate Pakistan's strong reliance on the Haqqani network as a tool to be used for these objectives.[58] Pakistani officials interviewed by Jane Perlez also provide a useful explanation for why Islamabad is reluctant to give the Haqqanis up: Pakistan does "not want to alienate Mr. Haqqani because they consider him an important player in reconciliation efforts that they would like to see get under way in Afghanistan immediately ..."[59] The fact that Pakistan publicly announced (as early as mid-2010) its ability to broker a deal between the Haqqani network, the United States, and Afghan President Hamid Karzai only solidifies the political utility of the group as a venue for Pakistani influence inside Afghanistan.[60] It is revealing that Pakistan put the Haqqanis forward as the agent it can deliver in these proposed talks and not the Quetta Shura Taliban. This confirms the distinctiveness of the Haqqani network vis-à-vis the Quetta Shura Taliban and suggests that Pakistan has a closer relationship with, or arguably more influence over, the Haqqanis. Historically, the Taliban's Kandahari leadership was often suspicious of Pakistani motives in their dealings with them, which were by no means warm, as evidenced in the memoir of former Taliban minister Abdul Salam Zaeef.[61] This suggests that Pakistan actually has more limited options to influence and affect Afghanistan's political landscape than has publicly been recognized, and thus Islamabad will likely go to great lengths to protect the group.

These examples, from the Taliban period to today, demonstrate the Haqqani network's historic value to Pakistan as an effective military and diplomatic force. When viewed collectively these examples reveal that the Haqqani network is not a rogue insurgent group, but rather is a fighting group that at times acts as a paramilitary and diplomatic arm of the Pakistani government.[62] The intimacy of relations and the value the Haqqani network provides to the Pakistani state also sheds light on Pakistan's refusal to move against the group, and why US efforts to facilitate such a shift have thus far yielded few tangible results.

Haqqani Network Incentives and Benefits to Maintain their Regional Value Proposition

The Haqqani network provides these services to the ISI for a variety of reasons and motivations. On one level, Haqqani assistance is tied to a history of shared interests, common experience, pragmatism, and ideological affinity. The Haqqani network understands, and has a deep appreciation for, Pakistan's regional security interests. The group has also proven itself willing to support those interests.

A statement made by Jalaluddin Haqqani in October 2001 puts this into context.

Let me remind you that on Pakistan's Eastern border is India—Pakistan's perennial enemy. With the Taliban in Afghanistan, Pakistan has an unbeatable 2,300 km strategic depth ... Does Pakistan really want a new government, which will include pro-India people in it, thereby wiping out its strategic depth? I tell you, the security and stability of Pakistan and Afghanistan are intertwined. Together, we are strong but separately we are weak.[63]

Such a statement reveals that the Haqqani network and Pakistan view their security as linked, a partnership which is in direct conflict with India and its strategic goals for the region.[64] Haqqani assistance to the Pakistani state is also driven by pragmatic considerations as the Haqqani family is at least partially dependent upon the ISI to maintain its stronghold in North Waziristan and ensure the smooth movement of logistics.[65] In exchange for services rendered, the Haqqani network receives a number of important benefits that enhance the organization's effectiveness and ensure its coherency and survival. The three most important are protection (i.e., safe haven), operational support, and noninterference with the Haqqani network's logistics/business enterprises.

Sanctuary and Protection

A significant amount of debate and conflicting information exists about the protection Pakistan provides the Haqqani network. On the one hand, some argue that Pakistan's inaction or reluctance to launch a full-scale assault in North Waziristan against the Haqqani network is entirely pragmatic and reflects the limits of Pakistan's army and security services which, in the context of their other campaigns in the KPP and FATA, need to consolidate their gains and are in danger of being overstretched.[66] Such an operation also carries the risk of provoking a broader conflict between the state and militants in Pakistan's Punjab province.[67] As Musharraf noted above, Pakistan needs to prioritize and tackle various insurgent groups one at a time. And "[a]s long as they're not attacking Pakistani targets, say several Pakistani experts, the Haqqanis are not a priority."[68] One also cannot overlook the fact that Pakistan lost 2,421 of its security personnel in the tribal areas fighting against militant entities that threaten the state between 2004 and 2010.[69] Cooperation between some elements of the ISI and US representatives, while challenging, has also been productive, at least as it relates to the capture or killing of al-Qa'ida operatives in Karachi, Baluchistan, and in some cases Peshawar.[70] Pakistan's noninterference with US drone strikes in the FATA has also indirectly led to the death of a number of Haqqani fighters, who were either killed alongside al-Qa'ida or TTP fighters or—in the case of Haqqani logistician and communications specialist Jan Baz Zadran—targeted directly.[71]

People on the other side of the debate point to what Pakistan has not done (i.e., the passive or indirect protection it provides) and evidence that ISI elements are actively sheltering Haqqani family members and other key leaders. Critics point to Pakistan's "soft" approach to militancy in North Waziristan, the historical resource base and power center of the Haqqani network in Pakistan. The Peace Accord reached in North Waziristan in 2006 (hereafter the "Accord") serves as one example of how Pakistan has turned a blind eye to and exacerbated the militancy problem in the agency.[72] While the Accord halted hostilities and temporarily benefited Pakistan, some of the agreement's tenets called upon the Pakistani army to dismantle its checkpoints in the agency, release militants it had arrested, and halt air and land operations.[73] Pakistan also reportedly agreed to take the names of the two militants driving much of the violence off its "Most Wanted" list.[74] In return, the militants agreed to cease all cross-border attacks into Afghanistan and to refrain from sheltering foreign militants.[75] These latter two components of the pact were quickly broken—the first as early as mid-September, when a signatory to the Accord was killed alongside several other militants during an operation in Paktika Province.[76] Not surprisingly, the demands Pakistan accepted were also viewed as acts that would only strengthen the writ of the Haqqanis in the agency and allow both the Haqqani network and its global jihadist allies to consolidate their primary safe haven. At the time such sentiments were expressed by Khalid Aziz, the NWFP's (now Khyber Pakthunkhwa Province) former chief secretary: "The Agreement is bound to fail as it will add to the Taliban's strength ... the Taliban will now enjoy greater flexibility in organizing their operations inside Afghanistan because their bases in Waziristan are no longer imperiled."[77]

By almost all accounts this is exactly what happened. Several months after the Accord, North Waziristan was described—even by al-Qa'ida members—as having evolved into a Taliban mini-state, a status which it arguably still enjoys today.[78] So instead of actively pursuing these entities before the TTP even posed a serious threat, Pakistan posed little resistance and arguably created the space for North Waziristan's dangerous jihadist cocktail to further coalesce and ramp up their campaign in Afghanistan. That December the commanding general of US forces in Afghanistan acknowledged a 200 percent increase in the number of cross-border attacks being conducted from Pakistan, a dramatic rise from the previous year.[79] While such an increase could also be due to enhanced reporting, the trend is still a significant one. Less than two years later, in 2008, the Pakistani government reached a similar and more secretive peace deal with North Waziristan militants. The deal reportedly contained many of the same provisions as that reached in 2006.[80]

Since that time the Haqqani network has been left largely unaffected and free to consolidate its influence across North Waziristan. The most detailed account of the freedom and influence the Haqqani network and other militants enjoy in the agency is provided by David Rohde, a *New York Times* journalist who was kidnapped and held by the Haqqanis in Pakistan for seven months.[81] His comments about North Waziristan and the Haqqani network's control in the area are worth quoting at length:[82]

> It [North Waziristan] is an absolute Taliban mini-state. They completely control the area. There are Pakistani bases throughout the area, but I saw very little evidence that the Pakistanis were getting out and doing any patrolling. I mean, it was very clear that the Taliban totally controlled the area.
>
> At one point a Taliban commander [Badruddin Haqqani, Sirajuddin's brother] took me on a drive in north Waziristan for three hours in broad daylight. While we were on that drive, we actually ran into a Pakistani army re-supply convoy. The vehicle in front of us, which had local civilians

> in it, pulled over when they saw the convoy, and all of the civilians got out of the car.
>
> With our car, we pulled to the side of the road, and suddenly the driver of the car, who was a well-known Taliban commander, just he got out, and we stayed in the back seat. Our guard loaded his Kalashnikov rifle and ordered me to cover my face and to not move. I was thinking, and he correctly guessed, that maybe Tahir and Asad and I could make a run for it, and the convoy might save us. But you know, I was amazed to watch this convoy drive by.
>
> The Pakistani soldiers did look very nervous. They drove by our vehicle and the Taliban commander driving our car simply smiled and waved hello to the Pakistani soldiers as this convoy drove past. He was completely confident and didn't seem to see them as any major threat.
>
> He then got back in the car and instructed me that that was, in fact, the Pakistani army that had just driven by. And he explained that under a truce with the army, all civilian vehicles, you know, have to get out. All the civilians, you know, as the people did in front of us, have to get out of their vehicle when the army drives past. But for Taliban vehicles, only the driver has to get out. And to me, that allowed the Taliban to transport prisoners around the tribal areas that would never be seen and also allowed foreign militants to hide in the back seat of cars and not be seen. ...
>
> What was amazing was the breadth of what the Taliban were carrying out in the area. I saw [Taliban] road crews, you know, doing road construction. There were Taliban sort of police patrolling the roads ... it was a completely functioning state and society. ...

Rohde's conclusion was that the Haqqanis controlled the area with "the de-facto acquiescence of the Pakistani military."[83] His account has been confirmed by a number of Pakistani journalists who have spent time in the agency or have contacts there, as well as several aspiring jihadis who received training in the agency.[84] At this point, there can be no doubt that North Waziristan functions as a militant stronghold and an important safe haven for the Haqqani network and a dangerous mix of local and foreign fighters, including al-Qa'ida. Pakistan's continued willingness to overlook North Waziristan's militant mix has a number of implications for Pakistan, Afghanistan, and the United States. Pakistan's inaction is not only fueling the Afghan insurgency, but is also providing space for the Haqqani network to sustain itself financially and for anti-Pakistan militants and global jihadis to further coalesce, a dynamic which is in turn helping to sustain groups like al-Qa'ida. It is revealing that many of the international terrorist plots disrupted within the last several years have had direct ties to al-Qa'ida leaders, training facilities, or other militants based in North Waziristan.[85] The case of Faisal Shahzad, the failed Times Square bomber, and his ties to the TTP and North Waziristan are particularly instructive in this regard.[86] Given these dynamics, it seems all too convenient that as "far as the Pakistani military is concerned, there's always a compelling reason why now isn't the right time to go there [i.e., North Waziristan]."[87]

A mixture of sources suggests that Pakistan is not just turning a blind eye to militancy in North Waziristan, but that it is actively assisting the Haqqani network. Accounts provided by Taliban commanders tell of how the ISI is helping to facilitate their movement from Afghanistan to their bases in North Waziristan. One Taliban commander described how this assistance works: "If I go across the border, even if the Pakistani authorities know I am a commander they open the way for me, all the way to the base."[88] A Haqqani subcommander similarly reported that he only had to phone his minder to get the roads cleared.[89] A former Taliban minister from southern Afghanistan also claimed to have seen written communication from Taliban members to Pakistani officials requesting safe passage across the border. Veteran Pakistani journalist Ahmed Rashid has documented the existence of communication intercepts which serve the same purpose.[90] Diplomatic cables from the Taliban period (late 1990s) also highlight the ISI's issuance of permits and special licenses to facilitate the movement of vehicles in and out of Afghanistan.[91] Pakistan's record on this issue demonstrates a historical pattern of behavior and suggests that the claims made by a number of Taliban and Haqqani commanders today might not be that far-fetched.

Other sources indicate that Haqqani network leaders are even being protected by elements of the Pakistani state.[92] A Taliban commander recently described Sirajuddin Haqqani's comfort in North Waziristan in the following way: "He [Sirajuddin] seems to feel invulnerable ... The ISI protects him."[93] Such activity is not without precedent as it is believed that Jalaluddin Haqqani was protected by Pakistan and at times even resided at a Pakistani officer compound during the 1980s.[94] Today, senior members of the Haqqani network are believed to reside in Pakistan's settled areas, including the capital Islamabad.[95] In 2010, Khalil and Nassir Haqqani were both seen at the Haqqaniya madrassa in Akora Khattak with a car that had Islamabad plates, suggesting that senior members of the Haqqani family are able to travel across Pakistan freely.[96] Nassir also reportedly maintains "residences in the immediate vicinity of ISI headquarters in Islamabad" and spends time in Karachi.[97] Sirajuddin's other brother, Muhammad, who was not believed to be associated with militancy, also lived and studied in Islamabad before being killed by a drone-fired missile in North Waziristan in February 2011.[98] Actions taken by the Haqqani network in 2010–11 to secure peace between warring tribes in Kurram Agency have led many to conclude that this activity is part of an ISI-linked effort to diversify the Haqqanis' access routes into Afghanistan and to develop additional safe havens that will allow the group to relocate resources and personnel to this area.[99]

There is also evidence suggesting that ISI elements have provided the Haqqani network with advance warning of raids and drone attacks. Mullah Nasrullah, a Taliban commander interviewed by *Newsweek* in 2008, said that individuals believed to be ISI officers used to visit Haqqani facilities in Miranshah and meet Sirajuddin regularly.[100] Taliban commanders from other areas have described having a similar relationship with the ISI.[101] A Haqqani defector also claimed that "Pakistanis used to tip off Sirajuddin whenever a US missile strike was imminent."[102] A separate document captured in Afghanistan makes similar accusations.[103] While statements such as these are difficult to corroborate, a former CIA officer interviewed by Matthew Cole shared an account which appears to confirm the Haqqani network defector's claims. The story unfolds as follows:

> The CIA had long known about a mosque and madrassa that the Haqqanis used as a headquarters in Miran Shah [Pakistan]. The CIA readied a plan to raid the mosque when surveillance indicated Sirajuddin Haqqani was present. The CIA plan required approval of a Pakistan Army commander

in Peshawar. But there was never any Pakistani response, which killed the plan. This refusal to cooperate, however, was no longer a surprise to American operatives. A year earlier, it had been. The CIA's first attempt to raid Haqqani, in 2005, had netted nothing. CIA officers discovered that an ISI officer had warned Haqqani in advance about the raid. "Our guys couldn't believe it," the former CIA officer told me. "CIA had worked on this thing for some time, and the son of a bitch tipped Haqqani off." They presented their evidence to the ISI general in charge, who responded with embarrassment and apologies.[104]

According to individuals that *New York Times* journalist David Sanger interviewed about the incident, "The account of the warning sent to the school [madrassa] was almost comical. It was something like, 'Hey we're going to hit your place in a few days, so if anyone important is there, you might want to tell them to scram.'"[105] The main mosque and madrassa complex that these individuals are referring to is the Manba' 'Ulum madrassa in Danday Darpa Khel, North Waziristan, one of several madrassa facilities in the tribal areas run by the Haqqani network.[106] Since its establishment in the 1980s Manba' 'Ulum has functioned as a mechanism through which the Haqqani network can provide services such as religious instruction to the local community, dimensions of which are likely positive and benign. Yet at the same time, for a significant period Manba' 'Ulum also functioned as the de facto military headquarters of the Haqqani network in Pakistan—a key operational hub and meeting place to coordinate militant activities.[107]

Pakistani security forces have reportedly raided Manba' 'Ulum multiple times within the past several years. In 2005, Pakistani security forces reportedly captured a large cache of weapons and ammunition, as well as a small remote-controlled "drone" at the facility.[108] Several years later, in 2008, the seminary was raided again by "hundreds of Frontier Corps and Levies personnel" who found the facility completely abandoned.[109] While it is dangerous to draw precise conclusions from these two, poorly sourced accounts, it is still surprising that this important facility was left vacant, leaving one to speculate that the Haqqanis did receive some form of advance warning. Press reports about a drone attack against Manba' 'Ulum (carried out in September 2008), however, suggest that the issue of early warning might be more nuanced and complex, or that the United States is conducting these operations unilaterally with increased precision.[110] Take, for example, local reports indicating that two wives and a sister of Jalaluddin Haqqani were killed alongside twenty militants during the drone strike, or the fact that Badruddin Haqqani was believed to have been present and to have only narrowly escaped.[111] Stories such as these, if true, indicate that Pakistan is playing both sides of the conflict: that it is doing just enough to appease the United States, but not enough to degrade a lethal militant proxy upon which it still relies to project its power and achieve its interests.[112]

Operational Support—Logistics, Materiel, Training, Advising, and Financial Resources

Of equal importance to the Haqqani network—and its effectiveness—is the operational support it receives from Pakistan and its intelligence services. As has been well documented, Pakistan has a long and rich history of providing operational support to various insurgent groups, ranging from anti-Soviet resistance commanders and Mullah Omar's Taliban to Lashkar-e-Taiba and a mix of other Kashmiri and sectarian insurgent entities.[113] Historically, Pakistan did not just provide these groups with funds, weapons, and other materiel, such as communications platforms, to wage war on the battlefield. The type of operational support and backing that Pakistan provided these groups during the 1990s was a lot more encompassing. It was also very intentional and strategic, as Pakistan saw the value of developing a cadre of ideologically committed militant proxies that it could deploy across the Durand Line and Kashmir's Line of Control. In support of this policy, Pakistan actively facilitated the logistics and the movement of fighters and materiel to key battlefronts. The ISI provided strategic direction to many of these militant groups and lent its facilities and military expertise to help train them, before turning on several of them post-9/11. During various conflicts the ISI deployed small teams of Pakistani military and intelligence personnel to serve as tactical-level advisors to Afghan fighting units.

Due to its effectiveness and reliability, the Haqqani network has been one of the key recipients of this assistance for the past three decades. Pakistan's political and military establishment publicly dismisses the claim that it is still actively supporting the Haqqani network today, and even charges that these claims are unfounded and without merit.[114] Sirajuddin Haqqani has similarly denied having any ties to the ISI.[115] It is worth noting that for a larger part of the Taliban period Pakistan similarly denied their support for the movement.[116] Even before the US invasion of Afghanistan the ISI reportedly told senior members of the Taliban that they could count on their support for any future jihad against the Americans.[117] Unfortunately for the Afghan government and the United States, these assurances were not an empty promise. A growing body of evidence, derived from multiple sources, indicates that Pakistan continues to provide support to the Haqqani network. The support offered today mirrors that which Pakistan provided in the past, and ranges from training and the deployment of tactical advisors in the field to financial resources and materiel. This assistance is very practical and helps to sustain the Haqqani group and enhance its effectiveness on the battlefield. To avoid any diplomatic or military blowback from its allies, such as the United States, Pakistan carefully manages how it operationally assists the Haqqani network. The testimonials of a number of Taliban and Haqqani fighters reveal the contours and some details of this assistance, however. A review of Pakistan's history of support for Afghan insurgent actors is equally useful as it situates Pakistan's behavior and demonstrates a number of patterns. One of the most insightful is that it appears that ISI and Frontier Corps personnel still use many of the same deceptive tactics honed during the Soviet jihad to mask Pakistan's support for the Haqqani network and others today.

Strategic and Operational Direction

There are a number of indications that the ISI provides, or at least attempts to provide, strategic direction to the Haqqani network.[118] While details are murky, it is likely that the ISI provides direction to the Haqqani network in ways that mirror the guidance it provided to the group in the past. During the anti-Soviet jihad the ISI was credited with "uniting the mujahidin and forcing them to adopt a unified strategy."[119] The Haqqani network was an important hub of this strategy. Pakistan's power to control and direct the insurgency against the Soviets is revealed by a number of letters to and from Haqqani network leaders that were captured in Afghanistan. For example, in a personal letter to Nizamuddin Haqqani in 1980, Fathullah Haqqani explains the reason why they need to halt their activity temporarily: "For a few days, the government of Pakistan has prohibited the mujahideen from carrying logistical or combat operations. But we will, Inshallah, load up some weapons and equipments in three to four days [after the prohibition is lifted]."[120] Communication logs between Haqqani network leaders and the ISI from 1989 to 1992 are even more insightful. They show the ISI providing tactical-level direction and shaping the activity of an interlinked network of mujahidin commanders spread across Afghanistan.[121] One message, sent in English the same month Soviet forces withdrew from Afghanistan, is emblematic of the type of strategic direction the ISI provided:[122]

PLEASE ACCEPT HEARTIEST CONGRATULATIONS ON YOUR SUCCESS ... THE SOVIET [*sic*] WERE UNABLE TO BREAK THE WILL OF GREAT AFGHANISTAN FREEDOM FIGHTER. AFGHANS NEVER GIVE IN DICTAT [*sic*] OF A SUPER POWER. AT THIS JUNCTURE I REQUEST YOU TO UNITE FURTHER DIRECTION YOUR ENERGIES AGAINST [Afghan President] NAJIB[ullah] SO THAT HIS GOVT IS FORCED TO TRANSFER POWER TO THE GOVT ANNOUNCED BY THE MUJAHIDEEN.

Another message addressed specifically to Commander Haqqani in 1988 is even more specific, and it illustrates the type of direction and intelligence the ISI gave to Jalaluddin and his other lieutenants. The Soviets "HAVE LAUNCHED MAJ[OR] OFFENSIVE IN KANDAHAR. INTENSIFY YOUR JEHAD AND CAPTURE GARDEZ ASP [As Soon as Possible]."[123] Other messages are more tactical and request Jalaluddin's presence in Islamabad for a meeting or for other commanders to attend a shura at Haqqani's house in Miranshah.[124] These communications also functioned as a way for Jalaluddin and other Haqqani commanders to request assistance and equipment and provide intelligence updates to the ISI.

Similar claims are made about the ISI's influence over the Taliban and the Haqqani network today. Several Taliban commanders have suggested that during 2003–4 senior Taliban leaders, foreign fighters, and the ISI all helped the Haqqani network, and more broadly the Taliban, to regroup and fight.[125] The ISI is also believed to have played a role in shaping the two suicide attacks that the Haqqani network has conducted against the Indian Embassy in Kabul. Although difficult to confirm, some Taliban commanders assert that the ISI has representatives on and resources the Miranshah Shura, a regional decision-making body led by Sirajuddin Haqqani which is used to coordinate Taliban activity.[126] These claims are interesting in that they suggest that the Haqqani network enjoys less autonomy and receives more direction from the ISI than previously thought. Given the history of relations between the Haqqani network and the ISI, it is likely that the ISI provides some form of direction to the Haqqani network today, but just how much strategic direction Pakistan's intelligence agency offers still remains unclear.

Training

As noted in Part I, Pakistan has a rich history of training Afghan and Kashmiri mujahidin units. The Haqqani network has often been a central partner in these initiatives. During the 1990s the ISI helped numerous Kashmiri militant groups to establish training camps to prepare Pakistani youth for operations in Indian-occupied Kashmir.[127] Some of these camps—including two Harakat-ul Ansar (HUA) training facilities struck by US cruise missiles in 1998—overlapped with those run by Osama bin Laden and al-Qa'ida.[128] Intelligence officials were so confident about the ISI's support for HUA that one of them described it in the following way: "We know without any doubt that Harakat-ul-Ansar is very heavily backed by ISI."[129] Other documents declassified by the US government confirm Pakistan's support for HUA.[130] A document that Pakistan provided to the Taliban in late 1998 illustrates that the ISI had intimate knowledge of who was training at these camps, indicating that the intelligence group had operatives at those locations or was at least collecting on them.[131]

After 9/11, al-Qa'ida and the ISI's training camp infrastructure in Loya Paktia was either destroyed or dismantled. But according to various sources it did not take long for a conglomeration of militant actors, including al-Qa'ida, the Haqqani network, other Afghan Taliban segments, local Pakistani fighters, and the ISI, to build new training facilities across the border in the mountains of North and South Waziristan. Elements of the ISI are believed to have supported new Taliban and Haqqani network camps as early as 2004. An account provided by a former Haqqani network commander about the composition of these camps and the ISI's "train the trainer role" in them is particularly revealing.[132] To protect his identity the former Haqqani network commander uses the pseudonym "Muhammed."[133]

The ISI also began to provide assistance in the Taliban's own training camps. The training camps inside both North and South Waziristan, said Muhammed, required new recruits to go through all the same training. After the ISI began helping, the labor was divided. In addition to leading attacks inside Afghanistan, Muhammed helped train young Afghan and Pakistani men in basic weapons. "I was good at some things, like teaching how to fire weapons." While he did that, an Arab or Uzbek trainer might school a smaller group in remote-controlled bombs or IEDs. An ISI officer, meanwhile, might teach an even smaller group how to gather intelligence.

Muhammed himself also received training from the ISI that allowed him to launch more sophisticated attacks across the border. During late 2005, Muhammed and his platoon operated on the Shawal mountain range in North Waziristan. From the Shawal peaks he and his men could see Afghanistan just a few miles away. An ISI captain named Asif Khan trained him to use a 6-foot rocket called the Sakar-20, a Russian-made device that is roughly 6 feet long and requires several days to perfect firing.

Capt. Khan, who took orders from another ISI officer whom Muhammed knew as "Major Doctor Sajit," spent a week teaching Muhammed how to position the rocket on the Shawal's ridgeline to get its maximum range of 30 kilometers. Khan, Muhammed said, also gave the Taliban fighters GPS devices, taught the men how to calibrate them, and then paid Afghans to take the device across the border to nearby American and Afghan bases to pinpoint their locations. With those coordinates, Muhammed could fire the Sakar-20 with decent precision. "Once I was taught, then I trained my men."

Other sources appear to corroborate Muhammed's account of the ISI's role, as well as the existence of Haqqani training facilities in the Shawal region.[134] The Haqqani network is also believed to run training facilities with the TTP in Spinkai Raghzai and Kotkai,

South Waziristan.[135] While little is known about who controls which camps, the ISI's presence is reportedly pervasive and the training provided at ISI-sponsored camps runs the gambit—with one exception. According to a Taliban commander from Loya Paktia "The trainers [at the camps] are all Pakistan ISI—they are well trained, well educated ... Training is in all military tactics: attacks, ambushes, IEDs—but not suicide bombers. This training is separate, very specialist."[136] Most of this specialized training is believed to have been done by Qari Hussain Mehsud (before his reported death in October 2010) or at camps associated with him. Given the overlapping ties between militant groups in the FATA this is not surprising, and it goes without saying that ISI training assistance has one primary goal—to increase the lethality and military effectiveness of Haqqani and other fighters. The ISI–Haqqani connection must be considered at least partly responsible for the markedly more advanced techniques, tactics, and procedures of the Haqqani network in the Afghan insurgency as compared to other elements, including the southern Afghan Taliban, who, though also historically supported by the ISI, do not have the advantage of the contiguity of out-of-country training areas and in-country operational theaters, as the Haqqanis do in North Waziristan and Loya Paktia, respectively.

Operational Advising and Tactical Field Assistance

Pakistan has a history of embedding ISI and Frontier Corps officers with the Taliban and Haqqani fighting units, and there are several indications which suggest that this practice might also be occurring today. During the anti-Soviet jihad some of these Pakistani officers just wanted to fight, while others served as advisors.[137] In his book, *Bear Trap*, the former head of the ISI's Afghan bureau Muhammad Yousaf explained that: "The men we sent into Afghanistan were not spies. They were soldiers from the Pakistan Army serving with the Afghan Bureau of ISI." Their mission, he noted, "was to accompany the mujahideen on special operations."[138] These officers were usually deployed in three-man teams and were often attached to Afghan mujahidin units.[139] The ISI masked the deployment of these soldiers through various forms of deception, which allowed Pakistan to maintain a plausible level of deniability.[140] During the Taliban period, members from the Frontier Corps proved useful for these assignments because they could "easily blend in with the Afghan Pashtun population" due to their tribal background and local knowledge.[141] For example, shortly after the US invasion of Afghanistan, Pakistan airlifted—with US approval—a sizeable number of "Pakistani Army officers, intelligence advisers, and volunteers who were fighting alongside the Taliban" from Kunduz, Afghanistan.[142]

Two poorly sourced accounts suggest that Pakistan has deployed officers to support the Haqqani network and the Quetta Shura Taliban during the post-2001 period. According to an uncorroborated account told by Anthony Shaffer, a US lieutenant colonel who was part of a leadership targeting cell in Afghanistan, in 2003 the 10th Mountain Division captured a female operating as part of a Taliban unit in Khost.[143] Although this female did not admit to being an ISI agent during her interrogation, she was carrying (unspecified) Pakistani documents. Other (unspecified) intelligence reportedly indicated that she was active with the ISI.[144] Another trace of ISI embedding its operatives emerged in 2007 after a British Special Forces team conducted a raid in Sangin (Helmand Province) to capture a Taliban commander based there. The Taliban commander was killed during the raid, but when British soldiers searched his belongings they reportedly found his Pakistani military ID.[145] The event led to a rift between Afghan President Hamid Karzai and British officials who for reasons unknown chose not to disclose what their soldiers had found.[146] Afghanistan's former intelligence chief—Amrullah Saleh—has also publicly revealed the capture of several other serving ISI officers.[147] Taliban commanders interviewed by Matt Waldman have similarly described the presence of Pakistani field advisors, many of whom are reported to be Pakistanis from Punjab Province.

Given the risk of alienating the United States and its allies, Pakistan needs to hide and mask the presence of these advisors. It does so by employing simple deception tactics used since at least the anti-Soviet jihad. Two separate accounts provided by a Haqqani and a Taliban commander indicate that to blend-in these soldiers do not wear uniforms and keep their beards long.[148] One of these commanders remarked that, "from their looks they were mujahedin."[149] Yet local fighters still know who they are "because of their particular appearance and manner."[150] According to a Taliban commander interviewed by Matt Waldman, these officers participate in important operations and are "'well educated, well trained, give strong orders ... use advanced techniques ... and develop good plans'." Similar to the account provided by Muhammad Yousaf about the anti-Soviet jihad, when these officers participate in major operations "there might be up to three such [Pakistani] commanders involved."[151]

Financial Assistance

Contributions from Pakistan have played an important role in helping to sustain the Haqqani network since the 1980s.[152] Haqqani communication logs from the anti-Soviet jihad reveal that the ISI paid the Haqqanis on a monthly basis. Some of this money likely filtered to the group from the United States. One such message sent out to all mujahidin stations is typical: "BRS [Brothers] I HAVE HANDED OVER YOUR SALARY FOR THE MONTH OF FEB[RUARY] TO YOUR PARTY REP[RESENTATIVE] TODAY. PLS CONFIRM YOU RECEIVED IT ... MAY ALLAH HELP YOU IN JIHAD."[153] Soon thereafter a message was sent back—the money had been received.[154] But just like the Taliban, the Haqqani network has historically never been dependent upon one source of funding. For example, during the anti-Soviet jihad the Haqqanis received financial donations from Pakistan, the Gulf States, the United States, Iran, and wealthy private donors, such as Osama bin Laden, and even individuals from Japan.[155] The historical sophistication and reach of the Haqqani network's fundraising machine is best illustrated by *Manba' al-Jihad*, the subscription-based magazine established by Jalaluddin Haqqani, which, as we have seen, served as a communications and fundraising tool that was specifically tailored to different audiences.[156] As specified in each magazine, all donations were to be made directly to a Haqqani network bank account in Peshawar or to a number of Haqqani representatives in the Gulf.[157] Although the number of *Manba'* subscriptions is not known, the Urdu version of Jalaluddin's publication was distributed to a number of influential mosques and madrassas throughout Pakistan, including Dar al-'Ulum Haqqaniyya.[158] Even if the magazine was not a strong source of revenue it at least helped the Haqqanis to solidify their ties to Pakistan's Islamist parties and religious establishment, which in turn might have facilitated other donations to the organization. For instance, limited evidence suggests that Jamiat Ulema-e-Islam (JUI-S) supported Jalaluddin financially.[159] The Haqqani network also likely made money by reselling scrap metal, guns, and other weapons they had taken from the battlefield.

Today, the Haqqani network likely still maintains a diverse funding stream, and the ISI is believed to play a role in sustaining the group.[160] Like most information pertaining to the ISI, details and sources on this issue are slim and at times they vary, and it is not clear whether Pakistan's security establishment provides funds to the group directly, or just facilitates the movement of funds or looks the other way. According to one Haqqani source, the ISI provided Jalaluddin cash not long after the US invasion of Afghanistan and helped him kick-start his jihad against the Americans.[161] Pakistan's financial support is believed to be so pervasive that one of these commanders even remarked that "Everyone knows Pakistan gives money."[162] (According to US government documents obtained by the *Guardian* and other newspapers in 2008, the US national intelligence officer for South Asia, Dr Peter Lavoy, possessed evidence to support this view.)[163] Statements made by Haqqani and other Taliban commanders from the southeast also suggest that Pakistan, similar to the past, is "paying the salaries of regular fighters and commanders."[164] Information gleaned from the interrogations of Taliban fighters appears to contradict this latter point, however, as regular Taliban soldiers are not believed to "receive salaries or other financial incentives for their work."[165] More likely are payments to the Haqqani senior leadership or the ISI's facilitation of materiel.

It is also believed that the Haqqanis continue to receive money from private donors in the Gulf.[166] The Haqqani network also profits from a sophisticated kidnapping and extortion ring in Pakistan's tribal areas, but little is known about how much money the organization receives from these criminal ventures.[167] Some analysts have speculated that al-Qa'ida financially supports the Haqqani network; however, no evidence exists to substantiate this claim, although it is not outside the realm of possibility.

Extremely little is known about how funds from Pakistan are disbursed to the Haqqani network, or what role the ISI potentially plays in facilitating other sources of funding, such as those from chromite smuggling or private donors in Pakistan and the Gulf. It is reasonable to assume that better financial intelligence and enforcement since 9/11 has made it harder for the Haqqani network to receive and manage its funds, especially those being sent directly to the group and its leaders from abroad.[168] If this assumption is correct, it is likely that the Haqqani network's fundraising streams are not as diverse as they were in the past, potentially leaving the group more financially dependent upon a small group of donors, illicit and licit income streams, and/or Pakistan and its intelligence services (and intermediaries).

Weapons and Materiel

A number of sources suggest that Pakistan has also been supplying the Haqqani network with weapons and other materiel.[169] As has already been established, North Waziristan—specifically Miranshah—has historically functioned as a key logistics and rear supply base for the Haqqani network during numerous conflicts. It is also well known that Pakistan used a strategic supply line linking Miranshah and Khost to resupply the Haqqani network and other fighters during and after the anti-Soviet jihad. The importance of this terrain is best illustrated by the fact that Jalaluddin Haqqani's main headquarter in Zhawara was positioned along this route, and was conveniently located so Haqqani could defend and benefit from it. In 1991, Jalaluddin himself remarked on the region's importance: "Khost is one of four strategic places in Afghanistan. It is very important because Khost has more than tens of routes to Pakistan, and more than eleven routes into other parts of Afghanistan. These routes are strategically important because we use them for shipping weapons and ammunition into the country, and taking our wounded and dead out."[170] Captured Haqqani communication logs from the 1989 to 1992 period indicate that when Haqqani fighters needed equipment they would request it from Pakistan and it would be delivered. One request sent from Jalaluddin in October 1989 is typical: "THE FOLLOWING AMMO VERY NEED FOR CITY GARDEZ: ONE—SMG 7.62 SHELL, TWO—122M GUN, THREE—THE 107 MM SHELL ..."[171]

Given this history, it is not surprising that Pakistan used the same supply routes between Miranshah and Khost to ferry equipment to the Taliban during the latter half of the 1990s.[172] There are even some indications that Pakistan continues to provide weapons and other materiel to Haqqani fighters today. Haqqani and Taliban commanders recently interviewed by the press tell how the ISI has been supplying them with weapons and other materiel since at least 2004. One story recounted by a former Haqqani network commander is particularly illustrative: "The rockets were delivered at night by an ISI logistics officer to a house in Miran Shah. The next morning ... [we] would retrieve them and transport them to the Shawal peaks."[173] ISI agents reportedly taught Haqqani and other fighters how to calibrate and use these rockets against US, Afghan, and Coalition forces in Afghanistan at training camps nestled in the mountains of Shawal (see the section on training above). These rockets were fired into Afghanistan "whenever we could get supplied," according to the former Haqqani commander.[174]

Another account relayed by a different Haqqani commander highlights how Pakistan is helping to facilitate the movement of this materiel and Taliban foot soldiers along old supply routes to the Afghan border. Pakistani "Police or military vehicles transport fighters to the border at night ... Other trucks loaded with guns and ammunition arrive separately, which are distributed at the border. The Pakistani Army, police, intelligence all cooperate ..."[175] It is worth noting that Pakistan used similar tactics (i.e., moving materiel at night) during the Taliban period to obfuscate the movement of equipment and their direct role.[176]

Pakistan's historical use of supply lines in North Waziristan and Khost to assist the Haqqani network and the Taliban lend credence to these firsthand testimonials. Such assistance is useful to the Haqqani network in that it directly facilitates its kinetic activity and enhances its operational capabilities. Even if these accounts are not true, Pakistan is at the very least overlooking the movement of this materiel as the ISI is intimately familiar with supply routes in this region. One should not forget that the ISI heavily used these supply routes for twenty years to supply the Haqqani network and other armed actors.

Conclusion

Pakistan's support for the Haqqani network is complicated and responsive to environmental factors, but time and again during periods of conflict or instability Pakistan has turned to the Haqqani network—and others—to protect its interests in the tribal areas and Afghanistan. Some rationalize the ISI's role in Afghanistan by arguing that it is "unrealistic to expect ISI not to be engaged [in Afghanistan], given its interests in regional foreign policy."[177] The need for the ISI's regional role in Afghanistan is not in dispute, but what is at issue is how the ISI is engaged in Afghanistan and the role it plays as an enabler of groups that operate with al-Qa'ida. The difference today is that the support provided by Pakistan is no longer being deployed against the Soviet Union or the Northern Alliance, but is instead being deployed against Pakistan's stated ally—the United States. The implications of this support are equally concerning as a correlation almost surely exists between the assistance Pakistan provides the Haqqani network and the group's military effectiveness, lethality, and its endurance on the battlefield.

Since 9/11 the United States has provided billions of dollars in military aid to Pakistan to help degrade al-Qa'ida. Pakistan's assistance has led to the capture and/or death of a number of senior al-Qa'ida operatives, and it has come at a significant human cost to Islamabad. Yet Pakistan's favored Afghan proxy is also the very same actor that has served as al-Qa'ida's primary local enabler for over two decades (for details see Part I and the next chapter). Given the ISI's historical sponsorship of the Haqqani network, it is highly unlikely that Pakistan has not been aware of this history. Although less clear, there is some evidence that the ISI helped, and continues to a lesser degree, to facilitate these ties, suggesting that Pakistan could have played a more influential role in the development of al-Qa'ida than has thus far been recognized.

More tangible is Pakistan's reluctance to conduct a military operation against the Haqqani network and the milieu of jihadist actors sheltered in North Waziristan. Pakistan's inaction is fueling the Afghan insurgency and it is also providing space for the Haqqani network to sustain itself and for anti-Pakistan militants and global jihadis to further coalesce and influence one another. Left unchecked, North Waziristan will likely continue to function as an epicenter of international terrorism and thus only further strain US–Pakistan ties. The continued operational proximity between Haqqani and al-Qa'ida commanders also poses challenges for reconciliation efforts, indicating that it is unlikely that the Haqqani network will meaningfully disengage from al-Qa'ida and other global jihadist actors. The fact that Pakistan has offered up the Haqqani network as a way to end the conflict in Afghanistan is reflective of the group's importance and central role, and Islamabad's limited options, but it also makes clear that the United States' and Pakistan's future goals for Afghanistan are in tension. While no options should be taken off the table, any US or Afghan effort to reconcile with the Haqqani network must do so from a position that understands the richness of the Haqqani–al-Qa'ida relationship, and be informed by an acute awareness of the risks that any future negotiated settlement with the Haqqani network presents. The likelihood of the Haqqani option bringing peace to Afghanistan should also be assessed in relation to the failure of prior negotiated settlements orchestrated by Pakistan between it and tribal militants based in the FATA, such as the 2006 Miranshah Peace Accord.[178]

Fig. 1: Haqqani fighter using an anti-aircraft gun during the anti-Soviet jihad period (Source: *Manba al-Jihad*).

Fig. 2: Entrance to the Zhawara base (Source: *Manba al-Jihad*).

Fig. 3: Abdullah Azzam (Source: *Manba al-Jihad*).

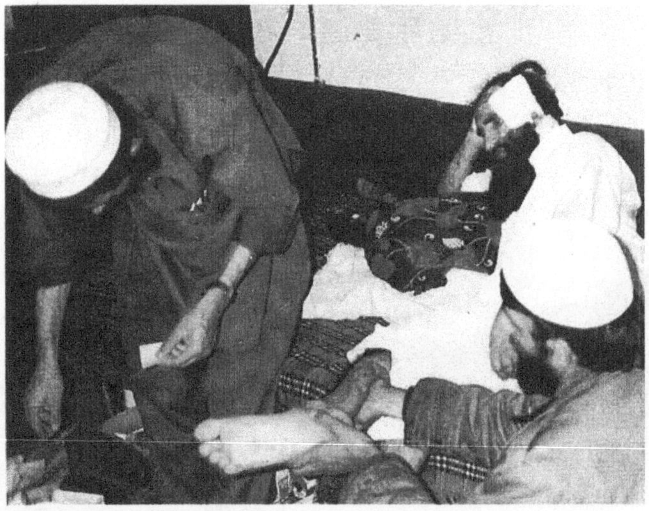

Fig. 4: Jalaluddin Haqqani recovering from injuries sustained during a Soviet and Afghan assault on his Zhawara base in 1987 (Source: *Manba al-Jihad*).

Fig. 5: *Nusrat al-Jihad* cover with Jalaluddin Haqqani and Zia ul-Haq (Source: *Nusrat al-Jihad*).

Fig. 6: Jalaluddin Haqqani and Sami ul-Haq in a General Gathering of the Jamiat-e-Ulama-e-Islam in Lahore, Pakistan, April 1991 (Source: *Manba al-Jihad*).

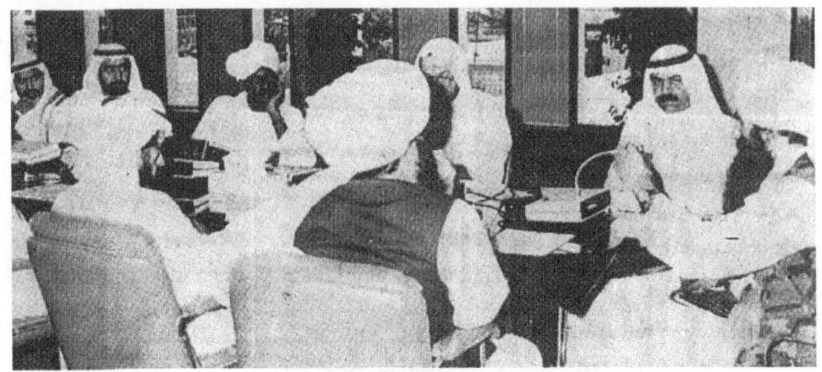

Fig. 7: Jalaluddin Haqqani with Gulf Sheikhs (Source: *Manba al-Jihad*).

Fig. 8: The Manba' 'Ulum madrassa, in North Waziristan, Pakistan circa 1989 (Source: *Manba al-Jihad*).

Fig. 9: Jalaluddin Haqqani (back seated row, third from right), Ahmed Shah Massoud (to his right), Abdul Haq (in white with Afghan pakool) and leaders at the National Commanders Shura, May 1990 (Source: *Manba al-Jihad*).

Fig. 10: Ibrahim Haqqani after the capture of Khost garrison in 1991 (Source: Robert Nickelsberg).

Fig. 11: Uighur fighters cleaning guns in Khost, 1990 (Source: Robert Nickelsberg).

Fig. 12: Ibrahim Haqqani being interviewed by Rahimullah Yusufzai and Lyse Doucet after the capture of Khost in 1991 (Source: Robert Nickelsberg).

Fig. 13: Burhanuddin Rabbani with Jalaluddin Haqqani in the weapons room at the Zhawara base (Source: *Manba al-Jihad*).

Fig. 14: Poster of Osama bin Laden captured at the Zhawara base after the U.S. invasion of Afghanistan in October 2001 (Source: Getty Images).

Fig. 15: Screen grab from a Haqqani network video of President Barack Obama giving the commencement address at the U.S. Military Academy at West Point, 22 May 2010 (Source: *Manba al-Jihad* video).

Fig. 16: Screen grab of the emir of the Pakistani Taliban, Hakimullah Mehsud, sitting with Jordanian suicide bomber, Humam Khalil Abu-Mulal al-Balawi (Abu Dujanah al-Khorasani) before his attack against Forward Operating Base Chapman in December 2009 (Source: *Manba al-Jihad* video).

6

GLOBAL

AL-QA'IDA AND OTHER GLOBAL JIHADIST GROUPS

In the summer of 2005, a diverse group of international militants staged a dramatic escape from a US military prison in Afghanistan. One—a Kuwaiti—had been arrested in Indonesia, another—a Libyan and protégé of veteran al-Qa'ida trainer Abu Laith al-Libi—had been picked up in Pakistan. They had been sharing Cell 119 with two other detainees—a Saudi and a Syrian, the latter having been captured two years earlier in Khost.[1] Due to their stature and experiences with al-Qa'ida, all were sent to the prison at Bagram—the large military base just north of Kabul. Two of them—the Kuwaiti, Omar al-Faruq, and the Saudi, Abu Nasir al-Qahtani—were awaiting transfer to Guantanamo Bay, Cuba.[2]

The details of their escape on 10 July 2005 are murky. After picking the locks to their cells, the detainees "changed out of their bright orange uniforms and made their way through a heavily guarded military base under the cover of night. They then crawled over a faulty wall where a getaway vehicle was apparently waiting for them."[3] Videos featuring the escapees describe their ordeal, and how they hid behind a pile of barley at one point to avoid being seen by local Afghan villagers.[4] The escape of the four al-Qa'ida operatives—believed to have been some of the most important in custody—was an embarrassment for the US military. The detainees either benefited from the "perfect storm" of security lapses or were extremely lucky.[5]

Some believe that the story is too good to be true, and it very well might be. An account shared by a Taliban commander claims that the four detainees did not escape at all, but rather were traded for a number of Coalition soldiers as part of a secret deal.[6] Regardless of what actually transpired, what matters most is where these detainees ended up (North Waziristan); who two of them partnered with (the Haqqani network); and what roles they would eventually play.[7] Perhaps most significant was the trajectory of the Libyan, Abu Yahya al-Libi (killed in a drone attack in North Waziristan in June 2012), who in a short period of time rose to become a key ideologue and one of al-Qa'ida's most important media personalities.[8] To many counterterrorism analysts it was Abu Yahya and not Ayman al-Zawahiri who represented the future of al-Qa'ida.

Given the Haqqani network's rich and storied history with al-Qa'ida and a wide range of foreign fighters, it makes sense that the Bagram escapees ended up in Waziristan and in the Haqqanis' orbit.[9] The Haqqani network walks a fine line though, as thus far the group has not been a direct participant in global jihadist activity—despite assisting al-Qa'ida over multiple decades. The group does not openly advocate for global jihad or publicly support international terrorist attacks against the United States and its allies abroad. In its public pronouncements since 9/11, the Haqqani network has instead expressed its concerns and fight in local terms. The United States is often described by the Haqqani network as an infidel power that is part of the Zionist–Crusader alliance, and is defined as an enemy due to its occupation of Afghanistan. America is also a target of hatred given its policies and actions, many of which are perceived as being an affront to and in direct conflict with Islam. Such rhetoric, while vitriolic and anti-American, reinforces the view that the Haqqani network is a local actor whose support for militancy is limited to Afghanistan. Yet Haqqani leaders have long viewed the United States as a broader enemy, and since at least 1991 the group has openly expressed their support for jihadis in other areas around the globe.

The Haqqani network's support for al-Qa'ida has remained consistent since 9/11. Lethal counterterrorism pressures have brought the two groups into even greater proximity, and a relentless campaign of drone strikes appears to have reinforced their sense of shared suffering and personal loss. This was perhaps most apparent to David Rohde, who along with his translator and driver were held hostage by the Haqqani network in North Waziristan. After spending seven months with his captors, Rohde realized that his Haqqani guards were "really committed to something far broader than simply driving American troops out of Afghanistan."[10] In addition to liberating Kabul, they also wanted to create a global Islamic caliphate that spanned the Muslim world.[11] The Haqqani network's appreciation for al-Qa'ida's worldview became most clear when Rohde's guards told him "how eager they were to carry out suicide attacks in the United States in revenge for the drone strikes."[12] These comments could be dismissed as frustration or mere posturing, or limited to the group's low-level guards, but they also reveal important contradictions between how the Haqqani network publicly portrays itself as a local actor and the broader jihadist interests it has long helped to facilitate. They also reveal that the ideology and vision of Haqqani network members is potentially evolving.

To be sure, Haqqani support for al-Qa'ida and its global jihad has not been limited to the ideological domain. As established in Part I, for the past twenty years the Haqqani network has consistently been al-Qa'ida's most important local partner and facilitator in the region, contributing to the operational development of Bin Laden's group in many ways. The reason why the Haqqani network's role has not been fully appreciated is because the assistance it provides to al-Qa'ida and others is locally oriented and most often transpires in the background. This support is also intentionally masked and hidden from public view.[13] Most important is the Haqqani network's continued willingness—even today—to "open up" its fronts, share its infrastructure (i.e., training camps, etc.), and serve as an operational bridge between local and foreign fighting communities. On a fundamental level, such openness helped to inspire and mobilize foreign fighters, and it distinguished Jalaluddin Haqqani very early on from other Afghan mujahidin commanders. This type of access has been of historic value to al-Qa'ida because "a majority of al-Qaida operatives began their militant careers as war volunteers, and most transnational jihadi groups today are by-products of foreign fighter mobilizations."[14]

Over the course of more than two decades the Haqqani network has been at the center of Afghan foreign fighter mobilizations, and it has been content to let al-Qa'ida and others leverage and use territory under its influence to plot and plan international terrorist attacks, develop their capabilities, and sell their message of global jihad. Haqqani network hosting has been of equal importance and enduring value to the security and survival of al-Qa'ida post-9/11. All of these elements of Haqqani support have continued largely unabated since the late 1980s. And it is revealing that even after al-Qa'ida's 1998 fatwa, its attacks on the US embassies in Africa, 9/11, and the slough of recent international terror plots that link back to North Waziristan and the Haqqanis' orbit, the Haqqani network has never severed its close operational ties to the group. The Haqqani network is therefore best understood as functioning as the most meaningful and enduring platform for the local expression, and continued incubation, of al-Qa'ida's global jihad.

The most valuable "service" that the Haqqani network currently provides foreign fighting entities is local partnering and access to its operational infrastructure in Loya Paktia and North Waziristan. As explained in Part I, this access is historic and has been of central significance to the operational development of al-Qa'ida and the formal launching of its global jihad.[15] A steady stream of statements made by Jalaluddin Haqqani, beginning as early as 1980 and continuing under Sirajuddin to this day, establish the Haqqani network's consistent willingness to open up its fronts and provide foreign fighters with an operational outlet in Afghanistan. One such statement recently made by Sirajuddin reveals this willingness: "The doors are open for all mujahadeen who fight to apply Allah's will ... We are ready to receive all foreigners, including Arabs, who want to fight alongside us."[16] While the policy Sirajuddin outlined is indicative of the Haqqani network's opportunism, it is immensely valuable for foreign fighters of all kinds who want to wage jihad against coalition forces in Afghanistan, especially given the Quetta Shura Taliban's efforts to distance themselves publicly from al-

Qa'ida or foreign fighters.[17] Indeed, the Haqqani network's open embrace of foreign fighters contrasts sharply with the Quetta Shura's reluctance to open its ranks to outsiders.

Access to Haqqani network fronts also provides a number of important secondary benefits to global jihadist organizations, such as al-Qa'ida and the IJU. On a very practical level, Haqqani network access allows transnational jihadis to test new recruits, hone their capabilities, and deepen their operational expertise.[18] It is not lost that Abu Hafs al-Masri and Abu Ubaydah al-Banshiri fought alongside Jalaluddin and his men during the anti-Soviet jihad, or that these men would later rise to become al-Qa'ida's first and most influential military commanders. By providing foreign fighters access to their fronts in Loya Paktia the Haqqani network is fostering transnational militancy and helping to develop the next generation of battle-tested al-Qa'ida commanders, individuals who, just like Abu Hafs and Abu Ubayda, could lend their expertise to future international terrorist plots. This is not to say that al-Qa'ida could not fight in Afghanistan without Haqqani assistance, but rather that al-Qa'ida's effectiveness and ability to operate in Afghanistan would be even more constrained than it already is without it.

An open invitation to join Haqqani network fighters on the battlefield also provides al-Qa'ida and the IJU with an opportunity to deepen their ties with the Haqqani family, making it all the more unlikely that the Haqqanis will not offer them protection and turn against those with whom they have suffered in battle. Even more important, access to the fight in Afghanistan (a classical jihad) is needed to sustain al-Qa'ida's relevance and branding as the leader of the global jihadist movement.[19] The access the Haqqani network facilitates would largely be for naught if it did not also provide a venue for al-Qa'ida and the IJU to create video footage—material that is later edited and sent around the world to communicate their contributions and sustain their campaigns with new financial and human contributions.

Operational Access and Local Partnering

An essential starting point, in light of debates about al-Qa'ida's limited presence in Afghanistan, is to identify the provinces/

regions where al-Qa'ida is most active inside Afghanistan. A useful tool in this regard is the attack and martyrdom videos released by al-Qa'ida through its main digital media production cell al-Sahab. Norwegian scholar Anne Stenersen recently conducted a review of over ninety films released by al-Sahab from 2005 to 2009 as part of its "Pyre for the Americans in the Land of Khorasan" series. Since most of these videos detail the attack location, she was able to establish, according to al-Qa'ida's own reporting, that the highest concentration of operational films released by al-Sahab during this time period were filmed in Khost (thirty), followed by Paktika (fourteen), and Kunar (twelve) provinces.[20] Put another way, footage of attacks in Khost and Paktika, territory where the Haqqanis are the "main executor of Taliban operations," account for 50 percent of all operational videos released by al-Qa'ida as part of this seminal series over a four-year period.[21] These "films do not necessarily mean that Arab or other foreign fighters took part in the attacks, but they do imply a connection between the fighting group and al-Qaeda's media operation[s]."[22] They also reveal that Loya Paktia functions as a central arena for al-Qa'ida's operational and media activity inside Afghanistan. A similar analysis conducted by Intel Center corroborates Stenersen's findings.[23]

Al-Qa'ida's operational footprint is believed to extend beyond Loya Paktia and Kunar to provinces such as Logar, Ghazni, Wardak, Kabul, Zabul, and Nuristan, the first three being areas where the Haqqani network is also active.[24] While these claims are more difficult to establish with certainty, in an interview in June 2009 the now deceased al-Qa'ida leader Mustafa Abu al-Yazid asserted that the group has assisted a number of martyrdom operations in Kabul.[25] The complex and strategic character of recent Haqqani network attacks in Kabul, as well as the tactics used and similar evolution of al-Qa'ida-linked attacks in Pakistan over the same period, suggest some level of overlap and collaboration between the two groups. A multipronged attack carried out in February 2009 against two Afghan ministries and the Directorate of Prisons in Kabul that has been tied to the Haqqani network is particularly illustrative. During the attack, eight individuals—all reportedly wired to suicide vests—deployed in three teams to their respective targets and killed at least twenty people.[26] It is noteworthy that the Kabul attack took place immediately before a visit by Special Envoy Richard Holbrooke and days before the Obama administration was supposed to decide whether to send an additional 30,000 soldiers to the country.[27] If al-Qa'ida cooperation extends as far as Kabul, it is most likely that al-Qa'ida provides training, technical expertise, and potentially suicide bombers to support Haqqani network operations via al-Qa'ida personnel. One good reason for this is operational security: the farther away from the border al-Qa'ida members get the more vulnerable, and dependent upon their Taliban hosts, they become.

The collaborative nature of al-Qa'ida's activity in Loya Paktia is confirmed by other material released by jihadist media outlets, as well as journalistic accounts, interviews with Taliban commanders, and Department of Defense press releases. Collectively, these sources prove that a number of al-Qa'ida and IJU fighting units are horizontally integrated with, and operate alongside, Haqqani network insurgents in Loya Paktia. Most Haqqani network operations in Loya Paktia are carried out by local fighting columns organized along subtribal lines. IJU and al-Qa'ida fighting groups are often small and consist of members from various nationalities, including local Afghans and Pakistanis, and—at least in the case of al-Qa'ida—are believed to be led by an Arab commander.[28] Although the Haqqani network and al-Qa'ida have different command and control hierarchies, al-Qa'ida and other foreign groups are usually operationally subordinate to the Haqqanis in Afghanistan. Al-Qa'ida leader Mustafa Abu al-Yazid explained the dynamics of this relationship in the following way: "our participation in Jihad inside Afghanistan is that we are under the command of the Islamic Emirate [of Afghanistan] and under the field leaders in the Islamic Emirate on the inside [in Afghanistan]. We participate with them ..."[29] A statement made by Sirajuddin Haqqani during an interview in 2008 described the relationship as functioning in the same manner.[30]

Historically, the Haqqani network either integrated foreign fighters into their fighting columns or allowed these fighters to operate semi-independently in separate teams alongside them.[31] The integration of al-Qa'ida with other foreign fighters is still guided by the same principles today. Several sources of information also indicate, however, that these local and foreign fighting groups are even more interwoven and that their command and control hierarchies are not only overlapping, but are also increasingly blurred, as an account provided by a Haqqani network defector in 2008 clearly suggests. After the Taliban's ouster in 2001, North Waziristan functioned as one of the main staging grounds for a complex mix of Afghan, Pakistani, and foreign fighters.[32] According to the Haqqani network defector, within this mix "there were two main and distinct groups. One was largely domestic and made up of Afghan and Pakistani Talibs. The other one was, and is, led by foreign fighters—Arabs, Uzbeks and Chechens." The defector claimed that even though "he served under ... Sirajuddin Haqqani" he was a member of the latter organization, which was led by Abu Laith al-Libi, a jihadist veteran who was killed in a drone attack in Mir Ali, North Waziristan in 2008.[33] Further, even though the defector fought alongside Abu Laith al-Libi he "did not consider himself al-Qaida ... he was Taliban—but the goal was the same."[34]

Specific insights into this integrated relationship can be gleaned by tracking the activity and statements of individuals, such as Abu Laith al-Libi, Abu Nasir al-Qahtani, Abu Yahya al-Libi, and Mustafa Abu al-Yazid, who are believed to have functioned as important nodes in the al-Qa'ida–Haqqani nexus before their reported deaths and/or detention.[35] According to a Haqqani commander, Abu Laith al-Libi had close ties with Nasiruddin Haqqani, Sirajuddin's brother.[36] After their escape from Bagram prison in July 2005, Abu Yahya al-Libi and Abu Nasir al-Qahtani announced the creation a sixty-member Afghan and Arab fighting force to wage jihad in Afghanistan.[37] Numerous videos indicate that this group conducted a number of attacks against Afghan and Coalition forces in Loya Paktia throughout 2005 and 2006.[38] During one of these operations Abu Nasir al-Qahtani led a group of fighters and attacked a US military position in Khost.[39] The joint nature of this attack was highlighted by al-Qahtani himself in a video released by al-Sahab, al-Qa'ida's media arm, in which he stated: "We, along with the brothers in the Taliban movement, carried out an operation against the US center ... in Khost province."[40] In another video released by al-Sahab in 2006, al-Qahtani noted that he had been "warmly received by Taliban" and that they "were happy to have their brothers from al-Qa'ida with them in their fight."[41] In this video al-Qahtani also gives instructions to fighters through a Pashto interpreter. Al-Qahtani's references to the Taliban in these videos are most likely references to Haqqani-linked fighters, given the Haqqani network's dominance and historical influence in Khost. (According to Thomas Ruttig, 95 percent of the commanders in Khost are linked to the Haqqani network.)[42] A similar video from 2006 shows Abu Yahya al-Libi leading a night operation into Afghanistan, while another video released by Labayk media shows Abu Yahya al-Libi teaching a class to local fighters, who in all likelihood were active with the Haqqani network.[43] Other information indicates that Abu Yahya al-Libi served as a liaison between al-Qa'ida and other Afghan and Pakistani militant groups in Waziristan and that he worked with Sirajuddin Haqqani to broker agreements between them.[44]

Even more convincing is al-Qa'ida's claim of responsibility for a multipronged suicide attack against FOB Salerno in Khost in August 2008.[45] During an interview in 2009, al-Qa'ida's commander for Afghanistan—Mustafa Abu al-Yazid—said that this attack was organized by al-Qa'ida and jointly executed with their Taliban partners.[46] On several occasions senior Haqqani network leaders have spoken openly about their close operational relationship with al-Qa'ida, revealing that there "is no distinction between us ... we are all one."[47] Many security analysts believe that the Haqqani network participated in, and likely directed, the botched assault on FOB Salerno.[48] The strongest indication of an al-Qa'ida role in the incident comes from Bryant Neal Vinas, an American al-Qa'ida operative, who was in North Waziristan at the time of the attack and met Mustafa Abu al-Yazid, Abu Yahya al-Libi, Yunis al-Mauritania, Saleh al-Somali, and Rashid Rauf.[49] In an interrogation conducted by Belgian authorities Vinas said that the attack had "been planned by al-Qa'ida leaders and that it went badly."[50] Vinas had such intimate knowledge of the attack that he was even able to identify one of the suicide attackers, with whom he had trained.[51]

A little less than two years later, in May 2010, the Haqqani network led approximately thirty fighters from the TTP, the Islamic

Movement of Uzbekistan (IMU), al-Qa'ida, and the Afghan Taliban to conduct a similar joint suicide attack against Bagram airbase.[52] Although the attack killed one American contractor and wounded nine NATO soldiers, it is largely believed to have been a failure as it resulted in the death of eleven of the attackers, including German al-Qa'ida/IMU operative Bekkay Harrach (also known as Al Hafidh Abu Talha al Almani), and the detention of several others.[53] Statements released by the IMU describe the attack as having been conducted in "coordination and cooperation with other jihadi groups" involving the participation of "Turks, Tajiks, Arabs, Pashtuns and Afghans."[54] Material recovered from Osama bin Laden's compound in Abbottabad, Pakistan, also reveals that Bin Laden knew of Harrach, and was impressed by him.[55] Before his death, Mustafa Abu al-Yazid had told Bin Laden that the young German fighter was on his way to conduct a suicide operation, illustrating that both al-Qa'ida leaders had awareness of the attack against Bagram discussed above.[56]

The death of a Haqqani network family member alongside a veteran al-Qa'ida leader during an attack in Loya Paktia further elucidates this close operational relationship. It is not a coincidence that Muhammed Omar Haqqani, the son of Jalaluddin and brother of Sirajuddin, was killed in a firefight in July 2008 along with Abu-Hasan al-Sa'idi in the Seta Kandao area of Paktia.[57] At the time, al-Sa'idi was believed to be al-Qa'ida's top military commander in southeastern Afghanistan. He also reportedly served as the head of al-Qa'ida's training camps in Loya Paktia for a period after the anti-Soviet jihad.[58] This incident speaks to the depth of Haqqani network and al-Qa'ida ties and illustrates how the intimacy of the personal relationships established during the 1980s and 1990s endure in the operational sphere today. It is likely that Jalaluddin Haqqani would not let his eighteen-year-old son fight with just anybody; Abu-Hasan al-Sa'idi was a trusted confidant. The deaths of other senior al-Qa'ida members in Loya Paktia also highlight the assistance likely provided to key al-Qa'ida affiliates and the Haqqani network's far-reaching ties. Take, for example, the deaths of Abu Dujanah al-Qahtani, the brother of Abu Nasir al-Qahtani, and Abu Sulayman al-Utaybi—two important al-Qa'ida members who were killed together in May 2008 in Paktia province.[59] Prior to his arrival in Afghanistan, Abu Sulayman al-Utaybi worked as a sharia official for the Mujahidin Shura Council and was a senior leader of al-Qa'ida in Iraq (AQI).[60] Given the close ties between al-Qa'ida and the Haqqani network, it is unlikely that the presence of such a high-profile AQI figure operating in Loya Paktia would have escaped Haqqani attention.

The record of joint operations between the IJU and the Haqqani network is equally strong, and it only reinforces the value foreign fighting groups derive from the access and local partnering the Haqqanis provide. The nexus between the Haqqani network, al-Qa'ida, and the IJU is believed to have been facilitated by individuals such as Abu Laith al-Libi.[61] According to Guido Steinberg, "from its headquarters in North Waziristan the IJU has joined the Haqqani network and its escalating fight against coalition forces in Afghanistan."[62] Similar to al-Qa'ida, the vast majority of the IJU's attacks in Afghanistan were conducted in Loya Paktia.[63] The best example of operational collaboration between the IJU and the Haqqani network took place in early March 2008 when a German-Turk drove his truck up to an American base in the Sabari district in Khost and detonated his suicide charge, killing four.[64] The attack was significant because the twenty-eight-year-old suicide bomber, Cüneyt Çiftçi, was Germany's first.[65] Before his arrival in North Waziristan, Cüneyt Çiftçi was already on the radar of German investigators due to his links with several of the Sauerland cell plotters.[66]

What was most revealing about the attack, however, was not the attack itself but the overlapping media response that transpired after it. Within several days, the Taliban, the IJU, and the Haqqani network all claimed responsibility for the incident. The Taliban moved first and their statement was followed by Sirajuddin Haqqani, who telephoned *The News* to provide attack details.[67] Sirajuddin said that he had personally planned the operation and that one of his fighters from Khost rammed the vehicle-borne suicide bomb into the base.[68] Zabihullah Mujahed, a moniker used by all Taliban spokespersons, also linked the attack to the Haqqani network.[69] After a number of days, the IJU issued a statement about the incident and released a martyr video of Cüneyt Çiftçi in which they described the operation as having been coordinated with the Taliban.[70] According to the IJU, the attack was conducted to avenge the death of Abu Laith al-Libi—who advised the group.[71] Then, several weeks later, Jalaluddin Haqqani claimed responsibility for the attack in a rare interview on a Taliban DVD.[72]

This media whirlwind (explored in further detail below) tells us a number of things about the relationship between these three parties and the Haqqani network's sophistication. The fact that all three parties—the Taliban, the Haqqani network, and the IJU—released statements around the same time tells us that the attack was either well integrated or that these actors are very opportunistic. From one perspective, the multiple claims of responsibility suggest that the relationships between the IJU, the Haqqani network, and the Taliban are so tight that it doesn't matter who takes credit for the attack. What is more important is the perception of their involvement and that they are all able to derive benefit from this single event. Another theory postulated by Einar Wigen is that the Haqqani network's claim of responsibility could be the cost the IJU has to pay for Haqqani network support and protection.[73]

The Haqqani network partners with and provides foreign fighting entities operational access to fronts in Afghanistan's southeast for two main reasons. First, on a very practical level, foreign fighting entities provide added manpower and diversify the Haqqani network's resource mobilization networks (for more detail see below). Foreign fighters are also useful as they bring a variety of technical skills that the Haqqani network can use to enhance its effectiveness. Second, and perhaps more importantly, the Haqqani network would not enable or serve as the main partner for foreign fighting entities in Afghanistan if it did not at least tacitly support what groups like al-Qa'ida aim to achieve, especially when one considers the risk that Haqqani leaders assume in being associated with these groups, and the historical ties between them. The Haqqani network remains attractive to al-Qa'ida and other foreign fighters because these groups have limited partnering options. According to Thomas Ruttig, the Haqqani network has also figured out the right formula for how to integrate small foreign fighting units by giving them enough flexibility while still maintaining a measure of command and control—as the wider Taliban networks do with their local networks.[74]

Local partnering and access to Haqqani network infrastructure helps al-Qa'ida and other transnational jihadist groups to remain operationally relevant in Afghanistan. Exposure to training camps and fighting fronts in territory associated with Haqqani units also functions as a "form of entryism" through which new recruits/ fighters can be further radicalized.[75] Therefore, by functioning as an operational bridge between local and foreign fighter mobilizations, the Haqqani network has—for the past two and half decades—been directly facilitating the radicalization of war volunteers.

Enabling Media and al-Qa'ida's Global Relevance to the Afghan Jihad

The operational access and local partnering that the Haqqani network provides has a number of important derivative benefits for al-Qa'ida, the IJU, and other foreign fighting units. One of the most meaningful is that it provides opportunities for al-Qa'ida and others to create local battlefield footage. This is not to say that al-Qa'ida and foreign fighters could not produce battlefield footage in Afghanistan without the Haqqanis, but rather that local partnering makes this a lot easier. This helps to explain why operational videos shot in Loya Paktia are so predominant in al-Qa'ida's media releases. After being filmed in Afghanistan, this digital material is smuggled back into Pakistan where it is edited, branded, and distributed around the world as part of a jihadist media campaign.[76] Time and again, senior al-Qa'ida leaders have commented on the importance of media to their operations. For example, in a personal letter to Mullah Omar, Osama bin Laden mentioned that "It is obvious that the media war in this century is one of the strongest methods; in fact, its ratio may reach 90% of the total preparation for the battles."[77] Ayman al-Zawahiri has made similar comments and identified al-Qa'ida's media activity as one of the group's most important accomplishments.[78] Al-Qa'ida, the Taliban, and the Haqqani network do not have to win tactical battles—they just need to create the perception that they are winning. With that in mind, operational videos from southeastern Afghanistan function as part of a web of segmented media products that are designed to influence public opinion from Dubai to Dallas. They are important precisely because they help al-Qa'ida and the IJU to communicate their relevancy and contributions to the fight in Afghanistan—a classical jihad.[79] In a practical sense, these videos also help al-Qa'ida and the IJU to attract new recruits and demonstrate value to private donors; inputs which are needed to sustain the global jihad.

Similar to al-Qa'ida, the Haqqani network has long recognized the value and importance of media.[80] Scholars have established the importance of Peshawar as a central media hub for jihadist actors during and after the anti-Soviet jihad.[81] Less historical attention, however, has been given to the media produced by militant leaders such as Jalaluddin Haqqani, who operated in places like Miran Shah. The fact that the academic and counterterrorism communities know so little about the Haqqani network's historical publications is reflective of how "old" jihadist print media produced from this region is critically understudied. This is surprising given the lethality and the important role the Haqqani organization plays today. Due to this considerable research gap these communities have largely failed to appreciate how some of the most important media initiatives conducted by these and other parties continue to be interlinked. An instructive example in this regard is Jalaluddin Haqqani's decision to partner with Abu'l-Walid al-Masri to produce his Arabic-, Pashto-, and Urdu-language magazine *Manba' al-Jihad*.[82] It is true that Abu'l-Walid al-Masri was never a formal member of al-Qa'ida, but—just like Abu Musab al-Suri—for close to a decade he served as a key al-Qa'ida advisor, strategist, and trainer.[83] Abu'l Walid was without question an intimate associate of al-Qa'ida's inner network, and one can imagine how Jalaluddin and Abu'l Walid's experiences with *Manba' al-Jihad* were shared and recounted to those who had access to these overlapping networks.

Perhaps because of their shared history, the Haqqani network appears to have been more understanding and lenient towards al-Qa'ida's media operations than Mullah Omar and the Quetta Shura. For instance, as established in Part I, it is not a coincidence that Osama bin Laden announced al-Qa'ida's 1998 fatwa—a declaration of war against the United States—and the launch of the World Islamic Front from the al-Siddiq training camp in Khost and not in Kandahar. Bin Laden's 1998 "fatwa" was a defining event in the history of al-Qa'ida and international terrorism, yet little attention has been given to the significance of where, specifically in whose backyard, this press conference was delivered.[84]

More recently, Sirajuddin and Badruddin Haqqani have shown an interest in media and both have worked hard to further develop the Haqqani network's capabilities in this area.[85] The rise in the status and prestige of Sirajuddin has been accompanied by a similar rise in the group's digital media profile, suggesting that the Haqqani network is learning from or is being advised by more experienced media hands. The slow, but steady, emergence of Manba' al-Jihad as a digital production company speaks to this trend, as does Sirajuddin's recent question and answer session in an Arabic-language jihadist forum (see below for more details), especially when one considers the connections that are required to facilitate such an event. By the authors' assessment, Sirajuddin Haqqani is the only known Taliban commander who has conducted this type of exchange on an Arabic-language forum; an act which is suggestively reminiscent of a question and answer session Ayman al-Zawahiri conducted on a forum back in December 2007.[86] It appears as though al-Qa'ida-linked media professionals could be assisting the Haqqani network in these efforts. In an interview in June 2009 Mustafa Abu al-Yazid alluded to such cooperation between the network and the Taliban.[87]

There are a growing number of indications that local Haqqani partnering also extends to the media sphere and that the group is part of an interlinked media nexus that involves Labayk media, al-Sahab, Badr-al-Tawheed/Elif Media, and Sawt al-Islam.[88] Each of these production companies function as an independent unit, but at the same time they also appear to be working together in what could be characterized as a media consortium. The make-up of production companies involved in this consortium directly reflects the major foreign groups sheltered in North Waziristan who fight alongside the Haqqani network in Loya Paktia. This suggests that Haqqani network cooperation is not limited to the operational sphere, but that it extends to some functional areas as well. The full extent of cooperation is not known; however, it appears that collaboration between these entities is mostly focused on the digital realm, and less on the production of print publications like al-Qa'ida's Arabic-language *Vanguards of Khorasan* magazine. Overlap between these entities has been revealed through testimonials and can be seen through their use of borrowed footage, cross-promotion, and guest appearances, and the connections and circumstances surrounding the martyrdom of a number of jihadist media personalities.

Before examining this evidence of integration, it is useful to establish how the media products released by these outlets are different and why these groups have an incentive to coordinate their activities and assist one another. An essential starting point is the concept of media segmentation. These entities cooperate with one another but do not necessarily compete because their media products are tailored to different audiences and segmented across a number of levels. At its most basic level, media products are segmented within groups between local (or internal) and global (or external) lines.[89] In a 2010 interview Sirajuddin Haqqani explained this concept and how it guides his group's approach to media:

> Media-wise, we work on two levels, internally and externally. On the internal level, we present our media materials in accordance with the traditions and culture of our Afghan people. Our enemies admitted that the Islamic Emirate has surpassed them in this field. As for the external level, the main reason for the media's weakness is the siege imposed on us by the international media, which is loyal to the United States and the West. Moreover, we have limited accesses to the necessary tools.[90]

This quote indicates that the Haqqani network is conscious of the different audiences it wants to affect and that it tries to tailor its messages accordingly. As terrorism scholar Brynjar Lia has noted, there are clear aims and benefits associated with this distinction: "Internally, it [jihadist media] seeks to increase and strengthen morale and provide ideological cohesion; externally, its aims are proselytising and recruitment, as well as waging psychological warfare."[91]

When viewed from a broader level, jihadist media products are also segmented across groups. For example, while the majority of al-Qa'ida's videos aim to influence "global" audiences in the Middle East and the West, Haqqani network videos are tailored to cultivate "local" influence with populations in Afghanistan and Pakistan. This is not to say that Manba' al-Jihad functions as al-Qa'ida's local media arm or that al-Qa'ida does not release locally oriented products, but rather that al-Qa'ida and the Haqqani network draw strength from this segmentation as their products are mutually reinforcing.[92] A third layer of segmentation occurs between categories of groups (i.e., local groups, global jihadist organizations). This dimension is illustrated by differences between the media operations of two global jihadist groups—al-Qa'ida and the IJU—who are mainly focused on influencing "external" audiences. The IJU primarily tailors many, if not most, of its messages to garner support from German and Turkish audiences. Al-Qa'ida, on the other hand, has released several media products tailored to influence these same audiences, but these audiences do not represent a primary line of effort for the group. Put more simply, the IJU is mostly focused on the German and Turkish market. The Turkistan Islamic Party (TIP) similarly tailors their messages to Uighur and Chinese audiences. Segmentation across these three different levels is useful as it allows each group to target their message and cultivate influence with the population they most want to affect. Segmentation also reduces the space for media competition between these actors. For these reasons, it is in the interests of al-Qa'ida, the IJU, and the Haqqani network to segment their products across the consortium.

The players involved in this media nexus are conscious of the need to separate their activities, minimize public overlap, and carefully manage the content of any messages that carry their brand. Such awareness could help to explain why they do not appear in one another's operational videos even though these groups fight together in Afghanistan. Doing so could distort how each militant group and its composition and role is seen and understood. For example, a recent video released by Manba' al-Jihad called the "Caravan of the Ghazis" highlights steps taken by the Haqqani network to ensure their videos project a local and not a regional or global image of the group. A significant portion of the video is devoted to statements by a number of "martyrs." All of the statements except three are directly recorded and delivered by each fighter in Pashto with accents from southeastern Afghanistan. However, the last three fighters—Shamsulhaq, Abdul Rahman, and Noorullah—seem to be foreigners because their statements are narrated in voiceover. It is not known what language they speak, as their own voices are silenced during the voiceover.[93] This could be read as an attempt by the Haqqani network to mask the involvement of outsiders so they can perpetuate their image as a local actor in Afghanistan's conflict.

Abu Laith al-Libi and a number of Arabs who operated within his orbit in Loya Paktia and North Waziristan were among the primary drivers of this media nexus after 9/11.[94] It appears that Labayk Media, a media organization that Abu Laith al-Libi founded, functioned as an important venue for al-Qa'ida, local Taliban fighters, and the IJU to learn from one another, develop their digital media capabilities, and distribute images of their battle exploits around the globe. Labayk first began releasing videos in 2005 and the group is believed to have remained quasi-independent for some time until integrating its operations with al-Sahab.[95] Abu Laith al-Libi's passion for media is reflected in a eulogy celebrating his death from an airstrike conducted in North Waziristan in February 2008. According to this testimonial, Abu Laith al-Libi: "afforded great importance to the media and his concern with spreading the news of the operations carried out by his brothers who were proficient in media issues ..."[96] The eulogy also commented on the importance of his media work and the broad impact it reportedly made.

The media appearances of two associates of Abu Laith al-Libi—Abu Yahya al-Libi and Abu Nasir al-Qahtani—reinforce Anne Stenersen's findings about the centrality of Loya Paktia to al-Qa'ida's media operations. They also highlight an unstated qualitative dimension to her analysis: that many of the videos featuring senior al-Qa'ida commanders and ideologues have primarily been filmed in areas where the Haqqani network exerts the most influence. After their escape from Bagram prison, Abu Yahya al-Libi and Abu Nasir al-Qahtani filmed attacks conducted in Loya Paktia for a number of operational videos released by al-Sahab and Labayk Media.[97] In one video released by Labayk Media in 2005, Abu Nasir al-Qahtani recounts and shows video of an attack that Abu Laith al-Libi and "some brothers from the Taliban" conducted against FOB Salerno earlier that year.[98] The physical presence of senior al-Qa'ida members and their media role in Loya Paktia is further illustrated by the arrest of Abu Nasir al-Qahtani by Coalition forces in Khost in November 2006. According to Abu Yahya al-Libi, al-Qahtani was arrested while videotaping the Khost airport.[99] Other independent news reports confirm al-Qahtani's capture and the recovery of a camera and a number of weapons during the raid.[100]

Given the nature of the Haqqani network's overall control in the region, there is reason to believe that the attacks carried out by Abu Laith al-Libi, Abu Yahya al-Libi, and Abu Nasir al-Qahtani inside Loya Paktia were conducted with Haqqani approval, direct support, and/or some form of oversight. The circumstances surrounding the death of Omar Haqqani, the son of Jalaluddin and brother of Sirajuddin, in Khost even suggest that the Haqqani network's and al-Qa'ida's media operations in Loya Paktia are integrated at the tactical level.[101] As mentioned previously, Omar was killed alongside veteran al-Qa'ida commander Abu-Hasan al-Sa'idi. According to local accounts, Omar was videotaping the operation when he died.[102] What remains unclear is for which group the younger Haqqani was filming and who would have access to his material. Additional evidence explored below sheds light on this issue and other areas of media collaboration between the Haqqani network, al-Qa'ida, and other foreign groups.

The Labayk videos featuring Abu Yahya al-Libi and al-Qahtani also provide a useful lens to understand how local footage shot in Loya Paktia is valuable for recruitment and even touches those convicted in international terrorism plots.[103] One of the many observers of Labayk videos was Hammad Khürshid, a young Danish citizen of Pakistani origin who was convicted in October 2008 of plotting to conduct a terror attack in Denmark using explosives.[104] Motivated by a desire to fight in Afghanistan, Khürshid left Denmark in 2007 and eventually made his way to an al-Qa'ida training camp in North Waziristan where he learned how to make explosives and is believed to have met Abu Nasir al-Qahtani and Abu Ubaydah al-Masri.[105] Police surveillance of Khürshid's apartment indicates that he and a co-conspirator watched "suicide bomber martyr videos, footage of a decapitation and other seditious material" to keep themselves occupied.[106] According to Danish investigators and notes taken at the court trial, while watching a clip of the four Bagram escapees Khürshid described al-Qahtani, who he saw in the video, as a very close friend.[107] Labayk media had produced the video. Captured al-Qa'ida operative Bryant Neal Vinas had linked in with the same group of trainers during his time in North Waziristan and had a similar experience. Vinas even appeared in an al-Qa'ida video with the group's ideologue Abu Yahya al-Libi.[108] The case of Hammad Khürshid indicates the value of al-Qa'ida's operational videos and how they can be used not only to recruit, but also to sustain the commitment of aspiring jihadis who aim to attack targets in the West.

Borrowed Footage and Overlapping Attack Claims

The fact that media outlets run by al-Qa'ida, the IJU, and the Haqqani network have used the same video footage suggests that these groups are directly collaborating, or are at least leveraging one another's work. For example, a Labayk Media photo album released in December 2006 featured material borrowed from an al-Sahab film distributed several months prior.[109] Einar Wigen discovered similar overlap between the IJU and the Haqqani network. In its claim of responsibility for a suicide attack in Khost on 3 March 2008 the Haqqani network used the same footage of the event as the IJU.[110] However, the footage shown on the Haqqani DVD was branded by its own media outlet—Manba' al-Jihad—and not by the IJU's media production company Badr al-Tawheed.[111] Hanna Rogan has highlighted the implication of this type of behavior, noting that "the use of the same footage in productions by *Labbayk* and *as-Sahab* ... indicates a certain interaction between the two media foundations, despite their proclaimed distinctiveness."[112] The Haqqani–IJU example also illustrates the sophistication of the media consortium's operations, and specifically, how local and global actors are leveraging the same attack to build cachet with different audiences. Take, for instance, the fact that both the IJU and the Haqqani network used different names for the suicide bomber who conducted the 3 March attack. In material distributed on the Internet, the IJU identified the bomber as a German-Turk, while Sirajuddin Haqqani told a Pakistani newspaper that the bomber was named Abdullah and was a local resident of Khost.[113] By acting in this way, both groups appealed to their primary support base and were able to portray the same attack to different audiences as being both local and global. It is as though the attack occurred twice.

Cross-Promotion and Guest Appearances

A more clear and visible indicator of media collaboration among al-Qa'ida, the IJU, the Pakistani Taliban, and the Haqqani network is cross-promotion.[114] While each of these organizations maintains their own digital media outlets, a number of guest interviews indicate that al-Sahab, Labayk media, and Badr-al-Tawheed/Elif Media operate in close proximity to one another and are leveraging each other's brands. This activity revolves around a number of key commanders and strategists who appear in videos produced both by their respective organizations and by other aligned groups. For example, on an internal level, al-Qa'ida members Abu Laith al-Libi, Abu Yahya al-Libi, and Abu Nasir al-Qahtani have been featured prominently in a number of Labayk and al-Sahab media productions.[115] Abu Yahya al-Libi's appearance in a May 2009 IJU video, which also featured the IJU's leader, is one example of how cross-promotion works external to al-Qa'ida.[116] The separate appearances of Mullah Dadullah, Hafiz Gul Bahadur, and Hakimullah Mehsud in al-Sahab videos illustrates the dual nature of this dynamic and the use of al-Qa'ida's media platform to promote Afghan and Pakistani Taliban leaders. Al-Sahab's video interview with Haqqani subcommander Mullah Sangeen suggests that the Haqqani network also has access to and is benefiting from al-Qa'ida's media expertise. When viewed in isolation these guest interviews are not that revealing, but when looked at collectively they demonstrate the existence of an interlinked media web, which is comprised of the major local and foreign groups that are based in North Waziristan and are operationally active with the Haqqani network in Loya

Paktia. Due to this it can reasonably be assumed that North Waziristan functions as the primary staging ground and facilitation point for this type of activity. As indicated above and below, media collaboration between these groups is not limited to cross-promotion but also includes less visible forms of assistance such as the sharing of resources and technical expertise.

Martyrdom Biographies and Connections of Jihadist Media Personalities

The network associated with the December 2009 suicide attack against FOB Chapman in Khost, which killed seven CIA officers, also speaks to the broader nature of the Haqqani network's media ties and the existence of an integrated media syndicate in Waziristan.[117] It also solidifies the close personal and operational ties between the Haqqani network, al-Qa'ida, and those who lead and continue to develop the TTP. The individual who conducted the attack, Humam Khalil Abu-Mulal al-Balawi (also known as Abu Dujanah al-Khorasani), was an influential writer on a prominent Arabic-language jihadist forum (al-Hesbah) who was recruited and sent by Jordanian and US intelligence agents to the FATA to collect intelligence on Ayman al-Zawahiri.[118] Instead of cooperating with these authorities, Abu Dujanah joined forces with the TTP and al-Qa'ida and turned on his intelligence contacts.[119] What was most revealing about the attack was which organization claimed responsibility for it, where it occurred, and the media activity that transpired afterword. The first organization to celebrate the attack publicly was al-Qa'ida, which noted in its media release that the "the appropriate media entity will publish his [the suicide bomber's] story ... in a proper production."[120] This statement suggests that al-Qa'ida had prior knowledge of the attack and that the TTP was soon planning to release a video about the incident.[121] Not long after, the TTP formally claimed responsibility for the attack through a series of videos that featured al-Balawi and TTP leader Hakimullah Mehsud.[122] The Haqqani network remained silent on this issue, but according to Michael Scheuer, "There is no way this operation would have occurred in Khost without the knowledge and active support of Jalaluddin Haqqani and/or his son."[123]

Direct Haqqani network ties to al-Balawi are hard to prove and an account told by Joby Warrick suggests that Sirajuddin Haqqani refused to meet with him due to his concerns that the Jordanian was a spy.[124] While this might be the case, other information illustrates that Haqqani network leaders were one person removed from a network of Arab foreign fighters and media operators linked to the Jordanian suicide bomber, suggesting that Sirajuddin's group was tied to the attack—or at least had knowledge of it. The centerpiece to this story involves an interview that Sirajuddin Haqqani conducted with al-Balagh media correspondent Abu-Dujanah al-San'ani (also known as Mohammed Naqaa al-Hamli) in April 2010.[125] Less than one month after conducting the interview, that very same correspondent was killed in North Waziristan while making a suicide bomb for himself.[126] Similar to the Jordanian suicide bomber, al-Hamali "was also a prolific contributor to web-based jihadist social networking forums, particularly the Falluja Islamic Network."[127] Even more revealing is the death and background of another jihadist writer from Yemen, Saddam Hussein al-Hussami (also known as Ghazwan al-Yemeni), who had ties to al-Balawi and al-Hamali and who was also killed in North Waziristan, albeit several months earlier.[128] An analysis of al-Hussami's online activity and the jihadist community's response to his death by Evan Kohlmann is worth quoting at length:

> In early October 2009, al-Yemeni [al-Hussami] had posted a flurry of requests via the chat forum on behalf of "the Jalaluddin Haqqani Organization in the Shadow of the Islamic Emirate of Afghanistan." In one such message, he appealed, "we, your brothers from the Jalaluddin Haqqani Organization, have encountered some problems in regards to the subjects *Tawheed* and *Aqeedah*, and we want the email or website of the renowned shaykhs in this field ..."[129]

Other analysis by Kohlmann confirms that al-Balawi, al-Hamali, and al-Hussami all knew one another and that al-Hussami had been trained by al-Qa'ida.[130] This suggests that the Haqqani network was not only connected to this group, but that it was working directly with it.

While the media connections between the Haqqani network, TTP, al-Qa'ida, and other groups allows these entities to share and/or leverage resources, this type of cooperation also poses risks for these groups as it illustrates how vulnerable media personnel could be to precise counterterrorism measures, and the potential cascading effects that could be achieved by targeting them.[131] Shared reliance on similar technicians or media resources suggests that recent calls made by Sirajuddin for media support might not be limited to the Haqqani network alone and could be a signal of more pervasive media problems. A plea made by Sirajuddin in April 2010 on an Arabic-language forum is illustrative:

> I would like to appeal to our Muslim brothers, in particular to the scholars, intellectuals, writers, businessmen, experts, youth, and media professionals to help us in our cause and jihad. This help could be by issuing fatwas, preparing fighters ... or by providing media expertise through TV satellite channels, Islamic news network websites on the Internet, newspapers and magazines, or by any possible means.[132]

Due to the Haqqani network's integration with al-Qa'ida on the battlefields of southeastern Afghanistan one could interpret Sirajuddin's call as also being a plea for media assistance from the latter group. Given al-Qa'ida's strong reliance on media (and it being an area where the group has usually been strong) such an admission would likely be more embarrassing for the group. It would also be an open indication that the group faced deep problems at the core of its capabilities. Even if this is not the case, Sirajuddin's statement establishes that his group faces a shortage of media equipment and experts which al-Qa'ida, the TTP, the IJU, or its other militant partners have not been able to fill. These dynamics remind of us of the blending of media capabilities between and across groups and the blurring of functional boundaries between militant groups based in North Waziristan.

"Brotherhood" and Safe haven

Another important benefit that the Haqqani network provides al-Qa'ida members and other foreign fighters is safe haven. Elements of the Pakistani state continue to protect the Haqqani family today because the Haqqani network is "good" Taliban (i.e., they do not attack the Pakistani state) and still holds value as a strategic asset and/or hedge. The central problem with Pakistan's calculus, however, is that it assumes the Haqqani network is limited to acting in a local capacity across the border in Afghanistan and that its activity can be neatly separated from a number of local and global jihadist groups, such as the TTP and al-Qa'ida, that are waging war against Pakistan and the United States. The trouble, as established in Part I, is that the Haqqani network has been intertwined with and has evolved alongside many of these entities for the past two decades.[133] Its ties are so deep that today the Haqqani network functions as a central nexus between them and is helping to facilitate their activity and survival.[134] It is not an accident that mid- and senior-level al-Qa'ida commanders are killed alongside Sirajuddin Haqqani's brothers in both Afghanistan and Pakistan.[135] Nor is it an accident that the Haqqani network has shared criminal infrastructure with the TTP.[136] David Rohde's account of the overlap between the Haqqani network and these other actors in North Waziristan is particularly revealing:[137]

> In terms of militancy, my [Haqqani network] guards took turns taking bomb making classes from foreign militants about how to make roadside bombs that would kill Afghan, American and NATO soldiers in Afghanistan. I also met and lived with suicide bombers who were coming out of local [Pakistani] religious schools known as madrases [*sic*], and clearly there was a lot of ideological indoctrination going on in local schools, and there were also foreign militants present even walking around in the bazaars in the local towns very confident.

One effect of Pakistan's support for the Haqqani network, given this overlap, is that ISI protection indirectly contributes to the security of groups like al-Qa'ida, the IJU, ETIM/Turkistan Islamic Party, and the TTP.[138] Haqqani sheltering of foreign fighters and al-Qa'ida personalities is historic, as during the anti-Soviet jihad Jalaluddin Haqqani provided residences in Miranshah, and likely in Peshawar, to a number of Arab war volunteers who would later play leading roles in al-Qa'ida.[139] According to Abu'l Walid, in the late 1980s the Arabs had two main houses in Miranshah, at least one of which was established by Jalaluddin. This guesthouse was located next to a "big hospital" and close to Jalaluddin's primary residence.[140] In April 1986, Abd al-Rahman and Abu Ubaydah attended a meeting at the guesthouse to plan operational matters as they were interested in "forming a group to attack the airport in Khowst."[141] Abu'l-Walid al-Masri also spent a significant amount of time there and described how the house functioned as a "workshop for mechanical and electrical works" to develop and modify weapons, including rockets.[142] A documented exchange between Abu'l Walid and Jalaluddin in the spring of 1988 is even more revealing, as it illustrates the elder Haqqani's clear willingness to provide additional facilities for the Arabs even when the jihad was drawing to a close and there was discussion of a settlement. It also indicates Jalaluddin's future operational plans to cooperate with Abu-'Abdallah, Osama Bin Ladin's *nom de guerre,* to reclaim the city of Khost.[143]

Abu'l Walid: What is the story with the settlement?

[J.] Haqqani: Failing, so far, each party is adamant about their opinion regarding the upcoming new government in Kabul.

Abu'l Walid: What about bringing our families to live in Miranshah after the settlement; so we can participate in Jihad?

[J.] Haqqani: We will purchase the land adjacent to *Manba' Al-Jihad* School ... you agree and decide on your needs as well as the number of families coming.*

Abu'l Walid: Does your next plan for Khowst include the seizure of Torgar Mountain?

[J.] Haqqani: We have a plan to attack Torgar in Ramadan and we will discuss that with Abu-'Abdallah [Osama Bin Laden]; so what do you think?

It is also believed that Jalaluddin was one of the key organizers of al-Qa'ida's escape from Afghanistan after the toppling of the Taliban and the events at Tora Bora.[144] Indeed, "Ayman al-Zawahiri's wife was taking refuge in a Haqqani-owned building on the Afghan side of the border when she was killed by a U.S. airstrike in late 2001."[145] Also well established is the fact that the Haqqani organization, along with other local partners, helped al-Qa'ida to establish a safe haven in Pakistan's tribal areas.[146] Some have even identified Jalaluddin Haqqani as the key organizer.[147] Given this history,

* The Manba' al-Jihad school is likely Haqqani's Manba' 'Ulum madrassa.

it should not come as a surprise that the Haqqani network continues to serve as an important protector of al-Qa'ida, IJU, IMU, and a number of smaller jihadist groups with which it operates in Afghanistan.[148]

It is revealing that several al-Qa'ida leaders and Haqqani family members have been killed alongside one another in drone attacks conducted in North Waziristan. For example, Abu Haris—al-Qa'ida's operations chief in Pakistan—and three other al-Qa'ida fighters and several Haqqani family members were reportedly killed in a drone attack against the Haqqani-controlled Manba' 'Ulum madrasa on 8 September 2008.[149] A document captured in Afghanistan in 2005 provides a very practical example of how the Haqqani network shelters a mix of foreign fighters and Pakistani militants.[150]

> Mullah Abdullah is from Logar and has 30 fighters of different nationalities: Afghans; Uzbeks; Chinese; Chechens; and two Arabs. They've received military training from the training camp ... It is managed by Mullah Dawood from Logar, and an Arab is the head of this camp. Under the supervisions of Mullah Dawood, they arrived in Miran Shah after spending a night at a Madrassa in the headquarters of Haqqani. Then, under the guidance of Mullah Dawood, they entered the south of Afghanistan via Babrak checkpoint. Because of a military clash with Afghan forces as they were crossing the border, three Pakistanis were injured and one was killed. After the battle only a limited number of people entered Afghanistan, and others returned to Miran Shah.

Additional revelation of these close ties also comes from Sirajuddin Haqqani himself. During an interview with an *NBC* journalist in 2008 Sirajuddin boasted that, unlike Afghan President Hamid Karzai, the Arab and other foreign groups operating alongside him were "under his control."[151] A recent statement by al-Qa'ida leader Mustafa Abu al-Yazid confirms Sirajuddin's claim. Haqqani network protection of al-Qa'ida leaders is not just historic, it is also being extended to the younger generation of al-Qa'ida fighters as well; individuals and groups who are likely to play an important role for al-Qa'ida and other like-minded groups in the future. For example, it is believed that before his death German-Moroccan al-Qa'ida fighter Bekkay Harrach lived under the protection of

Sirajuddin Haqqani in North Waziristan.[152] Members of the IJU are believed to enjoy similar forms of protection, but at some cost. German scholar Guido Steinberg suggests that to maintain their presence in Mir Ali, North Waziristan, the IJU "had to enter into an alliance with the Haqqani network."[153] Since the late 1990s members of TIP have been present and had infrastructure in territory controlled by Haqqani, and it is likely that the bonds of brotherhood between these organizations are just as strong today.[154] The death of Abdul Haq al-Turkistani, the leader of TIP, in a recent drone strike in North Waziristan is an important indication that this might be the case.[155]

Haqqani Network Incentives and Benefits to Maintain their Global Value Proposition

The Haqqani network receives a number of important benefits in exchange for the value it provides to foreign fighters and global jihadist groups. Broadly, the Haqqani network has an incentive to foster its ties to international jihadis and continue providing the services explored above because such connections diversify the resource mobilization networks to which the Haqqanis have access. The Haqqani network can then use these other networks to augment its capabilities and sustain its operations over the long term, as diversification makes the organization less susceptible to a single point of failure. In that sense, access to different resource streams contributes to the Haqqani network's resiliency and it can be used as a point of leverage over other actors, such as the ISI, upon which the Haqqani network also relies. The most important functional benefits that the Haqqani network derives from access to global jihadist resource mobilization networks include: financing, added manpower, access to technological innovations and technical experts, and organizational prestige.

Financing

Little public information exists about the financial relationship between the Haqqani network and global jihadist groups, specifically al-Qa'ida. While there is no "smoking gun" that al-Qa'ida has directly funded the Haqqani network, there is evidence that Osama bin Laden and al-Qa'ida have provided other critical forms of assistance to the Haqqani network, as well as facilitated financial contributions to the Afghan group. In most cases, this assistance took the form of services which held monetary value. Perhaps the best example is Bin Laden's provision of heavy-construction equipment during the anti-Soviet jihad to help Jalaluddin Haqqani build his elaborate headquarters at Zhawara and fortify other fighting positions in Khost.[156] As discussed in Part I, funds from al-Qa'ida continued to flow into Afghanistan throughout the 1990s, albeit at lower and sometimes frustrating levels given al-Qa'ida's presence in Sudan.[157] It is well known that al-Qa'ida bankrolled a number of jihadist training camps that operated in Khost with some form of Haqqani oversight.[158] Jalaluddin Haqqani likely would not have allowed al-Qa'ida to operate its camps in his control zones unless he received something in return. Although unproven, Steve Coll has speculated that Haqqani financially supported some of al-Qa'ida's training camps.[159] At a minimum, Jalaluddin Haqqani likely leveraged the trainers and recruits al-Qa'ida supplied at these camps to develop his organization's capabilities, broaden his global fundraising ties, and curry favor with anti-Kashmir jihadist groups and Pakistan's ISI who were also tied to several of these camps.

Funding from state sources dropped off precipitously at the end of the anti-Soviet jihad, making it likely that it was during the post-1989 period when donations from private sources and their business enterprises became all that more valuable to the Haqqani family.[160] Ever since the late 1970s Jalaluddin Haqqani has had strong ties to leaders and patrons in the Gulf, and he made numerous trips there before, during, and after the anti-Soviet jihad to raise funds. Some of these trips were for diplomatic and religious purposes (i.e., to attend the Hajj) but others had a fundraising component, and often the purposes of these trips blended together. According to Steve Coll, while in Saudi Arabia to participate in the Hajj Haqqani set up tents in Mecca to fundraise among those there for the pilgrimage.[161] Jalaluddin expressed his appreciation for Gulf support during a trip to the United Arab Emirates in 1991, where he remarked that his "brothers in the Gulf were the best help to the Mujahedeen in terms of money, supplies and men as well."[162]

To solicit and collect private donations in the region Jalaluddin Haqqani established a number of offices and facilitators based in the Gulf. Those who wanted to contribute could either reach out to someone in the network or call Haqqani fundraisers located in Saudi Arabia (Riyadh) or the United Arab Emirates (Abu Dhabi, Al-Aiyn, Al-Sharqa, Dubai, Bada Zayed) whose numbers were openly published in every Arabic-language issue of *Manba' al-Jihad*.[163] These representatives remained active until at least the early 1990s. This is not to suggest that all private donors who contributed money to the Haqqani enterprise also donated money to al-Qa'ida, although it is likely that some did, or that it was only local Arabs who provided funds through these channels.[164] That being said, given the depth of ties and the historical linkages between the Haqqani network and al-Qa'ida, it is not unreasonable to suspect that the former leveraged and benefited from al-Qa'ida's fundraising apparatus and list of wealthy Gulf contacts.

A Harmony document summarizing the interrogations of several Arabs detained by al-Qa'ida and the Taliban on suspicions that they were spying for foreign intelligence services during the late 1990s makes this overlap more clear. The document seems to indicate that a number of individuals who came to join al-Qa'ida during the late 1990s also collected funds for the Haqqani network from private donors in the United Arab Emirates. In an interview conducted after his release, one of those detained—Muhammad al-Bayid, who went by the alias Abu al-Mubtassim (a name which appears in the captured document)—repudiated the charges against him and stated that al-Qa'ida members Saif al-Adel, Abu Hafs al-Masri, and Abu Jandal interrogated him in secret prisons in Kandahar.[165] It was only after Jalaluddin Haqqani and Abu Hareth al-Urdani intervened that Mullah Omar pardoned Abu Mubtassim and let him go.[166] In a recent memoir Abu Jandal corroborated Abu Mubtassim's account and provided his own take on this episode.[167] Two different excerpts from the captured document help situate this overlap and are worth quoting at length:

Interrogation of Abu Talha[168]

Question: Who are the Afghans that you know and you met previously?

Answer: Jalal-al-Din Haqqani whom I met in the Emirates and his brother Khalil [Haqqani].

Question: What happened (illegible) and what was your role in the money paid to you?

Answer: I swear by Allah that I did not take any money from the Intelligence. But when I went to Pakistan I had a paper from Haqqani, then he sent Abu al-Harith [al-Urduni] the Jordanian because (illegible). He stayed at Haqqani's home. He wrote me a note, and Abu al-Harith [al-Urduni] met with Rustum Shah the [Pakistan] Minister of Interior in Islamabad.

In the morning, Abu al-Harith came to me accompanied by Haqqani's son whose name is Nasir[uddin], who is studying in Miram Shah (illegible), and I went to Towr Kham, and later to Peshawar, [where] I stayed at Abu Talha's (al-Assal) house.

Interrogation of Unidentified Individual[169]

Question: Who are the Afghans that you know and that you dealt with in the past?

Answer: I was in the Emirates in touch with the office of Haqqani and I sent the youth through them, I also collected money for them, and Jalal-al-Din Haqqani knows me when I was in the Emirates with him and Khost and Gardiz [*sic*].

Evidence presented in the trial *United State of America vs Enaam M. Arnaout* also highlights how the Benevolence International Foundation (BIF)—an Islamic charity that provided material support to al-Qa'ida and Gulbuddin Hekmatyar throughout the 1990s—also provided funds and materiel to Jalaluddin Haqqani's parent organization (Hezb-e-Islami) and the individual to whom he long reported (Yunis Khalis).[170] It is also worth mentioning that the chief executive of BIF—Enaam Arnaout—had personal letters from both Jalaluddin Haqqani and Yunis Khalis in his possession.[171]

More recent sources of information indicate that private financial contributions from the Gulf and al-Qa'ida still help to sustain the Haqqani organization. The "old" financial network built by Jalaluddin at the beginning of the anti-Soviet jihad appears to form the foundation for these donations. According to Gretchen Peters, "sources close to the Haqqani family name Abdullah Tanai, a commander based in Miram Shah, as the man responsible for distributing cash coming through the *Hawala* network from the Gulf among the commanders."[172] Comments recently made by one of these commanders is revealing in that he believed that his monthly operating expenses came from "Gulf countries, especially Saudi Arabia ... and from the ISI."[173] While it is difficult to corroborate this commander's claim, an estimate provided by Afghanistan's financial intelligence unit placed the value of private Saudi donor contributions to the Taliban at upwards of US$1 billion over the last four years.[174]

Some within the US government dispute that these are donations, arguing that it is instead laundered money from organized crime.[175] While speculative, the perception of a local politician from Pakistan's Khyber-Pakhtunkhwa Province about Haqqani network funding is just as revealing. When asked by a *PBS* journalist where Jalaluddin Haqqani received his money, Afrasiab Khattak replied: "I think it is Middle East money that is still coming in. He has very strong Arab connections. Supporters of al Qaeda think that they can bleed Americans in Afghanistan. And they think they can create a new front for the United States in [the] tribal areas. So they are investing money in this fighting."[176] Less speculative and more concrete is the US government's recent financial blacklisting of Nasiruddin Haqqani, the son of Jalaluddin who is referenced in the al-Qa'ida interrogation document above, on 22 July 2010. According to the US Treasury Department, from mid-2007 Nasiruddin Haqqani "reportedly received funding from donations from the Gulf region, drug trafficking, and payments from al-Qa'ida."[177] Nasiruddin's uncle and Jalaluddin's brother, Khalil al-Rahman Haqqani, was similarly designated on 9 February 2011 for his role in Haqqani financing and links with al-Qa'ida.[178] These designations confirm Nasiruddin's and Khalil's important role in facilitating these payments and the enduring reach of the Haqqani network's fundraising machine to private donors in the Gulf. The more recent designations of Fazl Rabbi and Ahmad Jan Wazir further refine this picture, which establishes yet another realm where al-Qa'ida and Haqqani network operations appear to still overlap.[179]

Ideologically Motivated Personnel and Knowledge and Technology Transfer

As has been shown, Jalaluddin Haqqani recognized the benefits of Arab and other foreign volunteers and how they could be used to strengthen his military campaign years before other Afghan commanders. Initially, Arab connections were viewed as a source of funding, but after Arab youth arrived Jalaluddin distinguished himself by providing them with operational opportunities and access to his facilities.[180] In doing so, Jalaluddin further integrated Arab and other foreign fighters into the kinetic and logistical infrastructure of the war. The legacy of this collaboration has been enduring, and for the past twenty-five years the Haqqani network has arguably been the most important local actor facilitating this process.[181] In return for leaving its doors open across multiple decades, the Haqqani network has received and benefited from additional resources and committed manpower, as well as the networks and technical skills that these foreign fighters have to offer. For the Haqqani network, the cost of this added personnel has been low, given that foreign fighters were historically supported by Islamic relief organizations and today many are believed to be self-financed, or at least partially so.[182] Put simply, foreign fighters function as personnel, resource, and technological force multipliers, inputs which require little financial investment from the Haqqani network and help the organization to wage a more effective and deadly campaign.

During the late 1980s and early 1990s the number of foreign war volunteers in Afghanistan was "never sufficient to swing the military balance," but there was still something qualitatively different about the Arabs and other foreigners who wanted to fight.[183] As noted by Anthony Davis and many others, "Arab and Sudanese fighters often fought with great, even suicidal, courage."[184] The same can be said about the ideological commitment of foreign volunteers who fight alongside the Haqqanis and their partners in Loya Paktia today. It is significant that some of the suicide bombers who participate in high-profile attacks in Loya Paktia are foreign war volunteers. The case of Cüneyt Çiftçi—discussed above—is particularly illustrative, as the benefit the Haqqani network derived from this attack can be seen in a long Taliban video that celebrated the operation and the last moments of his life. After seven years of silence, Jalaluddin Haqqani made a rare appearance to praise the attack, stating that: "With God's help, the United States will leave Afghanistan with their heads hung in shame."[185]

A Haqqani commander interviewed by *Der Spiegel* also reflected on the value of foreign fighters and how they assist his group in other operational areas. Sirajuddin Haqqani had reportedly been so impressed by German al-Qa'ida operative Bekkay Harrach's bomb-making skills and ability to draw up precise attack plans that Harrach, before his death in May 2010, is believed to have served as an advisor to the group.[186] Those foreign fighters who fall into the Haqqani network's orbit and return home are also likely of use to the Haqqanis, as they can solicit donations, distribute media products, and help other foreign recruits make their way to North Waziristan.

Positioned at the nexus of several foreign fighter mobilizations, the Haqqani network has historically been able to capitalize on the ideas, technology, and skills—such as digital editing experience—that these personnel flows have to offer. The most significant—and lethal—tactical innovations in Afghanistan since 2001 have been the proliferation of suicide attacks and the use of IEDs across the country. As some have noted, al-Qa'ida and its close allies are believed to have helped to introduce these tactics to the Afghan theater.[187] Given its history of close ties and operational collaboration, the Haqqani network and a variety of other Afghan Taliban commanders, such as Mullah and Mansour Dadullah, were well positioned to employ these tactics and take advantage of related technological innovations.[188] One account suggests that in 2004 Mullah Dadullah sent a team to Iraq to learn from Abu Musab al-Zaraqawi and al-Qa'ida in Iraq.[189] Iraqi groups also helped a local Taliban commander in Khost, Hamza Sangari, learn how to make shaped charges.[190]

Afghanistan's first indigenous suicide bomber—Hafez Abdallah—reportedly hailed from the region of Khost, suggesting that the individual responsible for the January 2004 attack in Kabul could have been recruited and supported by the Haqqani network.[191] Several years later, in September 2006, "a suicide bomber sent by the Haqqani network succeeded in killing the hightest-ranking Afghan official [at the time] ... Paktia's governor Hakim Taniwal."[192] The fact that the Haqqani network has emerged as the entity most often responsible for suicide and complex attacks in Kabul lends further credence to this potential linkage. It is also worth noting that a UN study on suicide attacks conducted in Afghanistan from 2001 to 2007 found that "over 80% of suicide attackers pass through recruitment, training facilities or safe houses in North or South Waziristan en route to their targets inside Afghanistan."[193] This finding is significant when one considers the organizational importance and centrality of the Haqqani network in North Waziristan and reports about the group's ties with al-Qa'ida and Pakistani Taliban suicide trainers, such as Qari Hussain Mehsud (before his death).[194] The Haqqani network's nexus position helps to ensure that the group will continue to be in a position to leverage new technologies, tactical innovations, and the trainers who help deploy them.

Prestige and Ability to Make a Broader Impact

Although currently in decline, al-Qa'ida remains the vanguard of the global jihadist movement, and association with the group—and several other groups that fall within its orbit in North Waziristan—bolsters the Haqqani network's jihadist credentials, and its reputation and standing—at least within the jihadist community. Through local partnering and providing back-end support the Haqqani network knows that their organization has directly contributed—over multiple decades—to the development and endurance of al-Qa'ida and its global jihad. The list of foreign fighters who fought with the Haqqani network reads like a "who's who" of al-Qa'ida and its major affiliates, and the international terrorist plots that link back to North Waziristan and Haqqani-associated training camps/infrastructure in Khost is equally revealing. By acting as a silent local partner, the Haqqani network has been able to drive and shape world events indirectly, and to contribute to a cause which is broader than its fight in Afghanistan.

Conclusion

The findings from this and the previous two chapters highlight a pattern of Haqqani network behavior that is in historical continuity with Part I of this book. This indicates that the Haqqani network cannot just be seen as a local actor that is only preoccupied with local concerns. The group's facilitation and enabling role of al-Qa'ida and other global jihadist groups is broader and more important than previously understood; it has also been a driving force for the group since the 1990s.

A review of the Haqqani network's value proposition also provides important insights into the logic behind the Haqqani network (and its nexus position) and the incentives of various actors, specifically detailing how and in which ways they cooperate with the group. Assessments of the Haqqani network usually focus on the military utility of the group, but as the chapters in this part of the book show, there are other important ways (i.e., by serving as an "office," maintaining an accessible platform for violence, etc.) through which the group is able to provide value to other actors and enhance their local standing. While some of the Haqqani network's local, regional, and global partners have different and conflicting interests, it appears that all of them have an interest in maintaining the Haqqanis' nexus position due to the benefits they receive.

Whether the Haqqani network will modify its behavior and/or continue to find value in its relationship with al-Qa'ida and the IJU (or their potential replacements) in the future remains an open question. The Haqqani network could find it in its interest to disengage from al-Qa'ida, as the costs for hosting al-Qa'ida and other jihadis in the 1990s were much lower, and their position in Afghanistan much stronger and relatively assured, than the reality they face in the next several years. Yet it is not known if these dynamics will be enough to sway the Haqqani network or if the sense of shared suffering and the group's deep history with al-Qa'ida will be a stronger pull and will help to ensure that the group will continue to play a behind-the-scenes facilitation role for those who aim to attack the United States and its allies.

7

ENTANGLEMENTS AND MANAGEMENT OF THE HAQQANIS' NEXUS POSITION

The Haqqani network is often described as the most lethal insurgent actor operating in Afghanistan today, and most analyses of the group point to this characteristic and the group's resiliency as indications of its sophistication and strength. While the Haqqani network's operational prowess is impressive and not in dispute, the real sophistication and endurance of the Haqqanis lies in the group's historic ability to manage its interests and maintain the nexus position upon which its military effectiveness is built. That the Haqqani network has proven able to provide value to local, regional, and global actors while simultaneously incorporating inputs from each actor group into a combined system of violence which, at least in theory, has been able to keep the interests of each segmented over time, is no small management feat. To that end, this chapter provides a brief overview of how the Haqqani network has been able to manage and maintain its nexus position since 2001 through careful conflict framing and by pursuing a non-threatening approach with key actors that often have varied and conflicting interests. In addition, this chapter explores some of the management challenges the Haqqani network confronts. It also provides unique insights into redline areas that pose risks for the group and illustrates how the Haqqani network's close ties to actors like the TTP and al-Qa'ida helps to facilitate other forms of militancy.

Strategy and Awareness of the Tension Inherent to its Nexus Position

The Haqqani network has maintained its nexus position over time by pursuing a strategy of extreme pragmatism. Due to the complexity of Afghanistan's conflict environment most militant groups are pragmatic actors, but given its nexus position and the various interests it must consider the Haqqani network needs to be even more judicious in how it evaluates the practical consequences of its actions. The success of such an approach is predicated on the Haqqani network's awareness of its position and the structural necessities, or internal and external constraints, which limit its public role and pursuit of power.[1] As illustrated in other chapters, the Haqqani network has limited political goals and it has a history of subordinating itself to other entities. Jalaluddin Haqqani's relationship with Hizb-e-Islami (Khalis) and the Taliban prior to 9/11 are indicative of the group's constrained approach, as is the Haqqani network's public deferment to the Afghan Taliban today. Unlike many other militant groups, the Haqqani network has little interest in nationally governing Afghanistan and seeks instead to maintain its autonomy, control, and influence locally in Loya Paktia and North Waziristan, while also enabling other entities that aim to spread jihad elsewhere. The Haqqani network appears confident in its capabilities and standing and the group is not overly concerned with receiving public recognition for its actions. The group's constrained approach also helps to explain why its central role in the development of al-Qa'ida and the emergence of global jihad has historically been underappreciated.

Careful Conflict Framing and Knowledge of Operational Redlines

Over the course of three decades the Haqqani network has been able to tell its own story and define its own role as a conflict actor. To limit the perception of its broad role and impact, the Haqqani network consciously portrays itself as a local actor preoccupied with local concerns. The group has been able to do so through a deceptive and segmented strategic communications campaign that masks the variety and depth of the relations it has with a broad mix of jihadist actors. This has allowed the Haqqani network to tailor its messages to different audiences. Perhaps the best historical example of this is the Haqqanis' treatment of the role of the Arabs in the siege and capture of Khost garrison in 1991. In the Pashto- and Urdu-language versions of *Manba'/Nusrat al-Jihad* the role of the Arabs is either ignored or specifically denied, while it is celebrated in the Arabic-language versions of the same magazine. Segmentation proved useful to the Haqqani network in this case as it bolstered its credentials with Gulf supporters while also distancing the group from pointed criticism made by Afghan President Najibullah about the presence of foreign fighters, specifically Pakistanis and Arabs, in this battle.[2]

Given the mutually antagonistic interests of entities like the TTP and Pakistan, and al-Qa'ida and Pakistan for that matter, the Haqqani network's knowledge of its red lines and how far it can push them is central to the success of its strategy and nexus position. An anecdotal analysis of the Haqqani network's communications post-2001 reveals that the group is guided by two primary redlines: direct association with either anti-Pakistan militancy or global jihad, despite having close operational ties with the two primary actors—the TTP and al-Qa'ida—that are driving these jihads. The Haqqani network typically only speaks in generalities about its relations with the TTP and al-Qa'ida and it sometimes rhetorically distances itself from these redlines for risk of jeopardizing its position in Pakistan. For example, in an interview conducted in 2009, Sirajuddin noted that: "We have asked our allies, whether living in Pakistan or any other part of the world, to carry out attacks against Americans only in Afghanistan and not in any other country. Our policy is that we would not interfere in the affairs of any other country whether it is an Islamic or non-Islamic country."[3]

Even more revealing was Sirajuddin's non-response to two direct questions that were asked of him about the Haqqani network's support for global jihad in a rare Arabic-forum interview.[4] Besides making a very vague reference to the TTP's suicide attack against FOB Chapman, Sirajuddin carefully sidestepped both questions. It is likely that Sirajuddin did not respond directly because crossing this redline would make the Haqqani network even more of a target than it already is. As noted by another Haqqani commander, "Pakistan can pull the rug out from under us at any moment."[5] While the reality of Pakistan's power is probably not that stark, if Pakistan was committed to doing so it could further restrict the Haqqani network's travel and the movement of its resources and materiel to and from the FATA. The Haqqani network would arguably not be walking such a fine line or managing its nexus position so closely if these associations did not pose challenges or vulnerabilities for the group. This suggests that while the Haqqani network's nexus position—and the nature of its various operational relationships—is a source of its strength it is also a potential weakness as its nexus position presents more ways to disrupt the group.

Managing Redlines: The Challenges of Entanglements, Spillover, and Blowback

Thus far, the Haqqani network has been able to manage the direction of its violence and the broader spillover associated with its ties with al-Qa'ida and the TTP. The Haqqani network does so at a local level by avoiding public association with the TTP and by issuing tactical and operational directives, which instruct its fighters to "stand down" when TTP or other elements conduct an attack against a Pakistani target.[6] According to a source with firsthand access, Haqqani fighters were ordered (via radio) in one case in 2009 to not participate in an expected clash with Pakistani soldiers. Haqqani fighters were told that Pakistani Taliban, not Afghan Taliban, would fight Pakistani military forces.[7] The Haqqanis do not retaliate against the Pakistani army in North Waziristan for drone attacks because Sirajuddin knows that doing so "would hurt them in Afghanistan and threaten their sanctuary if there was all out war in North Waziristan."[8] The need for such management and operational de-confliction illustrates the depth of Haqqani/TTP integration on both sides of the Durand Line. It also demonstrates the

Haqqani network's cognizance of this issue and the group's need to draw limits and manage where and how its fighters act. A review of various examples illustrates areas of spillover and how this poses a challenge for the group.

Association with anti-Pakistan Militancy—the TTP, IJU, and al-Qa'ida

The Pakistani Taliban has been the primary driver of anti-state violence in Pakistan since 2007.[9] The general statistics are staggering: between 2007 and 2009, Pakistan's Khyber Pakhtunkhwa Province saw a more than 300 percent increase in the number of terrorist attacks, with 2,586 attacks occurring across all of Pakistan in 2009 alone.[10] The number of suicide attacks—a method often used by the TTP—also rose dramatically, jumping from forty to eighty-four over the same 2007–9 time period.[11] The author was not able to find any evidence directly linking the Haqqani network to attacks conducted against the Pakistani state, and—given the protection and support the ISI provides—the group has little incentive to support anti-Pakistan militancy openly. That is not to say that such support does not exist or that members of the group have not crossed these lines, however, as the Haqqani network is well integrated with TTP factions active in Loya Paktia and both groups share infrastructure—including training camps—and draw from overlapping recruitment pools to replenish their ranks.

More relevant and concerning for Pakistan is the role the Haqqani network plays in maintaining the space for local and global actors to intermingle and coalesce. While this activity is less visible and on the surface more passive, the cumulative effect of this historical fostering has arguably proved more dangerous to Pakistan than any form of direct Haqqani support for TTP attacks. By continuing such support—and the web of relationships around which the Haqqani nexus is built—the Haqqanis have helped to deepen the operational marriage between local and global militants who are now leading the Pakistan jihad. According to American al-Qa'ida operative Bryant Neal Vinas, the relationship between the two most influential parties driving this jihad—al-Qa'ida and the TTP—is "so close that lines between the two organizations were sometimes blurred."[12]

Despite his claims that he sought to reorient their fight, Sirajuddin Haqqani has openly expressed his sympathy for the TTP and some of the ideological tenets underpinning their and al-Qa'ida's jihad against Islamabad. According to Sirajuddin, "Pakistan was once a pro-Mujahideen state and now is under U.S. pressure to kill its own people."[13] Sirajuddin has even gone so far as to publicly state his willingness to protect the TTP. In an interview in 2008 Sirajuddin proclaimed that "it has become my moral and religious responsibility to defend the Pakistani Taliban from US and Pakistani army attacks."[14] On one level these statements can be understood as a reflection of the Haqqani network's pragmatism and as an expression of local tribal solidarity, as the group needs local tribal support to ensure its long-term survival. Yet Sirajuddin's comments also illustrate how the Haqqani network—just like Pakistan—is hedging its own bets and playing both sides of the conflict.

Some might dismiss Sirajuddin's offer of defensive support to the TTP as mere posturing, but the danger of this occurring has Pakistan concerned and Islamabad is actively trying to manage the Haqqani network to make sure this does not take place. Take, for instance, the advice Pakistan gave Sirajuddin before launching its most recent operation in South Waziristan.[15] Pakistan specifically advised the Haqqani leader to "refrain from extending support to the TTP chief in the face of the military operation [in South Waziristan]."[16] The fact that Pakistan had to advise Sirajuddin not to support the TTP indicates Pakistan's misgivings and the local and tribal bonds that situate the Haqqani–TTP relationship.

Other evidence suggests that the Haqqani network's commitment to the TTP is not just pragmatic, but is also increasingly ideological. This is best demonstrated by the testimony of David Rohde, who, along with his translator and driver, were held captive by the Haqqani network in the FATA for seven months. According to Rohde, in March 2009, his Haqqani network guards "celebrated a suicide attack in a mosque in the Pakistani town of Jamrud [in Khyber Agency] that killed as many as 50 worshipers as they prayed to God. Those living under Pakistan's apostate government, they said, deserved it."[17] News reports about the attack indicated that the mosque was located "next to a tribal police checkpoint ...

and was crowded with about 250 worshippers, including many police."[18] The sentiments expressed by Rohde's Haqqani network guards are driven by a sense of shared suffering, a desire to strike back at Islamabad for the drone attacks, and an appreciation for the TTP and its fight. But this statement also demonstrates the ideological influence of al-Qa'ida and the TTP on younger Haqqani members, and the very real risk this poses for Islamabad.

It is also likely that the TTP has used materiel, equipment, training, and operational expertise provided by the Haqqani network in Afghanistan and the FATA to support and strengthen their campaign against the state. As noted by David Rohde, "One of the things that was clearest to me in my time in captivity was that the Haqqanis and the Pakistani-Taliban worked seamlessly together."[19] The level of TTP–Haqqani cooperation became most apparent to Rohde and his two colleagues when they were transferred from a Haqqani network safehouse in North Waziristan to one in South Waziristan in territory controlled by the late TTP leader Baitullah Mehsud.[20] The Haqqani network is able to mobilize and integrate TTP and other Pakistani Pashtun tribal fighting columns into their operations in Afghanistan, which begs the question: if Haqqani and TTP fighters have mutual respect for one another and are willing to die together on the battlefield in Loya Paktia, where else, and under what conditions, are they cooperating in the FATA? Several close Haqqani associates, such as Hafiz Gul Bahadur and Sadiq Noor, are members of the TTP and at times partake in anti-Pakistan militancy, but little is known about how these parties cooperate on the Pakistan side of the border.[21] Although speculative, it is not outside the realm of possibility that Haqqani fighters provide back-end support to some TTP elements and do so in a plausibly deniable way.

Similar spillover can be seen with global jihadist groups who are also attacking Pakistan and are integrated with the Haqqani network in Loya Paktia. The cases of the IJU and al-Qa'ida are particularly instructive of the blowback Pakistan faces from those with whom the Haqqani network is aligned and support. In October 2006, Pakistani authorities arrested a dozen Pakistanis after finding a number of rockets attached to cell phones near the president's residence and the ISI's headquarters in Islamabad. The group planned to use the rockets to attack these sensitive instillations.[22] The group's ringleader, Khalil Wyne, had trained in North Waziristan and had a close relationship with the IJU's late emir, Ebu Yahya Muhammed Fatih, who reportedly directed the plot.[23]

Even more telling is an event that transpired close to one year later. In December 2007, the IJU successfully carried out an attack against a Pakistani medical convoy in Swat. A video of the attack released by the IJU's media outlet—*Badr al-Tawhid*—clearly shows charred Pakistani military vehicles and the remains of at least half a dozen Pakistani soldiers who had been slaughtered.[24] While it is not clear which faction of the IJU conducted the attack, or how well integrated that element was with the Haqqanis, the Haqqani network did not cease its organizational support for the group after the event. According to a dataset compiled by the authors, IJU operatives were killed or captured in Loya Paktia alongside Haqqani network members as recently as May 2009.[25]

A nearly identical pattern of behavior can be seen with respect to the Haqqani network's willingness to serve as a partner for al-Qa'ida in Afghanistan and the FATA.[26] Al-Qa'ida recognizes the critical role Pakistan plays for the United States in its efforts to stabilize Afghanistan and the broader region, and since 2001 the group has been working to undermine this relationship and delegitimize the Pakistani government. Al-Qa'ida accomplishes this in three primary ways: (1) by providing religious justification and rallying support for anti-Pakistan militancy; (2) acting as a force multiplier and advisor to local groups; and (3) serving as a mediator and coalition builder for militant groups within Pakistan.[27] Although al-Qa'ida has only claimed responsibility for a small number of attacks in Pakistan, it is suspected of working with and through local groups to actively fight the Pakistani state. In 2003, for example, al-Qa'ida operative Abu Faraj al-Libi allegedly ordered an assassination attempt against then President Pervez Musharraf.[28] The double suicide attack that was executed on 25 December 2003 was reportedly planned by al-Qa'ida but conducted by the Kashmiri group Jaish-e-Muhammad.[29] Ilyas Kashmiri, an al-Qa'ida operative, is also believed to have played a role in the plot.[30] More recently, in June 2009, a "major terrorist cell" with plans to target Pakistani

President Asif Ali Zardari and a number of provincial chief ministers was reportedly disrupted in Karachi.[31] A member of al-Qa'ida was allegedly involved in the plot.[32]

These examples are provided not to suggest a primary Haqqani network role, but rather to illustrate the very dangerous game that Pakistan has been playing, and the spillover that has likely resulted from its continued support and protection of the Haqqani family. The Haqqani network is a distinct organization, yet at the same time it is also an important enabler of a larger system of violence that a mix of local and global jihadist actors leverage and plug into in southeastern Afghanistan. To facilitate this system of violence, the Haqqani network provides entities attacking and advocating for jihad against the Pakistani state with logistical and organizational support, at least as it pertains to Afghanistan. In doing so, the Haqqani network is directly contributing to the operational development of these groups and is reinforcing the strength of their networks in Pakistan's tribal areas, and by extension the protection they receive. These factors doubtless contribute to the durability and survival of these entities.

What is surprising is that the blowback associated with Pakistan's support for radical Islamists, including the Haqqani network, is predictable. It is both telling and concerning that one of al-Qa'ida's leading strategists and trainers outlined these dangers in the late 1990s. In a book published before 2001, Abu Musab al-Suri predicted that it was only a matter of time until jihadis would turn their guns on Islamabad.[33]

> I believe that the regional threat posed by the appearance of the [Afghan] Taliban and what it has brought about will not be contained. It will spread northward to the river and into the nations of Central Asia, where the Taliban or their influence will have the ability to mobilize Muslims. Meanwhile, its true influence has taken hold among the elite Muslims and religious movements in Pakistan that have been set aflame by virtue of the presence of the Taliban, their victories, and the cries for Jihad that have not been contained by the river on the Pakistan–Afghanistan border but have crossed over on the wind and have come to portend great things east of Afghanistan [in Pakistan] as well.

Unfortunately for Pakistan, al-Suri's prediction could not have been more right. His comments reveal that the opening of the

Pakistan jihad has been long in the making and that jihadist violence in Pakistan is to some degree a by-product of the country's own support for the Haqqani network and other militant actors. Al-Suri's statement could serve as a reminder to Pakistan that perpetuating the distinction between "good" and "bad" Taliban creates space for actors actively seeking to topple the government in Islamabad, and in the long-run is only likely to make matters worse. It also is a reminder that the Haqqani network cannot be meaningfully separated from the back-end production of this violence.

Association with Global Jihad and International Terrorism —al-Qa'ida and the IJU

As documented in Part I, the Haqqani network has long served as a local enabler of al-Qa'ida and its global jihad. Yet despite these close ties, the Haqqani network has carefully avoided any direct association with international terrorism or the targeting of Westerners outside of Afghanistan. The question of Haqqani support for incidents of international terrorism, however, needs to also be assessed through the context and contours of the Haqqani network's consistent support for al-Qa'ida—specifically, the former's connection to key events in al-Qa'ida's history and the Haqqanis' unwillingness to disengage meaningfully from the group since it formally declared war on the United States in 1998. This makes the Haqqani network a willing partner and an active participant in al-Qa'ida's global jihad, as the Haqqanis have consistently provided the local context and space for al-Qa'ida to sustain itself and—to a large extent—extend its jihad to other places. Whether the Haqqani network will alter its position and disengage from al-Qa'ida, given the death of Bin Laden and the decline of his group, remains to be seen.

As has been well documented by Paul Cruickshank, since 9/11 the vast majority of serious international terrorism plots have links back to Pakistan, and to North Waziristan specifically.[34] A review of several plots tied to al-Qa'ida and IJU members with whom Haqqani leaders are known to be associated highlight the danger of the Haqqanis' local support for these groups. Before reviewing these cases it is important to note that they do not form a representative sample. They were intentionally selected to illustrate the spillover associated with individuals that fall into the Haqqani network's immediate operational orbit. Further, the planning for these plots is likely compartmentalized and there is no direct evidence that the Haqqani network played a role in recruiting the plotters, or that Haqqani leaders even met them. However, due to the Haqqani network's known ties with specific al-Qa'ida commanders and the group's influence and control over significant operational resources and infrastructure in Loya Paktia and North Waziristan, these cases suggest, but do not prove, that these plotters likely received some form of local assistance (shelter, training, or operational assistance) from Haqqani members or their close intermediaries. We would be remiss if we also did not acknowledge that these plotters could just have easily have been supported by powerful local Pakistani Taliban commanders, such as Gul Bahadur or Mullah Nazir. While we acknowledge that suggestions of a Haqqani role in the training of these plotters is speculative, the history and evidence reviewed in other chapters of this book make clear that such a connection is not outside the realm of possibility. We believe these cases are useful as they illustrate the fine line the Haqqani network must walk and the group's close proximity to a number of transnational terrorism plots.

Sauerland Cell—Germany

The first case involves four Germans who were convicted of plotting to attack the Ramstein airbase and several other American-linked targets in Germany with hydrogen peroxide bombs.[35] Although the plotters originally aimed to fight elsewhere, they eventually made their way to North Waziristan where they were further radicalized and received training in explosives at camps affiliated with the Islamic Jihad Union.[36] One of the individuals they met there was the IJU's leader—Najmiddin Jalolov—who "personally asked cell member Fritz Gelowicz and his fellow militants to perpetrate a series of attacks on German soil."[37] Abu Laith al-Libi—who was serving as an advisor to the IJU—also reportedly helped to plan the attack.[38] As revealed earlier, Abu Laith had personal ties to Nasiruddin Haqqani.[39] According to court testimony, members of the group appeared in videos released by the IJU's media outlet—Badr al-Tawhid.[40] After returning to Germany, some of the plotters were communicating via email with the IJU's deputy commander who urged them to act and was growing increasingly impatient with their delays. German authorities disrupted the plot not long after in September 2007. This case is worth noting because it is largely recognized as the event which marked the IJU's emergence as a global jihadist actor. The four Germans implicated in this plot were also part of a wave of aspiring German jihadis who have settled in North Waziristan and have joined up with the IJU, Islamic Movement of Uzbekistan, and al-Qa'ida. Some of these recruits have been killed and the fate of others is not known, but a select few have held prominent positions within these organizations, such as Bekkay Harrach (killed in Afghanistan in January 2011), who was reportedly close to Sirajuddin Haqqani and was emerging as a junior leader within al-Qa'ida's and the IJU's ranks. It is also worth noting that after its split from the Islamic Movement of Uzbekistan (IMU) the IJU rose under the tutelage of al-Qa'ida leader Abu Laith al-Libi and operated in southeastern Afghanistan alongside the Haqqani network.

Glasvej—Denmark

The second case involves a smaller plot disrupted in Denmark in September 2007.[41] The plot's ringleader, Hammad Khürshid, sought to attack multiple targets in Denmark and potentially elsewhere in Europe using the explosive TATP. After the Pakistani-Dane arrived at Islamabad's Lal Masjid (Red Mosque) in the spring of 2007, he made his way to North Waziristan where he was trained in the construction and use of explosives by members of al-Qa'ida. According to intelligence sources, Khürshid is believed to have met Abu Nasir al-Qahtani and to have been trained by Abu Ubaydah al-Masri, al-Qa'ida's late chief of external operations and the architect of its failed 2006 transatlantic airliner plot.[42] (As documented in Chapter 6, al-Qahtani operated with local Haqqani and Taliban elements in southeastern Afghanistan.) After he returned to Denmark, Khürshid remained in contact with Muhammad Ilias Subhan Ali (a.k.a. Abu Ali), a Pakistani al-Qa'ida facilitator now detained in

Saudi Arabia.[43] Khürshid was arrested by Danish authorities after testing a batch of TATP in his apartment complex. Similar to the Sauerland cell, this case illustrates the close connection between this plot and an al-Qa'ida operative who operated with Haqqani fighters in Loya Paktia.[44]

Long Island Railroad—New York

The third case, involving American Muslim convert and al-Qa'ida operative Bryant Neal Vinas, is equally suggestive. Vinas travelled to Pakistan because he wanted to fight in Afghanistan. After spending some time in Pakistan's Mohmand Agency with a local insurgent group, Vinas—like the others plotters—made his way to North Waziristan where he met, took courses from, and was mentored by al-Qa'ida commanders. During an interrogation by Belgian authorities, Vinas described one course taught by Abu Hafith, an al-Qa'ida commander who reportedly served for a period as al-Qa'ida's external operations chief.[45] While in North Waziristan, Vinas also met Mustafa Abu al-Yazid, Rashid Rauf, Baitullah Mehsud, Yunis al-Mauritania, and Attiya Allah and appeared in an al-Sahab video with Abu Yahya al-Libi.[46] On two occasions Vinas attempted to infiltrate and conduct an operation against Coalition and Afghan forces in Afghanistan—the first into Kunar Province with a group led by Shaah Saab and the second into Loya Paktia.[47] The account Vinas provided to Belgian authorities of the second attempt is worth recounting due to the personalities involved:[48]

> Towards the beginning of Ramadan 2008 [September 2008], Vinas on the orders of A. S. went to a city known by him in Waziristan near the border with Afghanistan where he joined a group of fighters led by A. Y. Y. [Abu Yahya al-Libi]. He was the leader of this group following the death of AL [Abu Laith al-Libi] earlier in the year. He accompanied a group of Al Qaeda fighters in two attempts to [conduct] rocket attacks against a U.S. base in Afghanistan. The rockets were launched from a site in Pakistan. The first attack was not triggered because of problems with radio communication and the second [attempt] failed on the base.

It is not known if any Haqqani elements took part in or helped to facilitate this attack, although it is not outside the realm of possibility, especially since Vinas lived in North Waziristan for several months and was friends with one of the suicide bombers who attacked FOB Salerno in a coordinated Haqqani–al-Qa'ida assault in August 2008. Not long after proving himself in these operations, Vinas "consulted with a senior al Qaeda leader" who "provided detailed information about the operation of the Long Island Rail Road system."[49] Vinas agreed to return to the United States to conduct the attack, but he was arrested in Peshawar by Pakistani authorities before he was able to do so. This case is noteworthy because it also establishes a direct connection between Vinas and al-Qa'ida leaders, such as Abu Yahya al-Libi, who were known to operate in the Haqqani network's immediate orbit.

More Recent Threats against Europe

The death of two British Muslim converts, Abu Bakr and Mansoor Ahmed, in a drone attack in North Waziristan in December 2010 raises similar questions. Not much is known about these two Britons, but it is likely that they were killed due to their connection to the late Abdul Jabbar (another Briton who had ties to Omar Khyam—the ringleader of Operation Crevice—and was the supposed leader of a new splinter group called the Islamic Army of Great Britain) and other European plotters who intended to attack multiple targets in France, Germany, and the United Kingdom using small arms and Mumbai-style tactics.[50] According to press accounts, the two men were "handled by the Haqqani faction" and received training in North Waziristan.[51] Although details of the plot still remain murky, the plot was directed by al-Qa'ida, and some claim that it was supported by the IJU and the Haqqani network.[52] Western security services reportedly learned about the plot from multiple sources, including Ahmed Siddiqi, a German of Afghan origin captured by US forces in Kabul in July 2012.[53]

Collectively, these cases point to a trend of international terrorism plots emanating from North Waziristan that all have direct connections to senior al-Qa'ida and IJU leaders. The survival of these global jihadist groups and the space needed to plan, train, and prepare for these plots is rooted in, and dependent on, a local system of facilitators and protectors who make global jihad possible through the back-end support they provide. While not explicitly a global terrorist organization, the Haqqani network has long provided a region of refuge and the space for mobilization and training that others, like al-Qa'ida, have used to directly attack the United States, Pakistan, and many other countries. It remains telling that the Haqqani network has not ceased its support for these entities, despite a pattern of international terrorist attacks that stretch back as far as 1998. What can be established, therefore, is that the Haqqani network has made a conscious decision to continue to shelter and support these groups and—at least indirectly—enable their external operations.

Conclusion

The Haqqani network derives many benefits from its nexus position, and through careful conflict framing and awareness of its redlines it has proved skilled at managing the tension inherent to this position over several decades. The group still faces a number of considerable challenges, however. The most significant of which is the spillover associated with the Haqqani network's ties to TTP and al-Qa'ida, and specifically its proximity to anti-Pakistan militancy and acts of international terrorism—and what this means for both Pakistan and the United States in terms of common interests. As we move forward we can expect considerations, such as the efforts to further reduce al-Qa'ida's safe haven, the continuation of anti-Pakistan militancy, and mounting US pressure for Pakistan to conduct large-scale operations against the Haqqani network, to further stress the latter's ability to navigate its redlines and manage its nexus position. The push for a political "endgame" in Afghanistan and the likelihood of a diminished, but still very capable US counterterrorism presence in the region post-2014 could also create new and pragmatic incentives for the Haqqani network to alter its strategic calculus and ease the pressure, instead of just following the status quo.

CONCLUSION

This study is the first to systematically explore a trove of primary sources produced by the Haqqani network and a smattering of other al-Qa'ida-linked groups from the late 1980s onward. It is shocking and concerning that thousands of pages of these unique and revealing sources have been publically available for the last ten years at a local library in Kabul where, beyond the eyes of local Afghan readers, they have essentially sat gathering dust.[1] That it took a decade for any Western academic researcher or US and NATO official to discover and evaluate this material (or similar archival collections) says a lot about our naiveté, the challenges the West faced in Afghanistan after 9/11, and how much remains to be learned. It should also force one to take pause, particularly when we consider the challenges that lie ahead and that the "most important weapon we have against al-Qa'ida [or the Taliban for that matter] is knowledge."[2]

By leveraging these and other unique sources, this study has aimed to provide a more sophisticated and historically informed understanding of the Haqqani network—in however small a way. It has done so by outlining the contours of, and exploring many of the contextual dynamics associated with, the group's history, especially as it pertains to its association with regional and transnational Islamist militancy. This study has revealed how Jalaluddin Haqqani and the group that he led emerged as a central, nexus entity during the 1980s and early 1990s due to their flexible approach, long-term outlook, and skill in avoiding some of the inter-mujahidin fighting that plagued other Afghan Islamist party factions. The group's geographic position, ability to deliver battlefield results, and reliability has also endeared it to Pakistan's security establishment which—fearing broader conflict within its borders—currently views it as too risky to turn against the group, a dynamic which is not likely to change anytime soon. The second part of this study has also shown how the Haqqanis have operated as a system, or nexus, during the post-2001 period by providing value to its local, regional, and global partners across operational, diplomatic, and support functions.

Material presented in this publication challenges conventional narratives about the Haqqani network and al-Qa'ida's early development in the Afghanistan–Pakistan region in a number of important ways. Prior assessments, for example, have highlighted how Abdullah Azzam, Maktab al-Khidamat (the Services Bureau), and several Afghan Islamist party leaders, such as 'Abd al-Rabb Rasul Sayyaf and Gulbuddin Hekmatyar, have to varying degrees helped to shape al-Qa'ida's early and local trajectory. By broadening the geographic aperture and source base through which these dynamics have traditionally been examined, this study casts the spotlight on Jalaluddin Haqqani's enduring role in these developments and how his network provided critical assistance and support for al-Qa'ida at key moments. This book's contributions to what is known about the emergence of global jihadism are equally noteworthy, as they enhance our understanding about where and with whom these dynamics transpired in Afghanistan during the 1990s. They also highlight the role played by individuals like Abu'l-Walid al-Masri, who operated for an extended period in Jalaluddin Haqqani's inner circle and, according to the accounts of two al-Qa'ida insiders, played an important role in shifting al-Qa'ida's targeting strategy towards the West.

In revealing this history, this book provides a different and more nuanced view of the Haqqani network than that which previously existed on the subject. It is true that at its core the group is primarily a local actor with local concerns, and that the liberation of Loya Paktia and withdrawal of foreign forces from Afghanistan remain the group's immediate short-term goals. Yet such a view ignores other dimensions of the organization, as the Haqqani network's actions, outlook, and ties cannot be adequately explained solely in reference to the Afghan theater. The group has been a key facilitator of jihadi actors engaged in broader conspiracies and agendas that reach further afield. Indeed, as revealed in this book, al-Qa'ida's global jihad and elements of Kashmir's regional jihad have, for several decades, been shaped by the safe haven, training, combat experience, propaganda support, resource mobilization, and networking opportunities facilitated by the Haqqani network.

The Haqqani network, like other militant groups, is driven by complex motivations. Before publication of this book there were two primary narratives used to explain the Haqqani network's support for al-Qa'ida and its training camps during the mid-1990s. The first held that Jalaluddin Haqqani provided support to al-Qa'ida for personal reasons given his close ties to and respect for Osama bin Laden and other al-Qa'ida leaders, such as Abu Hafs al-Masri, who had assisted the Afghans and made a number of sacrifices during the anti-Soviet jihad. This explanation makes intuitive sense, especially since personal dynamics and the bonds of war have strong explanatory power in almost any context. Given the Haqqani network's integration of al-Qa'ida and other foreign fighters during the post-2001 period this logic likely also holds true to this day, as it makes sense that the Haqqanis—like any military entity—would support those brothers-in-arms with whom they have suffered in combat.

The second narrative suggests that economic or pragmatic considerations are what drove Jalaluddin to assist al-Qa'ida after Bin Laden's return to Afghanistan in 1996. This line of reasoning holds that Jalaluddin supported the development of al-Qa'ida and its training camps during this period because this "business" was a growth industry and another way for him to raise additional funds. There is some basis for these claims, as both before and after 9/11 Jalaluddin proved skilled at diversifying his income streams and in capitalizing on new financial opportunities. This explanation runs into problems though, as there is not much evidence that Jalaluddin made a lot of money from these training camps or from al-Qa'ida more broadly. Nor is there much information that outlines what the elder Haqqani spent his money on beyond his network of madrassas, even if these camps were a money-maker. Pragmatism undoubtedly played some role in motivating Jalaluddin and the other leaders of the network, but relying on this theory alone, especially in light of other evidence, is not sufficient to fully explain the reasons for the two groups' ties. It also does very little to answer a fundamental question about the Haqqani network's pragmatism: pragmatism in pursuit of what exactly?

A third explanation suggests that the Haqqani network's ties to al-Qa'ida were not just personal, pragmatic, or profit-motivated, but that they were also driven by Jalaluddin's and now Sirajuddin's religious views and ideological outlook. The content of magazines produced by Jalaluddin and the operational support and infrastructure provided by the Haqqani network lend credence to this view and show that the group's support for al-Qa'ida pre- and post-9/11 was driven—at least in some part—by sympathy for Bin Laden's group and what it aimed to achieve.

What can be learned from this discussion and our review of the available evidence is that when viewed alone none of these explanations—personal, financial, and ideological—can sufficiently explain the Haqqani network and its historical bonds with al-Qa'ida. All have played a role. The challenge for researchers lies in evaluating these and potentially other motivations to discover how each should be weighed in relation to the others.

This issue takes on particular relevance given the US plan to transition from Afghanistan in 2014 and current US and Afghan efforts to reach a political settlement with the Afghan Taliban and the Haqqanis. As discussed previously, there are very good reasons to question whether reconciliation with the Haqqanis is in the United States' long-term interests and to be skeptical that any political agreement with the group—if reached—will hold or actually mean much. Washington's search for a political solution to its Afghanistan imbroglio is understandable, but negotiations with the Haqqanis come with considerable risk given the group's historical and recent fostering of al-Qa'ida. There is also the risk that efforts to create peace through a broad-based political settlement for the Taliban will further fracture the country along ethnic lines, precipitate a coup within the country, or lead to greater conflict.[3] It can only be hoped that the decision to include the Haqqanis in such talks are made based upon facts, a deep understanding of the Haqqani network's history, and the reality of the situation on the ground, however hard and challenging that might make things for the relevant parties over the short term.

The American and NATO troop presence in Afghanistan and the US drone campaign across Pakistan's border have been critical to degrading al-Qa'ida since 9/11. The immediate threat to the United States has certainly been diminished as a result of these campaigns, but ten years of war will not be without its own share of new costs. In many ways, the environment the United States faces on both sides of the Durand Line is now more charged, complicated, and openly hostile than before October 2001. How the impact of war and a sense of shared suffering and personal loss will affect the region over the mid- to long-term and manifest itself in the development of new threats for the most part remains uncertain. The formation of the TTP and its attempts to attack the West are an indication that the road will be bumpy, and that the United States and its allies will face a new range of militant challenges with ties to the region in the decade ahead.

Any attempt to assess the future of violent jihad within and beyond the region is a messy and speculative exercise.[4] Yet if we are to use the aftermath of the Soviet departure from Afghanistan and its impact on the region as a guide, there are two central themes—change and outputs—that can inform our thinking. Indeed, two of the primary questions that must be asked are how will Pakistan's and Afghanistan's militant landscapes evolve post-2014 and, more specifically, what type of organizational and ideological outputs will emerge from these communities over the next decade as a result? These questions become more salient when one considers that the creation of many jihadi groups, the (re)opening of the Kashmir jihad, and the early development of al-Qa'ida and its shift in targeting calculus (from the near to the far enemy) largely transpired after the Soviets had left, not before. It is also worth remembering that the most important decade for al-Qa'ida—the 1990s—also started off as its quietest. Thus while the United States will likely shift some of its attention and assets to other areas of the globe, like Yemen and Africa, and engage other difficult problems, the next decade in the region could be even more important, and potentially as dangerous, as the previous one.

Change in the region's diverse jihadi landscape is a certainty. However, evaluating the direction, character, and intensity of that change—and what will motivate various actors, including the Haqqani network—is much more difficult. Many jihadis in the region will be emboldened by the US drawdown and eventual departure from Afghanistan, viewing the event as a victory in their quest to reclaim Muslim lands and rid those areas of Western influence. Inspired, some of these jihadis will continue their efforts to overthrow the Afghan government, while others will likely turn their attention and violence elsewhere. Some, if able, could return home, and yet others—tired from war—could disengage or decide to play a more positive and less violent role in their communities.

The options vary regarding where this violence may turn. Islamabad and its security forces will remain a consistent target of the TTP and other anti-state Pakistani jihadis if the former continues to conduct campaigns in the tribal territories and the latter can maintain their capabilities and manpower. If history is any guide, many of the jihadi groups active in the region will turn their sights to Kashmir, or support those that do, to reclaim Indian-occupied Kashmir from perceived Hindu dominance. Another likely option for some groups is reorientation to Afghanistan's neighboring countries, especially mainland India, where Lashkar-e-Taiba's three-day terrorist spectacular in November of 2008 against a mix of local, foreign, and symbolic targets reaffirmed the potential of active shooter plots and the value (and attention) gained by hitting hybrid targets. The pull towards India will most likely affect those groups with roots in Pakistan's Punjab or Kashmir. Like the events in Mumbai, future high-profile attacks in India will likely aim to manipulate security tensions between India and Pakistan with the hopes of provoking a broader conflict between the two countries, a scenario for which al-Qa'ida and others are already preparing.[5] The departure of US and NATO combat forces from the region could also make it easier for groups like the IMU and IJU to reinitiate their campaigns in Central Asia, particularly in Uzbekistan, Kyrgyzstan, and Tajikistan. In search of opportunities these groups could also try to hit softer US and Coalition targets there, using Afghanistan, Pakistan, or a pocket in one of the Central Asian countries as their base.

This assumes of course that the jihadis in the region will be able to hold things together and avoid infighting within their ranks, and to do so in the absence of such a visible foreign military presence in Afghanistan. History does not inspire much confidence in this regard, as tensions over tactics, access to resources, or local versus global targeting priorities are predictable points of disagreement and could derail plans to consolidate their gains.[6] Debates and conflict over sectarian issues could also create serious turmoil, especially if these dynamics are further unleashed in Pakistan's settled areas and in the Punjab particularly. One thing is certain: lacking the unifying factor of a full-scale American military presence, Afghanistan's and Pakistan's jihadis will struggle to retain the level of focus and cohesion that they hitherto enjoyed.

Given current dynamics, it remains an open question as to whether al-Qa'ida will continue to exist as a coherent or viable entity over the next several years in the region. It is also unclear how the group and its strategy will evolve, and who will guide it after the removal, death, or continued isolation of Ayman al-Zawahiri. Al-Qa'ida, if anything since 9/11, has certainly proven itself to be resilient, and Bin Laden's calls to shift its personnel to Kunar and Nuristan (more isolated areas), and to regions like Zabul and Ghazni, indicate that the group intends to persevere, lay low, and rebuild. There is also the issue of al-Qa'ida's seasoned members—personalities like Saif al-Adel and Adnan Shukrijumah—and the group's middle-managers and young turks, individuals who are likely known to counterterrorism operators but not the public, who will play a role in shaping the future trajectory of the group. The potential role played by family members of deceased senior al-Qa'ida militants, such as Bin Laden's son Hamza, cannot be discounted as well.

Al-Qa'ida's continued presence in Afghanistan and Pakistan for the past ten years, even if in small pockets, has also helped to ensure that the group's membership is now more local and potentially more deeply intermarried and interwoven into the tapestry of each place. Although an understudied phenomenon, al-Qa'ida has always had a Pakistani current running through its membership and it is therefore not unreasonable to assume that any future version of the group (or whatever potentially replaces it) will be markedly more Pakistani. An uptick in Urdu-language videos released by al-Qa'ida's media arm (targeted to Pakistanis) and a series of attacks allegedly involving insiders in Pakistan's military indicates that such a future is one that the group is actively working to cultivate. These dynamics suggest that the next generation of al-Qa'ida in the region could look much different than the first, and be even more integrated with other Afghan and Pakistani militant groups. Such a dynamic does not bode well for the future of the US–Pakistan relationship, especially if spoilers in Pakistan triumph over forces urging moderation.

So where does this leave the Haqqani network? Like other actors, the Haqqanis are approaching an inflection point. Given their position, the US drawdown, and their ability to withstand decades of war, the group arguably has little incentive to reconcile, since if they wait a little longer they will probably achieve their core interests in the region anyway. That is assuming, of course, that the status quo holds and the steps the United States is willing to take to achieve its goals in Afghanistan and North Waziristan do not change. Judging by the US commitment in pressing the Pakistanis on the Haqqani issue and Islamabad's unwillingness to budge and turn on the group, the latter is by no means a certainty. Significant change could also be driven by actions taken by the Haqqanis themselves, the removal of one or several of the group's senior leaders, shifts in the Afghan Taliban's hierarchy, or in response to Pakistani military operations.

As the clock ticks down to 2014, two central questions define the debate for the United States and its allies. First, what role does the Haqqani network want to play in Afghanistan and Pakistan in the next five to ten years and what does this mean for the West? Second, what type of relationship do the Haqqanis want to have with al-Qa'ida and like-minded transnational jihadist groups in the future? The answers to both of these questions are not straightforward, as the Haqqanis have publicly revealed little about either. The view provided by this book paints a fairly grim picture with respect to both of these issues, however, and it is not known how the Haqqani network will respond to the bundled mix of incentives and pressures that 2014 entails. Autonomy in Loya Paktia and nominal leadership of the area has always been prized by the Haqqani network, and the group is certain to play a strong direct or indirect role there, as well as in North Waziristan. The Haqqanis will also almost certainly remain a steady regional partner for the Afghan Taliban (and elements of the Pakistani state) in the years to come. Barring significant change, the Haqqanis' primary role in the conflict in Afghanistan will remain as a spoiler, a dynamic which is likely to further strain ties between Washington and Islamabad.

The al-Qa'ida question is one of incentives and at the moment it appears as though the Haqqani network has little motivation to maintain its relationship with the remnants of al-Qa'ida and other global jihadis. On the one hand, with al-Qa'ida's dwindling numbers and waning popularity around the world there does not appear to be that much in it for the Haqqanis, as maintaining such associations are sure to invite continued US pressure. The Haqqani network's relationship with Pakistan, while not always smooth, is also critical, and post-2014 the former's connections to transnational jihadism could be more problematic for Pakistan than they have been previously, especially when one considers the role that Pakistani ostensibly wants the Haqqanis to play politically in Afghanistan. On the other hand, the Haqqani network's historical and recent behavior does not inspire confidence that it will actually sever its ties to transnationally oriented jihadis in a meaningful or permanent way. Ideological sympathy and shared support for the broader goals that al-Qa'ida represents—surely held by at least some within the group—would be one important reason for not doing so, as would a desire to seek revenge for the losses that both groups have suffered over the last ten years. This skepticism is not to say that a shift in the Haqqanis' relationship with al-Qa'ida is impossible, but rather that such change would mark a significant break with the group's previous trajectory over the last two and half decades.

NOTES

INTRODUCTION

1. "Kabul siege ends after 20 hours," *Reuters*, 14 Sep. 2011, http://uk.reuters.com/article/2011/09/14/uk-afghanistan-attacks-idUKTRE78D0S720110914
2. http://armed-services.senate.gov/statemnt/2011/09%20September/Mullen%2009–22–11.pdf
3. Confidential cable from the US Embassy in Kabul dated 18 Jan. 2006, subject line "PRT/Khost: Bombings In Khost Target Civilians; New Tactic Aimed At 'anti-Islamic' Activities," released by WikiLeaks at http://wikileaks.org/cable/2006/01/06KABUL265.html. It is possible that the phrase appeared earlier in cables with a higher classification than those acquired and released by WikiLeaks.
4. Secret cable from US Embassy in Kabul dated 2 July 2006, subject line "NDS Director Saleh on Insurgency—Causes and Solutions," released by WikiLeaks at http://wikileaks.org/cable/2006/07/06KABUL2970.html. In this case the usage is attributed to Amrullah Saleh, director of the Afghan National Directorate of Security.
5. Admiral Moeller described the three main components of the Afghan insurgency as the Taliban, the "Haqqani Tribal Network," and Hizb-i-Islami Gulbuddin (HIG). A week later, the US State Department press office introduced the shortened appellation "Haqqani network" (David McKeeby, "Partnership Key to Progress in Afghanistan, U.S. General Says," *Washington File*, 16 Mar. 2006), though the phrase did not enter common usage in the Western press until late 2006, following Anthony Cordesman's editorial "One War We Can Still Win," *New York Times*, 13 Dec. 2006.
6. "Afghanistan: Progress Report. Joint Hearing before the Subcommittee on the Middle East and Central Asia and the Subcommittee on Oversight and Investigations of the Committee on International Relations," online at http://commdocs.house.gov/committees/intlrel/hfa26441.000/hfa26441_0f.htm. FATA stands for the Federally Administered Tribal Areas along Pakistan's border with Afghanistan.
7. Milt Bearden and James Risen, *The Main Enemy*, New York: Random House, 2003, p. 312. Bearden was the CIA station chief in Pakistan from 1986 to 1989.
8. Brigadier Mohammad Yousaf and Major Mark Adkin, *The Bear Trap: Afghanistan's Untold Story*, London: Leo Cooper, 1992, p. 164.
9. Arif Jamal, *Shadow War: The Untold Story of Jihad in Kashmir*, Brooklyn, NY: Melville House, 2009, p. 110.
10. Ayman Sabri Faraj, *Dhikriyyat 'Arab Afghan Abu Ja'far al-Masri al-Qandahari*, Cairo: Dar al-Shuruq, 2002, p. 25.
11. Syed Saleem Shahzad, "How Iran and al-Qaeda made a deal," *Asia Times*, 30 Apr. 2010. Shahzad was tortured and murdered in Pakistan on 31 May 2011, and US government officials and several human rights organizations have accused the ISI of his killing. Though undoubtedly a courageous journalist, Shahzad's reporting was often idiosyncratic and impossible to verify independently, and many of his claims—including this one about the Haqqani–Iran relationship—need to be treated with caution until further evidence emerges.
12. This is maintained by men who fought in the southeast for the Haqqani network or the Taliban in general in interviews with Ron Moreau and Sami Yousafzai; see Yousafzai and

Moreau, "The Taliban in Their Own Words," *Newsweek*, 26 Sep. 2009. A certain Muhammad Haqqani claims there that "Arab and Iraqi mujahedin began visiting us, transferring the latest IED technology and suicide-bomber tactics they had learned in the Iraqi resistance during combat with U.S. forces. ... Until 2004 or so, we were using traditional means of fighting like we used against the Soviets—AK-47s and RPGs. But then our resistance became more lethal, with new weapons and techniques: bigger and better IEDs for roadside bombings, and suicide attacks." See also the critical assessment of the so-called "Iraq effect" in Afghanistan in Alec D. Barker, "Improvised Explosive Devices in Southern Afghanistan and Western Pakistan, 2002–2009," Counterterrorism Strategy Initiative Policy Paper, New America Foundation, Apr. 2010. (And thanks to one of our anonymous readers for bringing this latter source to my attention.)

13. Manahi al-Shaybani, "Former Saudi Mujahidin Interviewed," *al-Riyadh*, 30 Dec. 2003.

1. SITUATING THE HAQQANIS: ORIGINS, POLITICAL CULTURE, REGIONAL CONTEXTS

1. There are four super-tribal confederacies of the Pashtun tribes, the other three being the Durrani, the Ghilzai, and the Ghurghusht. The Karlanri confederacy includes (among others) the Haqqanis' Zadran tribe as well as the Wazir, Mahsud, Orakzai, Afridi, Jaji, Tani, Mangal, Khattak, and Khugiani tribes, all of which are also comprised of numerous subtribal segmental clan units. Not all of the Pashtun tribes inhabiting this region are Karlanri—the Mohmand, for instance, are a Durrani tribe—but the Karlanri are the predominant population and it is in this region that all of the Karlanri are concentrated.
2. Quoted in James C. Scott, *Seeing Like a State*, New Haven, CT: Yale University Press, 1998, p. 396.
3. David B. Edwards, "Learning from the Swat Pathans: Political Leadership in Afghanistan, 1978–97," *American Ethnologist*, 25, 4 (1998), pp. 712–28, at p. 714. Edwards is summarizing the meanings of these terms among Pashtuns (= Pakhtuns) analyzed in the work of Akbar Ahmed, esp. *Millennium and Charisma among the Pathans*, London: Routledge and Kegan Paul, 1976.
4. Thomas Barfield, *Afghanistan: A Cultural and Political History*, Princeton, NJ: Princeton University Press, 2010, pp. 337f. Barfield is only describing Afghanistan in this passage, but the characterization holds true for the relationships between the British Raj and now the Pakistani state on the one hand and the highland Pashtuns of the tribal areas on the other.
5. David Edwards, *Before Taliban: Genealogies of the Afghan Jihad*, Berkeley, CA: University of California Press, 2002, pp. 64f. For details on the history of the "antistate violence" that Edwards alludes to here, see Louis Dupree, *Afghanistan*, Princeton, NJ: Princeton University Press, 1973, Chapters 18–21.
6. See, e.g., Olivier Roy, *Islam and Resistance in Afghanistan*, 2nd ed., Cambridge and New York: Cambridge University Press, 1990, p. 35, where, in emphasizing that "the status of the mullah is low in the tribal zones," Roy writes that "To be a Pashtun is to be integrated into a tribal structure. Priests are outside the tribal system ..." For a more nuanced view see Asta Olesen, *Islam and Politics in Afghanistan*, Richmond, UK: Curzon Press, 1995.
7. This observation is a commonplace in histories of the Taliban, but see, e.g., Ahmed Rashid, *Taliban*, New Haven and London: Yale Nota Bene, 2000, p. 87; and William Maley, "Interpreting the Taliban," in Maley (ed.), *Fundamentalism Reborn? Afghanistan and the Taliban*, New York: NYU Press, 1998, p. 20.
8. This insight is most fully elaborated in the work of David Edwards and, more recently, Sana Haroon's *Frontier of Faith: Islam in the Indo-Afghan Borderland*, New York: Columbia University Press, 2007. The latter writes, regarding the distinctive role of religious leaders in the highland Pashtun political economy in the early twentieth century: "In the absence of a government, there were no institutionalised legal or political systems in the frontier Tribal Areas. British political agents and Afghan authorities each had some authority over some tribes, but because no single authority extended over the different groups and their interactions in the Tribal Areas, these administrators could not arbitrate between the clans—even informally. It was this power vacuum that the *mullas* were able to fill" (p. 80).
9. While there is a rich anthropological literature on Pashtun political culture, both lowland and highland, the havoc wreaked on these societies since the Soviet invasion has not been systematically studied. The reader should thus be cautioned against assuming the applicability of my characterizations of Pashtun political culture to current dynamics on the frontier.

10. On the Hadda Mullah see David B. Edwards, *Heroes of the Age: Moral Fault Lines on the Afghan Frontier*, Berkeley, CA: University of California Press, 1996, Chapters 4 and 5; and Haroon, *Frontier of Faith, passim.*
11. Edwards, *Heroes of the Age*, p. 191.
12. Haroon, *Frontier of Faith*, pp. 60–2. On the history of the Deobandi movement in South Asia, see Barbara Metcalf, *Islamic Revival in British India: Deoband, 1860–1900*, Oxford and New York: Oxford University Press, 2005.
13. Haroon, *Frontier of Faith*, p. 89.
14. James C. Scott, *The Art of Not Being Governed: An Anarchist History of Upland Southeast Asia*, New Haven and London: Yale University Press, 2009. Scott did not invent either of these terms, though his is the first attempt to fully elaborate them as cross-cultural comparative categories.
15. Ibid., p. 23.
16. Ibid.
17. Ibid., p. 289. Scott glosses the function of religion in these contexts as "cosmologies of ethnic collaboration."
18. Contra analyses that identify supposedly inherent features of Islam as sufficient to explain anti-colonial and subsequent forms of political violence in the Muslim world; the classical statement of this view is Bernard Lewis, "The Revolt of Islam," in Lewis, *The Middle East and the West*, New York: Harper & Row, 1966, pp. 95–114.
19. Howard Hensman, *The Afghan War of 1879–80*, London: H. Allen and Co., 1881, p. 336. Hensman was an English journalist "embedded" with the Kurram Valley Field Force. The fiery cross was a signaling device of the highland Scots clans, used to summon urgent collective action, and was the historical antecedent of the cross burning by the Ku Klux Klan.
20. Scott, *The Art of Not Being Governed*, pp. 7f.
21. Ibid., p. 341 n. 25, where he writes that "analogies to the Pashtuns, Kurds, and Berbers are less apposite because, in these cases, the people in question have—or better, are assumed to have—a common culture."
22. On patterns of North Caucasus resistance from antiquity to the twentieth century, see Michael Reynolds, "Myth and Mysticism: A Longitudinal Perspective on Islam and Conflict in the North Caucasus," *Middle Eastern Studies*, 41, 1 (2005), pp. 31–54. The North Caucasus includes Chechnya and Dagestan, which remain centers of fierce Islamist resistance to Russian domination in the region.
23. These are both Durrani tribal groups, centered in Kandahar and the Swat Valley, respectively.
24. North-West Frontier Province of Pakistan, now called Khyber-Pakhtunkhwa.
25. Barfield, *Afghanistan*, p. 91. "Pakhtun" (actually pronounced *pukhtun*) is the highland and eastern pronunciation, while the major lowland groups in Afghanistan pronounce this "Pashtun." Linguistic divergence between different "Pashtun" groups is significant and extends not just to phonemic variation but also to broad lexical differences. See G. Morgenstierne, "The Place of Pashto among the Iranic Languages and the Problem of the Constitution of Pashtun Linguistic and Ethnic Unity," *Pashto Quarterly*, 1, 4 (1978), pp. 43–55.
26. The Turi, for instance, is a Shi'i tribe, as are significant segments of the Bangash and Orakzai, while the rest of the Karlanri groups are predominantly Sunni. Even among the latter there are variations, with different groups having reputations for greater or lesser conservatism in the practice of Sunni Islam—or, more precisely, one of the several "denominations" of Sunni Islam practiced in the region, including Hanafi, Deobandi (which is itself rooted in the Hanafi school), Ahl-i Hadith, and "Wahhabi."
27. "Paktika—Governor Katawazay Addresses Security, Development and Tribal Dispute in Gayan District," cable from US Embassy, Kabul, dated 25 May 2009, posted online by WikiLeaks at http://wikileaks.org/cable/2009/05/09KABUL1309.html
28. This is not to say that these people would necessarily self-identify as Karlanris. In comments made on an early draft of this chapter, Thomas Ruttig noted that in his fieldwork in the area he found that the highland Pashtuns that technically constitute the Karlanri confederacy do not use this nomenclature, but self-identify instead by tribal or segmental terms. My thanks to him for sharing this information. One of our anonymous readers seconded this view, writing that "I have never come across this kind of self-identification."
29. Various writers have given wildly varying estimates of Jalaluddin Haqqani's date of birth, but the latter himself identified his year of birth as 1939 in an interview with the Maktab al-Khidamat's magazine *al-Jihad* in 1985; see "Hiwar maftuh ma' Jalaluddin Haqqani," *al-Jihad*, 2, 13 (Nov. 1985), pp. 18–22 at p. 18. See also Thomas Ruttig, "Loya Paktia's Insur-

gency," in Antonio Giustozzi (ed.), *Decoding the New Taliban: Insights from the Afghan Field*, New York: Columbia University Press, 2009, p. 95 n. 22. In addition to the sources cited there, the first mention of Jalaluddin in the English-language Western press also indicates a birth year of 1939 (Richard Bill, "Afghan Guerrillas Set Sights on Key Target," *Associated Press*, 5 Dec. 1982).

30. On Jalaluddin's birthplace, see "Martyrs in the Path of Truth," obituary of Muhammad Isma'il Zabihullah Haqqani, *Manba' al-Jihad* (Pashto), 2, 2 (Aug. 1990). Thanks to Kevil Bell for assistance with the local geography. A map indicating the village of Karezgay can be found online here: http://www.aims.org.af/maps/provincial/paktya.pdf
31. This is according to an informant who visited the region in 2010 and wishes to remain anonymous. In his own fieldwork in the region, Thomas Ruttig was told by other locals that they believed Srana to have been the birthplace of Jalaluddin Haqqani; Ruttig, personal communication with the author, 3 Mar. 2011.
32. To be more precise, "the family belongs to the Sultankhel clan of the Prangai subtribe of the Mezi (a.k.a. Batkhel) subtribe of the Zadran"; Ruttig, "Loya Paktia's Insurgency," p. 95 n. 21.
33. "Portrait of a Mujahid," *Arabia* (Dec. 1985), p. 20. The fact that Jalaluddin comes from the family of a Zadran khan underscores the distinctive value placed on religious education among the Karlanri tribes and plainly contradicts the prevailing view in the literature; see, for instance, Roy, *Islam and Resistance*, p. 35, stating that "the son of a *khan* would never engage in religious studies (at least in the twentieth century...)."
34. "Necrology for Muhammad Isma'il," *Manba' al-Jihad* (Arabic), 4 (Nov. 1990). The Haqqani publications describe only the four brothers, with the birth order of Jalaluddin, Isma'il, Ibrahim, and Khalil, but other sources refer to other men—or perhaps the same men by different names—as brothers of Jalaluddin. Jere Van Dyk, for instance, mentions a Nurisam and an Islahan as younger brothers of Jalaluddin (*In Afghanistan: An American Odyssey*, New York: Coward-McCann, 1983, pp. 93 and 120), while Pakistani journalist Rafiq Afghan mentions a Sayyid Ahmad Shah as Jalaluddin's brother, "martyred early in the war against the communists," leaving three living brothers (as of 2002), Ibrahim, Yusuf, and Khalil; "Gardez, Gardez," *Ummat* (Urdu), 10 Mar. 2002. Sayyid Ahmad Shah was a Haqqani commander and does appear in the Haqqani publications—see, e.g, "Report on the Funeral of Jalaluddin Haqqani's Brother, Shahid Muhammad Isma'il in Miranshah," *Manba' al-Jihad* (Pashto), 2, 2 (Aug. 1990), which includes a photograph of Isma'il Haqqani leaning on Sayyid Ahmad's shoulder—but he is not identified there as a Haqqani sibling, and in any case as a "Sayyid" he was a descendent of the Prophet Muhammad, a line of descent never claimed by the Haqqani family.
35. On the Khost Rebellion and clerical and Karlanri resistance to Amanullah, see Olesen, *Islam and Politics in Afghanistan*, pp. 133–50; Barfield, *Afghanistan*, pp. 183ff.; and Dupree, *Afghanistan*, p. 449.
36. Olesen, *Islam and Politics in Afghanistan*, p. 149.
37. Ibid., pp. 180f.
38. Anthony Davis, "How the Taliban became a Military Force," in Maley (ed.), *Fundamentalism Reborn*, p. 60. This episode is further discussed below in Chapter 3.
39. Dupree, *Afghanistan*, p. 475.
40. With the one notable exception being the Shami Pir revolt, a failed assault on Khost in the year of Jalauddin's birth by highland tribesmen, led by an Iraqi relative of the deposed Amanullah's wife (the "Shami Pir," Sayyid Muhammad Sa'adi). See Dupree, *Afghanistan*, p. 479.
41. Haroon, *Frontier of Faith*, pp. 159–64.
42. Ibid., pp. 166–72.
43. Sadia Sulaiman and Syed Adnan Ali Shah Bukhari, "Hafiz Gul Bahadur: a Profile of the Leader of the North Waziristan Taliban," *Terrorism Monitor*, 2, 9 (Apr. 2009), pp. 4–6. According to one of our anonymous readers, some in the region dispute Gul Bahadur's descent from the Faqir of Ipi and maintain that he simply belongs to the same clan. Gul Bahadur's Waziri Taliban have had a tense and sometimes violent relationship with the Mehsud-dominated TTP and are also distinct from the Afghan Taliban led by Mullah Muhammad Omar.
44. Arnold Fletcher, *Afghanistan: Highway of Conquest*, Westport, CT: Greenwood Press, 1982 [1965], pp. 250f., who observes that "these Pushtoons had been separated by force from the Pushtoons of Afghanistan and were now limited, willy-nilly, to a choice between two successor states, one of which had no previous existence and thus no possible claim to the territory."
45. Universal adult suffrage was not extended to the Federally Administered Tribal Areas

(FATA) until 1996, and the ban on political parties in the FATA was not lifted until the summer of 2011.

46. Dennis Kux, *The United States and Pakistan, 1947–2000*, Washington, DC: Woodrow Wilson Center Press, 2001, p. 19; Rizwan Hussein, *Pakistan and the Emergence of Islamic Militancy in Afghanistan*, Aldershot, UK: Ashgate, 2005, Chapter 2.
47. See Jamal, *Shadow War*, pp. 45ff.
48. Fletcher, *Afghanistan*, p. 253.
49. Ibid., and Olesen, *Islam and Politics in Afghanistan*, p. 194.
50. On Pakistan's relations with the Soviets during this period, see the concise account in Fletcher, *Afghanistan*, Chapter 18.
51. Hussain, *Pakistan and the Emergence of Islamic Militancy in Afghanistan*, p. 71.
52. Henry Bradsher, *Afghanistan and the Soviet Union*, Durham, NC: Duke University Press, 1985, p. 22.
53. *Civil and Military Gazette* (Lahore), 1 Jan. 1960, quoted in Dupree, *Afghanistan*, pp. 534f. Dupree ends his discussion of this article with the observation, "One can only wonder which member of the Pakistan Tribal Affairs Department wrote this statement."
54. Hussain, *Pakistan and the Emergence of Islamic Militancy in Afghanistan*, p. 72; Dupree, *Afghanistan*, pp. 538ff.
55. On these developments see Thomas Ruttig, *Islamists, Leftists—and a Void in the Center: Afghanistan's Political Parties and where they came from (1902–2006)*, n.p.: Konrad Adenauer Stiftung, 2006; on the *Jawanan-i-Musulman*, see Edwards, *Before Taliban*, Chapter 6.
56. Oleson, *Islam and Politics in Afghanistan*, pp. 231f. Professor Niazi died in 1970.
57. The Kabuli Islamists were not, however, a Muslim Brotherhood movement in anything like a strict sense, nor can any of the mujahidin parties of the 1980s be considered as such, contrary to what is sometimes stated in the secondary literature. See, e.g., Peter Tomsen, *The Wars of Afghanistan*, New York: Public Affairs, 2011, p. 304, where four of the Sunni mujahidin parties are erroneously identified as politically affiliated with the Muslim Brotherhood. On this issue see Olesen, *Islam and Politics*, p. 253 n. 10.
58. On the symmetries of the Kabuli Islamists and their Marxist–Leninist enemies, see Barnett R. Rubin, *The Fragmentation of Afghanistan*, 2nd ed., New Haven and London: Yale University Press, 2002, pp. 84f., noting that "both groups believed that revolution would transform society through the agency of a strong state, yet neither had a program for structuring that state and financing its activities. Like the state they opposed, both groups ultimately relied on foreign aid in the struggle for power."
59. David B. Edwards, "The Evolution of Shi'i Political Dissent in Afghanistan," in Juan R.I. Cole and Nikkie R. Keddie (eds), *Shi'ism and Social Protest*, New Haven and London: Yale University Press, 1986, p. 218.
60. On the history of the JI, see Seyyed Vali Reza Nasr, *The Vanguard of the Islamic Revolution: The Jama'at-i Islami of Pakistan*, Berkeley and Los Angeles: University of California Press, 1994. On Maududi's influence on Qutb, see John Calvert, *Sayyid Qutb and the Origins of Radical Islamism*, New York: Columbia University Press, 2010, pp. 158 and 214.
61. Farshad Rastegar, "Education and Revolutionary Political Mobilization: Schooling versus Uprootedness as Determinants of Islamic Political Activism among Afghan Refugee Students in Pakistan," PhD thesis: University of California, Los Angeles, 1991, p. 11.
62. I take the phrase from Roxanne Euben, *Enemy in the Mirror: Islamic Fundamentalism and the Limits of Modern Rationalism*, Princeton, NJ: Princeton University Press, 1999. Euben discusses Marxist influences on Sayyid Qutb at p. 78
63. Olesen, *Islam and Politics in Afghanistan*, p. 232.
64. Edwards, *Before Taliban*, p. 238. The JIA would split in the late 1970s, and the offshoot that maintained the closest ties to the JI during the 1980s was Gulbuddin Hekmatyar's Hizb-e Islami Gulbuddin (HIG).
65. Also spelled *maulvi*, *maulana*, and other variants, the title literally means "master," akin to the English honorific "lord" (though there are nuances in local usage that distinguish between maulvi and mawlana, with the former sometimes having a pejorative sense). The exact date of Jalaluddin's enrollment in the Haqqaniyya madrassa is not stated in any of the primary sources available to me, though his date of graduation is, and he noted in an interview with 'Abdullah 'Azzam's *al-Jihad* magazine that he had studied there for six years; "al-Haj Jalaluddin Haqqani in an Interview with the al-Nasiha Magazine," *Manba' al-Jihad* (Pashto), 2, 5 (Nov. 1990), and "Hiwar maftuh ma' Jalaluddin Haqqani," *al-Jihad*, 2, 13 (Nov. 1985), p. 18.
66. Though now the surname of the family that leads the network, the name "Haqqani" is tra-

ditionally taken by many—but not all—graduates of the Haqqaniyya madrasa to indicate their membership in the elite confraternity of Haqqaniyya alumni.

67. The name of the school is often spelled Dar ul-Uloom; Haqqaniyya also has various alternate spellings. On this institution in the broader context of South Asian madaris, see Muhammad Qasim Zaman, *The Ulama in Contemporary Islam: Custodians of Change*, Princeton, NJ: Princeton University Press, 2002, Chapter 5.
68. See Mu'in-ud-Din Ahmad Khan, "Sayyid Ahmad Shahid's Campaign Against the Sikhs," *Islamic Studies*, 7, 4 (1968), pp. 317–38.
69. Jamal Malik, *Colonialization of Islam: Dissolution of Traditional Institutions in Pakistan*, New Delhi: Manohar, 1996, pp. 203–5.
70. Ibid., p. 209. Based on registry data from the madrassa covering the years 1977–84, Malik found that 16.7 percent of graduates came from Bannu/North Waziristan, and 16.2 percent from Afghanistan. In all, 87 percent of the graduates originated from the NWFP, the tribal areas, or Afghanistan. Malik also cites an article from the Haqqaniyya magazine *al-Haq* from 1981 stating that "an especially high number of students from the Afghan province of Paktia" were attending the school (ibid., p. 222 n. 92).
71. *Manba' al-Jihad* (Pashto), 1, 4–5 (Oct.–Nov. 1989).
72. See Edwards, *Before Taliban*, pp. 247f. One of Khalis' sons was a member of the Muslim Youth. According to recent research by Kevin Bell, it appears that Khalis completed his studies with Abdul Haq Akorwi prior to the formal establishment by the latter of the Dar al-'Ulum Haqqaniyya. While thus not technically a graduate of the Haqqaniyya school, Khalis was still very much a part of the clerical network associated with the madrassa. Bell, personal communication, 6 November 2012.
73. Roy, *Islam and Resistance*, p. 70. The work in question—Qutb's *Social Justice in Islam*, first published in Egypt in 1949—predates Qutb's prison years and is not representative of the advocacy for violent Islamist revolution that would characterize his later writings. On Khalis' complex relationship with the Muslim Brotherhood and other currents of Islamist thought, see Kevin Bell, "Yunis Khalis: The Tension between the Historiography and the Primary Sources," unpublished MA thesis: Princeton University, 2012.
74. Azmat Hayat Khan, "Factional Organization of the Afghan Mujahideens in Peshawar," *Central Asia* (University of Peshawar), 14 (1984), pp. 51–73, at p. 63.
75. *Gahez*, 40 (Dec. 1969), p. 1; trans. from Ashraf Ghani, "Afghanistan: Islam and Counterrevolutionary Movements," in John Esposito (ed.), *Islam in Asia: Religion, Politics, Society*, New York and Oxford: Oxford University Press, 1987, pp. 79–96, at p. 91. Brackets surrounding "state" in this quotation are from Ghani.
76. Edwards, *Before Taliban*, p. 249.
77. Ghani, "Afghanistan: Islam and Counterrevolutionary Movements," p. 91.
78. Khan, "Factional Organization," p. 55.
79. See Edwards, *Before Taliban*, Chapter 7.
80. Rastegar, "Education and Revolutionary Political Mobilization," p. 11. I do not intend to suggest in using this term that the "traditional Islamic culture" as articulated by groups such as the Haqqaniyya network is any less a modern construction than the Kabulis' revolutionary discourse, but simply that there was a very different way in which the two groups conceived of the status quo and its relation to particular constructions of "Islamic tradition."
81. On the relative "styles" of JUI and JI political activism, see Joshua White, *Pakistan's Islamist Frontier: Islamic Politics and U.S. Policy in Pakistan's North-West Frontier*, Arlington, VA: Center on Faith & International Affairs, 2008, p. 26 and *passim*.
82. Ibid., p. 28.
83. Illustrating the closeness of the JUI to the Haqqani Network, Sami ul-Haq, Member of the National Assembly and leader of one of the two wings of the JUI (JUI-S), at a JUI gathering in Lahore in Apr. 1991 attended by Jalaluddin Haqqani, declared that "Jamiat Ulema-e Islam considers Haqqani as of its own body; the JUI does not recognize territorial boundaries." "Al-Haj Mawlawi Jalaluddin Haqqani in a General Gathering of the Jamiat Ulema-e Islam in Lahore," *Manba' al-Jihad* (Pashto), 2, 11 (May 1991).
84. Ibid., and Hamid Mir, "The Attack on Maulana Samiul Haq," *Ausaf*, 20 Oct. 2001. On Abdul Haq's victory in this election, see Sayyid A.S. Pirzada, *The Politics of the Jamiat Ulema-i-Islam Pakistan, 1971–77*, Oxford and New York: Oxford University Press, 2000, p. 34; and the biographical profile of Abdul Haq at the Khyber.org website, online at http://www.khyber.org/people/ulema/MaulanaAbdulHaq.shtml
85. Jalaluddin established the Rahimiyya school with fellow Haqqaniyya alumnus Ahmad Gul, and was soon joined by other Haqqaniyya students from greater Paktia, all of whom went

on to join Jalaluddin in fighting the Kabul regime; "Interview with Commander Mawlawi Hanif Shah," *Manba' al-Jihad* (Pashto), 1, 4–5.

86. "Al-Haj Jalaluddin Haqqani in an Interview with the al-Nasiha Magazine," *Manba' al-Jihad* (Pashto), 2, 5 (Nov. 1990).
87. Radio Kabul broadcast, 17 July 1973, published in *Dawn* (Karachi), 18 July 1973; see Hussain, *Pakistan and the Emergence of Islamic Militancy in Afghanistan*, p. 78.
88. Hussain, *Pakistan and the Emergence of Islamic Militancy in Afghanistan*, p. 79.
89. On the ISI list, see Imtiaz Gul, *The Most Dangerous Place: Pakistan's Lawless Frontier*, New York: Viking, 2010, p. 2; the figure of 5,000 trainees is cited in Bradsher, *Afghan Communism*, p. 17.
90. Tomsen, *Wars of Afghanistan*, pp. 102 and 108. Tomsen was the US State Department special envoy to the mujahidin from 1989 to 1992.
91. Henry Kamm, "Pakistan Officials Tell of Ordering Afghan Rebel Push," *New York Times*, 23 Apr. 1989.
92. Kux, *The United States and Pakistan*, p. 209.
93. The town of Nika is currently located in Nika District in northeastern Paktika, contiguous with the Zadran district of Paktia. "Sahib" is an honorific and term of respect.
94. Gomal is located in Gomal District in central Paktika.
95. All four of these men became Haqqani commanders during the anti-Soviet jihad. Ahmad Gul, a Zadran from Nika, Paktika, graduated from the Haqqaniyya madrassa around 1970 and helped Jalaluddin establish their first madrassa in Paktika; he was killed in battle in Sep. 1985. Fathullah Haqqani, a Zadran from the Wazi Zadran district of Paktia, graduated from the Haqqaniyya madrassa in 1971 and, with his brother Nizamuddin Haqqani, fought alongside Jalaluddin from 1973 until his death in Sep. 1985. Fathullah was Jalaluddin's deputy and chief military commander of the Haqqani fronts in southeastern Afghanistan from 1980 to 1985. Mutiullah also fought with Haqqani from the early 1970s, served as battlefield commander in the 1980s, and went on to become the general director of military affairs for HIK before his death by landmine in June 1989. See "Martyrs of the Path of Truth," *Manba' al-Jihad* (Pashto), 1, 2–3.
96. The town of Urgun is in the south of the Urgun District of Paktika Province, just to the south of Nika District.
97. Qazi Amin Waqad, whose father was a disciple of the aforementioned Hadda Mullah, was one of the earliest Muslim Youth activists and was working during this period in Nangarhar as a madrassa teacher and clandestine Islamist activist. He joined the Peshawar émigrés in 1975 and later became Hekmatyar's deputy.
98. Mawlawi Aziz Khan, "The First Jihadi Operation in Afghanistan, and the Rising of the 'Ulama against the Communists," *Manba' al-Jihad* (Pashto), 1, 4–5 (Oct.–Nov. 1989).
99. Accounts of these events are given in Roy, *Islam and Resistance*, pp. 74ff., and Edwards, *Before Taliban*, pp. 235ff.
100. Ziruk is both a town and a district in northeastern Paktika, sharing borders with the Urgun and Nika districts of Paktika and the Zadran district of Paktia.
101. The 'Umar-e-Faruq Division was the name given to a group of Haqqani fighters stationed during the 1980s at a base in the Zhawara valley in Khost, at which al-Qa'ida also established a training camp known as al-Faruq.
102. i.e., west, toward Zarghun Shahr District in western Paktika.
103. On Mansur, see Ruttig, "Loya Paktia's Insurgency," pp. 78–83. Ruttig found that the "Mansur network" has operated independently of the Haqqani network in recent years, and the two networks fought under different mujahidin parties during the Soviet war though there is a long history of cooperation and integrated mobilizations by these two groups from the 1970s to the 1990s, richly documented in the *Manba' al-Jihad* volumes as well as the collection of Haqqani correspondence in the Harmony database.
104. "The Historic Battle of Paktia," *Manba' al-Jihad*, 3, 5 (Oct.–Nov. 1991), referencing "personal diary entries of Mawlawi Haqqani." An even more colorful account is given in "Portrait of a Mujahid," *Arabia* (Dec. 1985), p. 20, where Haqqani's men are said to have killed thirty government troops and to have survived in the mountains for a month on "roots, berries and even leaves and grass" before escaping into Pakistan.
105. "Al-Haj Jalaluddin Haqqani in an Interview with the al-Nasiha Magazine," *Manba' al-Jihad* (Pashto), 2, 5 (Nov. 1990); Edwards, *Before Taliban*, pp. 240 and 328 n. 20.
106. Edwards, *Before Taliban*, p. 241. Edward observes that, "Ironically, the assassination precipitated the street demonstrations that led President Daud [*sic*] to arrest Taraki and Hafizullah Amin, who then launched the Saur Revolution in April 1978."

107. "Portrait of a Mujahid," *Arabia* (Dec. 1985), p. 20. The author of the profile of Jalaluddin's life is not identified, though accompanying it is an interview with Jalaluddin conducted by Pakistani journalist Muhammad Salahuddin.
108. Ibid. (Note that the article refers to the Deh Mazang prison as the "Muzzang prison.") On the mass execution of Afghan Islamists that had been arrested under Daoud, see the "UN Mapping Report on Afghanistan," Kabul, 2005, p. 17. This UN human rights report was never officially released but was leaked online; see Sari Kuovo, "Facts for reconciliation: Human rights documentation needed," *Afghanistan Analysts Network*, 10 Oct. 2010, available online at http://aan-afghanistan.com/index.asp?id=1217
109. Hussain, *Pakistan and the Emergence of Islamic Militancy in Afghanistan*, p. 80.
110. Henry S. Bradsher, *Afghan Communism and Soviet Intervention*, Oxford and London: Oxford University Press, 1999, p. 20.
111. Edwards, *Before Taliban*, p. 241.
112. On the formation and character of the various Sunni parties, see Dorronsoro, *Revolution Unending: Afghanistan, 1979 to the Present*, New York: Columbia University Press, 2005, Chapter 4, and Rubin, *Fragmentation of Afghanistan*, Chapter 9.
113. See AFGP-2002-008624, pp. 49–56, "The High Command's Organizational Principles for the Mujahidin's Conduct of Jihad in the Areas of Paktia," no date. Of the nineteen principles of organization, eight have to do with defining the rights and responsibilities of the tribes. For instance, point 3 reads: "In the fronts there must be a tribal council and a base [i.e., a center of military leadership from the party]. The tribal council shall have responsibility for organizing the local mujahidin and the base shall have the responsibility for organizing the national and military mujahidin, as well as that of advisory issues. They shall conduct their administrative tasks in their respective areas." See also Edwards, *Before Taliban*, pp. 252f., noting that he personally witnessed this tribal integration during visits to Haqqani fronts in Paktia in 1984.
114. On these outreach attempts under Taraki, see Edwards, *Before Taliban*, p. 82.
115. "Afghan Cabinet Official Reported Slain by Villagers," *New York Times*, 15 Sep. 1980.
116. AFGP-2002-008629, p. 84. Parcham was one of two Afghan Marxist–Leninist parties.
117. "Afghan Cabinet Official Reported Slain by Villagers," *New York Times*, 15 Sep. 1980. Thomas Ruttig writes, on the basis of interviews with eyewitnesses, that Jalaluddin Haqqani personally had Faiz Muhammad killed, hosting the minister and his team for "negotiations" and serving them a rich meal, after which the guests fell asleep and were killed; Ruttig, "Loya Paktia's Insurgency," p. 65, and personal communication with the author, 3 Mar. 2011.
118. On JIA's failure to establish itself in Pashtun regions, see Roy, *Islam and Resistance*, p. 131.
119. Yousaf and Adkin, *Afghanistan: The Bear Trap*, p. 167.
120. Edwards, *Before Taliban*, p. 252.
121. Ibid., p. 249.
122. Van Dyk, *In Afghanistan*, p. 119.
123. Nasr, *Vanguard of Islamic Revolution*, p. 172.
124. See White, *Pakistan's Islamist Frontier*, pp. 30ff.
125. In one early survey of the Afghan resistance groups, the author lists ninety-five different resistance parties, representing every shade of the political spectrum in Afghanistan; see Azmat Hayat Khan, "Afghan Resistance and National Leadership," *Central Asia* (Peshawar), 9 (1981), pp. 163–77. The calculated limitations on ISI–CIA aid effectively eliminated over 90 percent of these groups, though a number of Shi'i parties managed to win support from Iran and were headquartered there during the conflict.
126. Rubin, *Fragmentation of Afghanistan*, p. 196.
127. Yousaf and Adkin, *Afghanistan: The Bear Trap*, p. 167.
128. On the Zakat system, see Malik's exhaustive analysis in *Colonialization of Islam*, Chapter 4.
129. See the data presented in ibid., Tables 3–4 (A–F); JUI-affiliated madrassas grew from 292 in 1971 to 1097 by Jan. 1984; JI-affiliated madrassas in the same period grew from forty-one to 107.
130. White, *Pakistan's Islamist Frontier*, p. 32.
131. According to Haqqani publications, but this could very well be an exaggeration. See Suhrat Nangyal, "Afghanistan' Jihad and the Virtuous Victory," *Manba' al-Jihad* (Pashto), 2, 8 (Jan. 1991), excerpting from a book by the same title published in Karachi in 1990 by a certain Mawlana Hafez Mushtaq Ahmad Abbasi.
132. "The Manba' al-'Ulum Madrasa as a Major Educational Center," *Manba' al-Jihad* (Pashto), 1, 1 (July 1989).

133. "Manba' al-'Ulum is a Resource to the Jihad," *Manba' al-Jihad* (Arabic), 1, 1 (Feb. 1990).
134. Edwards, *Before Taliban*, p. 260.
135. Rubin, *The Fragmentation of Afghanistan*, p. 194.
136. Ibid.
137. Edwards, *Before Taliban*, p. 262; Roy, *Islam and Resistance*, p. 124.
138. Roy, *Islam and Resistance*, pp. 152 and 129, notes that Jalaluddin Haqqani had "ousted the Babrakzay family from their position of influence in the powerful Jadran tribe," "by virtue of his energy and military skill," though he makes no reference in this connection to Pakistan's influence.

2. BIRTH OF THE NEXUS: THE HAQQANI NETWORK, FOREIGN FIGHTERS, AND THE ORIGINS OF AL-QA'IDA

1. Steve Coll, *Ghost Wars*, New York: Penguin Books, 2004, p. 238.
2. Milt Bearden and James Risen, *The Main Enemy*, New York: Random House, 2003, p. 312. Bearden was the CIA station chief in Pakistan from 1986 to 1989.
3. These debates are recounted in Abu'l-Walid al-Masri, "Jalaluddin Haqqani: Astura fi tarikh jihad Afghanistan (1)," *al-Sumud*, 45 (Feb.–Mar. 2010), pp. 34–9, at p. 35. This was the first of a three-part article on the life of Jalaluddin published by Abu'l-Walid in the Taliban's Arabic-language magazine, based on an unpublished book about the early years of the Afghan jihad that he had written in 1983. The early outreach of the Peshawar parties to the Arab world is described in 'Isam Diraz, *Malhamat al-Mujahidin al-'Arab fi Afghanistan*, Cairo, 1989, pp. 7ff.
4. The label "strategic asset" was applied to the Haqqanis in 2008 by Pakistani General Ashfaq Kayani, director of the ISI from 2004 to 2007, subsequently promoted to chief of army staff. See David Sanger, *The Inheritance*, New York: Harmony Books, 2009, p. 248.
5. The term "Afghan Arab" was applied to non-Afghan (and generally non-Pakistani) foreign Muslim volunteers who came to Afghanistan between 1979 and 1993, though in many cases these people were not Arabs but rather Southeast Asians, European, American, sub-Saharan Africans, etc.
6. Thomas Hegghammer, "The Rise of Muslim Foreign Fighters: Islam and the Globalization of Jihad," *International Security*, 35, 3 (2010–11), pp. 53–94, at p. 85; 'Isam Diraz, *Malhamat al-Mujahidin al-'Arab fi Afghanistan*, Cairo, 1989, pp. 5ff.
7. Muhammad, *al-Ansar al-Afghan fi Afghanistan*, p. 31. Tufail (d. 2009) led the JI until 1987 when he was succeeded by Qazi Hussein Ahmad.
8. See Camille Tawil, *al-Qa'ida wa akhawatuha: qissa al-jihadiyin al-'arab*, London: Saqi, 2007, 13ff.; 'Abdallah Anas, *Wiladat al-afghan al-'arab*, London: Saqi, 2002; Vahid Brown, "Foreign Fighters in Historical Perspective: The Case of Afghanistan," in Brian Fishman (ed.), *Bombers, Bank Accounts, and Bleedout: Al-Qa'ida's Road in and out of Iraq*, West Point, NY: Combating Terrorism Center at West Point, 2008, pp. 16–31; Hegghammer, "The Rise of Muslim Foreign Fighters." As noted below, however, Jalaluddin Haqqani claimed in 1980 that there were already "scores" of foreign fighters among his ranks. This estimate may have been meant to include Pakistani volunteers, who were indeed significantly represented in the Afghan war and are not included in the term "Afghan Arab."
9. There are some exceptions to this picture in the literature. For example, a declassified 2001 DIA assessment called Jalaluddin Haqqani "the Jadran [*sic*] tribal leader most exploited by ISI during the Soviet–Afghan war to facilitate the introduction of Arab mercenaries"; "Veteran Afghan Traveller's Analysis of Al Qaeda and Taliban." Coll, *Ghost Wars*, also acknowledges the Haqqanis' special relationship with the early Arab fighters. See also Hegghammer, "Muslim Foreign Fighters," p. 86.
10. For a partial translation of this book, including the text of the fatwa itself, see "The Defense of Muslim Territories Constitutes the First Individual Duty," trans. Thomas Hegghammer, in Kepel and Milelli (eds), *Al Qaeda in its Own Words*, Cambridge, MA: Belknap/Harvard, 2008, pp. 102–9. On the significance of the fatwa for the Afghan Arab phenomenon, see Hegghammer, "The Rise of Muslim Foreign Fighters," pp. 74f.
11. The organization referred to here is an early iteration of the Ittihad party, which was established under Sayyaf's leadership in 1980 and was meant to unite all of the mujahidin parties. It quickly fell apart as an umbrella organization and Sayyaf carried on the Ittihad as his own party, with the Haqqanis remaining under HIK.
12. "Jalaluddin Haqqani, interview with Sami 'Abd al-Muttalib," *Al-Ittihad* (Abu Dhabi), 11 June

1980 (FBIS trans.). Jalaluddin made similar appeals in other interviews over the course of the war and in the series of publications produced and distributed by the Haqqani network's "Manba' al-Jihad" publishing house; see, e.g., the "interview with Jalaluddin Haqqani during the siege of Khost," *Manba' al-Jihad* (Arabic), 7–8 (Feb.–Mar. 1991), in which Haqqani said, "Supporting the mujahidin is an obligated duty upon every Muslim because this war against the atheists and the agents in Kabul is a jihad that is made obligatory for them by God. The entire *umma* is in agreement upon this, and I believe it is my right to demand that all Muslims support the Afghan mujahidin with whatever they can: their money, their souls, and their prayers."

13. After his assassination, 'Azzam's will was published in *al-Jihad*, 63 (Jan. 1990), pp. 58ff., and at p. 58 it is headed with the inscription, "written April 20, 1986 in the home of the heroic Shaykh Jalaluddin Haqqani." The will was also published in the first issue of *Manba' al-Jihad* issued by the Haqqanis in 1989; Ahmad Zaydan, *The "Afghan Arabs" Media at Jihad*, Islamabad: PFI, 1999, p. 92.
14. 'Abdullah 'Azzam, *Ayat al-Rahman fi Jihad al-Afghanistan*, Iskandaria: Dar al-Da'wa, 1985 [1984], p. 30. On the significance of *Ayat al-Rahman* for 'Azzam's mobilization efforts, see Thomas Hegghammer, *Jihad in Saudi Arabia*, Cambridge and New York: Cambridge University Press, 2010, p. 41.
15. Haqqani was not the only Afghan leader to precede 'Azzam in declaring support for the Afghan jihad an individual duty, nor was he the first to reach out for Arab support. In Dec. 1980 several of the Peshawar-based party leaders visited Egypt to thank Sadat for his support and to seek further aid. Sayyid Ahmad Gilani, leader of one of the parties, was quoted in *al-Ahram* on 22 Dec. as saying that "jihad is a personal jihad (*jihad al-nafs*), a financial jihad (*jihad al-mal*), and is obligatory (*fard*) upon all Muslims." Muhammad Nabi Muhammadi, leader of Harakat, was quoted in the same paper on 27 Dec. as saying that "it is the duty (*wajib*) of every Muslim to support Afghanistan." See 'Isam Diraz, *al-'A'idun min Afghanistan*, Cairo: al-Dar al-Misriyya li'l-Nashr wa'l-I'lam, 1993, pp. 56f. These appeals, however, all emphasized material support and did not go to the extent of inviting volunteer fighters. Inayatullah Faizi, in "Afghan Political Literature in Peshawar," in Fazal-ur-Rahim Marwat and Sayed Wiqar Kakakhel (eds), *Afghanistan and the Frontier*, Peshawar: Emjay Books International, 1993, p. 281, lists *Farida al-Jihad 'ala al-jama'a wa'l-afrad* ("the duty of jihad upon the community and individuals") published in Arabic by Nabi Muhammadi's Harakat in 1978, but unfortunately I have been unable to locate a copy of this work.
16. Hegghammer argues that 'Azzam was the innovative advocator of "universal private military participation" in his *Jihad in Saudi Arabia*, p. 42.
17. Van Dyk, *In Afghanistan*, p. 109.
18. The Haqqanis also attempted to establish offices at some point in Mashhad, Iran, but in the one piece of correspondence in the Harmony database concerning this it is said that Iranian authorities had refused to permit this and that the effort "so far has produced no results"; AFGP-2002-008681, p. 24, undated letter addressed to Jalaluddin Haqqani.
19. "Interview with Commander Mawlawi Hanif Shah," *Manba' al-Jihad* (Pashto), 1, 4–5 (Oct.–Nov. 1989).
20. Mawlawi Aziz Khan, "The First Jihadi Operation in Afghanistan and the Rising of the 'Ulama Against the Communists," *Manba' al-Jihad* (Pashto), 1, 4–5 (Oct.–Nov. 1989).
21. Letter from Fathullah Haqqani to Nizamuddin Haqqani and other commanders, 3 July 1980 (AFGP-2002-008587, pp. 23–4). The rest of the letter makes clear that this was not simply for purposes of solicitation but rather that a program was already in place that had buy-in from donor communities in the Gulf.
22. Nearly all of the Afghan Arabs took new names, most often in the form of a *kunya* ("Abu So-and-So"), and this eventually became a universal practice in the Afghan Arab training camps and a central element of identity formation in the culture of the camps.
23. Abu'l-Walid al-Masri, "Chats from the Rooftop of the World 1," written at al-Faruq camp at Zhawara, Aug. 1994, AFGP-2002-600087, pp. 22f. The other two Egyptians who accompanied him to Afghanistan were a man identified only as "Isma'il" and Ahmad al-Minyawi, son of Husni al-Minyawi, a famous Muslim Brotherhood activist who fought in Palestine in 1947–8.
24. Haji Din Muhammad was a senior official in HIK and brother of Abdul Haq and Haji 'Abd al-Qadir, two of HIK's most capable commanders. All three later opposed the Taliban and, under Karzai, Haji Din Muhammad was made governor of Nangarhar Province. See Said Hyder Akbar and Susan Burton, *Come Back to Afghanistan*, New York: Bloomsbury, 2005, pp. 76ff.

25. This episode is also recounted in Basil Muhammad, *al-Ansar al-'Arab fi Afghanistan*, Riyadh: Lajnat al-Birr al-Islamiyya, 1991, p. 89. Abu'l-Walid dates his first meeting with Jalaluddin to June 1979 in "Jalaluddin Haqqani: Astura fi Jihad Afghanistan (1)," *al-Sumud*, 45 (Feb.–Mar. 2010), pp. 34–41, at p. 34.
26. Tomsen, *Wars of Afghanistan*, p. 143.
27. On Abu'l-Walid's career see Vahid Brown, "Abu'l-Walid al-Masri: A Biographical Sketch," online at http://www.ctc.usma.edu/posts/a-profile-of-abu%E2%80%99l-walid-al-masri. Abu'l-Walid maintains a blog on which he has made available his voluminous writings and memoirs, which are indispensable sources for the history of the Haqqanis, al-Qa'ida, and the Afghan Arab movement in Afghanistan; online at www.mafa.asia. He lived in Iran under house arrest from 2002 to 2011. After the "Arab Spring" overthrow of Mubarak in Egypt, Abu'l-Walid was released from Iran and repatriated to his homeland. He occasionally writes for the Taliban's Arabic journal *al-Sumud*, in recent issues of which (vols 45–6, 2010) he published a multipart hagiography of Jalaluddin Haqqani.
28. See below, Chapter 3.
29. 'Isam Diraz, *al-Qissat al-Damiyyah li'l-Ghazw al-Sufiyiti li-Afghanistan*, Cairo: Dar al-'Itisam, 1988, p. 18.
30. Zaydan, *The "Afghan Arabs" Media at Jihad*, p. 92.
31. Of the small number of prominent exceptions, mention should be made of 'Abdullah Anas, who fought with Ahmad Shah Massoud in the Panjshir Valley in 1984, and Abu Khubayb al-Masri, who fought for one of Sayyaf's commanders in Kandahar beginning in the same year; see Ayman Sabri Faraj (Abu Ja'far al-Qandahari), *Dhikriyyat 'Arab Afghan Abu Ja'far al-Masri al-Qandahari*, Cairo: Dar al-Shuruq, 2002, p. 49.
32. Van Dyk, *In Afghanistan*, pp. 98ff. Ken Guest published a photo of this "Engineer Abdul Rahman" in his chapter "Afghanistan" in Anthony Rogers et al., *Flashpoint: At the Front Line of Today's Wars*, London: Arms and Armour, 1995, p. 18.
33. Muhammad, *al-Ansar al-'Arab fi Afghanistan*, p. 80.
34. Ibid., p. 106 n. 8; *al-Jihad*, 44 (July 1988), p. 36. For Jalaluddin Haqqani's praise of 'Abd al Rahman, see 'Isam Diraz, *Malhamat al-Mujahidin al-'Arab fi Afghanistan*, Cairo, 1989, pp. 36f.
35. Ibid., p. 102. Abu Hafs was killed in the American aerial bombing of Afghanistan following the 9/11 attacks.
36. Ibid. Abu'l-Walid al-Masri provides a number of eyewitness accounts of the battles fought by this group at Haqqani fronts in the mid-1980s; see, e.g., Mustafa Hamid, *Ma'arik al-bawwaba al-sakhriyya*, al-Faruq Camp, Paktia: 1995, p. 40, which describes a battle fought in 1984 under the command of Fathullah Haqqani at which Abu Hafs and 'Abd al-Rahman "fought with a courage bordering on madness" and earned the epithets "the mad Arabs" (*al-'arab al-majanin*) among the Haqqanis' Afghan fighters.
37. 'Abdullah Anas, *Wiladat al-Afghan al-'Arab*, London: Dar al-Saqi, 2002, p. 19. When Anas recounted his story to Peter Bergen in 2005, he said "I'm the fourteenth Arabs [who arrived in Pakistan to help the Afghan jihad]"; see Bergen (ed.), *The Osama bin Laden I Know*, New York: Free Press, 2006, p. 29.
38. Muhammad, *al-Ansar al-'Arab fi Afghanistan*, p. 101. This is according to Salih al-Yemeni, who names another Yemeni, two Egyptians, two Algerians, a Libyan, a Qatari, a Jordanian, and a Saudi as composing this group.
39. Letter from Fathullah Haqqani, dated 3 July 1980 (AFGP-2002-008587, pp. 23–4). The trainers were Ma'afi Khan and Mawlawi 'Arabi, and the recipients of the letter are asked to treat them with deference; the recipients are asked to take special care of Mawlawi 'Arabi, to "treat [him] well with regard to everything: food, drink, etc." It is possible that this trainer was an Arab, as in other Haqqani correspondence field commanders are asked to treat the Arabs with special deference (see, e.g., AFGP-2002-008578, p. 9). That these camps were at Khost is indicated by the fact that they were set up at Mullah Abdul Rahman's center, the latter being indicated elsewhere (AFGP-2002-008576, p. 25) as the amir of the Khost front.
40. Details on the history of the Zhawara base are drawn from a 175-page book about the base written in 1991 by Shuhrat Nangyal, the editor of the Haqqanis' "Manba' al-Jihad" publications series; Nangyal, *Zhawara at the Dawn of History* (Pashto), n.p.: Public Relations Department of al-Haj Jalaluddin Haqqani's Fronts, 1991.
41. Yousaf and Adkin, *Afghanistan—The Bear Trap*, pp. 164 and 159.
42. Ibid., p. 167. There is an abundance of other primary source material that confirms Haqqani's status of overall commander and supply master in the region during the 1980s, particularly the Haqqani correspondence in the Harmony database. Jere Van Dyk, an American journalist

who visited the Haqqani fronts in Loya Paktia in 1981, encountered a former Pakistani army major fighting with Haqqani who told him that Jalaluddin Haqqani "has emerged among us. He is now the leader for all of Paktia Province and for all of southeast Afghanistan," and described the manner in which Haqqani had united the groups fighting for the various Peshawar parties under his command; Van Dyk, *In Afghanistan: An American Odyssey*, New York: Coward-McCann, 1983, p. 126. Mustafa Hamid, in his voluminous memoirs from the Afghan jihad, also confirms the impression of Haqqani's overall leadership.

43. Congressman Charlie Wilson visited the Zhawara base in 1987; see Yousaf and Adkins, *Afghanistan: The Bear Trap*, p. 62.
44. Mir Brahmanyar, *Afghanistan Cave Complexes 1979–2004: Mountain strongholds of the Mujahideen, Taliban & Al Qaeda*, Oxford: Osprey Publishing, 2004, p. 54. In addition to this and the above-cited text by Nangyal, see also Lester W. Grau and Ali Ahmad Jalali, "The Campaign for the Caves: the Battles for Zhawar in the Soviet-Afghan War," *Journal of Slavic Military Studies*, 14, 3 (2001), online at http://www.globalsecurity.org/military/library/report/2001/010900-zhawar.htm
45. On Operation Magistral, see Gregory Feifer, *The Great Gamble: The Soviet War in Afghanistan*, New York: HarperCollins, 2009, Chapter 6. Ali Ahmad Jalali and Lester W. Grau, *Afghan Guerrilla Warfare*, St. Paul, MN: MBI Publishing, 2001 [1995] includes several descriptions of the battles at Zhawara, including Operation Magistral, by prominent Haqqani commanders—indeed, much of this book consists of Haqqani commanders' descriptions of various engagements during the war.
46. Yousaf and Adkins, *Afghanistan: The Bear Trap*, pp. 164f. Abu'l-Walid, citing the *Bear Trap* book, takes exception to Yousaf's assertion that 40 percent of these supplies were routed through the Ali Khel base at Jaji in northern Paktia, which was under the primary control of Sayyaf's Ittihad party. If this was true, asks Abu'l-Walid, "why didn't the Soviets single out Jaji for attacks similar to the attacks on Zhawara?" *Ma'arik al-bawwaba al-sakhriyya*, p. 122.
47. DIA assessment, "Veteran Afghanistan traveller's analysis of Al Qaeda and Taliban, military, political and cultural landscape and its weaknesses," 24 Sep. 2001, quoted in B. Raman, "ISI–Bin Ladin Links: As Seen by the DIA," South Asia Analysis Group, paper no. 791 (17 Sep. 2003), available online at http://www.southasiaanalysis.org/papers8/paper791.html; cf. Barnett Rubin, *Fragmentation of Afghanistan*, p. 217. Jadran is a frequent alternate transliteration of Zadran. The assessment continues by observing that, as Zhawara (called Zahawa in the DIA document) became Bin Laden's base, "then serious questions are raised by the early relationship between bin Laden and Pakistan's ISI." According to Abu'l-Walid al-Masri, many of the contractors were actually Afghans, mostly from Wardak Province (AFGP-2002-600087).
48. See Steve Coll, *Ghost Wars*, pp. 156f., and Coll, *The Bin Ladens*, New York: Penguin, 2008, p. 293. Jamal Ismail, an "Afghan Arab" and journalist, recalls that, in contrast to 'Azzam, who was based in Peshawar, "Osama was spending most of his time on the Afghan frontline with commanders, especially general Jalaluddin Haqqani in Khost" (in Bergen, *The Osama bin Laden I Know*, p. 47).
49. George Crile, *Charlie Wilson's War*, New York: Grove Press, 2003, pp. 473ff.
50. Coll, *Ghost Wars*, p. 201.
51. Coll, *The Bin Ladens*, New York: Penguin, 2008, p. 294. As Coll notes, "Osama [bin Laden] would have had no reason to know about Haqqani's opportunistic work with the CIA, but he and his Arab volunteers benefitted from it."
52. Rubin, *Fragmentation of Afghanistan*, p. 243, makes a similar point.
53. Coll, *Ghost Wars*, p. 202.
54. Jamal, *Shadow War*, 2009, Chapter 4. According to a Maulana Abdul Bari, a JI official who was put in charge of this project, Zia had told him at a meeting in Rawalpindi in 1980 that "the biggest share of the international arms and American financial assistance" would be given to "whoever trains our boys from Kashmir." Ibid., p. 110.
55. According to one source, the Jihadwal base was named after Asadullah Jihadwal, a Zadran tribesman who was a close comrade of Hekmatyar's and who was killed early in the war; see Rafiq Afghan, "Gardez, Gardez," *Ummat* (Urdu) 10 Mar. 2002. Regarding the closeness of Hizb ul-Mujahidin to Hekmatyar, Masood Sarfraz, one of the founders of the former, stated that its name was derived from the latter's Hizb-i Islami (Jamal, *Shadow War*, p. 140).
56. Jamal, *Shadow War*, p. 169.
57. AFGP-2002-600088, pp. 16–20.

58. AFGP-2002-600088, p. 18. Mustafa Hamid calls them "jama'at al-mujahidin" and "jama'at al-jihad al-'alami," respectively, but it is clear from the details he provides that he is referring to the two groups better known in Pakistan as Harakat-ul Jihad al-Islami (HuJI) and Harakat-ul Mujahidin (HuM).
59. Nasrullah Mansur's collaboration with Haqqani in the 1970s anti-communist activities has been noted above; that they remained close into the 1990s is evidenced by an account of Abu'l-Walid of Mansur's accompaniment of Jalaluddin at the funeral of the latter's mother in Miranshah. Abu'l-Walid, the Jordanian Haqqani commander Abu'l-Harith al-Urduni, and Mansur sat together in the front row; AFGP-2002-600029, p. 54.
60. These details are confirmed in Mohammad Amir Rana, *Gateway to Terrorism*, London: New Millennium, 2003, pp. 240f., which describes Harakat-ul Mujahidin as having begun jihad in Afghanistan "under the leadership of the Afghan commander Jalaluddin Haqqani" in 1984; and p. 264f., which quotes Qari Saifullah Akhtar, the leader of HuJI, to the effect that HuJI worked with Nasrullah Mansur's Harakat party during the Afghan jihad.
61. "Harakatul Jihad Carried out Bombings on Udichi-Chhayanaut Cultural Function," *Prothom Alo* (Dhaka), 6 Feb. 2007.
62. By "significant numbers" is meant scores; none of our sources describe the contingent of Arabs at Zhawara in this battle as even approaching 100 men; Lawrence Wright, *The Looming Tower*, New York: Alfred A. Knopf, 2006, cites the figure of sixty in 'Azzam's group. It was not until the Battle of Jalalabad—see below—that the participation of Arabs numbered in the hundreds.
63. Secretary of State Clinton, "Testimony on Afghanistan and Pakistan," House Foreign Affairs Committee, 27 Oct. 2011. Online at http://www.state.gov/secretary/rm/2011/10/176281.htm
64. Yousaf and Adkin, *Afghanistan—The Bear Trap*, p. 167; Jalali and Grau, *Afghan Guerrilla Warfare*, p. 323. Additional accounts of the battle for Zhawara in English are given in Grau and Jalali, "The Campaign for the Caves"; Wright, *The Looming Tower*, p. 110, and Coll, *The Bin Ladens*, p. 285. Wright and Coll both rely on the accounts in Muhammad, *al-Ansar al-'Arab fi Afghanistan*, pp. 173ff. (and note that Coll refers to Zhawara as Jawr, a close transliteration of the name of the base in Arabic).
65. The presence of Pakistani military regulars and ISI officers is attested in all of the Arabic eyewitness sources cited below. Abu'l-Walid claims to have seen Brig. Yousaf inside the Zhawara base during the later stage of the siege, and directly challenges Yousaf's claim in *The Bear Trap* that the latter coordinated defenses from within Pakistan (*Ma'arik al-bawwaba al-sakhriyya*, p. 129).
66. Mustafa Hamid, *Ma'arik al-bawwaba al-sakhriyya*, al-Faruq Camp, Paktia: 1995, pp. 131f.; Muhammad, *al-Ansar al-'Arab fi Afghanistan*, pp. 174ff., which also mentions a number of other Arab fighters present at Zhawara during the battle before 20 Apr.
67. Hamid, *Ma'arik al-bawwaba al-sakhriyya*, p. 126. Julaydan describes these events himself in Muhammad, *al-Ansar al-'Arab fi Afghanistan*, p. 174. He was later a participant in the meetings in Peshawar during Aug. and Sep. 1988 at which al-Qa'ida was officially established as "an organized Islamic faction." See Bergen, *The Osama bin Laden I Know*, p. 80, where he appears under his *nom de guerre*, "Abu al Hasan al Madani."
68. Hamid, *Ma'arik al-bawwaba al-sakhriyya*, p. 132; and Abu Hafs' own account in Muhammad, *al-Ansar al-'Arab fi Afghanistan*, pp. 175f. See also the latter source, p. 179 n. 5, observing that this was the first contact of its kind between Arabs and Pakistanis on the Afghan battlefield, and that a Pakistani colonel involved in this episode later offered to provide Pakistani army training to Abu Hafs, who politely declined.
69. For the will—dated and indicating location in the first lines—see *al-Jihad*, 63 (Jan. 1990), p. 58.
70. Bin Laden audiocassette library, tape no. 1298, speaker not identified. Thanks to Flagg Miller for sharing this information with me. On this tape collection, see Flagg Miller, "Insights from Bin Ladin's Audiocassette Library in Kandahar," *CTC Sentinel* (Oct. 2011).
71. Abu'l-Fadl 'Umar al-Hadushi, "Nubdha mukhtasara 'an hayat mujaddid al-jihad al-shaykh al-imam 'Abdallah 'Azzam," posted to the al-Tahadi webforum and available online at http://www.archive.org/details/alt7dii
72. Or, according to Abu Mahmud al-Suri, the "Silent Brigade"; Diraz, *Ma'arik Ma'sada al-Ansar*, p. 24.
73. Muhammad, *al-Afghan al-'Arab fi Afghanistan*, p. 178. In this account, Bin Laden is noted to have been angered by 'Azzam's order to return to Peshawar, arguing instead that they should stay and fight.

74. Ibid. In Wright's account (*Looming Tower*, p. 110), this phrase (*katiba al-zurafa'*) is translated as "the Brigade of the Ridiculous."
75. This is according to Abu Mahmud al-Suri (Enaam Arnaout), who says that the "Silent Brigade" "was heavily involved in the battles; a large number of Arabs were wounded, and many were martyred" (Diraz, *Ma'arik Ma'sada al-Ansar*, p. 24).
76. Hamid, *Ma'arik al-bawwaba al-sakhriyya*, p. 136.
77. Diraz, *Malhamat al-Mujahidin al-'Arab*, p. 36.
78. Abu'l-Walid al-Masri, AFGP-2002-600096, p. 173, entry dated 14 May 1986. Later in the same diary Abu'l-Walid derisively describes these youths as war "tourists" on short visits from Saudi Arabia; ibid., pp. 177f.
79. Mustafa Badi (Abu Ibrahim al-Logari), *Afghanistan: Ihtilal al-dhakira*, Sana'a: 2003, available online at http://tokhaleej.jeeran.com/archive/2008/6/597637.html. Abu Ibrahim came to Afghanistan in 1986 and worked briefly for the MAK before aligning himself with Haqqani and establishing an independent training camp at Lezi ("Lija" in the Arabic sources), just north of the Zhawara base.
80. According to Bin Laden himself; see Bergen, *The Osama bin Laden I Know*, p. 74. The alternative notion that al-Qa'ida took its name from a "database" of the names of Afghan Arabs, a claim made to Jason Burke by Saudi intelligence sources (see his *Al-Qaeda*, London: I.B. Tauris, 2003, p. 293 n. 3) finds no support in the primary source evidence and should be laid to rest.
81. Sada was a MAK/Sayyaf camp located near the town of Sada in the Kurram tribal agency of Pakistan. According to Muhammad, *al-Ansar al-'Arab*, pp. 183f., Sada was established after the first battle at Zhawara in 1986. In an interview with Peter Bergen in 2005, 'Azzam's son Hudhayfa recalled having attended Sada in 1984; Coll repeats this date, citing this interview in *The Bin Ladens: An Arabian Family in the American Century*, New York: Penguin, 2008. However, there is evidence that Southeast Asian trainees began to attend the Sada camp as early as 1985 (see, e.g., International Crisis Group, "Jemaah Islamiyah in South East Asia: Damaged but Still Dangerous," 26 Aug. 2003, p. 4).
82. Faraj, *Dhikriyyat 'Arab Afghan*, p. 25. He did not end up joining al-Qa'ida after his training, and instead went on to fight with one of Sayyaf's commanders in Kandahar.
83. The Haqqani correspondence in the Harmony database documents the logistical coordination between the Haqqanis and the various other parties operating in the southeast; for supplying of Sayyaf's Ittihad, see AFGP-2002-008612, p. 49.
84. Ibid., p. 28. Abu Ja'far's guide from Zhawara to Jaji was an Iraqi Kurd, and he says that there were many such people in Afghanistan at the time who came in overland from Iran. Again, this is a population not likely to be accounted for in the Peshawar-centric view of Afghan Arab history.
85. Muhammad, *al-Ansar al-'Arab fi Afghanistan*, p. 236.
86. Ibid., p. 243, citing the memoirs of Abu Mahmud al-Suri (Enaam Arnaout), who took part in the establishment of the camp from the beginning. These same memoirs note that three days later an Arab returned to the camp "who had been dispatched by Abu 'Abdullah to work a bulldozer for Shaykh Jalaluddin Haqqani in Zhawara."
87. Muhammad, *al-Ansar al-'Arab fi Afghanistan*, p. 249.
88. Mustafa Hamid (Abu'l-Walid), *Ma'arik al-bawwaba al-sakhriyya*, p. 133. See also Michael Scheuer, *Through Our Enemies' Eyes*, rev. ed., Washington, DC: Potomac Books, 2006, pp. 108–10.
89. For an account of the encounter, see Wright, *Looming Tower*, pp. 115ff. Soviet Colonel (now General) Valerii Vostrotin confirms elements of the account, without mentioning Bin Laden. Vostrotin's forces were surprised while making their way down to Zhawara in May 1987 just south of the Parachinar Ledge (the same area as the Ma'sada camp) when they encountered a group of black-uniformed insurgents who engaged them in close combat, something nearly unheard of among Afghan mujahidin. After capturing some of them the Soviets discovered the fighters were Arab and African-American, armed with American M-14 rifles (Feifer, *Great Gamble*, p. 230).
90. See Hegghammer, *Jihad in Saudi Arabia*, p. 45.
91. The British cameraman Peter Jouvenal, describing a visit to the Zhawara base in 1982, says that "They [the Haqqanis] shot videos of executions of Russians and sent them to Saudi Arabia for fund-raising purposes"; Peter Bergen, *Holy War, Inc.*, New York: Touchstone, 2001, p. 57. According to one of our anonymous readers, other mujahidin parties also produced videos for foreign donor audiences during the war, though lacking evidence I am

unable to assess how widespread the practice was or whether the Haqqanis were innovators with regard to other Afghan resistance groups.
92. Hegghammer, *Jihad in Saudi Arabia*, p. 45.
93. Mustafa Hamid, *Ma'arika al-bawwaba al-sakhriyya*, pp. 229ff.
94. From a compilation of the writings and statements of 'Azzam in praise of Jalaluddin Haqqani, included in Husayn bin Mahmud's "Li-madha yurid al-Amrikan ightiyal Asad Khurasan?" (Why do the Americans want to assassinate the Lion of Khurasan [Jalaluddin Haqqani]?) posted to the Fajr forum in 2002, available online at naseh.net/vb/showthread.php?t=9246. Husayn bin Mahmud is a prominent Salafi-jihadi ideologue and al-Qa'ida supporter whose writings are popular in the jihad web forums.
95. See, e.g., *al-Jihad*, 1, 5 (Apr. 1985), p. 7; 1, 10 (Aug. 1985), pp. 25–7; 2, 13 (Nov. 1985), pp. 18–22; 2, 18 (May 1986), pp. 6–9; 2, 21 (Aug. 1986), pp. 28f.; 3, 28 (Mar. 1987), p. 23; 3, 29 (Apr. 1987), p. 16; 5, 56 (June 1989), p. 14; 7, 83 (Aug.–Sep. 1991), pp. 16f.; 8, 85 (Feb. 1992), pp. 12–15.
96. *al-Jihad*, 3, 31 (June 1987), p. 21. In the following issue, in an article about the Ramadan battle at Ma'sada, Bin Laden is again mentioned only in a passing reference at the very end of the article—though prominent attention is given in the body of the text to Abu 'Ubayda and his prior experience fighting at Zhawara. *Al-Jihad*, 3, 32 (July 1987), pp. 4–11, at p. 11.
97. For references to "Abu 'Abdullah" in later issues, see *al-Jihad*, 57–8 (July and Aug. 1989), stories on the Battle of Jalalabad, translated in Bergen, *The Osama bin Laden I Know*, pp. 87f.
98. On the negative reputation of the Arabs among other Afghan commanders, see Anthony Hyman, "Arab Involvement in the Afghan War," *Beirut Review*, 7 (1994), pp. 73–89, at p. 85. A Saudi volunteer who stayed at al-Qa'ida's Bayt al-Ansar in Peshawar before proceeding to train at the al-Faruq camp at Zhawara recalls: "The man in charge of the house explained to us during a meeting that when we got to Afghanistan, we would witness heresies and some idolatrous practices. He warned us not to discuss these issues with the Afghans because they would beat us up or even kill us because they were ignorant rabble." Manahi al-Shaybani, "Former Saudi Mujahidin Interviewed," *al-Riyadh*, 30 Dec. 2003.
99. AFGP-2002-008578, p. 9 (in Dari).
100. AFGP-2002-600096, p. 195. See also Van Dyk, *In Afghanistan*, pp. 99f., which describes the Egyptian whom Van Dyk encountered working for the Haqqanis in 1980–1 as having held "the Afghans … in contempt. They, he found, prayed only two or three times a day, and then only short prayers, and were ignorant of the religion to which they subscribed."
101. Haji Din Muhammad, *De Khalis Zhwand, Fan aw And*, Peshawar: Pir Chap Khuna, 2007, passage translated in Bell, "Yunis Khalis," p. 28.
102. The third of the five daily prayers in Islam, performed between mid-afternoon and sunset.
103. Faraj, *Dhikriyyat*, p. 28.
104. According to Abu'l-Walid al-Masri, al-Qa'ida had to rent the land for the latter two camps from Hekmatyar, though none of the sources mention any such remuneration required for the camps at Haqqani's facilities; see Mustafa Hamid, "Abu'l-Walid's dialogue with Egyptian researcher Leah Farral," http://allthingscounterterrorism.com/my-dialogue-with-abu-walid-al-masri/arabic-and-english-versions-of-abu-walids-answers-to-my-questions/english-trans-abu-walids-fifth-reponse/
105. See Nasser al-Bahri, *Dans l'ombre de Ben Laden*, Paris: Editions Michel Lafon, 2010, pp. 104ff.
106. Shuhrat Nangyal, *Zhawara at the Dawn of History* (Pashto), n.p.: Public Relations Department of al-Haj Jalaluddin Haqqani's Fronts, 1991, pp. 26ff. Prior to the name change of the Zhawara base, al-Faruq was known simply as the Zhawara camp.
107. Abu Jandal Nasir al-Bahri, in Khalid al-Hammadi, "Bodyguard Interviewed on First Meeting with Bin-Ladin, al-Qa'ida Beginnings," *al-Quds al-'Arabi*, 22 Mar. 2005 (FBIS trans.).
108. Abu Qudama Salih al-Hami, *Fursan al-farida al-ghayba* (posted to jihadi internet forums, 2007), pp. 802f. After Abu Binan the Khaldan camp was administered by Ibn al-Shaykh al-Libi and Abu Zubayda, though contrary to popular accounts it was run independently of al-Qa'ida. Abu Qudama al-Hami fought under the Haqqanis and was wounded at Khost, and later became a follower of Abu Mus'ab al-Zarqawi; see Jean Charles Brisard, *Zarqawi: The New Face of al-Qaeda*, New York: Other Press, 2005, p. 21.
109. See Abu'l-Walid's dialogue with Leah Farral, op. cit.
110. See Badi, *Afghanistan: Ihtilal al-dhakira*.
111. Hami, *Fursan al-farida al-ghayba*, pp. 688ff.; the amir of the training camp was Abu 'Abdullah al-Filistini and its Arab trainers included Khalil Mahmud Bashir al-Qaryuti, Abu Mahmud,

and 'Imad al-Din. Hami describes several of these men as veterans of the Haqqani campaigns at Khost and Gardez.

112. Hami, *Fursan al-farida al-ghayba*, p. 796.
113. Fazul, *al-Harb 'ala'l-Islam*, vol. 1, pp. 57f.
114. Salamat Ali, "Cause and Effect," *Far Eastern Economic Review* (23 May 1991), p. 24.
115. This fact was noted by the DIA in 2001: "For the first time, large numbers of Arabs were observed in Afghanistan during the Soviet withdrawal. One of the key features of the Paktia border province, in which they [the Arabs] were first established, was that it had no Russians. ... At that point, the Arab visitors were largely linked and reliant on Haqqani's mujahideen in Paktia"; DIA assessment, "Veteran Afghanistan traveler's analysis of Al Qaeda and Taliban, military, political and cultural landscape and its weaknesses," 24 Sep. 2001, quoted in B. Raman, "ISI-Bin Ladin Links: As Seen by the DIA."
116. For accounts of these battles and the Afghan Arab involvement, see Mustafa Hamid (Abu'l-Walid al-Masri), *Tharthara fawq saqf al-'alam* (distributed online, 2007–9), vols 4 (on the battle of Jalalabad), 8 (on Khost), and 9 (on Gardez). Lengthy accounts of these battles from another Afghan Arab can be found in Hami, *Fursan al-farida al-ghayba*.
117. 'Isam Diraz, *Usama bin Ladin yarwi ma'arik Ma'sada al-Ansar al-'Arab bi-Afghanistan*, Cairo: al-Manar al-Jadid, 1991, p. 71, quoting Abu Salman al-Ta'ifa, a Yemeni participant in the Jalalabad battle.
118. On the ISI/CIA planning for the siege, see Coll, *Ghost Wars*, Chapter 10.
119. On this see Vahid Brown, *Cracks in the Foundation*, West Point, NY: Combating Terrorism Center at West Point, 2007, pp. 4f.
120. AFGP-2002-600088, p. 13.
121. "Interview with Commander Haji Ma'afi Khan," *Manba' al-Jihad* (Pashto), 1, 1 (July 1989). In an interview with the MAK's *al-Jihad* magazine shortly after the Jalalabad battle, Khalil Haqqani—Jalaluddin's youngest brother and a senior leader within the network—also complained that the failed siege had "drained a huge quantity of materiel" from the mujahidin's stores in the southeast; *al-Jihad*, 54 (June 1989), p. 14.
122. See Mohammed Hafez, "*Jihad* after Iraq: Lessons from the Arab Afghans," *Studies in Conflict and Terrorism*, 32 (2009), pp. 73–94, at p. 75.
123. Mahan Abedin, "From Mujahid to Activist: An Interview with a Libyan Veteran of the Afghan Jihad," Jamestown Foundation *Spotlight on Terrorism*, 3, 2 (May 2005), online at http://www.jamestown.org/single/?no_cache=1&tx_ttnews[tt_news]=178. Benotman went on to fight at the Battle of Gardez.
124. "Martyrs of the Conquest of Khost (Arab Martyrs)," *Manba' al-Jihad* (Arabic), 10 (June 1991).
125. The siege of Khost became the stuff of jihadi legend and, as noted by Loretta Napoleoni, "For a mujahed, having participated in the battle of Khost is a sign of prestige; this is why some people have claimed that al Zarqawi was part of the Arab-Afghan brigade" led by Abu'l-Harith al-Urduni, though in fact Zarqawi arrived in Afghanistan a month after the fall of Khost; *Insurgent Iraq: Al Zarqawi and the New Generation*, New York: Seven Stories Press, 2005, p. 239 n. 2. On the Yemeni front, see Badi, *Afghanistan: Ihtilal al-dhakira*.
126. On al-Qa'ida's involvement, see Brown, *Cracks in the Foundation*, pp. 5f. The statement there that Haqqani "operated under the aegis of Gulbuddin Hekmatyar's Hizb-e Islami" is an error, and should read "Yunus Khalis' Hizb-e Islami." On the EIG's involvement, see Mustafa Hamid, *Jihad ma bayn nahrayn: Mashru' Tajikistan*, n.p., 2007, p. 9. This is the tenth volume of Hamid's *Tharthara fawq saqf al-'alam* series, posted online in Dec. 2007.

3. THE FOUNTAINHEAD: THE HAQQANI NETWORK, THE TALIBAN, AND THE RISE OF GLOBAL JIHAD

1. Rubin, *Fragmentation of Afghanistan*, p. 243.
2. Ibid., p. 251. Peter Tomsen, in *The Wars of Afghanistan*, pp. 335ff. and Chapter 17, reveals that there were two de facto US government policies toward the mujahidin at this time: the official policy of supporting a political settlement process, pursued by the State Department; and a conflicting policy pursued by the CIA, which continued to back the ISI in its support for a military solution via Hekmatyar.
3. Tomsen, *The Wars of Afghanistan*, p. 259, based on an account by Turki al-Faisal, then head of Saudi intelligence and chief liaison from the royal family to the mujahidin. A similar account, though lacking any mention of Jalaluddin grabbing a pistol and confronting Hekmatyar, is

given by 'Abdullah 'Azzam, who attended these meetings, in *al-Tarbiyya al-Jihadiyya*, Peshawar: Shahid 'Azzam Media Center, 1992, pp. 157–9.

4. Also known as the Interim Islamic Government of Afghanistan (IIGA). The presidency was given to Sibghatullah Mujaddidi and the prime minister post to Sayyaf, though an ISI bid to have Hekmatyar made the defense minister collapsed in a contentious dispute that ended the shura.
5. "Afghan Rebels Torn by New Quarrel," *New York Times*, 7 Apr. 1991.
6. See, e.g., *Nusrat al-Jihad* (Urdu). 1–2 (Nov.–Dec. 1991).
7. "Interviews with the Field Commanders," *Manba' al-Jihad* (Arabic), 16–17 (Feb.–Mar. 1992); Grau and Jalali, "The Campaign for the Caves," n. 49.
8. It was as leader of the NCS that Shaykh Zayid bin Sultan al-Nahyan, president of the UAE, welcomed Jalaluddin in 1991 in the first "state visit" accorded to any Afghan mujahidin leader by the Emirates; *Manba' al-Jihad* (Arabic), 11 (July 1991).
9. See *Afghanistan Forum*, 19, 3 (May 1991), p. 3, where the NCS was announced at a press conference in Quetta as a "new party" led by these three HIK commanders. Malang was the HIK's field commander for Kandahar, while Abdul Haq's area of operation was Kabul. Both later opposed the Taliban.
10. Rubin, *Fragmentation of Afghanistan*, p. 254. The Haqqanis publicized the involvement of Shi'a groups in *Manba' al-Jihad*, including an interview with Sayyid Muhammad Hasan Jagran, the most prominent Hazara Shi'i commander of the Revolutionary Council of the Islamic Union of Afghanistan, a Shi'a mujahidin party led by Sayyid 'Ali Beheshti. See "Interviews with the Field Commanders," *Manba' al-Jihad* (Arabic), 16–17 (Feb.–Mar. 1992).
11. *Afghanistan Forum*, 19, 3 (May 1991), p. 3.
12. See Neamatollah Nojumi, *The Rise of the Taliban in Afghanistan: Mass Mobilization, Civil War, and the Future of the Region*, New York: Palgrave, 2002, pp. 106 and 241 n. 3; Tomsen, *Wars of Afghanistan*, pp. 396ff.
13. "Interview with Mawlana Jalaluddin Haqqani," *Manba' al-Jihad* (Pashto), 1, 10 (Apr. 1990).
14. "Mawlawi Jalaluddin Haqqani on the Occasion of the Establishment of a Joint Governance Body in Khost," *Manba' al-Jihad* (Pashto), 5, 1–2 (Nov. 1993). When asked in an interview to explain his concept of Islamic government, Jalaluddin responded that "Those in power should be Muslim. The state law should be Islamic law, and the rulings of *shari'a* should be implemented, such as finding justice for the oppressed against the oppressor, rejecting adultery, applying the punishments, waging jihad, etc." "Interview with Shaykh Haqqani," *Manba' al-Jihad* (Arabic), 18 (1992).
15. Ibid. In 1994, at the height of the Afghan civil war, Jalaluddin even proposed the formation of "an interim government which will supervise elections under a transitional set-up"; Naseem Zehra, "Signs of Afghanistan-fatigue in Islamabad," *Inter Press Service* (Islamabad), 28 Feb. 1994.
16. See "Interview with al-Haj Nizamuddin Haqqani, Deputy Commander of the Southern Fronts," *Manba' al-Jihad* (Pasho), 3, 1 (July 1991).
17. "Mawlawi Jalaluddin Haqqani on the Occasion of the Establishment of a Joint Governance Body in Khost," *Manba' al-Jihad* (Pashto), 5, 1–2 (Nov. 1993). According to a 1994 letter from al-Qa'ida leader Abu 'Ata al-Sharqi, then amir of the al-Qa'ida camp at Jihadwal, to the al-Qa'ida leadership in Sudan, the Khost governor appointed during this process ('Abd al-Qayyum Khan) was "from the Haqqani organization" (*tanzim Haqqani*). To my knowledge, this is the first mention of anything akin to the "Haqqani network" in the sense of its current usage, though earlier Arabic sources sometimes refer to the "Haqqani group" (*jama'a Haqqani*).
18. Rubin, *Fragmentation of Afghanistan*, p. 277.
19. Ibid.
20. "On the Reconciliation between the Ahmadzai Tribe and the Nangarhar [Jalalabad] Shura," *Manba' al-Jihad* (Pashto), 5, 1–2 (Nov. 1993). The same article refers to Jalaluddin as one "who has always been the messenger of peace, the creator of stability, and the advocate of non-violence"!
21. Badi, *Afghanistan: Ihtilal al-dhakira*.
22. Ibid.
23. See Vahid Brown, "Classical and Global Jihad: al-Qa'ida's Franchising Frustrations," in Assaf Moghadam and Brian Fishman (eds), *Fault Lines in Global Jihad*, New York: Routledge, 2011, pp. 94f.
24. For the development of the polarization in Peshawar, see the volumes of *Afghanistan Forum* for 1990 and 1991.

25. "Interview with Jalaluddin Haqqani During the Siege of Khost," *Manba' al-Jihad* (Arabic), 7–8 (Feb.–Apr. 1991).
26. Badi, *Afghanistan: Ihtilal al-dhakira.*
27. On Bin Laden's offer, see Wright, *Looming Tower*, p. 157, where Bin Ladin is said to have offered 100,000 men. A more plausible account is provided by Bin Laden's son Omar, who recalls that his father offered 12,000 men; Najwa bin Laden et al., *Growing Up bin Laden*, New York: St. Martin's Press, 2009, p. 82.
28. "Afghan guerrillas for Riyadh," *Pakistan Times*, 9 Feb. 1991.
29. *Afghanistan Forum*, 19, 2 (Mar. 1991), p. 4.
30. Tomsen, *The Wars of Afghanistan*, p. 419.
31. See Mamoun Fandy, *Saudi Arabia and the Politics of Dissent*, New York: Palgrave, 2001, Chapter 6; AFGP-2002-000103. The reforms that Bin Laden proposed, however, were quite radical, and included calls for the immediate resignation of the king and his brothers.
32. "Interview with Shaykh Haqqani," *Manba' al-Jihad* (Arabic), 18 (1992); see also Sharon Herbaugh, "Mojaddidi Says Deal Near on Hekmatyar's Demand for Removing Militia," *AP*, 17 May 1992; and Anwar Iqbal, "Masoud, Hekmatyar refuse to acknowledge peace accord," *UPI*, 21 May 1992.
33. On Haqqani's reconciliation activities over this period, see, e.g., Anwar Iqbal, "Rival Afghan mujahideen leaders sign long-awaited peace accord," *UPI*, 25 May 1992; John Jennings, "Air Strikes, Artillery End Kabul Calm," 9 Feb. 1994; "Temporary cease fire begins in Kabul," *UPI*, 15 Feb. 1994; Anwar Iqbal, "Afghans reveal yet another peace plan," *UPI*, 28 Apr. 1994.
34. Sally Neighbour, *The Mother of Mohammed: An Australian Woman's Extraordinary Journey into Jihad*, Melbourne: Melbourne University Press, 2009, p. 198.
35. Salah Najm, "Osama bin Laden, the Destruction of the Base," *Al-Jazirah*, 10 June 1999, quoted in Michael Scheuer, *Through Our Enemies Eyes*, rev. ed., Dulles, VA: Potomac Books, 2007, p. 130 (ellipses in Scheuer).
36. "Important Statement from the Eritrean Islamic Jihad Movement in regards to the recent developments in the Ethiopian and Eritrean arenas," *Manba' al-Jihad* (Arabic), 11 (July 1991). The statement is notable for its framing of the Eritrean Islamist struggle as nested within a global confrontation between Islam and an alliance of "Crusaders and Zionists" and their Arab and Muslim regime "agents." The Haqqanis published Egyptian jihadist statements in a magazine that predated the *Manba'* series, on which see below.
37. Rohan Gunaratna, *Inside Al Qaeda*, New York: Berkley Books, 2002, pp. 201ff., based on late-1990s interviews with Eritrean Islamic Jihad leaders in the *Nida' al-Islam* magazine. The seized computer of Enaam Arnaout (see below) also contains an undated letter addressed by the EIJM to Osama bin Laden, outlining their history and goals and seeking support with training and the development of a recruitment infrastructure. Enaam Arnaout computer files, folder "Tareekh Osama," images 118–20. Thanks to J.M. Berger for sharing these files with me.
38. See "The Eritrean Islamic Jihad Movement," in *Al-Qai'da's (mis)Adventures in the Horn of Africa*, West Point, NY: United States Military Academy, Harmony Project, 2006, pp. 83–5. That communiqué has a distinctly "Salafi" tone, stating toward the end that the alliances between Arab and Muslim regimes and the "Crusaders and Jews" is in violation of the principle of *wala' wa'l-bara'* (loyalty and disavowal), a central tenet of Salafi ideology.
39. See *US v. Enaam Arnaout*, Government's Evidentiary Proffer, NDI Eastern Division, 02 CR 892, pp. 21 and 37–43; J. Millard Burr and Robert O. Collins, *Revolutionary Sudan*, Leiden: Brill, 2003, Chapter 3.
40. From the seized Enaam Arnaout computer, file folder "Jabal Daily Reports." The letterhead is in English, while the letter is in Arabic and bears Jalaluddin's signature.
41. *US v. Enaam Arnaout*, Government's Evidentiary Proffer, NDI Eastern Division, 02 CR 892, Exhibit 53. Note that these files also included the minutes and memoranda of the meetings during which al-Qa'ida was formally established; see Bergen, *The Osama bin Laden I Know*, pp. 75ff.
42. Ibid., exhibits 84–98.
43. Jalaluddin Haqqani, *Is the Afghanistan War a Russian–American War?* (Pashto), 2nd ed., n.p.: Manba' al-Jihad, 1988–9, p. 33. As the preface to this book states, it consists of a transcript of a long speech that Haqqani made to the HuJI conference.
44. Jamal Khashoggi, "Al Qaeda Organization: Huge Aims without Programs or Cells," *al-Hayat*, 12 Oct. 1998, as quoted in Scheuer, *Through Our Enemies Eyes*, p. 110.
45. The Haqqanis also published a Pashto weekly beginning in 1991 entitled "De Jihad Hindara,"

though we were unfortunately unable to obtain copies of this until after the completion of this book.

46. Jalaluddin complained of the dwindling American support to State Department envoy Peter Tomsen in a meeting at his home outside Miranshah in July of 1989; Tomsen, *The Afghanistan Wars*, p. 300.
47. Zaydan, *The "Afghan Arabs" Media at Jihad*, p. 78. Zaydan is our only source that links the Haqqanis to this magazine, copies of which we were unable to locate. Two knowledgeable sources in Afghanistan whom we contacted in search of copies of this magazine expressed skepticism on this point and, though they'd heard of the magazine, did not recall any connection to the Haqqanis.
48. "Text of al-Haj Haqqani's Interview with the Arab al-Murabitun Magazine," *Manba' al-Jihad* (Pashto), 2, 12 (June 1991).
49. "Highlights of Mawlawi Jalaluddin Haqqani's and Mawlawi 'Abdullah Zakeri's Speeches to a Joint Conference of Afghan Scholars and the Council of Commanders," *Nusrat al-Jihad* (Urdu), 3 (Jan. 1991).
50. Fazl ur Rahman, general secretary of the JUI, at a gathering of Islamist leaders in Karachi addressed by Jalaluddin Haqqani in 1992; "Al-Haj Jalaluddin Haqqani Visits Islamic Madaris and Societies in Karachi," *Manba' al-Jihad* (Pashto), 3, 9–10 (May 1992). At the same conference, Mawlawi Faruq Kashmiri, deputy head of Harakat-ul-Mujahidin, called on "all of you students (*taliban*) to prepare yourself for jihad, and go to Afghanistan under the leadership of Mawlana Haqqani on your summer recess time."
51. See, e.g., *Nusrat al-Jihad*, 3, 4 (Feb. 1991), in which the first article is a long editorial on the "American conspiracy," which argues: "America has been interfering in the internal affairs of the Muslim Gulf states in order to secure the stable flow of oil to the US. Now the opportunity has arisen to meet the objective. In this war, America has everything to gain and nothing to lose. Muslims die, their countries are destroyed, they pay for the costs of the war, while America gets control over the oil fields." See also the article "The New World Order," *Nusrat al-Jihad* (Urdu), 5 (Mar. 1991), which cites President George H.W. Bush and Henry Kissinger before arguing that with "the collapse of the Soviet Union, America does not face a communist threat, and it sees Islam as the next enemy. America is talking about this new world order as simply a means to repress Islam."
52. See also letters from Jalaluddin Haqqani calling for support of the mujahidin of Bangladesh, India, and Burma in AFGP-2002-800928; and the following Haqqani articles on the Burmese Jihad: "Arakan: The Islamic Movement of Burma," *Nusrat al-Jihad*, 1, 5 (Mar. 1991), providing a glowing account of the Rohingya Solidarity Organization (RSO) and its efforts to defend Burmese Muslims from state repression; and Muhammad Ayyub Munir, "Think about your Burmese Muslim Brothers," *Nusrat al-Jihad*, 2, 3–4 (Jan.–Feb. 1992), again providing awareness-raising information on the plight of Burma's Muslims.
53. Tomsen, *The Wars of Afghanistan*, p. 424, suggests direct ISI support for the camps but provides no evidence.
54. According to Ahmad Shah Massoud, who claimed that Beg laid out this vision to him; see Tomsen, *The Wars of Afghanistan*, p. 416.
55. In *The Muslim*, 21 Nov. 1990, quoted in Tomsen, *The Wars of Afghanistan*, pp. 417f.
56. On the establishment of these camps in 1991, see AFGT-2002–000079.
57. "Manba' al-'Ulum is a Resource to the Jihad," *Manba' al-Jihad* (Arabic), 1 (Feb. 1990).
58. B. Raman, "An Analysis of United States Bombing of Terrorist Camps in Afghanistan," 4 Nov. 1998, online at http://www.subcontinent.com/research/sapra_documents/tr_1998_11_001_s.html
59. Don Rassler interview with Bob Nickelsberg, 23 Sep. 2010. Journalist Anthony Davis was also present during this visit, and confirmed the presence of Uighurs at Zhawara, speaking with a group of them in Mandarin Chinese.
60. The man, identified only as Mutelip [i.e., Mutallab], when asked if the East Turkestan Islamic Movement (ETIM) leader Hassan Makhsum paid for the training, replied, "No, he did not. It was financed by the Arabs. (Reporter): Who provided the money? (Mutelip): Bin Ladin did. Bin Ladin took care of everything, including food, clothing, medical care, and living and other expenses." "A Decade of Terror: How are the 'East Turkistan' Elements Trained?" *Sohu* (Beijing), 25 July 2002.
61. Letters in the Harmony database from the al-Qa'ida members in Afghanistan addressed to the senior leadership in Sudan also attest to al-Qa'ida's (often ambivalent) involvement in this project; see Brown, *Cracks in the Foundation*, pp. 11f.

62. Mustafa Hamid, *Jihad ma bayn nahrayn: Mashru' Tajikistan*, p. 11. The two Egyptians were Abu Dujana al-Sharqawi and Abu Tamim al-Sharqawi.
63. Hamid, *Jihad ma bayn nahrayn*, p. 16. The Hanafi school is one of four Sunni schools of Islamic jurisprudence, historically predominant in Afghanistan and Central Asia, and is the school in which the Deobandi movement was originally rooted. Salafis generally reject the four schools and are hostile to Sufism as deviating from strict Islamic monotheism.
64. Ibid., pp. 20, 30.
65. Ibid., p. 48. The notorious commander was Mawlawi 'Abd al-Latif, who belonged to Nabi Muhammadi's Harakat.
66. Hamid, *Jihad ma bayn nahrayn*, p. 39.
67. Fazul, *al-Harb 'ala'l-Islam*, vol. 1, pp. 145f. and 167.
68. Bahri, *Dans l'ombre de Ben Laden*, pp. 111 and 128 (Bahri refers to Fazul here by the pseudonym "Yacoub al-Dusari").
69. Bahri, *Dans l'ombre de Ben Laden*, p. 128.
70. See Fazul, *al-Harb 'ala'l-Islam*, vol. 1, pp. 390ff.
71. Ibid.
72. "Abir Sabil" (a pseudonym), "Lasna 'ala ruq'a al-shatranj wa lasna ahjar," (We are not Pieces on a Chessboard), message to Abu'l-Walid dated 12 Jan. 2011, posted on 23 Feb. to http://www.mafa.asia/ar/temp.php?K_Mafa=1061&id1=6&detail=511&cnl=1
73. AFGP-2002-600053.
74. Ibid., p. 14 (quoting from the verbatim English translation provided with the declassified original document and prepared by the Department of Defense; both are available on the website of the Combating Terrorism Center at West Point).
75. Ibid., p. 2, letter dated 30 Sep. 1993.
76. See Fazul, *al-Harb 'ala'l-Islam*, vol. 1, pp. 168ff.
77. Ibid., p. 167.
78. See, for instance, the interview with Bin Laden conducted by John Miller for ABC at an al-Qa'ida camp near Zhawara in May 1998, online at http://www.pbs.org/wgbh/pages/frontline/shows/binladen/who/interview.html
79. To cite but one example, Mohamed Sadeek Odeh came to Khost from the Philippines in Oct. 1990 and trained at al-Faruq at Zhawara before swearing allegiance to Bin Laden in 1992. He went to Kenya in 1993, took part in the US embassy bombings in 1998, and is currently serving a life sentence in the United States; see Roy Gutman, *How We Missed the Story*, Washington, DC: United States Institute of Peace, 2008, pp. 16f. Fazul, the overall leader of the embassy bombing teams, also trained at al-Faruq before being sent to Africa on this mission; see my profile of Fazul in *Al-Qai'da's (mis)Adventures in the Horn of Africa*, West Point, NY: United States Military Academy, Harmony Project, 2006, pp. 89–105.
80. See Abu'l-Walid's dialogue with Leah Farrall, op. cit.
81. On the nationalism of the Taliban regime, see Robert D. Crews, "Moderate Taliban?" in Robert D. Crews and Amin Tarzi (eds), *The Taliban and the Crisis of Afghanistan*, Cambridge, MA: Harvard University Press, 2008, pp. 238–73, at pp. 263f.
82. On more recent conflicts between these various factions, see Vahid Brown, "Al-Qa'ida and the Afghan Taliban: Diametrically Opposed?" *Jihadica*, 21 Oct. 2009, available online at http://www.jihadica.com/al-qa%E2%80%99ida-and-the-afghan-taliban-%E2%80%9Cdiametrically-opposed%E2%80%9D/
83. On the predominance of Haqqaniyya graduates in the Taliban's upper ranks, see Rashid, *Taliban*, Appendix II.
84. See Akbar and Burton, *Come Back to Afghanistan*, pp. 76ff.; "Afghan elders ask Taliban to quit," *The News* (Islamabad), 16 Nov. 2001.
85. See Ahmed Rashid, *Descent into Chaos*, New York: Viking, 2008, p. 88. Former Taliban minister Mullah Zaeef refers to this group of Haqqani allies in his memoirs: "Some of the commanders—like Karzai, Abdul Haq, Mullah Malang and Gul Agha Shirzai—were in direct contact with America and were working with the CIA and FBI." Abdul Salam Zaeef, *My Life with the Taliban*, New York: Columbia University Press, 2010, p. 125.
86. Gutman, *How We Missed the Story*, p. 92.
87. "Resistance Commanders on the Situation Inside Afghanistan: Interview with Maulawi Haqani Commander of the Zadran Front," *Afghan Information Centre Monthly Bulletin*, 82 (Jan. 1988), p. 13, where Jalaluddin is quoted as saying, "At the beginning of the offensive I sent messages to the mujahideen [*sic*] commanders in other provinces to attack Russian troops in their own areas, such as Commander Qari Baba (Ghazni), Mullah Malang (Kandahar) and

Masoud (Panjsher). For that reason, they showed solidarity with our front by launching heavy attacks on the enemy ..."

88. See Davis, "How the Taliban became a Military Force," in Maley, *Fundamentalism Reborn?* p. 52.
89. Hamid, *Ma'arika al-bawwaba al-sakhriyya*, p. 137.
90. Rubin, *Fragmentation of Afghanistan*, p. 255.
91. Hamid, *Jihad ma bayn nahrayn*, p. 21; Abu 'Ata al-Sharqi letter to al-Qa'ida leadership in Sudan, 4 Sep. 1994, AFGP-2002-800581.
92. Letter from Abu 'Ata al-Sharqi on behalf of the "Jihadwal State" (*dawla Jihadwal*) to "the Military Official," dated 4 Sep. 1994, AFGP-2002-800581, p. 5. From the letter it is unclear exactly what Fayez Muhammad had done to the al-Qa'ida leaders in Khost, though it does describe the protestations made by the latter to both representatives of Hekmatyar in Kabul and to Qazi Hussein Ahmed, the leader of the Pakistani JI, during a visit to the Badr camps at Jihadwal.
93. AFGP-2002-800581.
94. Hamid, *Jihad ma bayn nahrayn*, p. 21.
95. Muhammad, *De Khalis Zhwand*, passage translated in Bell, *Yunis Khalis*, p. 61.
96. On the Iraqi tank transfers, see Coll, *Ghost Wars*, p. 227. Abu'l-Walid describes the Arabs' repairs of the Khost airstrip in *Jihad ma bayn nahrayn*, p. 24. He states that the funding for the repairs was provided by Abu 'Abd al-Rahman Khadr al-Kanadi. The latter's teenage son Omar Khadr was imprisoned in Guantanamo in 2002; see Michelle Shephard, *Guantanamo's Child: The Untold Story of Omar Khadr*, Mississauga, Ontario: Wiley, 2008.
97. Interview with journalist Anand Gopal, 5 Aug. 2011. Gopal was in Khost during this period and personally interviewed a number of the principals directly involved in these negotiations.
98. Interview with Anand Gopal, 5 Aug. 2011; Ruttig, "Loya Paktia's Insurgency," p. 65.
99. An ISI role is suggested by, e.g., Davis, "How the Taliban became a Military Force," p. 70; Anand Gopal also mentioned this in our interview, but said that if there was ISI pressure it was probably not the decisive factor.
100. Davis, "How the Taliban became a Military Force," p. 60.
101. Rashid, *Taliban*, p. 60, citing his interview with Haqqani in Kabul in July 1997.
102. Ibid.
103. See Najwa bin Laden et al., *Growing Up Bin Laden*, p. 174, where Saznur appears as "Mullah Nourallah."
104. Cable from American Consulate in Peshawar to SecState, "Afghanistan: Taliban Agree to Visits of Militant Training Camps, Admit Bin Ladin is their Guest," Jan. 1997, p. 2. Available online at http://www.gwu.edu/~nsarchiv/NSAEBB/NSAEBB295/doc06.pdf
105. Al-Bahri, *Dans l'ombre de Ben Laden*, pp. 83f. There are in fact strong indications that significant numbers of former Afghan communist (Khalqi) officers had joined the ranks of the Taliban by early 1995 and helped to fill "key gaps in the[ir] fighting capability" (Davis, "How the Taliban became a Military Force," p. 54). Haji 'Abd al-Qadir, Bin Laden's initial host in Jalalabad, also cited the presence of communist officers in Taliban ranks as one reason for his opposition to the movement; Kamal Matinuddin, *The Taliban Phenomenon: Afghanistan 1994–1997*, Karachi: Oxford University Press, 1999, p. 58.
106. Neighbour, *Mother of Mohamed*, p. 232.
107. Translated in Bruce Lawrence, *Messages to the World: The Statements of Osama bin Laden*, London: Verso, 2005, pp. 24–30.
108. Rahimullah Yusufzai and Sunil Narula, "Shifting Battle Lines: The Taliban face their toughest test as diplomatic and military pressures mount," *Outlook India*, 30 Oct. 1996.
109. Al-Bahri, *Dans l'ombre de Ben Laden*, p. 83.
110. Ibid., p. 84.
111. See Bergen, *Holy War, Inc.*, Prologue.
112. Al-Bahri, *Dans l'ombre de Ben Laden*, p. 82.
113. Gutman, *How We Missed the Story*, p. 110.
114. Abubakar Siddique, "Pakistani Chief's Death would have Broad Implications," *Radio Free Europe*, 7 Aug. 2009.
115. 'Umar 'Abd al-Hakim (Abu Mus'ab al-Suri), "Afghanistan, the Taliban, and the Battle for Islam Today," AFGP-2002-602383, p. 22.
116. State Department cable from Islamabad to SecState, "Afghanistan: Jalaluddin Haqqani's Emergence as a Key Taliban Commander," Jan. 1997. Available online at http://www.gwu.edu/~nsarchiv/NSAEBB/NSAEBB295/doc05.pdf

117. Marc Kaufman, "Schooling of Afghan Girls Goes Ahead," *Philadelphia Inquirer*, 28 Feb. 1997. The story also quotes a Mohammad Ibrahim, described as "a former mujaheddin commander" whose daughter was attending one of the schools. It is possible that this is Muhammad Ibrahim Haqqani, one of Jalaluddin's brothers. He is quoted as saying that "the Talibs do not know Islam or the knowledge of the age. So when it comes to schools, we will do what we think is the right thing."
118. Anand Gopal, Mansur Khan Mahsud, and Brian Fishman, "The Battle for Pakistan: Militancy and Conflict in North Waziristan," *New America Foundation*, Apr. 2010, pp. 7f., online at http://counterterrorism.newamerica.net/sites/newamerica.net/files/policydocs/northwaziristan.pdf
119. AFGP-2002-008585, p. 5 (Pashto), dated 4 July 1985, from "Jamila," who introduces herself as head of the local MSF mission, and which begins with well-wishes to "you and your mujahidin" in an impending attack on Khost. Jamila writes to Jalaluddin that "I was glad to hear of your decision that you wanted to appoint a doctor for Sarana. In about a month or so, I will send a Muslim doctor by the name of Ibrahim, who is originally French. He will visit your clinic and the Ziruk clinic," and closes by writing, "I hope to meet you in person and talk to you about our programs so that I will learn your opinion about Paktia and work here according to your instructions."
120. See Cable from American Consulate in Peshawar to SecState, "Afghanistan: Taliban Agree to Visits of Militant Training Camps, Admit Bin Ladin is their Guest," op. cit.; and the declassified National Intelligence Daily, Director of Central Intelligence, 30 Sep. 1996, which observed that "Taliban has closed militant training camps associated with Prime Minister Hikmatyar, factional leader Sayyaf, and Pakistan's Jamaat-i-Islami. Taliban has not closed other camps associated with Usama bin Ladin, Hizbi Islami (Khalis), Pakistan's Jamiat-Ulema-i-Islam, and Harakat ul-Ansar, including the HUA's main training camp at Khowst."
121. Michael Griffin, *Reaping the Whirlwind*, rev. ed., London: Pluto Press, 2003, p. 116.
122. Husain Haqqani, *Pakistan: Between Mosque and Military*, Washington, DC: Carnegie Endowment for International Peace, 2005, p. 236.
123. Rashid, *Descent into Chaos*, p. 113 and 422 n. 8. Rashid writes that journalists "said" that these ISI casualties were seen and that US diplomats later confirmed this to him, though I was unable to locate any published reports from the time in which a Pakistani journalist publicly reported this claim.
124. The nine wanted fugitives thus identified are Riaz Basra, his brother Ghulam Shabir, Muhammad Alsam Moavia, Ijaz Ahmad Tarar, Tariq Mahmud, Abdul Aziz "Kotana," Muhammad Zaki, Muhammad Ajmal ("Akram Lahori"), and Muhammad Tanveer Khan.
125. This refers to regions of Kashmir occupied by Pakistan and India, respectively.
126. AFGT-2002–000079 AFGP-2002-000079.
127. *The Nation* (Islamabad), 7 Oct. 1999.
128. *Manba' al-Jihad* (Arabic), 11 (July 1991).
129. *The Nation* (Islamabad), 12 Oct. 1999.
130. *Nusrat al-Jihad* (Urdu), 3 (Jan. 1991).
131. See J. Todd Reed and Diana Raschke, *The ETIM: China's Islamic Militants and the Global Terrorist Threat*, Santa Barbara, CA: Praeger, 2010, pp. 47f.; James Millward, *Violent Separatism in Xinjiang: A Critical Assessment*, Washington, DC: East–West Center, 2004, p. 14.
132. This is how his name is given in the TIP's own Arabic literature, though in secondary sources, such as the above-cited books by Reed and Raschke and Millward, his name is spelled Hasan Mahsum.
133. 'Abdullah Mansur, "Sira Abi Muhammad rahimuhu Allah," *Turkistan al-Islamiyya*, 1 (July 2008), pp. 28ff.
134. 'Abdullah Mansur, "Liqa ma'a Amir al-Hizb al-Islami al-Turkistani al-Akh al-Mujahid 'Abd al-Haqq," *Turkistan al-Islamiyya*, 2 (Oct. 2008), pp. 5–8; 3 (Feb. 2009), pp. 9–12; and 4 (June 2009), pp. 8–12.
135. Abu'l-Walid also confirms that one "Turkistani" was among the twenty-five people killed in the strikes on the camps; Mustafa Hamid, *Jihad ma bayn nahrayn*, p. 71.
136. On Saifurrahman Mansur, see Ruttig, "Loya Paktia's Insurgency," pp. 78ff.
137. Ibid., p. 79.
138. "Consultation du dossier de Mr BEYAYO," testimony of Walid Othmani, Jan.–Feb. 2009. Thanks to Sebastian Rotella for sharing this with me.
139. 'Abdullah Mansur, "al-Shahid al-Shaykh Bilal al-Turkistani," *Turkistan al-Islamiyya*, 4 (June 2009), pp. 19–22.
140. The TIP's recent media products, including the articles discussed above, are thus quite

explicit about the TIP's close connections to al-Qa'ida and the Haqqani network, which marks a departure from some of their earlier rhetoric. Before his death, the first leader of the TIP denied in an interview in 2002 that the TIP had any connection to al-Qa'ida or intentions to carry out international terrorist attacks. See Millward, *Violent Separatism in Xinjiang*, p. 23; Philip Pan, "U.S. Warns of Plot by Group in W. China," *Washington Post*, 29 Aug. 2002.

141. Abu'l-Walid al-Masri, *Qissat al-bay'at al-'arabiya li-amir al-mu'minin Mullah Muhammad 'Umar*, no date, posted to various jihadi internet forums on 19 and 20 July 2007. See also Vahid Brown, "The Facade of Allegiance: Bin Ladin's Dubious Pledge to Mullah Omar," *CTC Sentinel*, 3, 1 (Jan. 2010), pp. 1–6, and Brown, *Cracks in the Foundation*, p. 17.
142. Al-Bahri, *Dans l'ombre de Ben Laden*, p. 109.
143. For the text of the announcement of the Front, see Lawrence, *Messages to the World*, pp. 58ff. Lawrence confuses Fazlur Rahman Khalil of HuJI, one of the signatories to the Front, with the Pakistani parliamentarian Fazlur Rahman, who leads the Islamist political party JUI-F.
144. Al-Bahri, *Dans l'ombre de Ben Laden*, p. 88.
145. On these interviews, see Bergen, *The Osama bin Laden I Know*, pp. 194ff.; and Gutman, *How We Missed the Story*, pp. 128ff.
146. On this issue see Brown, "The Facade of Allegiance."
147. Gutman, *How We Missed the Story*, p. 129.
148. Ahmad Zaydan, *Usama Bin Ladin bi-la Qina'*, Beirut: al-Sharaka al-'Alami li'l-Kitab, 2003, p. 130.
149. Abu'l-Walid, *Qissat al-bay'at al-'arabiya*. For details on these organizations, see Abu Mus'ab Suri, *Da'wa al-muqawwama al-islamiyya al-'alamiyya*, n.p., n.d., pp. 727ff., portions of which are translated in Brynjar Lia, *The Architect of Global Jihad: The Life of al-Qa'ida Strategist Abu Musab al-Suri*, New York: Columbia University Press, 2008, pp. 247ff.
150. Abu'l-Walid, *Qissat al-bay'at al-'arabiya*, p. 5.
151. Ibid., p. 6.
152. Ibid. According to Wahid Mozhdeh, a former official within the Taliban government, the Taliban's Foreign Affairs Ministry was almost uniformly opposed to the extension of hospitality to Bin Laden and frequently lobbied Mullah Omar to place him under greater restrictions, to such an extent that Bin Laden was said to have claimed, "Two entities are against our jihad. One is the US, and the other is the Taliban's own foreign affairs ministry." Mozhdeh, *Afghanistan va panj sal-i sultah-i Taliban*, Tehran, 2003, unpublished English translation, p. 53 (thanks to Roy Gutman for kindly sharing this translation with me).
153. See al-Bahri, *Dans l'ombre de Ben Laden*; Gutman, *How We Missed the Story*, pp. 143ff.
154. Brown, "Facade of Allegiance."
155. The first interview was given to Jamal Ismail for al-Jazeera and subsequently published in English as "I Am Not Afraid of Death," *Newsweek*, 11 Jan. 1999. The interview on 22 Dec. was given to Rahimullah Yusufzai for BBC-Arabic, and an English transcript was published as "World's Most Wanted Terrorist: An Interview with Osama bin Laden," *ABC News*, 2 Jan. 1999. Neither of the stories indicated the location of the interview, but Gutman, *How We Missed the Story*, p. 157, claims they were given at "a mountain encampment in Helmand."
156. Al-Bahri, *Dans l'ombre de Ben Laden*, p. 179. Rahimullah Yusufzai relates that, according to Bin Laden himself, the Dec. interviews were given with Taliban permission; Yusufzai, "Taliban let Bin Laden Break his Silence," *The News*, 6 Jan. 1999. If both Nasir al-Bahri and Bin Laden are to be believed with regard to this episode, it may be that the content of Bin Laden's remarks in these interviews, rather than the fact of having given them, was what angered the Taliban leader.
157. See al-Bahri, *Dans l'ombre de Ben Laden*, pp. 181ff.; and Fazul, *al-Harb 'ala'l-Islam*, vol. 1, pp. 389ff.
158. See Brown, "Facade of Allegiance," p. 5.
159. Anand Gopal, "The most deadly US foe in Afghanistan," *Christian Science Monitor*, 31 May 2009, online at http://www.csmonitor.com/2009/0601/p10s01-wosc.html
160. Edwards, *Genealogies of the Afghan Jihad*, p. 299.
161. Crews, "Moderate Taliban?" p. 265.
162. Ibid., citing "Uprising in Eastern Afghanistan—Iranian Radio," BBC Summary of World Broadcasts, Voice of the Islamic Republic of Iran, Mashhad, in Persian, 23 Jan. 2000.
163. Mohammad Bashir, "Afghan Taliban Replace Unpopular Khost Governon," *AFP*, 27 Jan. 2000.

164. Ibid.
165. According to al-Bahri, *Dans l'ombre de Ben Laden*, p. 105, between 1998 and 1999, "the Taliban ordered all of the Arab training camps closed, with the exception of those of al-Qa'ida." Al-Bahri does not explain why al-Qa'ida's camps were exempted, but it is noteworthy that much of al-Qa'ida's training infrastructure during this period was centered in Haqqani-controlled territory, where, as has been seen, Taliban restrictions on al-Qa'ida could not be enforced. Other sources on the camp closures are noted in Brown, "Facade of Allegiance," p. 5.
166. See Brown, *Cracks in the Foundation*, pp. 17f.; Alan Cullison, "Inside Al-Qaeda's Hard Drive," *The Atlantic*, Sep. 2004, online at http://www.theatlantic.com/doc/200409/cullison; and Alan Cullison and Andrew Higgins, "Strained Alliance: Al Qaeda's Sour Days in Afghanistan," *The Wall Street Journal*, 2 Aug. 2002.
167. This is according to a diary of Abu Mus'ab al-Suri discovered in Afghanistan after the American invasion and dated 1999; the entry itself is not dated. AFGP-2002-002869, p. 40.
168. Kamil al-Tawil, "Interview with Nu'man bin 'Uthman (Noman Benotman)," *al-Hayah*, 1 Dec. 2006.
169. Ismail Khan, "Usama bin Laden Reprets Restrictions imposed by Taliban," *Dawn*, 3 Apr. 2001. Khan quotes from the letter in his article and notes that the senior Taliban official Tayyib Agha confirmed the meeting between Jalaluddin and Mullah Omar, while denying that Jalaluddin had delivered a letter from Bin Laden.
170. Translated into Arabic in al-Suri's 1999 diary (the next dated entry is early Jan. 2000), AFGP-2002-002869, pp. 43–8. Al-Suri refers repeatedly to the "thirteen points" decree throughout the diary, which also records his efforts to get Taliban officials to clarify certain of its provisions and to relax some of its restrictions.
171. Ibid., p. 48.

PART II: CONTINUITY, VALUE, CHANGE, AND THE HAQQANI NEXUS POST-2001

1. See Alex Strick van Linschoten and Felix Kuehn, *Separating the Taliban from al-Qaeda: The Core of Success in Afghanistan*, Center on International Cooperation, Feb. 2011; Interview with Anand Gopal, 9 Jan. 2011.
2. Attempts by Afghan authorities were also made around this time as well; see Ruttig, "The Haqqani Network as an Autonomous Entity," in Giustozzi, *Decoding the New Taliban*, pp. 57–88, at p. 66.
3. Joby Warrick, *The Triple Agent: The al-Qaeda Mole who Infiltrated the CIA*, New York: Doubleday, 2011, p. 111.
4. Kathy Gannon, *I is for Infidel*, New York: Public Affairs, 2005, p. 94. The CIA came to learn that Ahmed was giving similar advice to Mullah Omar and meeting with the latter frequently since mid-Sep.; see Rashid, *Descent into Chaos*, p. 77.
5. Gannon, *I is for Infidel*, p. 94.
6. "Interview with Taliban Commander Maulvi Jalaluddin Haqqani," *The News*, 20 Oct. 2001.
7. For background on Haq's initiative see Lucy Morgan Edwards, *The Afghan Solution: The Inside Story of Abdul Haq, the CIA and how Western Hubris Lost Afghanistan*, London: Bactria Press, 2011, pp. 198–9, 210, 302–3.
8. According to Thomas Ruttig, "After that, Omari [sc. Ibrahim Haqqani] was kept first in Logar in the Afghan army's headquarters for the Southeast by General Gul Haidar, a confidant of then Defense Minister (and not yet Marshal) Muhammad Qasem Fahim, and later in a government-run guesthouse in Kabul." See Thomas Ruttig, "Splitting the Haqqanis with NATO Reconciliation Air," Afghanistan Analysts Network, 1 Nov. 2010; Thomas Ruttig, "Talking Haqqani," Afghanistan Analysts Network, 1 July 2010, online at http://aan-afghanistan.com/index.asp?id=873; little information actually exists about the circumstances of Ibrahim Haqqani's arrest and his time spent in detention. For additional background see "Former Taliban Commander Surrenders in Eastern Afghanistan," *AFP*, 11 Mar. 2002; Jay Solomon, "Failed Courtship of Warlord Trips up U.S. in Afghanistan," *Wall Street Journal*, 8 Nov. 2007; Syed Saleem Shahzad, "Through the Eyes of the Taliban," *Asia Times*, 5 May 2004 www.atimes.com/atimes/Central_Asia/FE05Ag02.html; "Taliban Ready to Attack Indian Embassy," *Ummat* (Urdu), 12 July 2003; Dr Wazir Jaffer Zakori, "Jalaluddin Haqqani's brother, Ibrahim Haqqani arrested," *Pakistan* (Urdu), 19 May 2003; Seth G. Jones, *Reintegrating Afghan Insurgents*, RAND, 2011.

9. Jay Solomon, "Failed Courtship of Warlord Trips up U.S. in Afghanistan," *Wall Street Journal*, 8 Nov. 2007.
10. His name is spelled variously in the English sources (Badshah, Padshah, Bacha, and Pacha). Badshah Khan was a famous mujahidin leader during the anti-Soviet years, fighting as a subcommander under Jalaluddin Haqqani in the Saroti Pass, an important stretch of the Khost–Gardez road. American forces enlisted Khan and his men to aid in the search for al-Qa'ida leaders and the seizure of the Zhawara complex. In Dec. 2001 Karzai appointed Khan the governor of Loya Paktia, and Khan used the cash and arms supplied by the United States to move against Haqqani loyalists in these areas. In late Jan. 2002 Khan's men laid siege—unsuccessfully—to Khost city, and in late Apr. he unleashed a rocket attack on Gardez. Karzai responded in May by sacking Khan and appointing Hakim Taniwal as governor of Paktia. The United States also began to back off from its support to Khan after the Gardez bombardment. For background see Jalali and Grau, *Afghan Guerrilla Warfare*; see pp. 149–52; Griffin, *Reaping the Whirlwind*, pp. 339, 358, 373; Peter Baker, "Bacha Khan's Private War," *Washington Post*, 4 May 2002; "Afghanistan: Key road in the east reopens," IRIN, 4 Mar. 2003, www.irinnews.org/PrintReport.aspx?ReportId=19477; "Pakistan hands over Afghan rebel," *BBC*, 5 Feb. 2004, http://news.bbc.co.uk/2/hi/south_asia/3461351.stm; "Afghan spokesman blames Pakistan for bomb attacks," *Pajhwok Afghan News*, 24 Dec. 2006; Wolesi Jirga and Provincial Council Elections homepage, http://d8680609.u106.forthost.com/leadingCandidates.asp?ElectionID=1&ProvinceID=8
11. Jay Solomon, "Failed Courtship of Warlord Trips up U.S. in Afghanistan," *Wall Street Journal*, 8 Nov. 2007; Ruttig, "Splitting the Haqqanis with NATO Reconciliation Air"; Ruttig, "Talking Haqqani"; Ahmed Rashid, *Pakistan on the Brink: The Future of America, Pakistan and Afghanistan*, New York: Viking, 2012, pp. 133–6, 180; Rahimullah Yusufzai, "A Face-Saving Deal," *Newsline*, 1 Jan. 2012.
12. For background on this debate see John Walcott and Viola Gienger, "US Reviews Whether to Designate Pakistan's Haqqani Network as Terrorists," *Bloomberg*, 28 Sep. 2011; Congressional Record—Senate, "Haqqani Network Designation Act," S8781-S8782, 17 Dec. 2011.
13. Joshua Partlow, "Haqqani group poses resilient foe in Afghan war," *Washington Post*, 29 May 2011.
14. As Thomas Hegghammer notes, ideological hybridization is not a new phenomenon, even in Pakistan. See Thomas Hegghammer, "The Ideological Hybridization of Jihadi Groups," *Current Trends in Islamist Ideology*, 9, 18 (Nov. 2009), www.currenttrends.org/research/detail/the-ideological-hybridization-of-jihadi-groups
15. For a comprehensive overview of the value and role trust plays between organizations see Chapter 5 ("Trust Between Organizations") in Perri 6 et al., *Managing Networks of Twenty-First Century Organizations*, New York: Palgrave, 2006, pp. 83–118.
16. Value proposition is broadly defined as the unique value that a business offers its customers and/or partners. See Cindy Barnes, Helen Blake, and David Pinder, *Creating and Delivering Your Value Proposition: Managing Customer Experience for Profit*, London: Kogan Page, 2009. For analytical clarity, the "local" plane includes those militant groups that are indigenous to the tribal areas of Afghanistan and Pakistan, and who are primarily active in one of these two countries and seek to create change there. The "regional" plane is specifically devoted to the Pakistani state, given Islamabad's interests in shaping South Asia's security environment and historic use of proxies to counter Indian influence in the region. Groups such as al-Qa'ida and the Islamic Jihad Union who are primarily motivated by global jihad and directly engage in acts of international terrorism are included in the "global" plane. The authors recognize that these categories—while analytically useful—are also at times partially blurred due to the fluidity of the Afghanistan–Pakistan border, overlapping membership between groups, and the fact that the activity of several militant actors is not limited to one specific plane. For example, even though the Pakistani Taliban (TTP) is a local, indigenous militant group that is primarily concerned with attacking the Pakistani state, the TTP is also motivated by global jihad and has proven its desire to attack the United States.

4. LOCAL: PAKISTANI TALIBAN FACTIONS AND OTHER LOCAL INSURGENT UNITS

1. Interview with Taliban Commander Maulvi Jalaluddin Haqqani," *The News*, 20 Oct. 2001.
2. For background on other militant actors active in Loya Paktia see Ruttig, "The Haqqani Network as an Autonomous Entity"; Sébastien Trives, "Roots of the Insurgency in the Southeast," in Giustozzi, *Decoding the Taliban*, pp. 89–100; for a more recent perspective see Jeffrey

Dressler, *The Haqqani Network: A Strategic Threat*, Institute for the Study of War, Afghanistan Report, 9 Mar. 2012.

3. Mawlawi Aziz Khan, "The First Jihadi Operation in Afghanistan, and the Rise of the Ulema Against the Communists," *Manba' al-Jihad* (Pashto), 1, 4–5 (Oct.–Nov. 1989); "The Historic Battle of Paktia," *Manba' al-Jihad* (Pashto), 3, 5 (1991); "Martyrs of the Path of the Truth," *Manba' al-Jihad* (Pashto), 2, 2 (Aug. 1990); "Alhaj Jalaluddin Haqqani in an Interview with the *Al-Nasiha* Magazine," *Manba' al-Jihad* (Pashto), 2, 5 (Nov. 1990).
4. For example see Harmony documents AFGP-2002-008581 and AFGP-2002-008582 and the work of Abu'l-Walid al-Masri, specifically Harmony documents AFGP-2002-600090, pp. 23, 34, 45, 57, 86, 92; AFGP-2002-600092, pp. 1, 4, 47, 55, 57, 62, 67, 69, 70, 80, 91, 94, 96; AFGP-2002-600093, p. 103; AFGP-2002-600096 pp. 53, 64, 73, 304; AFGP-2002-600099, pp. 9, 13, 15, 41, 42, 71. All references to page numbers are to the English-language translations of these documents. Versions of these documents are available online via Abu Walid's blog http://mafa.maktoobblog.com/ and website http://mafa.asia/, and some of them in English at www.ctc.usma.edu
5. As established in the introduction to this part of the book, the local section provides a review of the Haqqani network's activity and relations with local tribal and militant entities in the Loya Paktia/Waziristan region. The Haqqani network's relations with the Pakistani state and ISI are reviewed in the regional subsection.
6. A detailed review of this issue follows. We give credit to Thomas Ruttig for analytically developing these points.
7. Shuhrat Nangyal, "Afghanistan's Jihad and the Virtuous Victory," *Manba' al-Jihad* (in Pashto), 8 (Jan. 1991). Shuhrat Nangyal, a prolific Afghan author, was the editor of and a contributor to the Pashto version of *Manba' al-Jihad* and its sister Urdu-language publication, *Nusrat al-Jihad*.
8. Some suggest that the Haqqani network also cultivates influence by providing financial support to local tribal elders in Loya Paktia, to include "cash payments, passports, houses in Pakistan and trips to the Gulf." See Ruttig, "The Haqqani Network as an Autonomous Entity," pp. 72–5; for an overview of traditional religious networks in the southeast see Sébastien Trives, "Roots of the Insurgency in the Southeast," pp. 89–100.
9. For reflections on the Haqqani network's ties to the Haqqaniyya madrassa see "Mawlana Abdul Haq, an unforgettable face in the Islamic World," *Manba' al-Jihad* (Pashto), 3, 4 (Sep. 1991); for reflections see "Alhaj Mawlawi Jalaluddin Haqqani in a General Gathering of the Jamiat-e-Ulama-e-Islam in Lahore," *Manba' al-Jihad* (Pashto), 2, 11 (May 1991).
10. For an example of a historic Haqqani recruitment advertisement see "Good News for the Prospective Taliban of the Course of Hadith-e Sharif!" *Manba' al-Jihad* (Pashto), 1, 11 (May 1990); see also "Interview with Mawlawi Aziz Khan, Head of the Manba-al Uloom Madrassa in Miranshah," *Manba' al-Jihad* (Pashto), 2, 1 (July 1990).
11. For confirmation of this see "Interview with Mawlawi Aziz Khan, Head of the Manba-al Uloom Madrassa in Miranshah," *Manba' al-Jihad* (Pashto), 2, 1 (July 1990).
12. Pir Zubayr Shah and Carlotta Gall, "For Pakistan, Deep Ties to Militant Network May Trump U.S. Pressure," *New York Times*, 31 Oct. 2011; personal interview with Pir Zubayr Shah, 13 Sep. 2010.
13. Personal interview with Pir Zubayr Shah, 13 Sep. 2010.
14. While this is the educational philosophy stressed by the Haqqani network, Manba' 'Ulum has also historically taught "new sciences like mathematics, English language, Islamic history, and few others about physics and medicine." See "Manba al Uloom is a Resource to the Jihad: A Beacon of Knowledge that Graduates Jihadist Ulema," *Manba' al-Jihad* (Arabic), 1, 1 (Feb. 1990).
15. "Manba al Uloom is a Resource to the Jihad: A Beacon of Knowledge that Graduates Jihadist Ulema," *Manba' al-Jihad* (Arabic), 1, 1 (Feb. 1990), pp. 5–8; "The Manba al-Uloom Madrasa as a Major Educational Center," *Manba' al-Jihad* (Pashto), 1, 1 (July 1989).
16. "The Manba al-Uloom Madrasa as a Major Educational Center," *Manba' al-Jihad* (Pashto), 1, 1 (July 1989).
17. "Interview with Mawlawi Aziz Khan, Head of the Manba-al Uloom Madrassa in Miranshah," *Manba' al-Jihad* (Pashto), 2, 1 (July 1990).
18. Jeffrey Goldberg, "Inside Jihad U.; the Education of a Holy Warrior," *New York Times Magazine*, 25 June 2000; Sami ul-Haq has given multiple perspectives on this issue, for examples see Imtiaz Ali, "The Father of the Taliban: an Interview with Maulana Sami ul-Haq," *Spotlight on Terror*, 4, 2 (23 May 2007); "Head of Islamic School that Spawned Taliban, Insurgents Offers to Help Afghan Talks," *Washington Post*, 1 Nov. 2011.

19. Ruttig, "The Haqqani Network as an Autonomous Entity."
20. Mohammad Osman Tariq Elias, "The Resurgence of the Taliban in Kabul: Logar and Wardak," in Giustozzi, *Decoding the New Taliban*, p. 50.
21. Some even suggest that this fault line is even greater than the Ghilzai–Durrani gap. See Ruttig, "The Haqqani Network as an Autonomous Entity," p. 73.
22. For examples, see ibid., p. 73.
23. Thomas Ruttig, "The Other Side: Dimensions of the Afghan Insurgency: Causes, Actors and Approaches to 'Talks'," Afghanistan Analysts Network, July 2009.
24. Ibid.
25. For an example of this see, "Open Interview with Sirajuddin Haqqani, a member of the Shura Council of the Islamic Emirate of Afghanistan and a commander in the southeastern provinces of Afghanistan," released by the Ansar al-Mujahidin Network, 27 Apr. 2010.
26. "Taleban Attack Kabul Luxury Hotel," *BBC*, 15 Jan. 2008, http://news.bbc.co.uk/2/hi/7187592.stm
27. Carol Grisanti, "Taliban commander: Afghan officials are helping kill Americans," *NBC News*, 30 July 2008.
28. A collection of Manba' al-Jihad videos can be viewed online on a number of video sharing sites, such as Youtube and LiveLeak.
29. Michael Georgy, "Haqqanis to Follow Taliban on Afghan Peace," *Reuters*, 17 Sep. 2011; Another potential explanation for Sirajuddin's statement, given the timing, is that the group was pressured by Pakistan's ISI (or representatives of it) not to claim credit for and/or associate itself with the attack due to political sensitivities between Pakistan and the United States. The Haqqani network's public association with this attack would have arguably only deepened the divide between the two countries. Admiral Mike Mullen publicly claimed that both the Haqqani network and individuals connected to the ISI were associated with the attack. See Elizabeth Bumiller and Jane Perlez, "Pakistan's Spy Agency is Tied to Attack on U.S. Embassy," *New York Times*, 22 Sep. 2011.
30. Ruttig, "The Haqqani Network as an Autonomous Entity," pp. 61–2.
31. As noted by Ruttig, "The Haqqani network stands out for its operational reach and impact," see Ruttig, "The Other Side: Dimensions of the Afghan Insurgency."
32. It is not clear how long Jalaluddin Haqqani held this position; John F. Burns, "Taliban Link Fate of Aid Workers to U.S. Action," *New York Times*, 7 Oct. 2001.
33. "Today's Encounter," Al-Jazeera (Arabic), 31 May 2006.
34. Antonio Giustozzi and Christoph Reuter, *The Insurgents of the Afghan North*, Afghanistan Analysts Network, Apr. 2011, pp. 20–4; Gretchen Peters, *Crime and Insurgency in the Tribal Areas of Afghanistan and Pakistan*, Combating Terrorism Center, 15 Oct. 2010, pp. 54–5; Jeffrey Dressler, *The Haqqani Network: A Strategic Threat*, Institute for the Study of War, Afghanistan Report 9, Mar. 2012, pp. 35–9; for another perspective on the Taliban's strategy in this area see Sippi Azarbaijani Moghaddam, "Northern Exposure for the Taliban," in Giustozzi, *Decoding the Taliban*, pp. 257–8.
35. The authors acknowledge that this issue is complicated by Jalaluddin Haqqani's partnership with Hizb-e-Islami Khalis.
36. Mawlawi Aziz Khan, "The First Jihadi Operation in Afghanistan, and the Rise of the Ulema Against the Communists," *Manba' al-Jihad* (Pashto), 1, 4–5 (Oct.–Nov. 1989); see also "Text of Alhaj Haqqani's Interview with the Arab Magazine *Al Marabtoon*," *Manba' al-Jihad* (Pashto), 2, 12 (June 1991); "Mawlawi Haqqani is great commander who, in addition to Khost and Paktia, has fighters in Ghazni, Wardak, Jalalabad and Herat" see "The Iron Man: Mawlana Jalaluddin Haqqani," *Manba' al-Jihad* (Pashto), 2, 6 (Dec. 1990).
37. See Jalaluddin's statement in FBIS JN111107, "Rebel Leader Statement," Doha QNA, 11 June 1980.
38. "Martyrs of the Path of the Truth," *Manba' al-Jihad* (Pashto), 1, 2–3 (Aug.–Sep. 1989); for information about the case of Mutiullah Muti, another of Jalaluddin's important commanders, see "The Islamic Revolution's Unforgettable Shaheed, Mutiullah Muti," *Manba' al-Jihad* (Pashto), 3, 7–8 (Jan.–Feb. 1992); see also "The Iron Man: Mawlana Jalaluddin Haqqani," *Manba' al-Jihad* (Pashto), 2, 6 (Dec. 1990).
39. For example, while spending time with Jalaluddin Haqqani in 1981 *New York Times* journalist Jere Van Dyk met fighters from all across Afghanistan who were waging jihad with the Haqqanis in Loya Paktia; see Jere Van Dyk, *In Afghanistan: An American Odyssey*, p. 125.
40. Given the lack of granular information about insurgent attacks in Afghanistan and the perpetrators of these attacks in various areas, it is difficult to assess whether the intensification of kinetic activity in certain provinces like Logar and Wardak is tied specifically to the

Haqqani network or reflects an intensification of the insurgency writ large; for an overview of the conflict's intensification see Anthony Cordesman, "The Afghan–Pakistan War: The Rising Intensity of Conflict 2007–2008," Center for Strategic and International Studies, 12 Aug. 2009; http://csis.org/files/publication/burke/090803_RisingIntensityConflict 20072008.pdf

41. Ruttig, "The Other Side: Dimensions of the Afghan Insurgency"; for a perspective on Hizb-e-Islami and Taliban integration in Logar see Elias, "The Resurgence of the Taliban in Kabul: Logar and Wardak," p. 53; for insights into the Taliban's post-2001 development in part of Ghazni and particularly the challenges between it and Hizb-e Islami Gulbuddin there see Christoph Reuter and Borhan Younus, "The Return of the Taliban in Andar District: Ghazni," in Antonio Giustozzi, *Decoding the Taliban*, pp. 101–18; see also Dressler, "The Haqqani Network: A Strategic Threat," pp. 24–9; as Giustozzi and Reuter note, the Taliban's expansion into northern Afghanistan was also due to their apparent success in reaching out and integrating non-Pashtun fighters. See Giustozzi and Reuter, *The Insurgents of the Afghan North*, p. 15.
42. For analysis of the Logar case see Antonio Giustozzi, "One or Many? The Issue of the Taliban's Unity and Disunity," Pakistan Security Research Unit, Brief Number 48, 23 Apr. 2009.
43. Although the two parties worked together, the relationship between Badruddin Haqqani and Tayeb was reportedly one of mistrust. See Gretchen Peters, "Haqqani Network Financing: The Evolution of an Industry," Combating Terrorism Center, July 2012.
44. Elias, "The Resurgence of the Taliban in Kabul: Logar and Wardak," pp. 48–9 and p. 55.
45. The authors recognize that this is a complicated issue and that the Haqqani network is not the only militant entity facilitating such integration, or that the integration of Pakistani fighters is always necessary.
46. These subtribal splits are typified by historical Mehsud and Wazir tribal rifts, see Akbar S. Ahmed, *Resistance and Control in Pakistan*, London: Routledge, 2004, p. 116.
47. See Alan Warren, *Waziristan, the Faqir of Ipi, and the Indian Army: The Northwest Frontier Revolt of 1936–1937*, London: Oxford University Press, 2000, p. 132; *Operations in Waziristan: 1919–1920*, compiled by the General Staff Army Headquarters, India, 1923 (originally published by the Delhi Central Government Press, 1923, pp. 30–1); Brian Robson, *Crisis on the Frontier: The Third Afghan War and the Campaign in Waziristan 1919–1920*, Staplehurst, UK: Spellmount, 2004, p. 101; Andrew M. Roe, *Waging War in Waziristan: the British Struggle in the Land of Bin Laden, 1849–1947*, Kansas: University Press of Kansas, 2010, p. 203.
48. Warren, *Waziristan, the Faqir of Ipi, and the Indian Army*, p. 85.
49. Ruttig, "The Haqqani Network as an Autonomous Entity," p. 72.
50. Ibid., p. 60.
51. The biography of Mawlana Qari Lal Mohammad, a fighter from Waziristan, is characteristic of this integration, see "Shaheed Lal Numa," *Nusrat ul-Jihad* (Urdu), 1, 3 (Jan. 1991).
52. For background on similar Pakistani integration with the Haqqanis during the Taliban period see Part I.
53. For another perspective on this see Claudio Franco, "The Tehrik-e-Taliban Pakistan," in Giustozzi, *Decoding the New Taliban*.
54. Ruttig, "The Haqqani Network as an Autonomous Entity," p. 76; Gul, *The Most Dangerous Place*, p. 37; Abubakar Siddique, "Pakistani Taliban Chief's Death Would Have Broad Implications," *Radio Free Europe/Radio Liberty*, 7 Aug. 2009, www.rferl.org/content/Pakistani_Taliban_Chiefs_Death_Would_Have_Broad_Implications/1794879.html; before his death Baitullah Mehsud is also believed to have had a close relationship with detained senior Haqqani commander Haji Mali Khan, see "Afghanistan Haqqani militant Haji Mali Khan captured," *BBC*, 1 Oct. 2011; for disputes on Baitullah's role during the Taliban period see Jason Burke, *The 9/11 Wars*, New York: Allen Lane, 2011, p. 374.
55. Ruttig, "The Haqqani Network as an Autonomous Entity," p. 71.
56. "Afghanistan Haqqani Militant Haji Mali Khan Captured," *BBC*, 1 Oct. 2011; "Nato claims capture of Haqqani group's leader," *Dawn*, 2 Oct. 2011.
57. "Translation of Hakimullah Mehsud's Handwritten Autobiographical Notes," NEFA, 3 Oct. 2009, www.nefafoundation.org/miscellaneous/Hakimullahnotetranslation.pdf; Baitullah Mehsud is also believed to have fought under Jalaluddin before the US invasion, see Imtiaz Ali, "Baitullah Mehsud—the Taliban's New Leader in Pakistan," *Terrorism Focus*, 9 Jan. 2008; Hakimullah also reportedly fought in Helmand province, see Mansur Khan Mahsud, "The Battle for Pakistan: Militancy and Conflict in South Waziristan," Counterterrorism Strategy Initiative, Apr. 2010; for background on Abdullah Mehsud and his death see "Former Guan-

tanamo Inmate Blows himself up in Pakistan," *Dawn*, 24 July 2007, www.dawn.com/2007/07/24/welcome.htm

58. For a perspective on this issue see Alex Spillius, "CIA suicide bomber 'worked with bin Laden allies'," *Telegraph*, 7 Jan. 2010.
59. Interview with Pir Zubayr Shah, 13 Sep. 2010.
60. Ibid.
61. Gopal, Mahsud, and Fishman, "The Battle for Pakistan: Militancy and Conflict in North Waziristan."
62. Integration between Gul Bahadur's group reportedly even extends to the Haqqanis' main seminary, the Manba' 'Ulum madrassa, where Bahadur's deputy—Sadiq Noor—is believed to serve as an administrator; for this reference and quote see ibid., pp. 13 and 15.
63. Bill Roggio, "Pakistani Taliban, Iraqi al Qaeda operatives killed in Afghanistan," *Long War Journal*, 11 May 2008; see also "Nine Militants Killed in Air Raid in Afghanistan," *The Hindu*, 11 May 2008, www.hindu.com/thehindu/holnus/003200805111441.htm
64. For example a number of documents recovered from Osama bin Laden's compound in Abbotabad, Pakistan, indicated that several al-Qa'ida leaders were concerned about these issues. For Adam Gadahn's view see SOCOM-2012-0000004, pp. 14–16; for Bin Laden's perspective see SOCOM-2012-0000010, p. 12; and for Abu Yahya al-Libi's and Attiyah's see SOCOM-2012-0000007, p. 1.
65. For background on Qari Amil, who was recently killed, see "Rebel Commander Killed in Afghan East," *Pajhwok News*, 2 Nov. 2010.
66. "The Miranshah shura, in particular, appears to integrate Afghan and Pakistani Taleban and, possibly, foreign fighters." See Ruttig, "The Other Side: Dimensions of the Afghan Insurgency," p. 62.
67. For background see Remy Ourdan, "The Terrorist Threat is in Pakistan," *Le Monde*, 5 Jan. 2010.
68. The development of the TTP's jihad against Pakistan is also an outgrowth of Pakistan's relationship with the United States, operations the Pakistani military has conducted in the FATA, and the US drone campaign.
69. According to Pir Zubayr Shah, the "local role of the Haqqanis is to make peace with the tribes." Interview with the authors, 13 Sep. 2010.
70. For example, during the siege of Khost there were at least six shuras, which were tribally oriented, and one overarching central shura to coordinate the mujahidin's campaign. Jalaluddin led the central shura. See "A Short Report on the Great Victory on Khost, and the Joint Operations Surrounding It," *Manba' al-Jihad* (Pashto), 2, 10 (Apr. 1991); after capturing Khost in 1991 the Haqqanis established two shuras to help ensure stability and political transition, as well as aid development, in the region; for detail see "Interview with Alhaj Nezamuddin Haqqani, Deputy Commander of the Southern Fronts," *Manba' al-Jihad* (Pashto), 3, 1 (July 1991).
71. "On the Reconciliation between the Ahmadzai Tribe and the Nangarhar Shura," *Manba' al-Jihad* (Pashto), 4, 1–2 (Nov. 1993); for background on the Ahmadzai see www.nps.edu/programs/ccs/Docs/Pakistan/Tribes/Ahmadzai_Wazir.pdf
72. "Pakistani Militants 'Call Truce'," *BBC*, 7 Feb. 2008, http://news.bbc.co.uk/2/hi/south_asia/7232203.stm; for background on the Sararogha deal see Hassan Abbas, "An Assessment of Pakistan's Peace Agreements with Militants in Waziristan (2004–2008)," in Daveed Gartenstein-Ross and Clifford D. May (eds), *The Afghanistan-Pakistan Theater: Militant Islam, Security and Stability*, Washington, DC: FDD Press, 2010, pp. 7–18.
73. Mohammad Jamshaid Baghwan, "Head of Islamic Movement of Uzbekistan Tahir Yeldshev escapes after coming in trap of Mullah Nazir," *Daily Express* (Urdu), 22 Mar. 2007; "130 foreigners killed in clashes: governor," *Dawn*, 24 Mar. 2007.
74. "Ceasefire Holding Between Locals, Foreign Militants in Waziristan," *The News*, 24 Mar. 2007; "130 foreigners killed in clashes: governor," *Dawn*, 24 Mar. 2007; S.H. Khan, "Taliban Commanders Try To Negotiate for Ending Battle With Pakistani Tribesmen," *Associated Press*, 22 Mar. 2007.
75. "Govt to hold talks with militants: Hamid," *The News*, 8 Feb. 2008; Gopal, Mahsud, and Fishman, "The Battle for Pakistan: Militancy and Conflict in North Waziristan."
76. On the SIM see ibid.; Raza Qazi and Sara A. Carter, "Pakistani Taliban Unite Against U.S.," *Washington Times*, 24 Feb. 2009; "Taliban 'receives $6M for Swat ceasefire'," Press TV (Iran), 24 Feb. 2009; the SIM was largely a notional organization and is now believed to be defunct; on Shura-e-Murakeba see Sailab Mehsud, "Taliban Groups Regroup to Fight US Forces," *Dawn*, 3 Jan. 2012, http://www.dawn.com/2012/01/03/al-qaida-taliban-ask-pakistani-

militants-for-help.html; Nadeem Sarwar and Safiullah Gul Mehsud, "Al-Qaeda Tries to Unite Pakistani Militants," *McClatchy-Tribune Regional News*, 22 Dec. 2011.
77. Matthew Rosenberg, "New Wave of Warlord Bedevils US," *Wall Street Journal*, 20 Jan. 2010.
78. "Haqqani's two sons mediating in Kurram," *Dawn*, 21 Oct. 2010, http://news.dawn.com/wps/wcm/connect/dawn-content-library/dawn/the-newspaper/front-page/haqqanis-two-sons-mediating-in-kurram-100; for additional background see Jeffrey Dressler and Reza Jan, "The Haqqani Network in Kurram: The Regional Implications of a Growing Insurgency," Institute for the Study of War, May 2011; Daud Khattak, "A Haqqani Brokered Peace in Kurram?" AF/PAK Channel, 16 Feb. 2011.
79. Don Rassler interview with Bob Nickelsberg, 23 Sep. 2010; while details are murky, the case of the former Ghazni provincial governor is interesting in this regard, see "US embassy cables: Afghan provincial governor accused of widespread corruption," *Guardian*, 2 Dec. 2010; for background on corruption in Ghazni and reports that officials in the province pay off Taliban fighters to not be attacked see Richard Opell, "Corruption Undercuts Hopes for Afghan Police," *New York Times*, 8 Apr. 2009; for additional background on the Haqqani network's financial ties to Ghazni see Gretchen Peters, *Haqqani Network Financing: The Evolution of an Industry*, Combating Terrorism Center, July 2012.
80. For background on the history of this region and the complex mix of actors there see "The Insurgency in Afghanistan's Heartland," International Crisis Group, Asia Report, no. 207, 27 June 2011.
81. Don Rassler interview with Bob Nickelsberg, 23 Sep. 2010.
82. Peters, *Crime and Insurgency in the Tribal Areas of Afghanistan and Pakistan*, p. 51.
83. Ibid., p. 50.
84. Ruttig, "The Haqqani Network as an Autonomous Entity," p. 71.
85. Gul, *The Most Dangerous Place*, p. 130.
86. Ibid.
87. Ruttig, "The Haqqani Network as an Autonomous Entity," pp. 64 and 77.
88. For additional background on this episode see "Suicide Attacks in Afghanistan (2001–2007)," United Nations Assistance Mission in Afghanistan, 9 Sep. 2007; this same study found that "recruitment for suicide attacks in the southeast region primarily takes place in madrassas in Pakistan's North Waziristan and those associated with Jalaluddin Haqqani are of particular salience." p. 66.
89. To protect his identity "Ahmad" is a pseudonym, see Anand Gopal, "The Most Deadly US Foe in Afghanistan," *Christian Science Monitor*, 1 June 2009.
90. David Rohde and Kristen Mulvihill, *A Rope and a Prayer: A Kidnapping from Two Sides*, New York: Viking, 2010, pp. 229–30.
91. Authors' interview with Pir Zubayr Shah, 13 Sep. 2010.
92. "Pakistan Releases 3 Relatives of Fugitive Taliban Commander Under Swap Deal," *The Frontier Post*, 14 Nov. 2007; for background on Mehsud's capture of these soldiers see Syed Shoaib Hasan, "Pakistan Rebels Display Hostages," *BBC*, 11 Oct. 2007, http://news.bbc.co.uk/2/hi/south_asia/7039101.stm
93. Authors' interview with Pir Zubayr Shah, 13 Sep. 2010.
94. Haji Mujtaba, "N. Waziristan militant leader threatens Pakistan government," *Reuters*, 12 Nov. 2011.
95. "North Waziristan drone strike: Tribesmen vow 'jihad' against US," *Dawn*, 19 Mar. 2011; see also "Tribesmen threaten the US with holy war," *AFP*, 27 Sep. 2011.

5. REGIONAL: THE PAKISTANI STATE AND ITS INTER-SERVICES INTELLIGENCE DIRECTORATE

1. For background on Hamza see Praveen Swami, "Kabul Attack: US Warming was Accurate," *The Hindu*, 3 Aug. 2008; www.hindu.com/2008/08/03/stories/2008080360650800.htm
2. "Scores Killed by Kabul Embassy Bomb," *al-Jazeera*, 7 July 2008.
3. Ibid.
4. "Kabul Car Blast Kills 41, Including Indian Envoys," *CNN*, 7 July 2008.
5. Praveen Swami, "Kabul Attack: US Warming was Accurate."
6. "In a transcript passed to Mike McConnell, the Director of National Intelligence in May 2008, Pakistan's army chief General Ashfaq Kayani was heard referring to Haqqani as 'a strategic asset.'" See Catherine Philp, "Pervez Musharraf was playing 'double game' with US," *The Times* (London), 17 Feb. 2009; for debates about Pakistan's policy see Jayshree Bajoria, "The ISI and Terrorism: Behind the Accusations," CFR Backgrounder, 28 May 2009.

7. "Pakistan can bring Haqqani to peace talks: official," *Daily Times*, 19 Aug. 2011.
8. See, for example, Muhammad Amir Rana, *Jihad and Jihadi*, Lahore: Mashal Books, 2003, pp. 32, 69; and the following Harmony documents written by Abu Walid al-Masri, AFGP-2002-600090, pp. 63, 74; AFGP-2002-600093, p. 79; AFGP-2002-600099, pp. 14, 26–7, 29, 33.
9. Yousaf and Adkin, *The Bear Trap*.
10. Harmony document AFGP-2002-008588, p. 13.
11. Mohammed al-Shafey, "A Talk with the 'Taliban-Maker,' Former Pakistani ISI Chief Hamid Gul," *Al Sharq al-Awsat*, Apr. 2009, www.aawsat.com/english/news.asp?section=3&id=16526
12. Zakiur Rahman Lakhvi is LeT's current operations chief and is also believed to be the mastermind behind the 2008 terrorist siege of Mumbai. Sources linking Lakhvi to Jalaluddin Haqqani are extremely thin and should be treated with some skepticism. During the Soviet period Lakhvi also spent a considerable amount of time in Nuristan. The one source known to the author is Rana, *Jihad and Jihadi*, pp. 32 and 105.
13. Don Rassler interview with Robert Nickelsberg, 23 Sep. 2010.
14. *Manba' al-Jihad* (Pashto), 3, 9–10 (May 1992); Jalaluddin Haqqani, *Is the Afghanistan War the Russian-American War?* (Pashto), edited by Abdulhadi Mullakhail (*Manba' al-Jihad*, 1988–9); for additional background see Roger Howard, "Wrath of Islam: HUA Analyzed," *Jane's Intelligence Review*, 1 Oct. 1997; Central Intelligence Agency, "Harakat ul-Ansar: Increasing Threat to Western and Pakistani Interests," DI TR 96–008, Aug. 1996, www.gwu.edu/~nsarchiv/NSAEBB/NSAEBB227/index.htm#10; Anthony Davis, "Pakistan's war by proxy in Afghanistan loses its deniability," *Jane's Intelligence Review*, 1 Oct. 1999.
15. *Manba' al-Jihad* (Pashto), 3, 9–10 (May 1992); Haqqani, *Is the Afghanistan War the Russian-American War?*
16. During a visit to HUA camps in Paktia in 1996, veteran Pakistani journalist Rahimullah Yusufzai estimated that there were 300 Pakistani fighters and fifty Arabs training for operations in Kashmir. Rahimullah Yusufzai's account is corroborated by Robert Nickelsberg and a British Journalist who visited Khost around the same time, see US Embassy (Islamabad) Cable, "Afghanistan: British Journalist Visits Site of Training Camps; HUA Activity Alleged," 26 Nov. 1996; Howard, "Wrath of Islam"; Central Intelligence Agency, "Harakat ul-Ansar: Increasing Threat to Western and Pakistani Interests," DI TR 96–008, Aug. 1996, www.gwu.edu/~nsarchiv/NSAEBB/NSAEBB227/index.htm#10; Jason Burke, *Al Qaeda: Casting a Shadow of Terror*, London: I.B. Tauris, 2003, p. 96; Davis, "Pakistan's war by proxy in Afghanistan loses its deniability."
17. Harmony document AFGP-2002-000079; for further analysis see Part I.
18. Don Rassler interview with Thomas Ruttig, 25 May 2010; see also FBIS LD2510195295, "Radio Reports on 'Fierce' Taliban Infighting," Kabul Radio Afghanistan Network (in Pashto), 25 Oct. 1995; and Ruttig, "The Haqqani Network as an Autonomous Entity," p. 65.
19. Pakistan's desire to diversify its influence in Afghanistan is best seen by the fact that during the Taliban period it is also believed to have maintained ties to the Northern Alliance. See Zaeef, *My Life with the Taliban*, p. 125.
20. AFGHANews, 11, 10 (Sep. 1995), p. 8 as cited in Davis, "How the Taliban Became a Military Force," pp. 43–64; Neamatollah Nojumi, *The Rise of the Taliban in Afghanistan: Mass Mobilization, Civil War and the Future of the Region*, New York: Palgrave, 2002, p. 146; US Embassy (Islamabad) Cable, "Afghanistan: Jalaluddin Haqqani's Emergence As a Key Taliban Commander," 7 Jan. 1997, Confidential, 14pp. [Excised], www.gwu.edu/~nsarchiv/NSAEBB/NSAEBB295/doc05.pdf; Griffin, *Reaping the Whirlwind*, p. 139; Harmony document AFGP-2002-602383; see also Ahmed Rashid, *Taliban: Islam, Oil and the New Great Game in Central Asia*, London: I.B. Tauris, 2001, p. 60; and US Embassy (Islamabad) Cable, "Afghanistan: Jalaluddin Haqqani's Emergence As a Key Taliban Commander," 7 Jan. 1997, Confidential, 14pp. [Excised].
21. Antonio Guistozzi, *Koran, Kalashnikov, and Laptop: The Neo-Taliban Insurgency in Afghanistan*, New York: Columbia University Press, 2008, p. 24; see also Shaun Gregory, "The ISI and the War on Terrorism," *Studies in Conflict and Terrorism*, 30, 12 (Oct. 2007), pp. 1013–31.
22. Harmony document, AFGP-2002-602383, "Afghanistan, the Taliban and the Battle for Islam Today," pp. 107–9. This document was authored by Abu Musab al Suri.
23. For example see "From [Excised] to DIA Washington, DC [Excised], Cable [Excised] Interservice Intelligence /Pakistan (PK) Directorate Supplying Taliban Forces," 22 Oct. 1996, Secret, 1 p. [Excised]; see also Mattieu Aikins, "State of the Taliban 2012: the Secret Report," *GQ*, 9 Mar. 2012.
24. For general background on the ISI see Gregory, "The ISI and the War on Terrorism," pp. 1013–31.

25. Julian Borger, "Taliban believe they will take over from US and Nato in Afghanistan—report," *Guardian*, 1 Feb. 2012; "Pakistan Helping Afghan Taliban—NATO," *BBC*, 1 Feb. 2012, www.bbc.co.uk/news/world-asia-16821218; Rod Nordland and Alissa J. Rubin, "Taliban Captives Dispute U.S. View on Afghanistan War," *New York Times*, 1 Feb. 2012; see also the concerns raised by Taliban leaders about repercussions and actions taken by the ISI in Rashid, *Pakistan on the Brink*, pp. 114–15, 119, 125–6.
26. Sanjoy Majumder, "India Renews Historic Afghan Ties," *BBC*, 25 Aug. 2005, http://news.bbc.co.uk/2/hi/4188462.stm; Steve Coll, "Letter from Afghanistan: 'War by Other Means,'" *New Yorker*, 24 May 2010.
27. "Afghan Bomb Strikes Indian Embassy," *BBC*, 8 Oct. 2009, http://news.bbc.co.uk/2/hi/south_asia/8296137.stm?ls
28. Simon Tisdall, "India and Pakistan's proxy war puts Afghanistan exit at risk," *Guardian*, 7 May 2010; Jayshree Bajoria, "India–Afghanistan Relations," CFR Backgrounder, 22 July 2009; Shantie Mariet D'Souza, "India's Aid to Afghanistan: Challenges and Prospects," *Strategic Analysis*, 31, 5 (Sep. 2007).
29. For another example see Stephen Tankel, *Laskhar-e-Taiba: Storming the World Stage*, London and New York: Hurst/Columbia University Press, 2011, p. 248; a press report from 2003 suggests that the Indian embassy has long been a target for Afghan insurgents, see "Taliban Ready to Attack Indian Embassy," *Ummat* (Urdu), 12 July 2003.
30. Praveen Swami, "Kabul Attack: US Warming was Accurate," *The Hindu*, 3 Aug. 2008; www.hindu.com/2008/08/03/stories/2008080360650800.htm; "The Spy Who Quit: A Conversation with Amrullah Saleh," *PBS Frontline*, 17 Jan. 2011, www.pbs.org/wgbh/pages/frontline/2011/01/video-amrullah-saleh-spy-who-quit.html
31. Mark Mazzetti and Eric Schmitt, "Pakistanis Aided Attack in Kabul, U.S. Officials Say," *New York Times*, 1 Aug. 2008; Jay Solomon, "US Ties Pakistani Intelligence to Attack in Kabul," *Wall Street Journal*, 2 Aug. 2008; Mark Mazzetti and Eric Schmitt, "Afghan Strikes by Taliban Get Pakistan Help, U.S. Aides Say," *New York Times*, 25 Mar. 2009.
32. "Secret Pakistan: Double Cross," *BBC* (Documentary), 26 Oct. 2011; see also the actions taken by Stephen R. Kappes, the CIA's deputy director, after this attack (as well as other cases), as referenced in Mark Mazzetti et al., "Pakistan Aids Insurgency in Afghanistan, Reports Assert," *New York Times*, 25 July 2010.
33. "The Spy Who Quit: A Conversation with Amrullah Saleh," *PBS Frontline*, 17 Jan. 2011, www.pbs.org/wgbh/pages/frontline/2011/01/video-amrullah-saleh-spy-who-quit.html
34. "Secret Pakistan: Double Cross," 26 Oct. 2011.
35. For example, a suicide truck bomb targeting Coalition forces killed thirteen US troops in the capital on 29 Oct. 2011. The Haqqani network was believed to have been the responsible party. See Rob Nordland, "12 Americans Die as Blast Hits Bus in Afghanistan," *New York Times*, 29 Oct. 2011; Rob Nordland, "Attacks on Foreigners in Capital get Afghan Faction's Message Across," *New York Times*, 30 Oct. 2011.
36. Official Transcript, "Hearing to Receive Testimony on the U.S. Strategy in Afghanistan and Iraq," Senate Armed Services Committee, 22 Sep. 2011, http://armed-services.senate.gov/Transcripts/2011/09%20September/11–70%20-%209–22–11.pdf
37. David Martin, "Cell Phones Link Pakistan to U.S. Embassy Attack," *CBS*, 23 Sep. 2011, www.cbsnews.com/stories/2011/09/23/eveningnews/main20110965.shtml
38. See www.youtube.com/embed/U1l6zJz6f7s; Lashkar-e-Taiba gunmen used a similar tactic during their Nov. 2008 siege of Mumbai. These phone conversations can also be downloaded from YouTube.
39. Gopal, Mahsud, and Fishman, "The Battle for Pakistan: Militancy and Conflict in North Waziristan"; M. Ilyas Khan, "The Afghan-Pakistan Militant Nexus," *BBC News*, 1 Dec. 2009.
40. Sadia Sulaiman, "Hafiz Gul Bahadur: A Profile of the Leader of the North Waziristan Taliban," *Terrorism Monitor*, 7, 9 (10 Apr. 2009); Gopal, Mahsud, and Fishman, "The Battle for Pakistan: Militancy and Conflict in North Waziristan"; Pazir Gul, "Waziristan Accord Signed," *Dawn*, 6 Sep. 2006; for the text of the Sep. 2006 North Waziristan Peace Accord, see "North Waziristan Peace Pact," *PBS Frontline*, 3 Oct. 2006, www.pbs.org/wgbh/pages/frontline/taliban/etc/nwdeal.html
41. Gopal, Mahsud, and Fishman, "The Battle for Pakistan: Militancy and Conflict in North Waziristan."
42. "Kidnapped envoy Tariq Azizuddin appeals for steps for his release," *The News*, 19 Apr. 2008, www.thenews.com.pk/updates.asp?id=43779; "Taliban hold kidnapped Pakistan envoy to Afghanistan," *Associated Free Press*, 19 Apr. 2008.

43. "Interview with Pervez Musharraf," *Der Spiegel*, 7 June 2009; see also "Pakistan Ambassador Freed," *BBC News*, 17 May 2008, http://news.bbc.co.uk/2/hi/south_asia/7406083.stm
44. According to Thomas Ruttig, Darim Sedgai acted as the Haqqani network's liaison to Baitullah Mehsud's faction of the TTP, see Ruttig, "The Haqqani Network as an Autonomous Entity," p. 72.
45. For a thorough review of this issue see Chapter 6 ("Good Jihadi/Bad Jihadi") in Tankel, *Laskhar-e-Taiba: Storming the World Stage*, pp. 119–72.
46. Mushtaq Yusufzai, "Kidnapped ambassador freed," *The News*, 18 May 2008; Ismail Khan, "Azizuddin is Home After 97 Days," *Dawn*, 18 May 2008; Candace Rondeaux and Pamela Constable, "Pakistan Launches Search For Missing Envoy to Kabul," *Washington Post*, 13 Feb. 2008; "Taliban Commanders Exchanges for Ambassador," *Jane's Terrorism and Security Monitor*, 10 June 2008.
47. Mian Abrar, "Pakistan swapped Dadullah for Tariq Azizuddin," *The News*, 28 May 2008.
48. Ismail Khan, "Forces, Militants Heading for Truce," *Dawn*, 23 June 2006, www.dawn.com/2006/06/23/top2.htm; Magnus Norell (ed.), "Militancy in the Pakistani Federally Administered Tribal Areas (FATA) and Afghanistan," Swedish Research Defense Establishment, FOI-R-2727-SE, Feb. 2010.
49. Intikhab Amir, "Holes in the Pact," *Herald*, 1 Oct. 2006.
50. Gopal, Mahsud, and Fishman, "The Battle for Pakistan: Militancy and Conflict in North Waziristan," p. 10; Raza Qazi and Sara A. Carter, "Pakistani Taliban Unite Against U.S.," *Washington Times*, 24 Feb. 2009; "Taliban 'receives $6M for Swat ceasefire'," Press TV (Iran), 24 Feb. 2009; the SIM was largely a notional organization and is now believed to be defunct.
51. Mark Hosenball, "More Forces for Afghanistan: Obama will send 17,000 U.S. troops," *Newsweek*, 17 Feb. 2009.
52. Haji Mujtaba, "Waziristan Taliban set up shura to wage jihad," *Daily Times*, 23 Feb. 2009; for the text of the SIM's official announcement, see *GEO TV*, 24 Feb. 2009.
53. BBC Monitoring, "Afghan Taliban chief asks militants to halt attacks on Pakistan Army," 25 Feb. 2009; "Mullah Omar orders halt to attack on Pak troops," *The News*, 24 Feb. 2009; "Mullah Omar asks Taleban not to attack Pakistani forces," *Ausaf*, 25 Feb. 2009.
54. Mushtaq Yusufzai, "No Moderates in Taliban Ranks: Haqqani," *The News*, 17 Apr. 2009, www.thenews.com.pk/top_story_detail.asp?Id=21576; although difficult to confirm, one source claims that Sirajuddin Haqqani, two deputies to Mullah Abdullah Zakir, Abu Yayha al-Libi, and a representative from the Eastern Turkistan Islamic Movement met with Baitullah Mehsud in June 2009 and urged him to reorient his fighters towards Afghanistan, see Bill Roggio, "Senior al Qaeda and Taliban Leaders Met with Baitullah," *Long War Journal*, 21 June 2009, www.longwarjournal.org/archives/2009/06/senior_al_qaeda_and.php
55. Afghan sources "say that at the behest of the ISI, Haqqani may now be trying to persuade his ally Mehsud to cease his attacks against Pakistan and to focus on Afghanistan instead," see Ron Moreau and Sami Yusufzai, "Pakistan's Dangerous Double Game," *Newsweek*; Raza Qazi and Sara A. Carter, "Pakistani Taliban Unite Against U.S.," *Washington Times*, 24 Feb. 2009.
56. In fact, one month after the SIM was forged Pakistani Taliban commander Mullah Nazir (a key signatory to the SIM) reaffirmed his commitment to wage jihad against the Pakistani state in a video released by al-Sahab.
57. According to some accounts, Abu Yahya al-Libi also played a key role in brokering the alliance. For background see Sailab Mehsud, "Taliban Groups Regroup to Fight US Forces," *Dawn*, 3 Jan. 2012, www.dawn.com/2012/01/03/al-qaida-taliban-ask-pakistani-militants-for-help.html; Nadeem Sarwar and Safiullah Gul Mehsud, "Al-Qaeda Tries to Unite Pakistani Militants," *McClatchy-Tribune Regional News*, 22 Dec. 2011; Amir Mir, "Siraj Haqqani exposes military-militants peace deal," *The News*, 14 Feb. 2012.
58. Jane Perlez, "Rebuffing U.S., Pakistan Balks at Crackdown," *New York Times*, 14 Dec. 2009.
59. Ibid.
60. Kathy Gannon, "Pakistan says it can bring Haqqani to peace talks," *Associated Press*, 18 Aug. 2011.
61. See Abdul Salam Zaeef, *My Life with the Taliban*.
62. The chairman of the Joint Chiefs of Staff, and thus by extension sections of the US intelligence community, have reached a similar conclusion. See Official Transcript, "Hearing to Receive Testimony on the U.S. Strategy in Afghanistan and Iraq."
63. "Interview with Taliban Commander Maulvi Jalaluddin Haqqani," *The News*, 20 Oct. 2001.
64. For more on the need to understand the geography of conflict in the south and India's goals

in the region see Robert Kaplan, *South Asia's Geography of Conflict*, Center for New American Security, Aug. 2010.

65. For a perspective on this issue see the statements of Admiral William H. McRaven in Nick Paton Walsh, "Tripling Afghanistan's 'community Watch with AK-47s'," Security Clearance (CNN blog), 11 Dec. 2011, http://security.blogs.cnn.com/2011/12/11/tripling-afghanistans-community-watch-with-ak-47s/
66. "Times Square Bomb Attempt Puts Focus on Pakistan," NPR Interview with David Rohde, Transcript, www.npr.org/templates/transcript/transcript.php?storyId=126536285; "Pakistan Army pays heavy price in Taliban war," *Dawn*, 20 May 2010.
67. For background see Mujahid Hussain, *Punjabi Taliban: Driving Extremism in Pakistan*, New Delhi, India: Pentagon Security International, 2012.
68. Ron Moreau and Sami Yusufzai, "Pakistan's Dangerous Double Game," *Newsweek*; see also Fareed Zakaria, "Terrorism's Supermarket: Why Pakistan keeps exporting jihad," *Newsweek*, 7 May 2010.
69. "Pakistan Army pays heavy price in Taliban war," *Dawn*, 20 May 2010.
70. For insights into some of these successes and the trials and tribulations of this relationship see Terry McDermott and Josh Meyer, *The Hunt for KSM*, New York: Little, Brown and Company, 2012, pp. 194–221, 242–8.
71. According to a dataset compiled by the New America Foundation, the Haqqani network is believed to have been targeted by at least twenty-six drone strikes since 2004, eleven of which occurred in 2010. Peter Bergen and Katherine Tiedemann, "The Year of the Drone: An Analysis of U.S. Drone Strikes in Pakistan, 2004–2010," Counterterrorism Strategy Initiative Paper, updated as of 11 Nov. 2010, http://counterterrorism.newamerica.net/drones
72. Pakistan has conducted several large military operations in North Waziristan, but the Haqqani network has never been the primary target of these larger operations, see Pazir Gul, "Further on Manhunt Launched for Clerics Behind Pakistan Tribal Clashes," *AFP*, 7 Mar. 2006; Behroz Khan, "5,000 more troops sent to Pak-Afghan border," *The News*, 14 Sep. 2005.
73. "North Waziristan Peace Pact," *PBS Frontline*, 3 Oct. 2006, www.pbs.org/wgbh/pages/frontline/taliban/etc/nwdeal.html; Rahimullah Yusufzai, "47 Tribal elders also signed peace accord," *The News*, 20 Oct. 2006.
74. "Arms swapped in Waziristan," *Dawn*, 7 Sep. 2006; Thomas H. Johnson and M. Chris Mason, "No Sign Until the Burst of Fire: Understanding the Afghanistan-Pakistan Frontier," *International Security*, 32, 4 (Spring 2008), p. 56.
75. "North Waziristan Peace Pact," *PBS Frontline*, 3 Oct. 2006, www.pbs.org/wgbh/pages/frontline/taliban/etc/nwdeal.html
76. See case of Maulana Abdul Kalam and four others in Intikhab Amir, "Holes in the pact," *Herald*, 1 Oct. 2006.
77. Ibid.
78. Carlotta Gall and Ismail Khan, "Taliban and Allies Tighten Grip in North of Pakistan, *New York Times*, 11 Dec. 2006, www.nytimes.com/2006/12/11/world/asia/11pakistan.html?_r=1; Guido Steinberg, "The Return of al-Qaida," SWP Comments, 22 (Dec. 2007); for al-Qa'ida's perspective on this see "A Statement Concerning Last Events in Waziristan," Palestine's Dialogue Forum, https://www.paldf.net/forum/showthread.php?p=457622, 9 Mar. 2006.
79. Andrew Gray, "Taliban step up cross-border attacks-U.S. military," *Reuters*, 17 Jan. 2007, www.reuters.com/article/idUSISL240273
80. Carlotta Gall, "Leadership Void Seen in Pakistan," *New York Times*, 24 June 2008 www.nytimes.com/2008/06/24/world/asia/24pstan.html?pagewanted=2
81. For an account of his captivity see David Rohde, "7 Months, 10 Days in Captivity," *New York Times*, 17 Oct. 2009, www.nytimes.com/2009/10/18/world/asia/18hostage.html
82. "A Reporter's Tale of Ambush and Captivity," NPR (Fresh Air), 27 Oct. 2009, www.npr.org/templates/transcript/transcript.php?storyId=114173568; see also Harmony document AFGP-2004-0011048; David Rohde, "'You Have Atomic Bombs, but We Have Suicide Bombers,'" *New York Times*, 19 Oct. 2009.
83. David Rohde, "'You Have Atomic Bombs, but We Have Suicide Bombers,'" *New York Times*, 19 Oct. 2009.
84. Gul, *The Most Dangerous Place*, Chapter 4; see comments made by Pakistani journalist Ashraf Ali in James Rupert, "'Biggest Threat' to U.S. in Afghanistan Is Aided by Pakistanis," *Bloomberg News*, 8 Oct. 2008; on the perspective of aspiring jihadis see Burke, *The 9/11 Wars*, p. 384.
85. For a breakdown of these plots and their ties to North Waziristan see Paul Cruickshank, "The

Militant Pipeline: Between the Afghanistan–Pakistan Border Region and the West," Counterterrorism Strategy Initiative Policy Paper, Feb. 2010.

86. As are the dynamics of several other plots. For more information see Chapter 7.
87. Fareed Zakaria, "Terrorism's Supermarket: Why Pakistan Keeps Exporting Jihad," *Newsweek*, 7 May 2010.
88. Matt Waldman, "The Sun in the Sky: The Relationship between Pakistan's ISI and Afghan Insurgents," Crisis States Discussion Papers, June 2010, p. 13.
89. Ruttig, "The Haqqani Network as an Autonomous Entity," p. 76.
90. Rashid, *Descent Into Chaos*, p. 223.
91. See Zaeef, *My Life with the Taliban*, p. 125; see also US Consulate (Peshawar) Cable, "Afghan-Pak Border-Relations at Torkham Tense," 2 Oct. 1996, Confidential, 6 pp. [Excised].
92. Bruce Riedel, "Pakistan and Terror: Eye of the Storm," *AAPSS*, July 2008, p. 32; the "ISI of Pakistan and other militias are clearly protecting the Taliban in the open," Harmony document AFGP-2004-011048.
93. Ron Moreau, "Pakistan's Dangerous Double Game," *Newsweek*, 13 Sep. 2008; see also http://armed-services.senate.gov/statemnt/2011/09%20September/Mullen%2009–22–11.pdf
94. Ruttig, "The Haqqani Network as an Autonomous Entity," p. 66.
95. For a reflection of this see Pir Zubayr Shah and Carlotta Gall, "For Pakistan, Deep Ties to Militant Network may Trump U.S. Pressure," *New York Times*, 31 Oct. 2011.
96. Interview with Pir Zubayr Shah, 23 Sep. 2010; for other claims about "Taliban leaders travelling in cars with official ISI license plates," see Graeme Smith, "We must do something about Pakistan," *Globe and Mail*, 2 Sep. 2006.
97. This quote is from "Pakistan Helping Afghan Taliban—NATO," *BBC*, 1 Feb. 2012; see also Madiha Sattar, "ANP leaders said military protected Haqqanis, other militants," *Dawn*, 23 May 2011; Rod Nordland and Alissa J. Rubin, "Taliban Captives Dispute U.S. View on Afghanistan War," *New York Times*, 1 Feb. 2012; and "2009: ANP on military's deals with militants," *Dawn*, 23 May 2011; Karachi data point is from author's interview with Pir Zubayr Shah, 23 Sep. 2010.
98. Interview with Pir Zubayr Shah, 23 Sep. 2010.
99. Dressler and Jan, "The Haqqani Network in Kurram."
100. Ron Moreau, "Pakistan's Dangerous Double Game," *Newsweek*, 13 Sep. 2008.
101. Waldman, "The Sun in the Sky," p. 14.
102. Moreau, "Pakistan's Dangerous Double Game."
103. Harmony document AFGP-2004-0011048.
104. Matthew Cole, "Killing Ourselves in Afghanistan," *Salon.com*, 10 Mar. 2008; James Rupert, "'Biggest Threat' to U.S. in Afghanistan Is Aided by Pakistanis," *Bloomberg News*, 8 Oct. 2008; Matthew Aid, *Intel Wars: The Secret History of the Fight Against Terror*, New York: Bloomsbury, 2012, pp. 108–13.
105. David E. Sanger, *The Inheritance: The World Obama Confronts and the Challenges to American Power*, New York: Harmony Books, 2009, p. 253. Given the context David provides it is likely that those he interviewed worked at the National Security Agency were those who processed the communications intercepts.
106. Harmony document AFGP-2004-0011048; according to other sources, the Haqqani network is affiliated with over eighty madrassas in Pakistan, see *Manba' al-Jihad* (Pashto), 2, 8 (Jan. 1991).
107. For background on the Manba' 'Ulum madrassa see Part I.
108. Behroz Khan, "5,000 more troops sent to Pak-Afghan border," *The News*, 14 Sep. 2005; Iqbal Khattak, "40 Militants Killed in North Waziristan," *Daily Times*, 30 Sep. 2005; "Pakistani Law Enforcers Intensify Hunt for Haqqani," *Pajhwok Afghan News*, 7 Mar. 2006.
109. Shaiq Hussain, "U.S. Missiles Said To Kill 20 in Pakistan Near Afghan Border," *Washington Post*, 9 Sep. 2008; "Forces raid Haqqani's madrassa in N Waziristan," *The News*, 30 July 2008.
110. Some sources suggest that a compound near Manba' 'Ulum was targeted by a drone strike in 2007. See Ismail Khan, "Missile Kills 5 in Northwest Pakistan; U.S. Denies Attack," *New York Times*, 3 Nov. 2007.
111. Shamim Shahid, "US Drones Bomb Madrassa in NW," *The Nation*, 9 Sep. 2008, www.nation.com.pk/pakistan-news-newspaper-daily-english-online/print/Politics/09-Sep-2008/US-drones-bomb-madrassa-in-NW
112. Pakistan has a rich history of betting on both sides. See Zaeef, *My Life with the Taliban*, pp. 125 and 126.

113. During the anti-Soviet jihad the United States and Saudi Arabia bankrolled and provided key weaponry to the Afghan resistance. It should also be noted that some of the sectarian groups previously fostered by the Pakistani state are now waging jihad against their former backer. For details on Pakistan's historic support for insurgent groups see Husain Haqqani, *Pakistan: Between Mosque and Military*, Washington, DC: Carnegie Endowment for International Peace, 2005; Jamal, *Shadow War*; Stephen Tankel, *Lashkar-e-Taiba: Storming the World Stage*; Praveen Swami, *India, Pakistan and the Secret Jihad: the Covert War in Kashmir (1947–2004)*, London: Routledge, 2007.
114. For example, see comments made by Lieutenant-General Ahmed Shuja Pasha in "Pakistan Never Backed Haqqani network: ISI Chief," *Reuters*, 30 Sep. 2011.
115. Interview with ABC-News, 1 Aug. 2008 as cited in Gul, *The Most Dangerous Place*, p. 162.
116. US Embassy (Islamabad), Cable, "[Excised] Believe Pakistan is Backing Taliban," 6 Dec. 1994, Secret, 3 pp.; US Embassy (Islamabad), Cable, "Senator Brown and Congressman Wilson Discuss Afghanistan with Pakistani Officials," 14 Apr. 1996, Confidential, 4 pp.
117. Zaeef, *My Life with the Taliban*, p. 147; the ISI also reportedly advised Jalaluddin Haqqani not to give up Osama bin Laden, see Gannon, *I is for Infidel*, p. 94.
118. Seth Jones, *In the Graveyard of Empires: America's War in Afghanistan*, New York: W.W. Norton & Co., 2010; Missy Ryan and Susan Cornwell, "U.S. says Pakistan's ISI supported Kabul embassy attack," *Reuters*, 22 Sep. 2011; "COMISAF's Initial Assessment," unclassified version, 30 Aug. 2009, pp. 2–10, available at: www.washingtonpost.com/wp-dyn/content/article/2009/09/21/AR2009092100110.html; Matthieu Aikins, "State of the Taliban 2012: The Secret Report," *GQ*, 9 Mar. 2012; Jason Burke, "Guantanamo Bay files: Pakistan's ISI spy service listed as a terrorist group," *Guardian*, 25 Apr. 2011.
119. Zaeef, *My Life with the Taliban*, p. 105.
120. Harmony document AFGP-2002-008587, pp. 23–4; another document captured in Afghanistan shows Pakistan's interest and involvement in more tactical and less strategic details, with the ISI instructing the Taliban to disrupt road-building in northeastern Afghanistan, see Harmony document AFGP-2005-0003302.
121. For examples see Harmony documents AFGP-2002-008582, pp. 9, 11, 12, 13; AFGP-2002-008581 p. 1.
122. Harmony document AFGP-2002-008581, p. 1.
123. Harmony document AFGP-2002-008582, p. 13.
124. Harmony document AFGP-2002-008581 and AFGP-2002-008582.
125. Matthew Cole, "Killing Ourselves in Afghanistan," *Salon.com*, 10 Mar. 2008; Sami Yusufzai, "Taliban in their Own Words," *Newsweek*, www.newsweek.com/2009/09/25/the-taliban-in-their-own-words.html; Waldman, "The Sun in the Sky," p. 17; Declan Walsh, "Taliban officials brought in from the cold: authorities pin hopes on reconciliation effort to break insurgency," *Guardian*, 19 May 2005.
126. Waldman, "The Sun in the Sky," p. 10; for additional suggestions of the ISI's role at other Taliban coordination meetings (not official shuras) see Jason Burke, "Guantanamo Bay files: Pakistan's ISI spy service listed as terrorist group," *Guardian*, 25 Apr. 2011.
127. Harakat-ul Mujahidin, Harakat-ul Jihad Islami, Hizb-ul Mujahidin, and Harakat-ul Ansar all had camps in Loya Paktia; the best source on the history of these camps is Muhammad Amir Rana's work, *Jihad in Kashmir and Afghanistan*, no date, and *Jihad and Jihadi*.
128. The two HUA camps hit were the Khalid-bin-Waleed and Muawia camps; see Rana, *Jihad in Kashmir*, pp. 127–8; one of the individuals at the al-Farouq camp during the cruise missile strike was Hassan al-Khamiri, who was the emir of the camp at that time, but would later serve as one of the suicide bombers for al-Qa'ida's attack against the USS Cole in 2000. See Ali H. Soufan, *The Black Banners: The Inside Story of 9/11 and the War Against al-Qaeda*, New York: Norton, 2011, p. 329.
129. Howard, "Wrath of Islam."
130. For example, see Central Intelligence Agency, "Harakat ul-Ansar: Increasing Threat to Western and Pakistani Interests," DI TR 96–008, Aug. 1996, www.gwu.edu/~nsarchiv/NSAEBB/NSAEBB227/index.htm#10
131. Harmony document AFGP-2002-000079.
132. Matthew Cole, "Killing Ourselves in Afghanistan," *Salon.com*, 10 Mar. 2008; Aid, *Intel Wars*, pp. 108–13; for another perspective on the ISI's support for the insurgency and training for Taliban units in the south of Afghanistan see Sarah Chayes, "Denying Pakistan," *Los Angeles Times*, 23 Nov. 2011, http://articles.latimes.com/2011/nov/23/opinion/la-oe-chayes-pakistan-role-in-afghanistan-20111123; and Ahmed Rashid, "Nato's top brass accuse Pakistan over Taliban aid," *Telegraph*, 6 Oct. 2006.

133. Cole, "Killing Ourselves in Afghanistan."
134. "All commanders reported that significant numbers of their fighters attend training camps in Pakistan that are run or backed by the ISI … Emphasizing the continued importance of such training, a south-eastern commander said that, 'of the 280 fighters in our district, some 80 percent were trained in Pakistan,'" Waldman, "The Sun in the Sky," p. 15; see also Gul, *The Most Dangerous Place*, p. 130.
135. See Appendix in Gul, *The Most Dangerous Place*.
136. Waldman, "The Sun in the Sky"; according to Matthew Aid, the US intelligence community held a similar view, see Aid, *Intel Wars*, pp. 111–12; for similar claims about Pakistani military assistance to insurgents in Zabul Province see Jason Burke, "Guantanamo Bay files: Pakistan's ISI spy service listed as a terror group," *Guardian*, 25 Apr. 2011.
137. Harmony document AFGP-2002-008588, p. 13.
138. Yousaf and Adkin, *The Bear Trap*.
139. Davis, "Pakistan's 'war by proxy' in Afghanistan loses its deniability."
140. Bajoria, "The ISI and Terrorism: Behind the Accusations."
141. "IIR [Excised] Pakistan Involvement in Afghanistan," 7 Nov. 1996, Confidential, 2 pp. [Excised].
142. Seymour Hersh, "The Getaway: Questions Surround a Secret Pakistani Airlift," *New Yorker*, 28 Jan. 2002; Jason Burke, *The 9/11 Wars*, pp. 61–2.
143. See the interviews of Lt Col Anthony Schaffer and Mullah Khasim in *Secret Pakistan*, BBC, www.bbc.co.uk/programmes/b016n0js/episodes/guide. The documentary can be viewed on Youtube; See also Lt Col Anthony Schaffer, *Operation Dark Heart*, New York: Thomas Dunne Books, 2010, p. 67.
144. Ibid.
145. Waldman, "The Sun in the Sky," p. 12; Christina Lamb, "Taliban leader killed by SAS was Pakistan officer," *Sunday Times*, 12 Oct. 2008, www.timesonline.co.uk/tol/news/world/asia/article4926401.ece
146. Ibid.; see also Guistozzi, *Koran, Kalashnikov, and Laptop*.
147. "The Spy Who Quit: A Conversation with Amrullah Saleh," *PBS Frontline*, 17 Jan. 2011, www.pbs.org/wgbh/pages/frontline/2011/01/video-amrullah-saleh-spy-who-quit.html
148. For a historical account of the ISI's use of this tactic see Yousaf and Adkin, *The Bear Trap*, p. 114.
149. Cole, "Killing Ourselves in Afghanistan."
150. Waldman, "The Sun in the Sky."
151. Ibid.
152. Rashid, *Descent Into Chaos*, p. 417.
153. Harmony Document AFGP-2002-008581, p. 17.
154. Harmony Document AFGP-2002-008582, p. 7.
155. For the Iran link see Harmony Document AFGP-2002-008681-24; for the link to Japan see Harmony Document AFGP-2002-008583, pp. 11–12.
156. The Urdu version of this magazine is titled *Nusrat al-Jihad*.
157. For confirmation of the existence of Haqqani offices in the Gulf, specifically in the United Arab Emirates, see any Arabic edition of *Manba' al-Jihad* and Harmony document AFGP-2002-800775.
158. In a letter published in *Manba' al-Jihad* (Pashto), 2, 10 (Apr. 1991), son of Abdul Haq Haqqani, Anwar-ul Haq Haqqani, and Mawlana Fazul Rahim from Jamia-e Ashrafiya in Lahore personally requested that copies of *Nusrat ul-Jihad* be sent to the Haqqania madrassa and Jamia-e Ashrafiya.
159. "Alhaj Mawlawi Jalaluddin Haqqani in a General Gathering of the Jamiat-e-Ulama-e-Islam in Lahore," *Manba' al-Jihad* (Pashto), 2, 11 (May 1991).
160. Cole, "Killing Ourselves in Afghanistan"; Waldman, "The Sun in the Sky"; Aid, *Intel Wars*, pp. 108–13.
161. Cole, "Killing Ourselves in Afghanistan."
162. Waldman, "The Sun in the Sky," p. 14.
163. Declan Walsh, "Wikileaks cables: 'US aid will not stop Pakistan supporting militants'," *Guardian*, 30 Nov. 2010, www.guardian.co.uk/world/2010/nov/30/wikileaks-us-aid-pakistan-militants; for the full context see "181529: Allies find briefing on Afghanistan NIE 'gloomy'," *The Hindu*, 19 Mar. 2011, www.thehindu.com/news/the-india-cables/the-cables/article1551330.ece
164. Waldman, "The Sun in the Sky," p. 19.
165. Matthieu Aikins, "State of the Taliban 2012: the Secret Report," *GQ*, 9 Mar. 2012; a "senior

Pakistani religious figure with close ties to the [Haqqani] network" who was interviewed by Gretchen Peters also believed that "the Haqqanis were no longer reliant on the ISI for funding, and did not take orders from the intelligence agency." Peters, *Haqqani Network Financing: the Evolution of an Industry*, p. 38.

166. For a review of the material related to this issue see Chapter 6 and specifically the US Treasury Department designations of several Haqqani leaders; see also Peters, *Crime and Insurgency in the Tribal Areas of Afghanistan and Pakistan*; Peters, *Haqqani Network Financing: The Evolution of an Industry*.
167. Peters, *Crime and Insurgency in the Tribal Areas of Afghanistan and Pakistan*.
168. For a discussion of this see Gul, *The Most Dangerous Place*, p. 195.
169. Waldman, "The Sun in the Sky," p. 19; see also Ahmed Rashid, "Nato's top brass accuse Pakistan over Taliban aid," *Telegraph*, 6 Oct. 2006.
170. "Text of Alhaj Haqqani's Interview with the Arab Magazine *Al Marabtoon*," *Manba' al-Jihad* (Pashto), 2, 12 (June 1991).
171. Harmony document AFGP-2002-008581, p. 11.
172. From [Excised] to DIA Washington, DC [Excised], Cable "[Excised]/Pakistan Interservice Intelligence/ Pakistan (PK) Directorate Supplying the Taliban Forces," 22 Oct. 1996, Secret, 1 p. [Excised].
173. Cole, "Killing Ourselves in Afghanistan"; Waldman, "The Sun in the Sky," p. 19; Mark Mazzetti et al., "Pakistan Aids Insurgency in Afghanistan, Reports Assert," *New York Times*, 25 July 2010; for similar accusations involving Pakistani border control posts "assisting insurgent attacks" in southeastern Afghanistan see Paul Watson, "On the trail of Taliban's support; more signs suggest a Pakistani role in aiding the Afghan insurgency," *Los Angeles Times*, 24 Dec. 2006.
174. Cole, "Killing Ourselves in Afghanistan."
175. Waldman, "The Sun in the Sky," p. 18; Watson, "On the trail of Taliban's support."
176. From [Excised] to DIA Washington, DC [Excised], Cable "[Excised]/Pakistan Interservice Intelligence/ Pakistan (PK) Directorate Supplying the Taliban Forces," 22 Oct. 1996, Secret, 1 p. [Excised].
177. US Embassy (Islamabad) Cable, "Afghanistan: [Excised] Criticizes GOP's Afghan Policy; Says It Is Letting Policy Drift," 16 June 1998, Confidential, 2 pp.
178. For background on these deals, see Abbas, "An Assessment of Pakistan's Peace Agreements with Militants in Waziristan (2004–2008)," pp. 7–18.

6. GLOBAL: AL-QA'IDA AND OTHER GLOBAL JIHADIST GROUPS

1. Bill Roggio, "Senior al-Qaeda Commander in Afghanistan Killed in US Airstrike," *Longwar Journal*, 31 July 2008.
2. Eric Schmitt and Tim Golden, "Details Emerge on a Brazen Escape in Afghanistan," *New York Times*, 4 Dec. 2005.
3. Ibid.
4. "Al-Qaeda Members Describe Escape from Bagram," *Al-Arabiya*, 18 Oct. 2005.
5. Schmitt and Golden, "Details Emerge on a Brazen Escape in Afghanistan."
6. Michael Hirsh, "Qaeda Prison Break," *Newsweek*, 13 Nov. 2005, www.thedailybeast.com/newsweek/2005/11/13/qaeda-prison-break.html
7. Omar al-Faruq, who served as al-Qa'ida's operations chief for Southeast Asia, was killed in Sep. 2006 by British Special Forces in Basra, Iraq. See "Senior Militant Killed in Iraq," *BBC*, 25 Sep. 2006; The Syrian—Abu Abdallah al-Shami—was killed in 2008 by an airstrike in the Afghanistan/Pakistan region. Abu Nasir al-Qahtani was captured again by US forces in Khost, Afghanistan, in Nov. 2006. See Roggio, "Senior al-Qaeda Commander in Afghanistan Killed in US Airstrike."
8. Declan Walsh and Eric Schmitt, "Drone Strike Killed No. 2 in Al-Qaeda, U.S. Officials Say," *New York Times*, 5 June 2012.
9. As Thomas Hegghammer and others have pointed out, foreign fighters are too often conflated with and assumed to be international terrorists or members of al-Qa'ida. Such conflation ignores variance in foreign fighter populations and their motivations, as not all foreign fighters aim to become members of al-Qa'ida. The cases of Najibullah Zazi and Hammad Khurshid are illustrative, as they both initially travelled to Pakistan to fight with the Taliban in Afghanistan and not with al-Qa'ida.
10. "A Reporter's Tale of Ambush and Captivity," NPR (Fresh Air), 27 Oct. 2009, www.npr.org/templates/transcript/transcript.php?storyId=114173568

11. David Rohde, "'You Have Atomic Bombs, but We Have Suicide Bombers,'" *New York Times*, 19 Oct. 2009.
12. "A Reporter's Tale of Ambush and Captivity."
13. Deception and cover and denial tactics play an important role in war. Evidence that speaks to these dynamics is reviewed below in this and the following chapter. See specifically, for example, Jalaluddin's role in obfuscating the role of Arabs in the 1991 battle for Khost (p. 221) and discrepancies between how the IJU and the Haqqani network represented a Mar. 2008 attack (pp. 193, 202–203).
14. Hegghammer, "The Rise of Muslim Foreign Fighters: Islam and the Globalization of Jihad," pp. 53–94.
15. See Part I for a thorough review of sources.
16. "Afghanistan: Taliban leader says Osama bin Laden still 'alive'," *Adnkronos International*, 14 Apr., no year; see also FBIS LD60927, "Abu-Dhabi Paper Interviews Rebel Leader," *al-Ittihad* (Arabic), 11 June 1980, p. 12; "Interview with Taliban Commander Maulvi Jalaluddin Haqqani," *The News*, 20 Oct. 2001; *Nawa-e-Afghan Jihad* (Urdu), 2, 10 (Nov. 2009).
17. Vahid Brown, "Al-Qa'ida and the Taliban: Diametrically Opposed?" *Jihadica*, 21 Oct. 2009.
18. For a discussion of how foreign fighter mobilizations empower transnational terrorist groups see the conclusion to this subsection and Thomas Hegghammer's work cited above.
19. For a perspective on this see Vahid Brown, "Classical and global jihad: Al-Qa'ida's franchising frustrations," in Assaf Moghadam and Brian Fishman (eds), *Fault Lines in Global Jihad: Organizational, Strategic, and Ideological Fissures*, New York: Routledge, 2011, pp. 88–117.
20. For a breakdown of all provinces see Anne Stenersen, "Al Qaeda's Allies: Explaining the Relationship between al Qaeda and Various Factions of the Taliban after 2001," Counterterrorism Strategy Initiative Paper, 19 Apr. 2010.
21. Guido Steinberg, "A Turkish al-Qaeda: The Islamic Jihad Union and the Internationalization of Uzbek Jihadism," *Strategic Insights*, July 2008; the most comprehensive assessment of actors in southeastern Afghanistan is provided by Ruttig, "The Haqqani Network as an Autonomous Entity," pp. 57–89.
22. Stenersen, "Al Qaeda's Allies: Explaining the Relationship between al Qaeda and Various Factions of the Taliban after 2001," p. 4.
23. Intel Center, "Jihadi Video Production Group Breakout by Afghan Province v1.0," 28 Oct. 2008.
24. The Haqqani network is not known to be active in Zabul, Kunar, or Nuristan. For background on ties that al-Qa'ida and other aligned foreign militant groups have to Zabul, Ghazni, and Kunar and Nuristan see Harmony document SOCOM-2012-0000015, p. 1; see also Sebastian Abbot, "Drone Strike Kills al-Qa'ida Leader," *Associated Press*, 30 May 2012; Paul Cruickshank and Tim Lister, "NATO on alert for influx of foreign fighters in southern Afghanistan," *CNN*, 24 May 2011.
25. "Mustafa Abu al-Yazid's Interview on al-Jazeera," NEFA, 22 June 2009.
26. Richard Oppel Jr., Abdul Waheed Wafa, and Sangar Rahimi, "20 Dead as Taliban Attackers Storm Kabul Offices," *New York Times*, 12 Feb. 2009; Anand Gopal, "Coordinated Kabul assault shows Taliban strength," *Christian Science Monitor*, 12 Feb. 2009.
27. Ibid.
28. Stenersen, "Al-Qaeda's Allies: Explaining the Relationship between Al-Qaeda and Various Factions of the Taliban post 2001."
29. "Mustafa Abu al-Yazid's Interview on al-Jazeera," NEFA Foundation, 22 June 2009.
30. Carol Grisanti and Mushtaq Yusufzai, "Taliban commander: Afghan officials are helping kill Americans," *NBC News*, 30 July 2008.
31. For examples see Part I and AFGP-2002-600088, p. 18; while several future leaders of al-Qa'ida had close ties to or at times fought under the direction of Haqqani in Paktia, there were a number of Arab fighters who rose to leadership positions under Haqqani but never joined al-Qa'ida. One such individual was Abu al-Hareth al-Urduni, a Jordanian, who Abu'l-Walid al-Masri described as being the "Emir (Commander) of the main Arab group at Khost." AFGP-2002-600090, p. 4.
32. Sami Yousufzai, "The Taliban in their Own Words," *Newsweek*, 26 Sep. 2009.
33. Abu Laith al-Libi is believed to have had a strained relationship with al-Qa'ida at times. For background see Guido Steinberg, "Renewing Leadership: The Role of Egyptians and Libyans in al-Qaeda's Senior Leadership," Janes IHS Defense, Jan. 2012, p. 11, www.swp-berlin.org/fileadmin/contents/products/fachpublikationen/sbgrenewingleadership_02.pdf; on his role during the early days of the US invasion of Afghanistan see Burke, *The 9/11 Wars*, p. 57; on Abu Laith's death see Rashid, *Descent into Chaos*, p. 390.

34. Cole, "Killing Ourselves in Afghanistan."
35. For example, in June 2009 Abu Yahya al-Libi and Sirajuddin Haqqani were both reportedly part of a delegation which tried to convince Baitullah Mehsud to negotiate a truce with Islamabad, as "Haqqani and al-Qaeda leaders were watching the army's advance through South Waziristan and worried that their territory might be next." Warrick, *The Triple Agent*, p. 72.
36. Gopal, Mahsud, and Fishman, "The Battle for Pakistan: Militancy and Conflict in North Waziristan," pp. 6–7.
37. "Arab Escapees Set up 60-Strong Group to Fight Coalition Forces in Afghanistan," *Pajhwok News* (in Dari), 8 Dec. 2005.
38. "Mujahideen Breaking in One of the Apostates' Centers," Jihad Archive, www.jarchive.info; "First Operation Against the Americans After the Escape From Baghram Prison," Jihad Archive, www.jarchive.info
39. "Terrorism Incident Report: Afghanistan, 2002–2007," IntelCenter, p. 203; "Holocaust of the Americans," al-Sahab, Dec. 2005.
40. "Breaking in an Apostates' Center in Khost," Jihad Archive, www.jarchive.info
41. "First Operation Against the Americans After the Escape From Baghram Prison," Jihad Archive, www.jarchive.info
42. Ruttig, "The Haqqani Network as an Autonomous Entity," p. 59.
43. "Mujahideen Breaking in One of the Apostates' Centers," Jihad Archive, www.jarchive.info; for additional reflections of Abu Yahya al-Libi's presence in Khost see Mushtaq Yusufzai, "US now says Somali, not al-Libbi killed in drone hit," *The News*, 13 Dec. 2009; for other video see Hanein Network, www.hanein.info/vb/showthread.php?t=139908&page=1
44. Nadeem Sarwar and Safiullah Gul Mehsud, "Al-Qaeda Tries to Unite Pakistani Militants," *McClatchy-Tribune Regional News*, 22 Dec. 2011; Declan Walsh and Eric Schmitt, "Drone Strike Killed No. 2 in Al Qaeda, U.S. Officials Say," *New York Times*, 5 June 2012.
45. "Mustafa Abu al-Yazid's Interview on al-Jazeera," NEFA, 22 June 2009; it is worth noting that the Taliban also claimed responsibility for this attack, see Matt Dupee, "FOB Salerno Withstands 2-Day Taliban On-Slaught," *Long War Journal*, 18 Aug. 2008.
46. "Mustafa Abu al-Yazid's Interview on al-Jazeera," NEFA, 22 June 2009.
47. "An Interview with the Director of Military Affairs in Paktika: Mawlawi Sangeen," al-Sahab, English translation provided by Dar al Murabiteen Publications, no date.
48. Ron Moreau, "Pakistan's Dangerous Double Game," *Newsweek*, 13 Sep. 2008; "Unravelling Haqqani's Net," *Jane's Terrorism and Security Monitor*, 30 June 2009.
49. Vahid Brown's interview with Sebastian Rotella 11 Aug. 2010; see also Sebastian Rotella and Josh Meyer, "A young American's journey into al-Qa'ida," *Los Angeles Times*, 24 July 2009; Paul Cruickshank, "Al-Qaeda's 2008 plan to hit Long Island Railroad Revealed," *CNN*, 23 Apr. 2012.
50. Belgian interrogation summary of Bryant Neal Vinas.
51. Paul Cruickshank, Nic Robertson, and Ken Shifman, "From Long Island to Lahore: The Plot to Bomb New York," *CNN*, 21 May 2010, http://edition.cnn.com/2010/CRIME/05/14/bryant.neal.vinas.part2/index.html; Sebastian Rotella and Josh Meyer, "A young American's journey into al-Qa'ida."
52. According to congressional testimony provided by General David Petraeus in June 2010, "the Hakkani [*sic*] network ... clearly commanded and controlled the operation ..." See "Hearing to Continue to Receive Testimony on the Situation in Afghanistan," Senate Armed Services Committee, 16 June 2010, p. 14, http://armed-services.senate.gov/Transcripts/2010/06%20June/10–53%20-%206–16–10.pdf
53. For background on the assault see Liam Stack, "Bagram Attack Kills U.S. Contractor, Wounds Nine NATO Soldiers," *Christian Science Monitor*, 19 May 2010; for background on Bekkay Harrach see the United Nations' "Al-Qaida and Taliban Sanctions Committee Record for Harrach" (at www.un.org/News/Press/docs/2009/sc9667.doc.htm); on his death see Yassin Musharbash, "Al-Qaida Fighter from Bonn Believed Dead," *Der Spiegel*, 19 Jan. 2011.
54. Bill Roggio, "IMU claims 2010 attack on Bagram airbase was executed 'in coordination and cooperation with other jihadi groups,'" *Long War Journal*, 19 Oct. 2011.
55. Harmony document SOCOM-2012-0000019, pp. 30–1. In the document Bekkay Harrach is referred to by his kunya: Abu Talha al-Almani.
56. Harmony document SOCOM-2012-0000019, pp. 30–1.
57. "Al-Qa'idah commander killed in Afghan east," *Pajhwok Afghan News* (in English), 13 July 2008; "Haqqani's son killed in Paktia," *The News*, 11 July 2008.

58. "Al-Qaeda Commander Dies in Fight with US and Afghan Forces," Jane's Terrorism and Insurgency Centre, 16 July 2008.
59. Evan F. Kohlmann, "Dossier: Shaykh Mustafa Abu al-Yazid (aka Shaykh Saeed)," NEFA, June 2008; "The 'Martyrdom' of Abu Sulaiman al-Otaibi," NEFA, 11 May 2008; Bill Roggio, "Al-Qa'ida Operatives Killed in Afghanistan were Saudis," *Long War Journal*, 13 May 2008.
60. Abu Musab al-Zarqawi, AQI's deceased leader, reportedly fought with Jalaluddin and his men in 1991 during their capture of Khost, see the article by Fu'ad Husayn in *Al Quds al Arabi*, 13 May 2005; Abu Sulayman al-Utaybi was reportedly dismissed from his position by Abu Omar al-Baghdadi before heading to Afghanistan. For background see Nibras Kazimi, "Interesting: Abu Suleiman al-'Uteibi Killed in Afghanistan," Talisman Gate (Blog), 11 May 2008, http://talismangate.blogspot.com/2008/05/interesting-abu-suleiman-al-uteibi.html
61. For reflections of Abu Laith al-Libi's role see Steinberg, "A Turkish al-Qaeda."
62. Ibid.
63. Wigen, "Islamic Jihad Union."
64. For a review of other joint attacks see ibid., specifically the cases of Abu Müslim Kurdi (June 2008) and Ebu Ömer Lezgi (Nov. 2008).
65. Matthias Gebauer, Yassin Musharbash, and Holger Stark, "Berlin's Worst Nightmare: Germany's First Suicide Bomber in Afghanistan?" *Der Spiegel Online*, 15 Mar. 2008.
66. Ibid.; Steinberg, "A Turkish al Qaeda."
67. Mushtaq Yusufzai, "Taliban Attack US Military Camp in Khost," *The News*, 4 Mar. 2008.
68. Ibid
69. Carlotta Gall, "Old-Line Taliban Commander Is Face of Rising Afghan Threat," *New York Times*, 17 June 2008.
70. "IJU Press Release," 6 Mar. 2008.
71. Ibid.
72. Wigen, "Islamic Jihad Union"; Carlotta Gall, "Old-Line Taliban Commander Is Face of Rising Afghan Threat," *New York Times*, 17 June 2008; www.spiegel.de/international/world/0,1518,543768,00.html
73. Wigen, "Islamic Jihad Union."
74. Don Rassler's interview with Thomas Ruttig, 25 May 2010.
75. This "form of entryism" concept is borrowed from Jason Burke, *Al Qaeda: The True Story of Radical Islam*, London: I.B. Tauris, 2004, p. 220.
76. As Hanna Rogan notes, "There appears to be not one jihadist media strategy and one media campaign, but rather a number of strategies ..." see Hanna Rogan, "Al-Qaeda's online media strategies: From Abu Reuter to Irhabi 007," Norwegian Research Defense Establishment, 2007, p. 117.
77. Harmony document AFGP-2002-600321; for similar reflections on how al-Qa'ida views media and its importance see seventeen of the internal al-Qa'ida documents that were recovered from Bin Laden's compound in Abbottabad, Pakistan, and were released by the Combating Terrorism Center. This material can be viewed and downloaded via www.ctc.usma.edu/posts/letters-from-abbottabad-bin-ladin-sidelined
78. "I say to you that we are in a battle, and that more than half of this battle is taking place in the battlefield of the media." See "Letter from al-Zawahiri to al-Zarqawi," http://ctc.usma.edu/harmony/pdf/CTC-Zawahiri-Letter-10–05.pdf; Ayman al-Zawahiri, *Exoneration*, no date.
79. Various scholars have noted that al-Qa'ida's strategic communications consistently emphasize three main points/goals: propagation, legitimization, and intimidation, see the work of Steve Corman and Jill S. Schiefelbein, "Communication and Media Strategy in the Jihadi War of Ideas," Consortium for Strategic Communication, 20 Apr. 2006; and Hanna Rogan, "Abu Reuter and the E-Jihad: Virtual Battlefronts from Iraq to the Horn of Africa," *Georgetown Journal of International Affairs* (Summer/Fall 2007), p. 94.
80. See Harmony document AFGP-2002-008575-47-48; Bergen, *Holy War, Inc*, p. 57.
81. See the work of Ahmed Zaidan, Brynjar Lia, and Thomas Hegghammer.
82. In addition to writing for *al Ittihad* newspaper, Abu Walid is also believed to have played a role in the production of *al-Mujahid*, which was produced by Jamiur Rahman, who primarily operated in Afghanistan's northeast. See Zaydan, *The "Afghan Arabs" Media at Jihad*, p. 92.
83. For additional background on Abu'l-Walid al-Masri see Vahid Brown, "Abu'l Walid al-Masri: A Biographical Sketch," Combating Terrorism Center, no date; for background on al-Suri see Lia, *The Architect of Global Jihad*, 2008.
84. This significance of this has been noted by Ahmed Zaydan, "I learned later from Afghan

Arab sources who were there that Usama had sought to sidestep the Taliban pressure on him by meeting the press in areas far away from the Taliban city of Kandahar, such as Jalalabad, where Hizb-i Islami leader Mawlawi Yunis Khalis enjoyed power and good relations with Usama since the days of the Afghan jihad, or in Paktia, where Shaykh Jalaluddin Haqqani, the Taliban Minister of Borders and Tribes, had strong ties with Bin Ladin as well ... This might explain why the declaration of the World Islamic Front for Jihad Against the Jews and Crusaders in May of 1998 by Bin Ladin, Zawahiri, and Pakistani figures, was issued in Khost, not Kandahar, or other areas where the Taliban and Mullah Muhammad Omar enjoyed significant influence." It is also believed that Bin Laden asked Jalaluddin's former boss, Yunis Khalis, for permission to hold the press conference; see Ahmad Zaydan, *Usama Bin Ladin bi-la Qina'*, Beirut: al-Sharaka al-'Alami li'l-Kitab, 2003, p. 130.

85. For information on Badruddin Haqqani's media role see David Rohde, "'You Have Atomic Bombs, but We Have Suicide Bombers,'" *New York Times*, 19 Oct. 2009; Rohde and Mulvihill, *A Rope and a Prayer*, pp. 157–61.
86. For background on Zawahiri's question and answers session see Jarret Brachman, Brian Fishman, and Joseph Felter, "The Power of Truth? Questions for Ayman al-Zawahiri," Combating Terrorism Center, 21 Apr. 2008.
87. See "Mustafa Abu al-Yazid's Interview on al-Jazeera," NEFA, 22 June 2009.
88. Labayk media and al-Sahab are productions companies affiliated with al-Qa'ida; Badr-al-Tawheed and Elif media are production companies associated with the IJU; Sawt al-Islam is a production company associated with the Eastern Turkistan Islamic Movement (ETIM), recently renamed as the Turkistan Islamic Party (TIP). Earlier videos released by ETIM were branded with the logo "Turkistan."
89. As Hanna Rogan notes, another useful distinction is segmentation between friendly and adversarial audiences; see Rogan, "Al-Qaeda's online media strategies."
90. "Open Interview with Sirajuddin Haqqani, a member of the Shura Council of the Islamic Emirate of Afghanistan and a commander in the southeastern provinces of Afghanistan," released by the Ansar al-Mujahidin Network, 27 Apr. 2010.
91. Brynjar Lia, "Al-Qaeda Online: Understanding Jihadist Internet Infrastructure," *Jane's Intelligence Review*, 1 Jan. 2006.
92. Ustadh Ahmad Farooq serves as al-Qa'ida's head of dawah and media in Pakistan, and the Urdu-language videos that feature him are a reflection of al-Qa'ida's efforts to influence local audiences in Pakistan.
93. "Caravan of the Ghazis," *Manba' al-Jihad* (in Pashto), second video, Sep. 2009, available at http://www.youtube.com/watch?v=A4abacEjO4A, accessed on 29 July 2010.
94. Abu Laith al-Libi is believed to have worked as an independent commander before officially joining al-Qa'ida in 2007. According to Anne Stenersen, "Abu al-Layth al-Libi's soldiers were known as *majmu'at Abu al-Layth* (Abu al-Layth's group)." See "Al Qaeda's Allies: Explaining the Relationship between al Qaeda and Various Factions of the Taliban after 2001," Counterterrorism Strategy Initiative Paper, 19 Apr. 2010.
95. Brynjar Lia, "Jihadi Web Media Production: Characteristics, Trends, and Future Implications," paper presented at "Check the Web" Conference on "Monitoring, Research and Analysis of Jihadist Activities on the Internet—Ways to Deal With the Issue" in Berlin on 26 and 27 Feb. 2007; "Lessons from the Life of Abu-al-Layth," Shumukh Al-Islam Network, https://shamikh1.net/vb/showthread.php?t=16023
96. "Lessons from the Life of Abu-al-Layth," Shumukh Al-Islam Network, https://shamikh1.net/vb/showthread.php?t=16023
97. "Mawlawi Nur Muhammad Raid in Khost," Jihad Archive, www.jarchive.info
98. "Abu-Nasir al-Qahtani, the Mujahid Poet," Jihad Archive, www.jarchive.info, 21 Oct. 2005; according to a foreign fighter who served under Abu Laith al-Libi, the al-Qa'ida leader commanded a group of 300 to 500 fighters; Belgian interrogation document provided to the authors.
99. "Tora Bora Interview with Sheikh Abu Yahya al-Libi," www.al-jahafal.com/vb/showthread.php?t=676; Abu Nasir al-Qahtani's media role is revealed in al-Sahab videos and its "Holocaust of the Americans" series.
100. "U.S.: Senior al Qaeda leader captured in Afghanistan," *CNN*, 13 Nov. 2006, www.cnn.com/2006/WORLD/asiapcf/11/13/afghan.capture/index.html; Rahimullah Yusufzai, "Al-Qaeda man rearrested," *The News*, 13 Nov. 2006; see also Fahd al-Riya'I, "Interview with Saudi Tribal chief Shaykh Ja'far al-Qahtani, father of Terror Suspect 'Abu Nasir' al-Qahtani," *Ukaz* (Arabic), no date.

101. "Al-Qa'idah commander killed in Afghan east," *Pajhwok Afghan News*, 13 July 2008; "Haqqani's son killed in Paktia," *The News*, 11 July 2008.
102. Ruttig, "The Haqqani Network as an Autonomous Entity," p. 74.
103. They have also helped to enhance the reputation and personal brand of all three al-Qa'ida members, especially Abu Yahya al-Libi.
104. Soren Astrup and Moren Skjoldager, "Prosecutor: 22 Year-Old Knew al-Qa'ida Leader," *Politiken*, 4 Sep. 2008.
105. Interview with Morten Skoldager, 5 Aug. 2010; Morten Skoldager, *Truslen indefra: De danske terrorister*, Lindhardt og Ringhof, Denmark, 2009; see also Laura Marie Sorensen, "Al-Qaeda-leder trænede dansk terrorist," *Politiken* (Danish), 11 Oct. 2009, http://politiken.dk/indland/article807742.ece
106. Julian Isherwood, "Guilty of Planning Terrorism," *Politiken* (in English), 21 Oct. 2008.
107. Interview with Morten Skoldager, 5 Aug. 2010.
108. Sebastian Rotella and Josh Meyer, "A young American's journey into al-Qa'ida," *Los Angeles Times*, 24 July 2009.
109. Rogan, "Al-Qaeda's online media strategies."
110. Wigen, "Islamic Jihad Union"; Carlotta Gall, "Old-Line Taliban Commander Is Face of Rising Afghan Threat," *New York Times*, 17 June 2008; Matthias Gebauer, "Bavarian Taliban Video: The Smiling Suicide Bomber," *Der Spiegel*, 27 Mar. 2008, http://www.spiegel.de/international/world/0,1518,543768,00.html
111. International Crisis Group, "Taliban Propaganda: Winning the War of Words?" 24 July 2008.
112. Rogan, "Al-Qaeda's online media strategies."
113. German officials have noted that the bomber, Cüneyt Çiftçi, also went by the name Saad Ebu Furkan; see Matthias Gebauer, Yassin Musharbash, and Holger Stark, "Berlin's Worst Nightmare: Germany's First Suicide Bomber in Afghanistan?" *Der Spiegel Online*, 15 Mar. 2008; Sirajuddin Haqqani identified the bomber as Abdhullah, see Mushtaq Yusufzai, "Taliban Attack US Military Camp in Khost," *The News*, 4 Mar. 2008.
114. The concept of cross-promotion is borrowed from Joanna Nathan, "Reading the Taliban," in Giustozzi, *Decoding the New Taliban*, p. 33.
115. The official status and affiliation of Labayk media is not entirely clear. Some have speculated that Labayk media is affiliated with the Taliban, others argue that it is closer to al-Qa'ida and al-Sahab. The authors believe the latter affiliation is now more accurate.
116. Jeremy Binnie and Joanna Nathan, "The Evolving Role of Uzbek-led Fighters in Afghanistan and Pakistan," *CTC Sentinel*, 2, 8 (Aug. 2009).
117. FOB Chapman reportedly functions as a CIA outpost used to collect intelligence, see Mark Mazzetti, "CIA Takes on Bigger and Riskier Role on Front Lines," *New York Times*, 31 Dec. 2009.
118. For background on al-Balawi's biography and his jihadist media credentials see Warrick, *The Triple Agent*.
119. During his time in North Waziristan, al-Balawi met al-Qa'ida's operations chief for Pakistan—Abdullah Said al-Libi—who invited al-Balawi to stay in his compound; "drank tea with [al-Qa'ida leader] Atiyah Abd al-Rahman" (now deceased); was introduced to al-Qa'ida's operations chief for Afghanistan Sheikh Saeed al-Masri (also known as Mustafa Abu al-Yazid; also now deceased); and served as a doctor for TTP leader Baitullah Mehsud. Al-Balawi was also interviewed by al-Qa'ida's *Vanguards of Khorasan* magazine. See Warrick, *The Triple Agent*, particularly p. 154.
120. "Statement on the Abu-Dujanah Al-Khurasani Raid (May God Accept Him) To Infiltrate the Fortresses of the Americans," Al-Qa'ida General Command, 6 Jan. 2010.
121. Such integration is not surprising. See quote from Bryant Neal Vinas in Cruickshank, "The Militant Pipeline."
122. For example, see http://www.youtube.com/watch?v=RTZQTC6ucVI
123. Alex Spillius, "CIA suicide bomber 'worked with bin Laden allies'," *Telegraph*, 7 Jan. 2010.
124. Warrick, *The Triple Agent*, pp. 79–80.
125. "Interview with Sirajuddin Haqqani," al-Balagh Media Center, 13 Apr. 2010.
126. "Yemeni Bombmaker Martyred in Waziristan," *Flashpoint Partners*, 9 May 2010. For background on al-San'ani, see Evan Kohlmann, "Al-Qa'ida's Yemeni Expatriate Faction in Pakistan," *CTC Sentinel*, 4, 1 (Jan. 2011).
127. Kohlmann, "Al-Qa'ida's Yemeni Expatriate Faction."
128. Ibid.
129. Ibid.

130. For example, as noted by Kohlmann, "Allah awarded them to spend Eid there in the highest levels of Paradise, with their beloved ones and brothers Ghazwan al-Yemeni, Abu Dujanah al-Sanaani, and Abu Dujanah al-Khorasani. Just as He gathered them in life, He has gathered them in the afterlife." Ibid.
131. The Nov. 2011 death in Karachi of an al-Qa'ida-linked Global Islamic Media Front (GIMF) official Abd al Moeed bin Abd al Salam (from Yemen) could serve as an important example here, as Moeed "created local media groups and Jihadi websites and forums in ... Urdu, English, Bengali, and Pashto." Moeed's death was announced through a statement issued by GIMF in Dec. 2011, which praised him for his work supporting al-Qa'ida and the TTP. Interestingly, several weeks after Moeed's death the TTP released a statement claiming responsibility for the death of three Pakistani Rangers in Karachi, who were reportedly killed to avenge the death of Moeed. These dynamics suggest that Moeed was a fairly important and well-known player in GIMF. For background on all of these details see "Statement on the Martyrdom of One of Its Commanders and Knight of Knights: The Brother Abu Umar—May Allah Accept Him," GIMF statement, 8 Dec. 2011, in the author's possession; Bill Roggio, "Al Qaeda announces death of Karachi-based media operative," *Long War Journal*, 8 Dec. 2011; Adil Jawad and Faraz Khan, "Gulistan-e-Jauhar grenade suicide: FIA report casts doubts on Rangers' claims," *Express Tribune*, 5 Dec. 2011; Bill Roggio, "Pakistani Taliban take revenge for slain al Qaeda media operative," *Long War Journal*, 15 Dec. 2011.
132. "Open Interview with Sirajuddin Haqqani, a member of the Shura Council of the Islamic Emirate of Afghanistan and a commander in the southeastern provinces of Afghanistan," released by the Ansar al-Mujahidin Network, 27 Apr. 2010; see also "Interview with Siraj Haqqani," al-Balagh Media Center, 13 Apr. 2010.
133. For an exploration of this history see Part I of this book.
134. One of our anonymous readers suggested that there have been instances where the Haqqanis abandoned foreign fighters, leaving them to be captured or killed by Pakistani security forces. Unfortunately, we were not able to locate any evidence or accounts of such occurrences. It is unclear if this has transpired.
135. "Al Qaeda commander dies in fight with US and Afghan forces," *Jane's Terrorism and Insurgency Centre*, 16 July 2008; "US Drone Kills Key al-Qa'ida Commander in Waziristan," *Geo TV*, 20 Feb. 2010, www.geo.tv/2–20–2010/59655.htm
136. David Rohde, "A Drone Strike and Dwindling Hope," *New York Times*, 20 Oct. 2009.
137. "A Reporter's Tale of Ambush and Captivity," NPR (Fresh Air), 27 Oct. 2009, www.npr.org/templates/transcript/transcript.php?storyId=114173568
138. Bruce Riedel made a similar point in 2008, stating that "the environment Pakistan tolerates inside its borders has allowed bin Laden and al Qaeda to continue to thrive there." See Bruce Riedel, "Pakistan and Terror: Eye of the Storm," *AAPSS*, 618, July 2008; for another perspective see Gul, *The Most Dangerous Place*, pp. 165–6.
139. Jalaluddin Haqqani had a political office in Peshawar, see "Interview with Commander Haji Mohammad Ibrahim," *Nusrat al-Jihad* (Urdu), 1, 9 (July 1991); he also had a number of residences there, see Harmony document AFGP-2002-600099, p. 33; see also Harmony document AFGP-2002-800775, p. 53; for historical examples of the Haqqanis providing facilities for Arab fighters and future members of al-Qa'ida see the writing of Abu Walid al-Masri, specifically, AFGP-2002-600099, pp. 12 and 17; AFGP-2002-600096, p. 75; AFGP-2002-600099, pp. 12–14. All references to page numbers are to the English-language translations of these documents. Versions of these documents are available online via Abu Walid's blog http://mafa.maktoobblog.com/ and website http://mafa.asia/
140. Harmony document AFGP-2002-600099, pp. 12 and 17.
141. Harmony document, AFGP-2002-600096, p. 75.
142. Harmony document, AFGP-2002-600099, pp. 12–13.
143. Harmony document AFGP-2002-600099, p. 14.
144. For background and various perspectives on the actors involved see accounts provided by Peter Bergen, "The Battle for Tora Bora," *The New Republic*, 240, 23/24 (30 Dec. 2009); Philip G. Smucker, *Al-Qaeda's Great Escape: The Military and the Media on Terror's Trail*, Dulles, VA: Brassey's, 2004; Dalton Fury, *Kill bin Laden: A Delta Force Commander's Account of the Hunt for the World's Most Wanted Man*, New York: St. Martin's Press, 2008; Lucy Morgan Edwards, *The Afghan Solution: The Inside Story of Abdul Haq, the CIA and how Western Hubris Lost Afghanistan*, Bactria Press: London, 2011, p. 79; Burke, *The 9/11 Wars*, pp. 61–72; Gary Bernsten and Ralph Pezzullo, *Jawbreaker: the Attack on Bin Laden and al-Qaeda—a Personal Account*

by the CIA's Field Commander, New York: Crown Publishers, 2005; Najwa bin Laden, Omar bin Laden, and Jean Sasson, *Growing up Bin Laden*; John Kerry, "Tora Bora Revisited: How we Failed to Get Bin Laden and Why it Matters Today," A Report To Members of the Committee on Foreign Relations, US Senate, 30 Nov. 2009.

145. Rashid, *Descent Into Chaos*, pp. 99 and 268.
146. Mark Mazzetti and Eric Schmitt, "CIA Outlines Pakistan Links with Militants," *New York Times*, 30 July 2008; it also appears that the Haqqani network provided protection to the IMU and its leaders after they moved to North Waziristan, given tensions in South Waziristan. See Gul, *The Most Dangerous Place*, pp. 58 and 69.
147. Rashid, *Descent Into Chaos*, p. 268.
148. These global jihadist groups hosted a range of different actors, including Hafiz Gul Bahadur and a number of Pakistani Taliban leaders, for details see Barbara Sude, "Al Qaeda Central: An Assessment of the Threat Posed by the Terrorist Group Headquartered on the Afghanistan–Pakistan Border," Counterterrorism Strategy Initiative Paper, Feb. 2010, p. 6; see also Magnus Norell (ed.), "Militancy in the Pakistani Federally Administered Tribal Areas (FATA) and Afghanistan," Swedish Research Defense Establishment, FOI-R-2727-SE, Feb. 2010.
149. "Guard: Al Qaeda Chief in Pakistan Killed," *CNN*, 9 Sep. 2008; Mushtaq Yusufzai, "Three more US attack victims succumb to injuries," *The News*, 10 Sep. 2008; Isambard Wilkinson, "Pakistan condemns US troop crossborder raids from Afghanistan," *Telegraph*, 11 Sep. 2008; three years after Abu Haris' death his replacement (Abu Hafs al-Shahri) was also killed in North Waziristan. According to one account he was killed with a Haqqani commander who went by the name Hafezullah. See Bill Roggio, "Abu Hafs al Shahri confirmed killed in Predator strike in Pakistan," *Long War Journal*, 17 Sep. 2011.
150. Harmony document, AFGP-2005-0003302.
151. Carol Grisanti and Mushtaq Yusufzai, "Taliban commander: Afghan officials are helping kill Americans," *NBC News*, 30 July 2008.
152. "German security forces name citizen as leading Al Qaeda attack planner," *Jane's Terrorism and Insurgency Centre*, 27 Jan. 2009.
153. Guido Steinberg, "A Turkish al Qaeda"; Wigen, "Islamic Jihad Union."
154. For background on this relationship see Part I and Jin Yan and Wu Qi, "Asan Mahsum and his East Turkistan Islamic Movement Plan, Carry Out Terrorist Activities in China," *Sanlian Shenghuo Zhoukan*, no date; "How are 'East Turkistan' Elements Trained?" *Sohu*, 25 July 2002.
155. "Militant Leader Killed in N. Waziristan Drone Strike," *Dawn*, 1 Mar. 2010.
156. Fathullah Haqqani initially established facilities in Zhawar for Jalaluddin in 1981, see "Inside Afghanistan—The Strongest Jihadi Center in Zhwar is Named After Hazrat-e Omar," *Nusrat al-Jihad* (Urdu), 1, 9 (July 1991); see also Scheuer, *Through our Enemies' Eyes*, pp. 96–7; for videos, satellite imagery, and photos of Zhawar see: www.globalsecurity.org/military/world/afghanistan/zhawar-kili.htm
157. Local frustrations of those who remained in Afghanistan during this period are best captured by Abu'l-Walid al-Masri, see Brown, *Cracks in the Foundation*; and Harmony document AFGP-2002-60053, p. 31.
158. Harmony documents AFGP-2002-600106 and AFGP-2002-800581; according to Steve Coll, "The first infrastructure [i.e., training camps] of Al Qaeda was essentially supervised by Haqqani," see www.pbs.org/wgbh/pages/frontline/taliban/interviews/coll.html
159. According to Steve Coll, "He was their Afghan patron in many ways," see ibid.
160. During the 1990s Jalaluddin Haqqani still received some state funding. For example, in the early 1990s Saudi Arabia provided Jalaluddin Haqqani with money to build a number of schools and a university in Khost; see "Mawlawi Jalaluddin Haqqani in an Interview with Manba-al Jihad," *Manba' al-Jihad* (Pashto), 4, 1 (Sep. 1992); Jere Van Dyk corroborated these findings, "it is an open secret that the Haqqanis built the main mosque in Khost with Saudi money," interview with Don Rassler, 1 Apr. 2010; there is some evidence that the CIA funded initiatives during the 1990s—such as the Commanders' Shura—in which Jalaluddin Haqqani played a major role. But there is no evidence that covert funding from the United States was earmarked specifically for Haqqani during this period, although this is possible.
161. See www.pbs.org/wgbh/pages/frontline/taliban/interviews/coll.html
162. "To Our Muslim Girls," *Manba' al-Jihad* (Arabic), 1, 5 (Dec. 1990).
163. The first delegation sent by Jalaluddin Haqqani to fulfill these duties in the Gulf was headed

by Mawlawi Aziz Khan. He and a number of other "brothers" worked in the Gulf for five years until they were replaced by several other people, see Mawlawi Aziz Khan, "The First Jihadi Operation in Afghanistan, and the Rising of the Ulama Against the Communists," *Manba' al-Jihad* (Pashto), 1, 4–5 (Oct.–Nov. 1989).

164. One must also consider that the UAE is the home of the world's largest Pashtun diaspora community outside of Pakistan, see Doris Buddenberg and William A. Byrd (eds), "Afghanistan's Drug Industry: Structure, Functioning, Dynamics and Implications for Counter-Narcotics Policy," UNODC, Nov. 2006, p. 166.
165. Muhammad al-Shafi'i, "Five Arabs, including a Saudi, are Detained by al-Qa'ida Organization on Charges of Spying," *Al-Sharq al-Awsat*, 20 June 2000.
166. Ibid.
167. Nasser al-Bahri, *Dans l'ombre de Ben Laden*, pp. 161–5; for additional insight into this issue see Kevin Jackson's three-part blog series "'A believer is not stung twice out of the same hole': the longstanding issue of security within the ranks," Alleyesonjihadism (blog), http://alleyesonjihadism.wordpress.com/2012/06/
168. Harmony document AFGP-2002-800775, p. 3.
169. Harmony document AFGP-2002-800775, p. 38.
170. "Government's Evidentiary Proffer Supporting the Admissibility of Coconspirator Statements," 02 CR 892, United States District Court, Northern District of Illinois, Eastern Division; for an overview of al-Qa'ida's use and affiliation with various Islamic charities, including BIF, see Victor Comras, "Al Qaeda Finances and Funding to Affiliated Groups," in Jeanne K. Giraldo and Harold A. Trinkhunas (eds), *Terrorism Financing and State Responses: A Comparative Perspective*, Stanford: Stanford University Press, 2007, pp. 115–32.
171. "Government's Evidentiary Proffer Supporting the Admissibility of Coconspirator Statements," 02 CR 892.
172. Peters, "Crime and Insurgency in the Tribal Areas of Afghanistan and Pakistan," Combating Terrorism Center, Oct. 2010, p. 37.
173. Waldman, "The Sun in the Sky," p. 19.
174. Anthony Loyd, "Terror link alleged as Saudi millions flow into Afghanistan war zone," *The Times*, 31 May 2010; "The CIA recently estimated that Taliban leaders and their allies received $106 million in the past year from donors outside Afghanistan," see Craig Whitlock, "Diverse Sources Fund Insurgency In Afghanistan," *Washington Post*, 27 Sep. 2009.
175. Don Rassler's interview with Gretchen Peters, 22 Jan. 2011.
176. Senator Afrasiab Khattak is the president of the Awami National Party in the recently renamed Khyber-Pakhtunkhwa Province of Pakistan; see interview with Afrasiab Khattak, www.pbs.org/wgbh/pages/frontline/taliban/etc/script.html
177. "Treasury Targets Taliban and Haqqani Network Leadership: Treasury Designates Three Financiers Operating in Afghanistan and Pakistan," US Treasury Press Release, 22 July 2010; other sources confirm Nasiruddin's financial role, Interview with Pir Zubayr Shah, 23 Sep. 2010; see also Gopal, Mahsud, and Fishman, "The Battle for Pakistan: Militancy and Conflict in North Waziristan."
178. "Treasury Targets the Financial and Support Networks of al-Qa'ida and the Taliban, Haqqani Network Leadership," US Treasury Department Press Release, 9 Feb. 2011.
179. For background on Fazl Rabbi see www.treasury.gov/resource-center/sanctions/OFAC-Enforcement/Documents/taliban_notice_06212011.pdf; www.un.org/sc/committees/1988/NSTI15712E.shtml; for background on Ahmad Jan Wazir see www.treasury.gov/resource-center/sanctions/OFAC-Enforcement/Documents/taliban_notice_06212011.pdf; www.un.org/sc/committees/1988/NSTI15912E.shtml
180. Harmony document AFGP-2002-600096, p. 228; see also Harmony document AFGP-2002-600093, p. 57.
181. As noted in Part I, other Afghan political and mujahidin leaders, such as Ahmed Shah Masoud and Abdul Rasul Sayyaf, also played important roles facilitating the movement and integration of foreign fighters, although not as early or as consistently as Jalaluddin Haqqani.
182. Although it is not known if similar practices are followed in Afghanistan/Pakistan, internal al-Qa'ida in Iraq records illustrate how foreign fighters were contributed to al-Qa'ida after their arrival, see Brian Fishman (ed.), *Bombers, Bank Accounts and Bleedout: al-Qa'ida's Road in and out of Iraq*, Combating Terrorism Center, July 2008.
183. Anthony Davis, "Foreign Combatants in Afghanistan," *Jane's Intelligence Review*, 1 July 1993.
184. Ibid.

185. Matthias Gebauer, "'Bavarian Taliban' Video: The Smiling Suicide Bomber," *Der Spiegel*, 27 Mar. 2008.
186. "The Threat from Within: A German Islamist Rises up Al-Qaida's Ranks," *Der Spiegel*, 27 Jan. 2009; Bin Laden was impressed by Harrach as well. See Harmony document SOCOM-2012-0000019, p. 30.
187. For a reflection of this see the mention of Mullah Dadullah's interview with al-Jazeera in 2006, "Suicide Bombings in Afghanistan," *Jane's Islamic Affairs Analyst*, 1 Sep. 2007.
188. Mullah Dadullah, who served as a suicide attack trainer for the Afghan Taliban, later went on to wage a brutal campaign of violence in southern Afghanistan, see Johnson and Mason, "No Sign Until the Burst of Fire," pp. 41–77.
189. Franco, "The Tehrik-e-Taliban Pakistan," p. 283.
190. Seth Jones, "Pakistan's Dangerous Game," *Survival*, 49, 1 (Spring 2007), p. 22; for a more skeptical analysis of these claims see Alec D. Barker, "Improvised Explosive Devices in Southern Afghanistan and Western Pakistan, 2002–2009," Counterterrorism Strategy Initiative Policy Paper, New America Foundation, Apr. 2010.
191. "Suicide Bombings in Afghanistan," *Jane's Islamic Affairs Analyst*, 1 Sep. 2007.
192. Ruttig, "The Haqqani Network as an Autonomous Entity," p. 69.
193. Christine Fair, "Suicide Attacks in Afghanistan (2001–2007)," United Nations Assistance Mission to Afghanistan, 9 Sep. 2007.
194. Gul, *The Most Dangerous Place*, pp. 138–9.

7. ENTANGLEMENTS AND MANAGEMENT OF THE HAQQANIS' NEXUS POSITION

1. Limited research has been done on "constrained pragmatism." For two perspectives see H. Elaine Mayo, "Toward Collective Praxis in Teacher Education: Complexity, Pragmatism and Practice," thesis, University of Canterbury, 2003 and Richard Posner, *How Judges Think*, Cambridge, MA: Harvard University Press, 2008.
2. In a series of televised speeches to Pashtun and Tajik elders during this period President Najibullah criticized the role of foreigners fighting in Afghanistan, Khost, and Jalalabad, www.youtube.com/watch?v=pnvIrb8L9hk&NR=1. He gives speeches to the gatherings of Pashtun and Tajik elders in the country, appealing to them to support the government because the foreigners are there fighting to destroy Afghanistan. He mentions that every night he shows Arab and Pakistani captives on national television, pleading guilty of fighting in Afghanistan. He mentions Khost and Nangarhar; we would like to thank Ahmed for helping us to understand this point.
3. "Taliban's Sirajuddin Haqqani Shrugs Off $5m Bounty," *AfPax Insider*, 4 July 2009.
4. "Interview with Sirajuddin Haqqani," al-Balagh Media Center, 13 Apr. 2010.
5. Gopal, Mahsud, and Fishman, "The Battle for Pakistan: Militancy and Conflict in North Waziristan," p. 13.
6. Authors' interview with anonymous source, Mar. 2010.
7. Ibid.
8. Authors' interview with Pir Zubayr Shah, 13 Sep. 2010.
9. For an overview of this problem see Christine Fair and Seth G. Jones, "Pakistan's War Within," *Survival*, 51, 6 (Dec. 2009–Jan. 2010), pp. 161–88.
10. Derived from statistics provided in Ian S. Livingston and Michael O'Hanlon, "Pakistan Index: Tracking Variables of Reconstruction and Security," Brookings Institution, 8 Dec. 2010; for attack numbers see "Pakistan Security Report 2009," Pak Institute for Peace Studies, Jan. 2010.
11. Lolita C. Baldor, "Terrorist Attacks Spike in Pakistan, Afghanistan," *Huffington Post*, 26 Apr. 2010, www.huffingtonpost.com/2010/04/29/terrorist-attacks-spike-i_n_556343.html; for a breakdown of these attacks see https://wits.nctc.gov/ or http://www.start.umd.edu/gtd/
12. Cruickshank, "The Militant Pipeline."
13. Carol Grisanti and Mushtaq Yusufzai, "Taliban commander: Afghan officials are helping kill Americans," *NBC News*, 30 July 2008.
14. Ibid.
15. For a review of Pakistani military operations in South Waziristan and the FATA see Fair and Jones, "Pakistan's War Within."
16. Shaiq Hussain, "Ditch Mehsud or face action," *The Nation*, 29 July 2009.
17. David Rohde, "You Have Atomic Bombs, but we have Suicide Bombers," *New York Times*, 19 Oct. 2009.

18. "Deadly Blast Hits Pakistan Mosque," *BBC*, 27 Mar. 2009, http://news.bbc.co.uk/2/hi/7967594.stm; see also "Death Toll in Jamrud Mosque Suicide Attack Hits 70," *Pakistan Tribune*, 27 Mar. 2009, www.paktribune.com/news/index.shtml?212987
19. NPR interview, 6 May 2010, www.npr.mobi/templates/transcript/transcript.php?storyId=126536285
20. David Rohde, "A Drone Strike and Dwindling Hope," *New York Times*, 20 Oct. 2009.
21. Gul, *The Most Dangerous Place*, p. 37; Gopal, Mahsud, and Fishman, "The Battle for Pakistan: Militancy and Conflict in North Waziristan."
22. Ronald Sandee, "The Islamic Jihad Union (IJU)," NEFA, 14 Oct. 2008; Steinberg, "A Turkish al-Qaeda."
23. A Pakistani investigator with intimate knowledge of the case explained the ties back to North Waziristan in the following way: "while the fingers were in Islamabad, the tail was in Mirali." See Ismail Khan, "Rocket Attack Plan was Approved by Al Qaeda," *Dawn*, 4 Nov. 2006; Ebu Yahya Muhammed Fatih was killed in a drone attack in Mir Ali, North Waziristan in Sep. 2009.
24. IJU video: *Islami Cihad Ittehad Operasyonlari: Murtedlerin Sonu.*
25. This dataset is current as of June 2010.
26. For background on this integration see Chapter 6.
27. For background see Don Rassler, "Al-Qa'ida's Pakistan Strategy," *CTC Sentinel*, June 2009.
28. "Attack on Musharraf; 5 Get Capital Punishment," *Pakistan Times*, 28 Aug. 2005; "Arrests Follow Musharraf Attack," *BBC*, 27 Dec. 2003.
29. B. Raman, "Jihadis Strike at Pak Army and ISI Again," South Asia Analysis Group, 25 Nov. 2007.
30. Bruce Riedel, *Deadly Embrace: Pakistan, America and the Future of Global Jihad*, Washington, DC: Brookings Institution Press, 2011, p. 77.
31. "Seven Qaida Commanders Enter Pakistan," *Daily Times*, 4 June 2009; "ISI is Not a Rogue Agency: Riedel," *Dawn*, 6 June 2009; the *Long War Journal* claims that Prime Minister Gilani and General Kiyani were also targets. For more, see Bill Roggio, "Al Qaeda Operatives Targeting Pakistani Leaders," *Long War Journal*, 4 June 2009.
32. Ibid. It should also be noted that significant disagreements exist among academics and counterterrorism professionals about the strength of the links between al-Qa'ida and Lashkar-e-Taiba.
33. Harmony document AFGP-2002-602383.
34. Cruickshank, "The Militant Pipeline."
35. For background on the plot see Simone Kaiser, Marcel Rosenbach, and Holger Stark, "Operation Alberich: How the CIA helped Germany foil terror plot," *Der Spiegel*, 10 Sep. 2007; Guido Steinberg, "Trial and Error: How a Failed Plot Revealed a Movement," *Jane's Intelligence Review*, 16 Apr. 2010.
36. Steinberg, "A Turkish al-Qaeda"; Souad Mekhennet and Michael Moss, "Europeans Get Terror Training Inside Pakistan," *New York Times*, 10 Sep. 2007, www.nytimes.com/2007/09/10/world/europe/10germany.html
37. Yassin Musharbash, "Mastermind behind German Terror Plot: Jihadi Leader Reported Killed in US Drone Attack," *Der Spiegel*, 18 Sep. 2009, www.spiegel.de/international/world/0,1518,649978,00.html
38. Guido Steinberg, "Al-Qaida and Jihadist Terrorism post 2001," in Mark Pieth, Daniel Thelesklaf, and Radha Ivory (eds), *Countering Terrorist Financing: The Practitioner's Point of View*, Basel: Basel Institute on Governance, 2009, p. 8.
39. For a review of the IJU/Abu-Laith al-Libi linkage see Chapter 6; for insight into the link between Abu Laith al-Libi and the Haqqani network see Gopal, Mahsud, and Fishman, "The Battle for Pakistan: Militancy and Conflict in North Waziristan," pp. 6–7.
40. Yassin Musharbash and Marcel Rosenbach, "Explosions in the Sand," *Der Spiegel* (German), 10 Aug. 2009.
41. We personally thank Morten Skoldager and representatives from the Danish Defense Intelligence Service for the assistance and information they provided about this plot.
42. Morten Skoldager, *Truslen indefra: De danske terrorister*, Lindhardt og Ringhof, Denmark, 2009; see also Laura Marie Sorensen, "Al-Qaeda-leder trænede dansk terrorist," *Politiken* (Danish), 11 Oct. 2009, http://politiken.dk/indland/article807742.ece; Sebastian Rotella, "A Look Inside al-Qaeda," *Los Angeles Times*, 2 Apr. 2008; al-Masri reportedly trained Bekkay Harrach during the same timeframe.
43. "According to the U.S. authorities, Abu Ali was a liaison between the senior leadership of al-Qaeda and its rank-and-file members around the world. Abu Ali arranged travel, pro-

cured false documents and assisted in other ways the rank and file al-Qaeda members who were sent out into the world to carry out terrorist actions." [Translated from Danish]; see Skoldager, *Truslen indefra*.

44. Abu Nasiruddin al-Qahtani was captured in Khost and is now detained in Saudi Arabia, see sources above.
45. As Cruickshank notes, "Abu Hafith" could be a reference to Bekkay Harrach; see Cruickshank, "The Militant Pipeline," footnote 148; Belgian interrogation summary of Bryant Neal Vinas.
46. Vahid Brown interview with Sebastian Rotella; see also Sebastian Rotella and Josh Meyer, "A young American's journey into al-Qa'ida," *Los Angeles Times*, 24 July 2009; see also Paul Cruickshank, Nic Robertson, and Ken Shifman, "From Long Island to Lahore: The Plot to Bomb New York," *CNN*, 21 May 2010, http://edition.cnn.com/2010/CRIME/05/14/bryant.neal.vinas.part2/index.html
47. For background see Paul Cruickshank, "Al-Qaeda's 2008 plan to hit Long Island Railroad Revealed," *CNN*, 23 Apr. 2012.
48. Belgian interrogation summary of Bryant Neal Vinas.
49. Paul Cruickshank, Nic Robertson, and Ken Shifman, "From Long Island to Lahore: The Plot to Bomb New York," *CNN*, 21 May 2010, http://edition.cnn.com/2010/CRIME/05/14/bryant.neal.vinas.part2/index.html
50. For background on Abdul Jabbar and his ties see "UK and Taliban links of drone death man Abdul Jabbar," *BBC Newsnight*, 11 Oct. 2010, http://news.bbc.co.uk/2/hi/programmes/newsnight/9080165.stm
51. "Two al-Qaeda Leaders Arrested in Pakistan Last Month," *Daily Times*, 21 Dec. 2010.
52. "Al-Qaida Plans: Bin Laden Said to have Financed European Terror Plot," *Der Spiegel*, 2 Oct. 2010, www.spiegel.de/international/europe/0,1518,720879,00.html; Amir Mir, "Drones Trying to Wipeout White Jihadis in Waziristan," *The News*, 9 Oct. 2010.
53. Matthias Bartsch, Yassin Musharbask, and Holger Stark, "Fears of Mumbai Redux: The Story behind Germany's Terror Threat," *Der Spiegel*, 22 Nov. 2010, www.spiegel.de/international/germany/0,1518,730377,00.html

CONCLUSION

1. Many of these sources are also currently being digitized in partnership with the University of Arizona by a grant sponsored by the US National Endowment for the Humanities.
2. Soufan, *The Black Banners*, p. xxii.
3. For good background see Dexter Filkins, "After America: Will civil war hit Afghanistan when the U.S. leaves?" *New Yorker*, 9–16 July 2012, pp. 54–67.
4. As reviewed in the introduction, the author recognizes that the term jihad has multiple meanings. For clarity all references to jihad in the following paragraphs refer to violent jihad.
5. For background on al-Qa'ida's posturing vis-à-vis India see Mustafa Abu al-Yazid, "Speech to the People of Pakistan," al-Sahab, 26 Mar. 2009.
6. For reflections of disagreements over tactics in Waziristan see SOCOM-2012-0000007. For a broader investigation of fault lines within and external to the region's jihadi community see Assaf Moghadam and Brian Fishman (eds), *Fault Lines in Global Jihad*, New York: Routledge, 2011.

BIBLIOGRAPHY

European-language sources

Abbas, Hassan, "An Assessment of Pakistan's Peace Agreements with Militants in Waziristan (2004–2008)," in Daveed Gartenstein-Ross and Clifford D. May (eds), *The Afghanistan-Pakistan Theater: Militant Islam, Security and Stability*, Washington, DC: FDD Press, 2010, pp. 7–18.

Abedin, Mahan, "From Mujahid to Activist: An Interview with a Libyan Veteran of the Afghan Jihad," Jamestown Foundation, *Spotlight on Terrorism*, 3, 2 (May 2005); http//www.jamestown.org/single/?no_cache=1&tx_ttnews[tt_news]=178

Ahmed, Akbar S., *Millennium and Charisma among the Pathans*, London: Routledge and Kegan Paul, 1976.

——— *Resistance and Control in Pakistan*, London: Routledge, 2004.

Aid, Matthew, *Intel Wars: The Secret History of the Fight Against Terror*, New York: Bloomsbury, 2012.

Akbar, Said Hyder and Susan Burton, *Come Back to Afghanistan*, New York: Bloomsbury, 2005.

Ali, Imtiaz, "Baitullah Mehsud—the Taliban's New Leader in Pakistan," *Terrorism Focus*, 9 (Jan. 2008).

——— "The Father of the Taliban: an Interview with Maulana Sami ul-Haq," *Spotlight on Terror*, 4, 2 (23 May 2007).

Ali, Salamat, "Cause and Effect," *Far Eastern Economic Review* (23 May 1991).

'Azzam, 'Abdullah, "The Defense of Muslim Territories Constitutes the First Individual Duty," trans. Thomas Hegghammer, in Gilles Kepel and Jean-Pierre Milelli (eds), *Al Qaeda in its Own Words*, Cambridge, MA: Belknap/Harvard, 2008, pp. 102–9.

Al-Bahri, Nasser, *Dans l'ombre de Ben Laden*, Paris: Editions Michel Lafon, 2010.

Bajoria, Jayshree, "India–Afghanistan Relations," CFR Backgrounder, 22 July 2009.

——— "The ISI and Terrorism: Behind the Accusations," CFR Backgrounder, 28 May 2009.

Barfield, Thomas, *Afghanistan: A Cultural and Political History*, Princeton, NJ: Princeton University Press, 2010.

Barker, Alec D., "Improvised Explosive Devices in Southern Afghanistan and Western Pakistan, 2002–2009," Counterterrorism Strategy Initiative Policy Paper, New America Foundation, Apr. 2010.

Barnes, Cindy, Helen Blake, and David Pinder, *Creating and Delivering Your Value Proposition: Managing Customer Experience for Profit*, London: Kogan Page, 2009.

Bearden, Milt and James Risen, *The Main Enemy*, New York: Random House, 2003.

Bell, Kevin, "Yunis Khalis: The Tension between the Historiography and the Primary Sources," unpublished MA thesis: Princeton University, 2012.

Bergen, Peter, "The Battle for Tora Bora," *The New Republic*, 240, 23/24 (30 Dec. 2009).

——— *Holy War, Inc.*, New York: Touchstone, 2001.

——— (ed.), *The Osama bin Laden I Know*, New York: Free Press, 2006.

Bergen, Peter and Katherine Tiedemann, "The Year of the Drone: An Analysis of U.S. Drone Strikes in Pakistan, 2004–2010," Counterterrorism Strategy Initiative Paper, updated as of 11 Nov. 2010; http://counterterrorism.newamerica.net/drones

Bernsten, Gary and Ralph Pezzullo, *Jawbreaker: the Attack on Bin Laden and al-Qaeda—a Personal Account by the CIA's Field Commander*, New York: Crown Publishers, 2005.

BIBLIOGRAPHY

Bin Laden, Najwa, Omar bin Laden, and Jean Sasson, *Growing Up bin Laden*, New York: St. Martin's Press, 2009.

Binnie, Jeremy and Joanna Nathan, "The Evolving Role of Uzbek-led Fighters in Afghanistan and Pakistan," *CTC Sentinel*, 2, 8 (Aug. 2009).

Brachman, Jarret, Brian Fishman, and Joseph Felter, "The Power of Truth? Questions for Ayman al-Zawahiri," Combating Terrorism Center, 21 Apr. 2008.

Bradsher, Henry, *Afghan Communism and Soviet Intervention*, Oxford and London: Oxford University Press, 1999.

——— *Afghanistan and the Soviet Union*, Durham, NC: Duke University Press, 1985.

Brahmanyar, Mir, *Afghanistan Cave Complexes 1979–2004: Mountain strongholds of the Mujahideen, Taliban & Al Qaeda*, Oxford: Osprey Publishing, 2004.

Brisard, Jean Charles, *Zarqawi: The New Face of al-Qaeda*, New York: Other Press, 2005.

Brown, Vahid, "Abu'l Walid al-Masri: A Biographical Sketch," Combating Terrorism Center, 1 Jan. 2008; http://www.ctc.usma.edu/posts/a-profile-of-abu%E2%80%99l-walid-al-masri

——— "Al-Qa'ida and the Afghan Taliban: Diametrically Opposed?" *Jihadica*, 21 Oct. 2009; http://www.jihadica.com/al-qa%E2%80%99ida-and-the-afghan-taliban-%E2%80%9Cdiametrically-opposed%E2%80%9D/

——— "Classical and Global jihad: Al-Qa'ida's Franchising Frustrations," in Assaf Moghadam and Brian Fishman (eds), *Fault Lines in Global Jihad: Organizational, Strategic, and Ideological Fissures*, New York: Routledge, 2011, pp. 88–117.

——— *Cracks in the Foundation*, West Point, NY: Combating Terrorism Center at West Point, 2007.

——— "The Facade of Allegiance: Bin Ladin's Dubious Pledge to Mullah Omar," *CTC Sentinel*, 3, 1 (Jan. 2010).

——— "Foreign Fighters in Historical Perspective: The Case of Afghanistan," in Brian Fishman (ed.), *Bombers, Bank Accounts, and Bleedout: Al-Qa'ida's Road in and out of Iraq*, West Point, NY: Combating Terrorism Center at West Point, 2008, pp. 16–31.

Buddenberg, Doris and William A. Byrd (eds), "Afghanistan's Drug Industry: Structure, Functioning, Dynamics and Implications for Counter-Narcotics Policy," United Nations Office on Drugs and Crime, Nov. 2006.

Burke, Jason, *Al Qaeda: Casting a Shadow of Terror*, London: I.B. Tauris, 2003.

——— *The 9/11 Wars*, New York: Allen Lane, 2011.

——— *Al Qaeda: The True Story of Radical Islam*, London: I.B. Tauris, 2004.

Burr, J. Millard and Robert O. Collins, *Revolutionary Sudan*, Leiden: Brill, 2003.

Calvert, John, *Sayyid Qutb and the Origins of Radical Islamism*, New York: Columbia University Press, 2010.

Central Intelligence Agency, "Harakat ul-Ansar: Increasing Threat to Western and Pakistani Interests," DI TR 96–008, Aug. 1996; www.gwu.edu/~nsarchiv/NSAEBB/NSAEBB227/index.htm#10

Coll, Steve, *The Bin Ladens: An Arabian Family in the American Century*, New York: Penguin, 2008.

——— *Ghost Wars*, New York: Penguin Books, 2004.

Comras, Victor, "Al Qaeda Finances and Funding to Affiliated Groups," in Jeanne K. Giraldo and Harold A. Trinkhunas (eds), *Terrorism Financing and State Responses: A Comparative Perspective*, Stanford: Stanford University Press, 2007, pp. 115–32.

Cordesman, Anthony, "The Afghan–Pakistan War: The Rising Intensity of Conflict 2007–2008," Center for Strategic and International Studies, 12 Aug. 2009; http://csis.org/files/publication/burke/090803_RisingIntensityConflict20072008.pdf

Corman, Steve and Jill S. Schiefelbein, "Communication and Media Strategy in the Jihadi War of Ideas," Consortium for Strategic Communication, 20 Apr. 2006.

Crews, Robert D., "Moderate Taliban?" in Robert D. Crews and Amin Tarzi (eds), *The Taliban and the Crisis of Afghanistan*, Cambridge, MA: Harvard University Press, 2008, pp. 238–73.

Crile, George, *Charlie Wilson's War*, New York: Grove Press, 2003.

Cruickshank, Paul, "The Militant Pipeline: Between the Afghanistan-Pakistan Border Region and the West," Counterterrorism Strategy Initiative Policy Paper, Feb. 2010.

Cullison, Alan, "Inside Al-Qaeda's Hard Drive," *The Atlantic*, Sep. 2004, online at http://www.theatlantic.com/doc/200409/cullison

Davis, Anthony, "How the Taliban became a Military Force," in William Maley (ed.), *Fundamentalism Reborn? Afghanistan and the Taliban*, New York: NYU Press, 1998.

——— "Pakistan's war by proxy in Afghanistan loses its deniability," *Jane's Intelligence Review*, 1 Oct. 1999.

BIBLIOGRAPHY

Dorronsoro, Gilles, *Revolution Unending: Afghanistan, 1979 to the Present*, New York: Columbia University Press, 2005.

Dressler, Jeffrey, *The Haqqani Network: A Strategic Threat*, Institute for the Study of War, Afghanistan Report 9, Mar. 2012.

Dressler, Jeffrey and Reza Jan, "The Haqqani Network in Kurram: The Regional Implications of a Growing Insurgency," Institute for the Study of War, May 2011.

D'Souza, Shantie Mariet, "India's Aid to Afghanistan: Challenges and Prospects," *Strategic Analysis*, 31, 5 (Sep. 2007).

Dupee, Matt, "FOB Salerno Withstands 2-Day Taliban On-Slaught," *Long War Journal*, 18 Aug. 2008.

Dupree, Louis, *Afghanistan*, Princeton, NJ: Princeton University Press, 1973.

Dyk, Jere Van, *In Afghanistan: An American Odyssey*, New York: Coward-McCann, 1983.

Edwards, David B., *Before Taliban: Genealogies of the Afghan Jihad*, Berkeley, CA: University of California Press, 2002.

——— "The Evolution of Shi'i Political Dissent in Afghanistan," in Juan R.I. Cole and Nikkie R. Keddie (eds), *Shi'ism and Social Protest*, New Haven and London: Yale University Press, 1986.

——— *Heroes of the Age: Moral Fault Lines on the Afghan Frontier*, Berkeley, CA: University of California Press, 1996.

——— "Learning from the Swat Pathans: Political Leadership in Afghanistan, 1978–97," *American Ethnologist*, 25, 4 (1998), pp. 712–28.

Edwards, Lucy Morgan, *The Afghan Solution: The Inside Story of Abdul Haq, the CIA and how Western Hubris Lost Afghanistan*, London: Bactria Press, 2011.

Elias, Mohammad Osman Tariq, "The Resurgence of the Taliban in Kabul: Logar and Wardak," in Antonio Giustozzi (ed.), *Decoding the New Taliban: Insights from the Afghan Field*, New York: Columbia University Press, 2009.

Euben, Roxanne, *Enemy in the Mirror: Islamic Fundamentalism and the Limits of Modern Rationalism*, Princeton, NJ: Princeton University Press, 1999.

Fair, Christine, "Suicide Attacks in Afghanistan (2001–2007)," United Nations Assistance Mission to Afghanistan, 9 Sep. 2007.

Fair, Christine and Seth G. Jones, "Pakistan's War Within," *Survival*, 51, 6 (Dec. 2009–Jan. 2010), pp. 161–88.

Faizi, Inayatullah, "Afghan Political Literature in Peshawar," in Fazal-ur-Rahim Marwat and Sayed Wiqar Kakakhel (eds), *Afghanistan and the Frontier*, Peshawar: Emjay Books International, 1993.

Fandy, Mamoun, *Saudi Arabia and the Politics of Dissent*, New York: Palgrave, 2001.

Feifer, Gregory, *The Great Gamble: The Soviet War in Afghanistan*, New York: HarperCollins, 2009.

Fishman, Brian (ed.), *Bombers, Bank Accounts and Bleedout: al-Qa'ida's Road in and out of Iraq*, Combating Terrorism Center, July 2008.

Fletcher, Arnold, *Afghanistan: Highway of Conquest*, Westport, CT: Greenwood Press, 1982 (1965).

Franco, Claudio, "The Tehrik-e-Taliban Pakistan," in Antonio Giustozzi (ed.), *Decoding the New Taliban: Insights from the Afghan Field*, New York: Columbia University Press, 2009.

Fury, Dalton, *Kill bin Laden: A Delta Force Commander's Account of the Hunt for the World's Most Wanted Man*, New York: St. Martin's Press, 2008.

Gannon, Kathy, *I is for Infidel*, New York: Public Affairs, 2005.

Ghani, Ashraf, "Afghanistan: Islam and Counterrevolutionary Movements," in John Esposito (ed.), *Islam in Asia: Religion, Politics, Society*, New York and Oxford: Oxford University Press, 1987, pp. 79–96.

Giustozzi, Antonio (ed.), *Decoding the New Taliban: Insights from the Afghan Field*, New York: Columbia University Press, 2009.

——— *Koran, Kalashnikov, and Laptop: The Neo-Taliban Insurgency in Afghanistan*, New York: Columbia University Press, 2008.

——— "One or Many? The Issue of the Taliban's Unity and Disunity," Pakistan Security Research Unit, Brief Number 48, 23 Apr. 2009.

Giustozzi, Antonio and Christoph Reuter, *The Insurgents of the Afghan North*, Afghanistan Analysts Network, Apr. 2011, pp. 20–4.

Goldberg, Jeffrey, "Inside Jihad U.; the Education of a Holy Warrior," *New York Times Magazine*, 25 June 2000.

Gopal, Anand, "Coordinated Kabul assault shows Taliban strength," *Christian Science Monitor*, 12 Feb. 2009.

——— "The Most Deadly US Foe in Afghanistan," *Christian Science Monitor*, 1 June 2009; http://www.csmonitor.com/2009/0601/p10s01-wosc.html

Gopal, Anand, Mansur Khan Mahsud, and Brian Fishman, "The Battle for Pakistan: Militancy and Conflict in North Waziristan," *New America Foundation*, Apr. 2010; http://counterterrorism.newamerica.net/sites/newamerica.net/files/policydocs/northwaziristan.pdf

Grau, Lester W. and Ali Ahmad Jalali, "The Campaign for the Caves: the Battles for Zhawar in the Soviet-Afghan War," *Journal of Slavic Military Studies*, 14, 3 (2001); http://www.globalsecurity.org/military/library/report/2001/010900-zhawar.htm

Gregory, Shaun, "The ISI and the War on Terrorism," *Studies in Conflict and Terrorism*, 30, 12 (Oct. 2007), pp. 1013–31.

Griffin, Michael, *Reaping the Whirlwind: The Taliban Movement in Afghanistan*, rev. ed., London: Pluto Press, 2003.

Guest, Ken, "Afghanistan," in Anthony Rogers, Ken Guest, and Jim Hooper, *Flashpoint: At the Front Line of Today's Wars*, London: Arms and Armour, 1995.

Gul, Imtiaz, *The Most Dangerous Place: Pakistan's Lawless Frontier*, New York: Viking, 2010.

Gunaratna, Rohan, *Inside Al Qaeda*, New York: Berkley Books, 2002.

Gutman, Roy, *How We Missed the Story*, Washington, DC: United States Institute of Peace, 2008.

Hafez, Mohammed, "*Jihad* after Iraq: Lessons from the Arab Afghans," *Studies in Conflict and Terrorism*, 32 (2009), pp. 73–94.

Hamid, Mustafa, "Abu'l-Walid's Dialogue with Egyptian Researcher Leah Farral," http://allthingscounterterrorism.com/my-dialogue-with-abu-walid-al-masri/arabic-and-english-versions-of-abu-walids-answers-to-my-questions/english-trans-abu-walids-fifth-reponse/

Haqqani, Husain, *Pakistan: Between Mosque and Military*, Washington, DC: Carnegie Endowment for International Peace, 2005.

Harmony Project, *Al-Qai'da's (mis)Adventures in the Horn of Africa*, West Point, NY: United States Military Academy, 2006.

Haroon, Sana, *Frontier of Faith: Islam in the Indo-Afghan Borderland*, New York: Columbia University Press, 2007.

Hegghammer, Thomas, "The Ideological Hybridization of Jihadi Groups," *Current Trends in Islamist Ideology*, 9, 18 (Nov. 2009); www.currenttrends.org/research/detail/the-ideological-hybridization-of-jihadi-groups

——— *Jihad in Saudi Arabia*, Cambridge and New York: Cambridge University Press, 2010.

——— "The Rise of Muslim Foreign Fighters: Islam and the Globalization of Jihad," *International Security*, 35, 3 (2010–11), pp. 53–94.

Hensman, Howard, *The Afghan War of 1879–80*, London: H. Allen and Co., 1881.

Howard, Roger, "Wrath of Islam: HUA Analyzed," *Jane's Intelligence Review*, 1 Oct. 1997.

Hussain, Mujahid, *Punjabi Taliban: Driving Extremism in Pakistan*, New Delhi, India: Pentagon Security International, 2012.

Hussein, Rizwan, *Pakistan and the Emergence of Islamic Militancy in Afghanistan*, Aldershot, UK: Ashgate, 2005.

Hyman, Anthony, "Arab Involvement in the Afghan War," *Beirut Review*, 7 (1994), pp. 73–89.

International Crisis Group, "Jemaah Islamiyah in South East Asia: Damaged but Still Dangerous," 26 Aug. 2003.

International Crisis Group, "Taliban Propaganda: Winning the War of Words?" 24 July 2008.

Jalali, Ali Ahmad and Lester W. Grau, *Afghan Guerrilla Warfare*, St. Paul, MN: MBI Publishing, 2001 [1995].

Jamal, Arif, *Shadow War: The Untold Story of Jihad in Kashmir*, Brooklyn, NY: Melville House, 2009.

Johnson, Thomas H. and M. Chris Mason, "No Sign Until the Burst of Fire: Understanding the Afghanistan-Pakistan Frontier," *International Security*, 32, 4 (Spring 2008).

Jones, Seth, *In the Graveyard of Empires: America's War in Afghanistan*, New York: W.W. Norton & Co., 2010.

——— "Pakistan's Dangerous Game," *Survival*, 49, 1 (Spring 2007).

——— *Reintegrating Afghan Insurgents*, RAND, 2011.

Khan, Azmat Hayat, "Afghan Resistance and National Leadership," *Central Asia* (Peshawar), 9 (1981), pp. 163–77.

——— "Factional Organization of the Afghan Mujahideens in Peshawar," *Central Asia* (University of Peshawar), 14 (1984), pp. 51–73.

Khan, Mu'in-ud-Din Ahmad, "Sayyid Ahmad Shahid's Campaign Against the Sikhs," *Islamic Studies*, 7, 4 (1968), pp. 317–38.

Kohlmann, Evan, "Al-Qa'ida's Yemeni Expatriate Faction in Pakistan," *CTC Sentinel*, 4, 1 (Jan. 2011).

Kuovo, Sari, "Facts for reconciliation: Human rights documentation needed," *Afghanistan Analysts Network*, 10 Oct. 2010; http://aan-afghanistan.com/index.asp?id=1217

Kux, Dennis, *The United States and Pakistan, 1947–2000*, Washington, DC: Woodrow Wilson Center Press, 2001.

Lawrence, Bruce, *Messages to the World: The Statements of Osama bin Laden*, London: Verso, 2005.

Lewis, Bernard, "The Revolt of Islam," in Bernard Lewis, *The Middle East and the West*, New York: Harper & Row, 1966, pp. 95–114.

Lia, Brynjar, "Al-Qaeda Online: Understanding Jihadist Internet Infrastructure," *Jane's Intelligence Review*, 1 Jan. 2006.

——— *The Architect of Global Jihad: The Life of al-Qa'ida Strategist Abu Musab al-Suri*, New York: Columbia University Press, 2008.

——— "Jihadi Web Media Production: Characteristics, Trends, and Future Implications," paper presented at "Check the Web" Conference on "Monitoring, Research and Analysis of Jihadist Activities on the Internet—Ways to Deal With the Issue" in Berlin on 26 and 27 Feb. 2007.

Linschoten, Alex Strick van and Felix Kuehn, *Separating the Taliban from al-Qaeda: The Core of Success in Afghanistan*, Center on International Cooperation, Feb. 2011.

Livingston, Ian S. and Michael O'Hanlon, "Pakistan Index: Tracking Variables of Reconstruction and Security," Brookings Institution, 8 Dec. 2010.

Mahsud, Mansur Khan, "The Battle for Pakistan: Militancy and Conflict in South Waziristan," Counterterrorism Strategy Initiative, Apr. 2010.

Maley, William, "Interpreting the Taliban," in William Maley (ed.), *Fundamentalism Reborn? Afghanistan and the Taliban*, New York: NYU Press, 1998.

Malik, Jamal, *Colonialization of Islam: Dissolution of Traditional Institutions in Pakistan*, New Delhi: Manohar, 1996.

Matinuddin, Kamal, *The Taliban Phenomenon: Afghanistan 1994–1997*, Karachi: Oxford University Press, 1999.

Mayo, H. Elaine, "Toward Collective Praxis in Teacher Education: Complexity, Pragmatism and Practice," PhD thesis, University of Canterbury, 2003.

Metcalf, Barbara, *Islamic Revival in British India: Deoband, 1860–1900*, Oxford and New York: Oxford University Press, 2005.

Meyer, Josh, *The Hunt for KSM*, New York: Little, Brown and Company, 2012.

Miller, Flagg, "Insights from Bin Ladin's Audiocassette Library in Kandahar," *CTC Sentinel* (Oct. 2011).

Millward, James, *Violent Separatism in Xinjiang: A Critical Assessment*, Washington, DC: East–West Center, 2004.

Moghadam, Assaf and Brian Fishman (eds), *Fault Lines in Global Jihad*, New York: Routledge, 2011.

Moghaddam, Sippi Azarbaijani, "Northern Exposure for the Taliban," in Antonio Giustozzi (ed.), *Decoding the New Taliban: Insights from the Afghan Field*, New York: Columbia University Press, 2009.

Morgenstierne, G., "The Place of Pashto among the Iranic Languages and the Problem of the Constitution of Pashtun Linguistic and Ethnic Unity," *Pashto Quarterly*, 1, 4 (1978), pp. 43–55.

Napoleoni, Loretta, *Insurgent Iraq: Al Zarqawi and the New Generation*, New York: Seven Stories Press, 2005.

Nathan, Joanna, "Reading the Taliban," in Antonio Giustozzi (ed.), *Decoding the New Taliban: Insights from the Afghan Field*, New York: Columbia University Press, 2009.

Neighbour, Sally, *The Mother of Mohammed: An Australian Woman's Extraordinary Journey into Jihad*, Melbourne: Melbourne University Press, 2009.

Nojumi, Neamatollah, *The Rise of the Taliban in Afghanistan: Mass Mobilization, Civil War, and the Future of the Region*, New York: Palgrave, 2002.

Norell, Magnus (ed.), "Militancy in the Pakistani Federally Administered Tribal Areas (FATA) and Afghanistan," Swedish Research Defense Establishment, FOI-R-2727-SE, Feb. 2010.

Olesen, Asta, *Islam and Politics in Afghanistan*, Richmond, UK: Curzon Press, 1995.

Pak Institute for Peace Studies, "Pakistan Security Report 2009," Jan. 2010.

Peters, Gretchen, *Crime and Insurgency in the Tribal Areas of Afghanistan and Pakistan*, Combating Terrorism Center, 15 Oct. 2010.

——— *Haqqani Network Financing: The Evolution of an Industry*, Combating Terrorism Center, July 2012.

Pirzada, Sayyid A.S., *The Politics of the Jamiat Ulema-i-Islam Pakistan, 1971–77*, Oxford and New York: Oxford University Press, 2000.

Posner, Richard, *How Judges Think*, Cambridge, MA: Harvard University Press, 2008.

Raman, B., "An Analysis of United States Bombing of Terrorist Camps in Afghanistan," 4 Nov. 1998; http://www.subcontinent.com/research/sapra_documents/tr_1998_11_001_s.html

——— "ISI-Bin Ladin Links: As Seen by the DIA," South Asia Analysis Group, 791 (17 Sep. 2003); http://www.southasiaanalysis.org/papers8/paper791.html

Rana, Mohammad Amir, *Gateway to Terrorism*, London: New Millennium, 2003.

——— *Jihad and Jihadi*, Lahore: Mashal Books, 2003.

Rashid, Ahmed, *Descent into Chaos*, New York: Viking, 2008.

——— *Pakistan on the Brink: The Future of America, Pakistan and Afghanistan*, New York: Viking, 2012.

——— *Taliban*, New Haven and London: Yale Nota Bene, 2000.

——— *Taliban: Islam, Oil and the New Great Game in Central Asia*, London: I.B. Tauris, 2001.

Rassler, Don, "Al-Qa'ida's Pakistan Strategy," *CTC Sentinel*, June 2009.

Rastegar, Farshad, "Education and Revolutionary Political Mobilization: Schooling versus Uprootedness as Determinants of Islamic Political Activism among Afghan Refugee Students in Pakistan," PhD thesis: University of California, Los Angeles, 1991.

Reed, J. Todd and Diana Raschke, *The ETIM: China's Islamic Militants and the Global Terrorist Threat*, Santa Barbara, CA: Praeger, 2010.

Reuter, Christoph and Borhan Younus, "The Return of the Taliban in Andar District: Ghazni," in Antonio Giustozzi (ed.), *Decoding the New Taliban: Insights from the Afghan Field*, New York: Columbia University Press, 2009, pp. 101–18.

Reynolds, Michael, "Myth and Mysticism: A Longitudinal Perspective on Islam and Conflict in the North Caucasus," *Middle Eastern Studies*, 41, 1 (2005), pp. 31–54.

Reza Nasr, Seyyed Vali, *The Vanguard of the Islamic Revolution: The Jama'at-i Islami of Pakistan*, Berkeley and Los Angeles: University of California Press, 1994.

Riedel, Bruce, "Pakistan and Terror: Eye of the Storm," *AAPSS*, 618, July 2008.

Robson, Brian, *Crisis on the Frontier: The Third Afghan War and the Campaign in Waziristan 1919–1920*, Staplehurst, UK: Spellmount, 2004.

Roe, Andrew M., *Waging War in Waziristan: the British Struggle in the Land of Bin Laden, 1849–1947*, Kansas: University Press of Kansas, 2010.

Rogan, Hanna, "Abu Reuter and the E-Jihad: Virtual Battlefronts from Iraq to the Horn of Africa," *Georgetown Journal of International Affairs* (Summer/Fall 2007).

——— "Al-Qaeda's online media strategies: From Abu Reuter to Irhabi 007," Norwegian Research Defense Establishment, 2007.

Roggio, Bill, "Pakistani Taliban, Iraqi al Qaeda operatives killed in Afghanistan," *Long War Journal*, 11 May 2008.

——— "Senior al-Qaeda Commander in Afghanistan Killed in US Airstrike," *Long War Journal*, 31 July 2008.

——— "Senior al Qaeda and Taliban Leaders Met with Baitullah," *Long War Journal*, 21 June 2009; www.longwarjournal.org/archives/2009/06/senior_al_qaeda_and.php

Rohde, David and Kristen Mulvihill, *A Rope and a Prayer: A Kidnapping from Two Sides*, New York: Viking, 2010.

Roy, Olivier, *Islam and Resistance in Afghanistan*, 2nd ed., Cambridge and New York: Cambridge University Press, 1990.

Rubin, Barnett R., *The Fragmentation of Afghanistan*, 2nd ed., New Haven and London: Yale University Press, 2002.

Ruttig, Thomas, "The Haqqani Network as an Autonomous Entity," in Antonio Giustozzi (ed.), *Decoding the New Taliban: Insights from the Afghan Field*, New York: Columbia University Press, 2009, pp. 57–88.

——— *Islamists, Leftists—and a Void in the Center: Afghanistan's Political Parties and where they came from (1902–2006)*, n.p.: Konrad Adenauer Stiftung, 2006.

——— "Loya Paktia's Insurgency," in Antonio Giustozzi (ed.), *Decoding the New Taliban: Insights from the Afghan Field*, New York: Columbia University Press, 2009, pp. 78–83.

——— "The Other Side: Dimensions of the Afghan Insurgency: Causes, Actors and Approaches to 'Talks'," Afghanistan Analysts Network, July 2009.

——— "Splitting the Haqqanis with NATO Reconciliation Air," Afghanistan Analysts Network, 1 Nov. 2010.

——— "Talking Haqqani," Afghanistan Analysts Network, 1 July 2010; http://aan-afghanistan.com/index.asp?id=873

Sanger, David E., *The Inheritance: The World Obama Confronts and the Challenges to American Power*, New York: Harmony Books, 2009.

Schaffer, Anthony, *Operation Dark Heart*, New York: Thomas Dunne Books, 2010.

BIBLIOGRAPHY

Scheuer, Michael, *Through Our Enemies Eyes*, rev. ed., Dulles, VA: Potomac Books, 2007.

Scott, James C., *The Art of Not Being Governed: An Anarchist History of Upland Southeast Asia*, New Haven and London: Yale University Press, 2009.

——— *Seeing Like a State*, New Haven, CT: Yale University Press, 1998.

Shephard, Michelle, *Guantanamo's Child: The Untold Story of Omar Khadr*, Mississauga, Ontario: Wiley, 2008.

Siddique, Abubakar, "Pakistani Chief's Death would have Broad Implications," *Radio Free Europe*, 7 Aug. 2009.

Skoldager, Morten, *Truslen indefra: De danske terrorister*, Lindhardt og Ringhof, Denmark, 2009.

Smucker, Philip G., *Al-Qaeda's Great Escape: The Military and the Media on Terror's Trail*, Dulles, VA: Brassey's, 2004.

Soufan, Ali H., *The Black Banners: The Inside Story of 9/11 and the War Against al-Qaeda*, New York: Norton, 2011.

Stack, Liam, "Bagram Attack Kills U.S. Contractor, Wounds Nine NATO Soldiers," *Christian Science Monitor*, 19 May 2010.

Steinberg, Guido, "Al-Qaida and Jihadist Terrorism post 2001," in Mark Pieth, Daniel Thelesklaf, and Radha Ivory (eds), *Countering Terrorist Financing: The Practitioner's Point of View*, Basel: Basel Institute on Governance, 2009.

——— "Trial and Error: How a Failed Plot Revealed a Movement," *Jane's Intelligence Review*, 16 Apr. 2010.

——— "A Turkish al-Qaeda: The Islamic Jihad Union and the Internationalization of Uzbek Jihadism," *Strategic Insights*, July 2008.

——— "Renewing Leadership: The Role of Egyptians and Libyans in al-Qaeda's Senior Leadership," Janes IHS Defense, Jan. 2012; www.swp-berlin.org/fileadmin/contents/products/fachpublikationen/sbgrenewingleadership_02.pdf

——— "The Return of al-Qaida," SWP Comments, 22 (Dec. 2007).

Stenersen, Anne, "Al Qaeda's Allies: Explaining the Relationship between al Qaeda and Various Factions of the Taliban after 2001," Counterterrorism Strategy Initiative Paper, 19 Apr. 2010.

Sude, Barbara, "Al Qaeda Central: An Assessment of the Threat Posed by the Terrorist Group Headquartered on the Afghanistan-Pakistan Border," Counterterrorism Strategy Initiative Paper, Feb. 2010.

Sulaiman, Sadia and Syed Adnan Ali Shah Bukhari, "Hafiz Gul Bahadur: a Profile of the Leader of the North Waziristan Taliban," *Terrorism Monitor*, 2, 9 (Apr. 2009), pp. 4–6.

Swami, Praveen, *India, Pakistan and the Secret Jihad: the Covert War in Kashmir (1947–2004)*, London: Routledge, 2007.

Tankel, Stephen, *Laskhar-e-Taiba: Storming the World Stage*, London and New York: Hurst/Columbia University Press, 2011.

Tomsen, Peter, *The Wars of Afghanistan*, New York: Public Affairs, 2011.

Trives, Sébastien, "Roots of the Insurgency in the Southeast," in Antonio Giustozzi (ed.), *Decoding the New Taliban: Insights from the Afghan Field*, New York: Columbia University Press, 2009, pp. 89–100.

United Nations, "UN Mapping Report on Afghanistan," Kabul, 2005.

Waldman, Matt, "The Sun in the Sky: The Relationship between Pakistan's ISI and Afghan Insurgents," Crisis States Discussion Papers, June 2010.

Warren, Alan, *Waziristan, the Faqir of Ipi, and the Indian Army: The Northwest Frontier Revolt of 1936–1937*, London: Oxford University Press, 2000.

Warrick, Joby, *The Triple Agent: The al-Qaeda Mole who Infiltrated the CIA*, New York: Doubleday, 2011.

White, Joshua, *Pakistan's Islamist Frontier: Islamic Politics and U.S. Policy in Pakistan's North-West Frontier*, Arlington, VA: Center on Faith & International Affairs, 2008.

Wigen, Einar, "Islamic Jihad Union: al-Qa'ida's Key to the Turkic World," Norwegian Defense Research Establishment, 23 Feb. 2009.

Wright, Lawrence, *The Looming Tower*, New York: Alfred A. Knopf, 2006.

Yousaf, Mohammad and Mark Adkin, *The Bear Trap: Afghanistan's Untold Story*, London: Leo Cooper, 1992.

Zaeef, Abdul Salam, *My Life with the Taliban*, New York: Columbia University Press, 2010.

Zaman, Muhammad Qasim, *The Ulama in Contemporary Islam: Custodians of Change*, Princeton, NJ: Princeton University Press, 2002

Zaydan, Ahmad, *The "Afghan Arabs" Media at Jihad*, Islamabad: PFI, 1999.

BIBLIOGRAPHY

Non-European Language Sources

Afghan Information Centre Monthly Bulletin, "Resistance Commanders on the Situation Inside Afghanistan: Interview with Maulawi Haqani Commander of the Zadran Front," 82 (Jan. 1988).

Afghan, Rafiq, "Gardez, Gardez," *Ummat* (Urdu), 10 Mar. 2002.

Anas, 'Abdullah, *Wiladat al-Afghan al-'Arab*, London: Dar al-Saqi, 2002.

Ansar al-Mujahidin Network, "Open Interview with Sirajuddin Haqqani, a member of the Shura Council of the Islamic Emirate of Afghanistan and a commander in the southeastern provinces of Afghanistan," 27 Apr. 2010.

'Azzam, 'Abdullah, *Ayat al-Rahman fi Jihad al-Afghanistan*, Iskandaria: Dar al-Da'wa, 1985 (1984).

——— *al-Tarbiyya al-Jihadiyya*, Peshawar: Shahid 'Azzam Media Center, 1992.

Badi, Mustafa (Abu Ibrahim al-Logari), *Afghanistan: Ihtilal al-dhakira*, Sana'a: 2003; http://tokhaleej.jeeran.com/archive/2008/6/597637.html

Al-Balagh Media Center, "Interview with Sirajuddin Haqqani," 13 Apr. 2010.

Diraz, 'Isam, *al-'A'idun min Afghanistan*, Cairo: al-Dar al-Misriyya li'l-Nashr wa'l-I'lam, 1993.

——— *Malhamat al-Mujahidin al-'Arab fi Afghanistan*, Cairo, 1989.

——— *al-Qissat al-Damiyyah li'l-Ghazw al-Sufiyiti li-Afghanistan*, Cairo: Dar al-'Itisam, 1988.

——— *Usama bin Ladin yarwi ma'arik Ma'sada al-Ansar al-'Arab bi-Afghanistan*, Cairo: al-Manar al-Jadid, 1991.

Faraj, Ayman Sabri (Abu Ja'far al-Qandahari), *Dhikriyyat 'Arab Afghan Abu Ja'far al-Masri al-Qandahari*, Cairo: Dar al-Shuruq, 2002.

Al-Hami, Abu Qudama Salih, *Fursan al-farida al-ghayba* (posted to jihadi internet forums, 2007).

Hamid, Mustafa (Abu'l-Walid al-Masri), *Jihad ma bayn nahrayn: Mashru' Tajikistan*, n.p., 2007.

——— *Ma'arik al-bawwaba al-sakhriyya*, al-Faruq Camp, Paktia: 1995.

——— "Jalaluddin Haqqani: Astura fi tarikh jihad Afghanistan (1)," *al-Sumud*, 45 (Feb.–Mar. 2010), pp. 34–9.

——— *Qissat al-bay'at al-'arabiya li-amir al-mu'minin Mullah Muhammad 'Umar*, no date, posted to various jihadi internet forums on 19 and 20 July 2007.

——— *Tharthara fawq saqf al-'alam* (distributed online, 2007–9); vol. 4 (on the battle of Jalalabad), vol. 8 (on Khost), and vol. 9 (on Gardez).

Haqqani, Jalaluddin, *Is the Afghanistan War a Russian-American War?* (Pashto), 2nd ed., n.p.: Manba' al-Jihad, 1988–9.

Al-Ittihad (Arabic), "Abu-Dhabi Paper Interviews Rebel Leader," 11 June 1980.

Al-Jazeera (Arabic), "Today's Encounter," 31 May 2006.

Al-Jihad, 1, 5 (Apr. 1985).

——— 1, 10 (Aug. 1985).

——— "Hiwar maftuh ma' Jalaluddin Haqqani," 2, 13 (Nov. 1985), pp. 18–22.

——— 2, 18 (May 1986).

——— 2, 21 (Aug. 1986).

——— 3, 28 (Mar. 1987).

——— 3, 29 (Apr. 1987).

——— 3, 31 (June 1987).

——— 3, 32 (July 1987).

——— 44 (July 1988).

——— 5, 56 (June 1989).

——— 54 (June 1989).

——— 57–8 (July and Aug. 1989).

——— 63 (Jan. 1990).

——— 7, 83 (Aug.–Sep. 1991).

——— 8, 85 (Feb. 1992).

Khan, Mawlawi Aziz, "The First Jihadi Operation in Afghanistan, and the Rise of the Ulema Against the Communists," *Manba al-Jihad* (Pashto), 1, 4–5 (Oct.–Nov. 1989).

Mahmud, Husayn bin, "Li-madha yurid al-Amrikan ightiyal Asad Khurasan?" [Why do the Americans want to assassinate the Lion of Khurasan (Jalaluddin Haqqani)?]; (posted to the Fajr forum, 2002); naseh.net/vb/showthread.php?t=9246

Manba' al-Jihad (Pashto), "The Manba al-Uloom Madrasa as a Major Educational Center," 1, 1 (July 1989).

——— (Pashto), "Martyrs of the Path of the Truth," 1, 2–3 (Aug.–Sep. 1989).

——— (Pashto), "Interview with Commander Mawlawi Hanif Shah," 1, 4–5 (Oct.–Nov. 1989).

BIBLIOGRAPHY

——— (Arabic), "Manba al Uloom is a Resource to the Jihad: A Beacon of Knowledge that Graduates Jihadist Ulema," 1, 1 (Feb. 1990).
——— (Pashto), "Interview with Mawlana Jalaluddin Haqqani," 1, 10 (Apr. 1990).
——— (Pashto), "Good News for the Prospective Taliban of the Course of Hadith-e Sharif!" 1, 11 (May 1990).
——— (Pashto), "Interview with Mawlawi Aziz Khan, Head of the Manba-al Uloom Madrassa in Miranshah," 2, 1 (July 1990).
——— (Pashto), "Martyrs in the Path of Truth," obituary of Muhammad Isma'il Zabihullah Haqqani, 2, 2 (Aug. 1990).
——— (Pashto), "Report on the Funeral of Jalaluddin Haqqani's Brother, Shahid Muhammad Isma'il in Miranshah," 2, 2 (Aug. 1990).
——— (Pashto), "Alhaj Jalaluddin Haqqani in an Interview with the *Al-Nasiha* Magazine," 2, 5 (Nov. 1990).
——— (Arabic), "Necrology for Muhammad Isma'il," 4 (Nov. 1990).
——— (Arabic), "To Our Muslim Girls," 1, 5 (Dec. 1990).
——— (Pashto), "The Iron Man: Mawlana Jalaluddin Haqqani," 2, 6 (Dec. 1990).
——— (Pashto), 2, 8 (Jan. 1991).
——— (Arabic), "Interview with Jalaluddin Haqqani During the Siege of Khost," 7–8 (Feb.–Apr. 1991).
——— (Pashto), "A Short Report on the Great Victory on Khost, and the Joint Operations Surrounding It," 2, 10 (Apr. 1991).
——— (Pashto), "Alhaj Mawlawi Jalaluddin Haqqani in a General Gathering of the Jamiat-e-Ulama-e-Islam in Lahore," 2, 11 (May 1991).
——— (Pashto), "Text of Alhaj Haqqani's Interview with the Arab Magazine *Al Marabtoon*," 2, 12 (June 1991).
——— (Arabic), "Martyrs of the Conquest of Khost (Arab Martyrs)," 10 (June 1991).
——— (Arabic), "Important Statement from the Eritrean Islamic Jihad Movement in regards to the recent developments in the Ethiopian and Eritrean arenas," 11 (July 1991).
——— (Pashto), "Interview with al-Haj Nizamuddin Haqqani, Deputy Commander of the Southern Fronts," 3, 1 (July 1991).
——— (Pashto), "Mawlana Abdul Haq, an unforgettable face in the Islamic World," 3, 4 (Sep. 1991).
——— (Pashto), "The Historic Battle of Paktia," 3, 5 (Oct.–Nov. 1991).
——— (Pashto), "The Islamic Revolution's Unforgettable Shaheed, Mutiullah Muti," 3, 7–8 (Jan.–Feb. 1992).
——— (Arabic), "Interview with Shaykh Haqqani," 18 (1992).
——— (Arabic), "Interviews with the Field Commanders," 16–17 (Feb.–Mar. 1992).
——— (Pashto), "Al-Haj Jalaluddin Haqqani Visits Islamic Madaris and Societies in Karachi," 3, 9–10 (May 1992).
——— (Pashto), "Mawlawi Jalaluddin Haqqani in an Interview with Manba-al Jihad," 4, 1 (Sep. 1992).
——— (Pashto), "On the Reconciliation between the Ahmadzai Tribe and the Nangarhar Shura," 4, 1–2 (Nov. 1993).
——— (Pashto), "Mawlawi Jalaluddin Haqqani on the Occasion of the Establishment of a Joint Governance Body in Khost," 5, 1–2 (Nov. 1993).
Mansur, 'Abdullah, "Liqa ma'a Amir al-Hizb al-Islami al-Turkistani al-Akh al-Mujahid 'Abd al-Haqq," *Turkistan al-Islamiyya*, 2 (Oct. 2008), pp. 5–8; 3 (Feb. 2009), pp. 9–12; and 4 (June 2009), pp. 8–12.
——— "al-Shahid al-Shaykh Bilal al-Turkistani," *Turkistan al-Islamiyya*, 4 (June 2009), pp. 19–22.
——— "Sira Abi Muhammad rahimuhu Allah," *Turkistan al-Islamiyya*, 1 (July 2008).
Mozhdeh, Wahid, *Afghanistan va panj sal-i sultah-i Taliban*, Tehran, 2003.
Muhammad, Basil, *al-Ansar al-'Arab fi Afghanistan*, Riyadh: Lajnat al-Birr al-Islamiyya, 1991.
Muhammad, Haji Din, *De Khalis Zhwand, Fan aw And*, Peshawar: Pir Chap Khuna, 2007.
Munir, Muhammad Ayyub, "Think about your Burmese Muslim Brothers," *Nusrat al-Jihad*, 2, 3–4 (Jan.–Feb. 1992).
Nangyal, Shuhrat, "Afghanistan' Jihad and the Virtuous Victory," *Manba' al-Jihad* (Pashto), 2, 8 (Jan. 1991).
——— *Zhawara at the Dawn of History* (Pashto), n.p.: Public Relations Department of al-Haj Jalaluddin Haqqani's Fronts, 1991.
Nusrat al-Jihad (Urdu), "Highlights of Mawlawi Jalaluddin Haqqani's and Mawlawi 'Abdullah

Zakeri's Speeches to a Joint Conference of Afghan Scholars and the Council of Commanders," 3 (Jan. 1991).
——— (Urdu), "Shaheed Lal Numa," 1, 3 (Jan. 1991).
——— 3, 4 (Feb. 1991).
——— (Urdu), "The New World Order," 5 (Mar. 1991).
——— "Arakan: The Islamic Movement of Burma," 1, 5 (Mar. 1991).
——— (Urdu), "Inside Afghanistan—The Strongest Jihadi Center in Zhwar is Named After Hazrat-e Omar," 1, 9 (July 1991).
——— (Urdu), "Interview with Commander Haji Mohammad Ibrahim," 1, 9 (July 1991).
——— (Urdu), 1–2 (Nov.–Dec. 1991).
Al-Riya'i, Fahd, "Interview with Saudi Tribal chief Shaykh Ja'far al-Qahtani, father of Terror Suspect 'Abu Nasir' al-Qahtani," *Ukaz* (Arabic), no date.
Sabil, Abir [pseudonym], "Lasna 'ala ruq'a al-shatranj wa lasna ahjar," [We are not Pieces on a Chessboard] (message to Abu'l-Walid dated 12 Jan. 2011), posted on 23 Feb. to http://www.mafa.asia/ar/temp.php?K_Mafa=1061&id1=6&detail=511&cnl=1
Shumukh Al-Islam Network, "Lessons from the Life of Abu-al-Layth," https://shamikh1.net/vb/showthread.php?t=16023
Suri, Abu Mus'ab, *Da'wa al-muqawwama al-islamiyya al-'alamiyya*, n.p., n.d.
Tawil, Camille, *al-Qa'ida wa akhawatuha: qissa al-jihadiyin al-'arab*, London: Saqi, 2007.
'Umar al-Hadushi, Abu'l-Fadl, "Nubdha mukhtasara 'an hayat mujaddid al-jihad al-shaykh al-imam 'Abdallah 'Azzam," posted to the al-Tahadi webforum; http://www.archive.org/details/alt7dii
Ummat (Urdu), "Gardez, Gardez," 10 Mar. 2002.
——— (Urdu), "Taliban Ready to Attack Indian Embassy," 12 July 2003.
Al-Yazid, Mustafa Abu, "Speech to the People of Pakistan," al-Sahab, 26 Mar. 2009.
Zakori, Wazir Jaffer, "Jalaluddin Haqqani's brother, Ibrahim Haqqani arrested," *Pakistan* (Urdu), 19 May 2003.
Al-Zawahiri, Ayman, *Exoneration*, no date.
Zaydan, Ahmad, *Usama Bin Ladin bi-la Qina'*, Beirut: al-Sharaka al-'Alami li'l-Kitab, 2003.

Harmony Documents

AFGP-2002-000079
AFGP-2002-000103
AFGP-2002-002869
AFGP-2002-008576
AFGP-2002-008578
AFGP-2002-008582
AFGP-2002-008583
AFGP-2002-008587
AFGP-2002-008588
AFGP-2002-008612
AFGP-2002-008624
AFGP-2002-008629
AFGP-2002-008575-47-48
AFGP-2002-008681
AFGP-2002-008681-24
AFGP-2002-60053
AFGP-2002-600029
AFGP-2002-600053
AFGP-2002-600087
AFGP-2002-600088
AFGP-2002-600090
AFGP-2002-600092
AFGP-2002-600093
AFGP-2002-600096
AFGP-2002-600099
AFGP-2002-600106
AFGP-2002-600321
AFGP-2002-602383
AFGP-2002-800581

BIBLIOGRAPHY

AFGP-2002-800775
AFGP-2002-800928
AFGP-2004-0011048
AFGP-2004-011048
AFGP-2005-0003302
SOCOM-2012-0000004
SOCOM-2012-0000007
SOCOM-2012-0000010
SOCOM-2012-0000015
SOCOM-2012-0000019

INDEX

Abdallah, Hafez: first indigenous Afghan suicide bomber, 216
al-'Adl, Sayf: 98, 241
Afghan Civil War (1989–92): 83; Battle of Jalalabad (1989), 81–2; Battle of Khost (1990–1), 81–2; Battle of Gardez (1991), 81–2
Afghan Interim Government (AIG): 89; creation of, 85; members of, 88
Afghan Services Bureau (MAK): 72–4, 236; *al-Jihad*, 77; establishment in Peshawar (1984), 65; founding of (1979), 64; members of, 61, 77; training camps of, 80
Afghanistan: 10–11, 15, 21, 23, 33, 71, 76–7, 82, 157, 181, 187–8, 199, 219, 225, 236; Baluchistan, 110, 120, 157, 164; borders of, 5, 69, 74, 81, 125, 131, 140, 148, 160, 225; Durand Line, 4, 22, 32, 35, 51, 122, 129 30, 138, 154, 222, 239; Ghazni Province, 137, 188; government of, 5, 9–10, 33, 48, 123–4, 152, 171, 240; Herat, 50, 137, 145; Indian embassy bombing (2008), 2, 9, 150, 157, 173; Jalalabad, 5, 87, 105–6; Kabul, 1, 5, 9, 27, 30–2, 36–42, 48–9, 55, 57, 63, 71, 82, 84, 89, 101, 103, 105, 107, 112, 119, 123–4, 134, 136–9, 145, 150, 154–6, 159, 173, 183, 188, 216, 232, 235; Kandahar, 24, 35, 73, 101, 108, 110, 162; Khost Province, 2, 5, 9, 13, 51, 65–7, 76, 80, 85–6, 89, 91, 97, 100, 103, 105, 111, 113–15, 117, 124, 126, 139–41, 176, 179, 183, 188, 190–1, 201–2, 204, 218; Kunar Province, 22, 85, 231; Logar Province, 40, 137–8, 188; Loya Paktia, 5, 9, 13, 22, 34, 66, 81, 108, 121, 129–31, 133–4, 136, 138, 140, 143–4, 148, 153–4, 173, 175, 186, 188–9, 192, 197, 200–1, 223, 225, 229, 231, 243; military of, 34–5, 52, 67, 72, 152; Nangarhar Province, 105–6, 137; NATO/ISAF presence in, 16–17, 135, 137, 156–8, 240; Nuristan Province, 188; Operation Enduring Freedom (2001–), 71, 124, 136, 139, 158, 178, 240;

Paktia Province, 28, 42, 67–8, 75, 86–7, 91, 117, 124, 137, 140, 164, 188, 193; Paktika, 22, 27; Soviet Invasion of (1979–89), 4–7, 13, 17, 21, 31, 40, 53, 56, 59–61, 63–4, 67–8, 70–1, 76, 78, 83, 90, 96, 139, 153–4, 171–2, 176–7, 192, 196, 239; Takhar Province, 118; Taloqan Province, 96; Tora Bora, 107, 208; Wardak Province, 137–8, 188; Zabul Province, 188
Ahmadzai: 87
Ahmed, Mahmud: Director General of ISI, 123
Ahmed, Mansoor: associates of, 232; death of (2010), 232
Ahmed, Qazi Hussein: amir of JI, 103
Akhtar, Saifullah: 111
Akhund, Mullah Obaidullah: member of Quetta Shura Taliban, 160
Akorwi, Abdul Haq: family of, 39; founder of Dar al-'Ulum Haqqaniyya, 38
Allah, Attiya: 231
Algeria: 28
Ali, Muhammad Ilias Subhan (Abu Ali): 230–1
Amil, Qari: 140
Ammanullah, King: 56
Anas, 'Abdullah: memoirs of, 66
AQI, *see* al-Qa'ida in Iraq
Arnaout, Enaam: (Abu Mahmud al-Suri): 92; chief executive of BIF, 213; co founder of al-Qa'ida, 90
Atatürk, Mustafa Kemal: 29
Aziz, Khalid: former chief secretary of NWFP, 164
Azizuddin, Tariq: former Pakistani Ambassador to Afghanistan, 159; kidnapping of, 159–60
'Azzam, 'Abdullah: 8, 73, 75, 236; fatwa issued by (1984), 62–3; leader of MAK, 61, 64, 77; *The Defense of Muslim Territories* (1983), 62; *The Signs of the Merciful in the Jihad in Afghanistan* (1983), 62

Baba, Qari: 102
Bahadur, Hafiz Gul: 143–4, 146, 225, 229; family of, 31; media appearances of, 203; member of SIM, 160; TTP commander in North Waziristan, 140, 148
al-Bahri, Nasir: 114; bodyguard to Osama Bin Laden, 79, 98, 116
Bakr, Abu: associates of, 232; death of (2010), 232
al-Balawi, Humam Khalil Abu-Mulal (Abu Dujanah al-Khorasani): alleged connection to Haqqani network, 205; influence of, 204
Baluch: insurgency movements, 21; nationalism, 43
Bangladesh: 32, 70, 94; Liberation War (1971), 21, 42
al-Banshiri, Abu 'Ubayda (Ali Amin al-Rashidi): 72, 75, 90, 207–8; first military leader of al-Qa'ida, 66
Basayev, Shamil: 97
Basra, Riaz: 111
al-Bayid, Muhammad(Abu al-Mubtassim): pardoned by Mullah Muhammad Omar, 212

Beg, Mirza Aslam: Pakistani chief of army staff, 94
Belgium: 231
Benevolence International Foundation (BIF): funding of Hezb-e-Islami, 213; personnel of, 213
Benotman, Noman: former leader of Libyan Islamic Fighting Group, 82
Bhutto, Benazir: electoral victory of (1993), 102; murder of, 159
Bhutto, Zulfikar Ali: administration of, 43; President of Pakistan, 42, 44; trial and execution of (1979), 53; visit to USA (1973), 44
Bin Laden, Osama: 7–8, 64, 68, 73, 75, 79, 87–90, 94, 98, 118, 192, 195, 211, 237, 241; as Abu 'Abdullah, 77, 208; assassination of (2011), 228; CNN interview (1997), 107, 113–14; 'Expel the Polytheists from the Arabian Peninsula' (1996), 106; family of, 241; fatwa issued by (1998), 196–7; founding of Advice and Reform Committee (1990), 89; leader of World Islamic Front for Jihad Against Jews and Christians, 70, 114, 197; move to Afghanistan (1996), 105–6; relationship with Taliban, 107–8, 114, 116, 118; supporters of, 60, 237–8
Bosnia and Herzegovina: Sarajevo, 90
Brezhnev, Leonid: General Secretary of Central Committee of CPSU, 50
Buddhism: 26
Bush, George W.: administration of, 158

CARE International: schools built by, 108
Carter, Jimmy: foreign policy of, 64
Chechnya: 95, 97
Cheney, Dick: US Vice President, 157–8
China: 83, 94, 111; financial aid provided for anti-Soviet jihad by, 59; Muslim population of, 3, 112; Xinjiang, 112
Çiftçi, Çüneyt: 215; suicide bombing conducted by (2008), 193–4
Clinton, Bill: foreign policy of, 110
Cold War: 21, 59
Commonwealth of Independent States (CIS): 95
Cuba: Guantanamo Bay, 183

Dadullah, Mullah: 203, 216; death of (2007), 137
Daoud Khan, Muhammad: 35, 46, 49, 51, 55, 129; Afghan Defense Minister, 33; Afghan Prime Minister, 33; anti-*purdah* measures, 35; coup d'état led by (1973), 36, 43; reform policies of, 34
Dar al-'Ulum Haqqaniyya: 39, 49, 132–3, 178; founding of (1947), 38; graduation ceremonies of, 132; students of, 38, 40, 42, 55, 63; ties to Haqqani network, 131
Dawar: 146
Denmark: 201, 230

Egypt: 7; Cairo, 37; military of, 65, 76

Egyptian al-Jama'a al-Islamiyya (EIG): 82; factions of, 90; members of, 90; *al-Murabitun*, 93
Engels, Friedrich: writings of, 40

Falluja Islamic Network: 205
al-Faruq, Omar: imprisonment of, 183
Fatemi, Tariq: former Pakistani Ambassador to USA, 161
Fazul, 'Abdullah Muhammad: death of (2011), 80, 98; leader of al-Qa'ida operations in East Africa, 80, 97
First Gulf War (1990–1): belligerents of, 12; Invasion of Kuwait (1990), 88; political impact of, 87–8
Foreign Broadcast Information Service (FBIS): 15
France: 232
Free Pashtunistan movement: members of, 32

Gahez: 39
Gahez, Minhajuddin: founder of *Gahez*, 39
Gandhi, Mohandas: 30
Garang, John: military forces led by, 90
Gelowicz,Fritz: 229
Germany: 28, 192, 232; Ramstein airbase attack plot (2007), 229–30
Giustozzi, Antonio: 15
Gopal, Anand: 15–16
Gorbachev, Mikhail: speeches of, 71
Gul, Hamid: former chief of ISI, 153
Haq, Abdul: 85, 123; member of HIK, 101
Haq, Mawlana Sami-ul: 133; family of, 38–9; head of JUI-S, 38
Haqqani, Badruddin: 170; death of (2012), 138
Haqqani, Fathullah: 39, 63; fighting units led by, 137
Haqqani, Ibrahim Khan: family of, 29, 96, 123, 143; participation in Qatar meeting (2011), 124
Haqqani, Jalaluddin: 7, 30, 39, 45–6, 48–9, 52, 55, 61, 67–8, 70–1, 78, 81, 87, 91, 93, 102–4, 111–12, 114, 118, 129, 139, 153, 155, 172, 177, 180, 185–6, 194, 196, 207–8, 211–12, 214–15, 235, 238; background of, 28, 31, 38, 42; capture of Khost garrison (1991), 142, 221; declaration of jihad (1973), 31, 33, 46, 129; family of, 14, 28–9, 31, 96, 117, 123, 139, 143, 147, 168, 170, 201, 204, 214; founder of Haqqani network, 28; ideology of, 91; Islamabad meetings (2001), 122–3; leader of NCS, 85–6; visit to Saudi Arabia, 211
Haqqani, Khalil: 168; family of, 29, 143, 147, 214
Haqqani, Mawlawi Nizamuddin: 39, 72, 153, 172
Haqqani, Muhammad: death of (2011), 168; family of, 168
Haqqani, Nasiruddin: 168; associates of, 229; family of, 190
Haqqani, Omar: death of (2008), 192, 201
Haqqani, Sirajuddin: 124–5, 141–2,

144, 147, 160–1, 167, 171, 189, 191, 197–8, 203, 205–6, 209–10, 221; family of, 14, 117, 168, 186, 190, 201; leader of Miranshah Shura, 173; military leader of Haqqani network, 13; role in creation of SIM (2009), 160; support for TTP, 224; training of suicide bombers, 146

Haqqani network: 1–3, 8–9, 15, 17–18, 22–3, 27, 30, 38, 41, 45, 48, 51–2, 56–60, 101, 105, 121, 124, 127, 129, 132, 134, 142–3, 148, 153, 155, 157, 162, 171, 174, 179, 181, 184, 194–5, 198–9, 202–3, 210, 215–18, 223, 227, 232, 235, 237, 243; alleged connection to Humam Khalil Abu-Mulal al-Balawi, 205; alliance with al-Qa'ida, 11–12, 75, 113, 115, 121–2, 126, 178–9, 182, 185, 195, 204–5, 211–12, 214, 218, 222, 226, 228–9, 233, 237–8; assault on FOB Salerno (2008), 232; clients of, 6–7, 9, 15; designated as Foreign Terrorist Organization (2012), 124; former US direct support for, 4–6, 104; funding of, 5, 214; ideology of, 12–13, 100–1, 138, 184, 236; madrassas network of, 131, 168, 209; *Manba' al-Jihad*, 3, 14, 45–6, 65, 81, 85, 90, 92, 94, 100, 131, 135, 177–8, 196–7, 199, 202, 212, 221; members of, 13, 24, 53, 78, 95, 113, 121, 126, 130, 139–40, 142, 147, 160, 167, 172, 174, 185, 190, 216, 222, 225–6, 228–9; *Nusrat al-Jihad*, 14, 92, 139, 221; relationship with IJU, 193, 195, 202, 219; relationship with Pakistani state, 11, 152–3, 159, 161–3, 170–3, 206, 228, 242–3; relationship with TTP, 126, 146–8, 205, 222–3, 233; role in Indian embassy bombing (2008), 152; smuggling activity of, 145; support provided to Taliban, 107–8, 131, 135–6, 148; supporters of, 33; territorial presence of, 5, 12, 117, 119–20, 129–30, 137, 140, 145, 164, 169, 189, 203, 219, 225; *The Voice of Global Jihad*, 92; ties to Dar al-'Ulum Haqqaniyya, 131; Zhawara facility, 5–6, 8, 66–70, 72–5, 79–80, 85, 91, 95, 99–100, 106, 109, 113–14, 116, 179, 211

Harakat-i Inqilab-i Islami: 40–1, 52, 101; members of, 51

Harakat ul-Ansar (HUA): 110; formation of, 109; training camps operated by, 109, 154, 173

Harakat-ul Jihad al-Islami (HuJI): 94, 109–10; branches of, 70; Gujrat City conference (1988), 92

Harkat-ul Jihad al-Islami al'Alami (HuJI): members of, 70

Harkat ul-Mujahidin (HuM): 94, 109–10, 154; members of, 70

Harrach, Bekkay (Al Hafidh Abu Talha al Almani): 216; death of (2011), 192, 209–10, 216, 230

Hazaras: 137

Hekmatyar, Gulbuddin: 14, 37, 44, 48, 73, 84, 86, 88–9, 96, 102–3, 109, 142, 213, 236; leader of HIG, 50, 52–3, 70; supporters of, 65, 84

Hinduism: 33, 240
Hizb-i Islami Afghanistan: collapse of, 50
Hizb-i Islami-Gulbuddin (HIG): 88, 102; arsenal of, 103; financial aid provided by ISI, 53; Jihadwal facility, 70; members of, 50, 52, 56, 70; offices of, 103
Hizb-i Islami-Khalis (HIK): 40–1, 52, 81, 86, 101, 137, 220; members of, 50, 85, 101, 104; funding of, 213
Hizb ul-Mujahidin: associates of, 69
ul-Haq, General Zia: 6, 53–4, 56–7; alliance with JI, 69; background of, 53; coup d'état led by (1977), 53; Zakat Ordinance (1980), 54–5
al-Hussami, Hussein (Ghazwan al-Yemeni): 205
Hussein, Saddam: 88

improvised explosive device (IEDs): use in Iraq, 12
India: 1, 9, 24, 29, 42, 151; British Raj, 23; Congress Party, 30; conflict with Pakistan, 3, 163; military of, 138; Mumbai attacks (2008), 232, 240; Partition (1947), 30–1; political influence in Afghanistan, 156–7; presence in Kashmir, 154, 158, 173, 240; support for Northern Alliance, 10
Indonesia: 28, 183
International Security Assistance Force (ISAF): bombing of headquarters of (2011), 158; presence in Afghanistan, 135
Iqbal, Maulana: death of (2008), 140
Iraq: Baghdad, 88; military of, 88; use of IEDs in, 12
al-'Iraqi, Abu 'Ubayda: 66, 72, 74, 76
Iran: 11, 43, 177
Iraq: Operation Iraqi Freedom (2003–11), 124
Islam: 33, 184; Hajj, 211; political use of, 7; Qur'an, 26, 52, 104; Ramadan, 54; Shi'a, 11, 110, 143; Sunni, 11, 24, 38, 41, 49
Islamic Jihad Union (IJU): 18, 187, 194, 196, 200, 203, 206–7, 209, 232, 240; attack on medical convoy in Swat (2007), 226; *Badr al-Tawheed*, 197, 202, 226, 230; members of, 10, 189, 210, 226, 228–30; relationship with Haqqani network, 193, 195, 202, 219
Islamic Movement of Uzbekistan (IMU): 191–2, 209, 230, 240; formation of (1998), 97; media created by, 199
Islamism: 4, 17, 37–42, 44, 48, 50, 178, 236; Deobandi, 13, 30; militant, 8, 28, 82, 84, 87, 235; Pashtun, 38, 56; radical, 57; revolutionary, 90; Sunni, 38, 41, 49
al-Ittihad al-Islami: training of, 99
Ittihad Party: financial aid provided by ISI, 53; formation of (1980), 51

Jabbar, Abdul: associates of, 232
Jaish-e-Mohammad: 125–6; attempted assassination of Pervez Musharraf (2003), 226

Jaji: 29
Jalil, Mullah: 116
Jalolov, Najmiddin: leader of IJU, 229
Jamiat-i Islami (JI): 38, 41, 53, 109; founding of (1941), 37; ideology of, 37; madrassas network of, 70; members of, 37–8, 53, 103; political alliances of, 69–70
Jamiat-i Islami Afghanistan (JIA): financial aid provided by ISI, 53; formation of (1972), 38; members of, 50
Jamiat Ulema-e-Hind: branches of, 30
Jamiat Ulema-e-Islam (JUI): 30, 38, 91; factions of, 38, 178; madrassa run by, 54; member of MRD, 53; members of, 38–40, 42, 93, 154
Jamiat Ulema-e-Sarhad (JUS): branch of Jamiat Ulema-e-Hind, 30
Jan, Mawlawi Bakhta: 142; role in creation of SIM (2009), 160
al-Jaza'iri, Abu Binan: death of (1991), 80
jihadism: 8, 132, 198; global, 7–8, 12, 88, 120, 207, 236; national, 82; revolutionary, 98; Salafi, 13
Julaydan, Wa'il (Abu'l-Hasan al-Madani): director of Saudi Red Crescent, 72

Karzai, Hamid: 123, 161, 176; administration of, 124, 152, 160; attempted assassination of, 135; exile of, 102; President of Afghanistan, 135, 162, 209
Kashmir: 31, 33, 41, 60, 83, 94, 112, 156, 237, 239; Indian military presence in, 154, 158, 173, 240; Line of Control, 170; use of proxy groups in, 158
Kashmiri, Ilyas: role in attempted assassination of Pervez Musharraf (2003), 226
Kenya: Nairobi 100; US embassy bombing (1998), 100, 109, 113, 115, 118
Khalil, Maulana Fazlur Rahman: 70, 154
Khalis, Yunis: 40, 50, 57, 78, 91, 104, 108, 213; background of, 39; founder of HIK, 40
Khan, Abdul Ghaffar: leader of Khudai Khidmatgar, 32
Khan, Babrak: family of, 56
Khan, Ghazi: family of, 29, 147
Khan, Haji Mali: detained by Coalition forces (2011), 139; family of, 139
Khan, Isma'il: commander of JIA, 50
Khan, Khwaja Muhammad: family of, 28–9
Khan, Ma'afi: forces led by, 81
Khan, Mawlawi 'Aziz: 39, 63; writings of, 45
Khan, Mirza 'Ali: Faqir of Iqi, 31–2, 138; leader of Free Pashtunistan movement, 32
Khan, Muhammad Isma'il: family of, 29
Khan, Shamali: death of (1993), 87; Governor of Jalalabad, 87
al-Khorasani, Abu Dujanah: suicide bombing conducted by (2011), 140
Khost Rebellion (1924–5): 56; impact of, 29

Khrushchev, Nikita: visit to Kabul, 34
Khudai Khidmatgar: 33; members of, 32
Khugiani: 29
Khürsid, Hammad: arrest and conviction for plotting attack in Denmark (2008), 201–2, 230–1; background of, 230
Khyam, Omar: leader of Islamic Army of Great Britain, 232
Khyber, Mir Akbar: assassination of (1978), 49
Kuwait: Iraqi Invasion of (1990), 88
Kyrgyzstan: 240

Lakhvi, Zakiur Rahman: 154
Lashkar-e-Taiba (LeT): 154, 170; suicide bombers trained by, 157
Lenin, Vladimir: writings of, 40
al-Libi, Abu Faraj: role in attempted assassination of Pervez Musharraf (2003), 226
al-Libi, Abu Laith: 183, 201, 203; associates of, 229; death of (2008), 190, 194
al-Libi, Abu Yahya: 184, 191, 201, 232; death of (2012), 184; escape from prison (2005), 190, 200; media appearances of, 200, 203
Libyan Islamic Fighting Group: members of, 82
al-Logari, Abu Ibrahim (Mustafa Badi): 88; training camps established by, 80, 87

Makhdum, Hasan: death of (2003), 112
Malang, Mullah: 85; death of (2001), 102; member of HIK, 101
Mansur, Nasrullah: 49–50; family of, 112–13; members of Harakat-i Inqilab-i Islami, 51
Mansur, Saifurrahman: family of, 112–13
Marx, Karl: writings of, 40
Marxism: 40
al-Masri, Abd al-Rahman: 66, 74; death of (1988), 65
al-Masri, Abu Hafs: 72, 75, 98, 108, 237
al-Masri, Abu Ubaydah: 201; chief of external operations for al-Qa'ida, 230
al-Masri, Abu'l Walid (Mustafa Hamid): 72, 74, 77–8, 95–7, 103, 115, 196, 208; background of, 64–5; 'Five Letters to the Africa Corps' (1993–4), 99–100; influence of, 98
Massoud, Ahmad Shah: 37, 44, 84, 86, 89, 96; assault on Kabul (1996), 107; commander of JIA, 50; territory controlled by, 118
Maududi, Abu'l-'Ala: founder of JI, 37, 53; writings of, 37, 53
al-Mauritania, Yunis: 191, 231
Médecins Sans Frontières (MSF): personnel of, 108–9
Mehsud, Abdullah: death of (2007), 139
Mehsud, Baitullah: 139, 143, 147, 160, 231; leader of TTP, 108, 159; member of SIM, 160; support for Uzbek militants, 142; territorial influence of, 225
Mehsud, Hakimullah: commander

of TTP, 139, 204; media appearances of, 203
Mehsud, Qari Hussain: specialized training conducted by, 175, 217; training of suicide bombers, 146
Mehta, Brigadier Ravi Datt: death of (2008), 151
Mengal, Sardar Ataullah: 43
Moeller, Rear Admiral Robert: testimony to US Senate, 2
Movement for the Restoration of Democracy (MRD): members of, 53
Muhammad, Faiz: Afghan Minister of Frontier and Tribal Affairs, 51; Afghan Minister of Interior, 51; assassination of (1980), 52
Muhammad, Haji Din: 49, 78–9; deputy leader of HIK, 104
Muhammad, Khalid Shaykh: role in planning of 9/11 attacks, 98
Muhammad, Prophet: 27
Muhammadi, Muhammad Nabi: 39, 57; background of, 40; founder of Harakat-i Inqilab-i Islami, 40, 51
Mujahid, Zabihullah: spokesperson moniker for Taliban, 135, 193
Mujahidin Shura Council: members of, 193
Mujaddidi, Sibghatullah: 142
mujahidin: 12, 15, 30, 37, 40–1, 53, 61–2; financial aid and training provided to, 5, 59, 64, 68–9; members of, 14, 54, 59, 65, 67; supporters of, 7; *Voice of Afghanistan*, 67
Mullah-I Lang: leader of Khost Rebellion, 29
Mullen, Admiral Mike: chairman of US Joint Chiefs of Staff, 1, 158
Musharraf, Pervez: 159; attempted assassination of (2003), 226; President of Pakistan, 123; rise to power (1999), 111
Muslim Brotherhood: 7; *al-Mutjama*, 62; wings of, 37
Muslim Youth (Jawanan-i-Musulman): 39–40; formation of (1969), 36; members of, 48–9

bin al-Nahyan, Sheikh Zayed: Emirati Prime Minister, 111
Najibullah, Muhammad: 84, 221; President of Afghanistan, 71; removed from power (1992), 82, 89
Najmuddin, Mullah: 24
Nasrullah, Mullah: 168
National Awami Party (NAP): coalition with JUI parties, 43
National Commanders Shura (NCS): 86, 93; capture of Gardez (1991), 86; creation of (1990), 85; members of, 101; Rawalpindi meeting (1990), 94
National Directorate of Security: 158
National Islamic Revolutionary Council: formation of (1980), 56
nationalism: 105; Baluch, 43; ethno-, 43; Pashtun, 43, 57
Nazir, Mullah: 141–3, 229; member of SIM, 160
Niazi, Ghulam Muhammad: background of, 37

Nickelsberg, Bob: 15
Nixon, Richard: administration of, 44; foreign policy of, 44–5
Noor, Sadiq: 225; alleged role in preparations of car bombs, 146
Northern Alliance: 133, 181; members of, 10, 107; supporters of, 10
North Atlantic Treaty Organization (NATO): 145, 235; military forces of, 192; presence in Afghanistan, 16–17, 135, 137, 156–8, 240
North Waziristan Peace Accord (Miranshah Peace Accord) (2006): 160, 182; signatories of, 159, 164

Obama, Barack: 161; announcement of US troop surge in Afghanistan (2009), 160
Omar, Mullah Muhammad: 105–6, 111, 114, 116, 118, 125, 136–7, 155, 160–1, 170, 195; attempted assassination of (1999), 116; background of, 101; leader of Taliban, 101; pardoning of Abu Mubtassim, 212

Pakistan: 15, 21–3, 32, 34, 39, 44, 48, 52, 68, 76, 84, 94, 109, 119, 121–2, 124, 141, 147–8, 169, 177–8, 182, 195, 199, 207–9, 233, 236, 241–2; Abbottabad, 192; Bajaur, 22; borders of, 5, 69, 74, 81, 125, 131, 146, 148, 160, 225, 239; conflict with India, 3, 163; Durand Line, 4, 22, 30, 32–3, 122, 129–30, 138, 154, 170, 222, 239; Federally Administered Tribal Areas (FATA), 22, 125–6, 130, 148–9, 152, 163, 182, 204, 222, 225; Frontier Corps, 44, 46, 170–1, 175; government of, 34, 41, 44, 109, 131, 142, 154–5, 162, 226, 228; Gujrat City, 92; Independence of (1947), 30–1; Inter-Services Intelligence Directorate (ISI), 1, 5–6, 14, 44, 51–5, 67–9, 71–2, 84, 94, 102–3, 105, 109–10, 121, 123, 126, 136, 153, 155–6, 158, 161–4, 167–8, 170–5, 178, 180–2, 207, 210–11, 214, 223, 225; Islamabad, 10, 23, 41, 68, 113, 122, 125–6, 130, 142, 147–8, 151–3, 160–1, 163, 224–5, 228, 240, 242; Karachi, 93, 154, 164, 227; Khyber Pakhtunkhwa Province (KPP)/North-Western Frontier Province (NWFP), 32–4, 43, 55, 125, 163, 214; Lahore, 153; madrassas in, 54–5, 131–2; military of, 5, 9, 12, 14, 42, 57, 68–9, 113, 147, 153, 166, 170, 176, 180, 222, 226; National Assembly, 38; North Waziristan, 2–3, 5–6, 8–9, 12, 27, 30–1, 39, 45–6, 57, 67, 97, 104, 113–14, 121, 126, 129–30, 138–40, 143–4, 148–9, 152, 163–7, 169, 174–5, 179–80, 182, 184–6, 190, 193, 197, 200, 202–7, 209–10, 216–17, 220, 228–32, 242; Peshawar, 4, 11, 30, 35, 38, 46–7, 51, 56, 59–61, 65–7, 73, 77, 80, 85, 89, 92–3, 95, 97, 146, 153, 159, 164, 168, 196, 207, 232; Punjab Province, 43, 146, 163, 176, 240–1; Quetta, 56, 102;

Rawalpindi, 84, 94, 130; relationship with Haqqani network, 11, 152–3, 159, 161–3, 170–2, 206, 228, 242–3; Sindh, 43; South Waziristan, 22, 80, 97, 113, 130, 138–9, 142, 160, 174–5, 217, 224
Pakistan Peoples Party (PPP): electoral performance of, 42–3; ideology of, 41
Pashtun: 17, 26–8, 46, 48, 50, 55–6, 86–7, 118, 192; Durrani, 26; Ghilzai, 26; Ghurghusht, 26; insurgency movements, 21; Islamism, 38, 56; *nang*, 22, 24–5; nationalism, 43, 57; *qalang*, 22, 25; territory inhabited by, 22–5, 31–3, 35–6, 55, 108
Pathan, Merajuddin: Governor of Khost, 2
People's Democratic Party of Afghanistan (PDPA): formation of (1965), 36, 38; Khalq faction, 36; members of, 50; Parcham faction, 36
purdah: concept of, 29; opposition to, 35

al-Qadir, Haji 'Abd: 86
al-Qahtani, Abu Dujanah: death of, 192; family of, 192
al-Qahtani, Abu Nasir: 191, 201; escape from prison (2005), 190, 200; family of, 192; imprisonment of, 183, 190; media appearances of, 200–1
al-Qa'ida: 2, 9–10, 15, 17–18, 71, 81–2, 92, 97, 101, 123, 166, 174, 181–2, 189–91, 199, 210–11, 218, 220–1, 230, 235–6, 240–3; alliance with Haqqani network, 11–12, 75, 113, 115, 121–2, 126, 178–9, 182, 185, 195, 204–5, 211–12, 214, 218, 222, 226, 228–9, 233, 237–8; assault on FOB Salerno (2008), 232; ideology of, 84, 116, 119, 125, 186, 224, 226, 228, 233; influence of Battle of Ramadan (1987) on, 76; members of, 11, 15, 64, 66, 73, 80–1, 87, 90–1, 95, 97, 100, 103, 113, 121, 149, 164–5, 183–4, 186–9, 191–2, 201–3, 206–7, 209, 216, 223, 225, 227–31, 237, 241; military committee of, 65; origins of, 79; tactics of, 11–12, 89, 98; presence in Sudan, 87, 95, 99; al-Sahab, 188, 190, 197, 202–3; supporters of, 214, 224; training camps of, 6, 8, 13, 64, 79–80, 84, 91, 97, 100, 103, 106, 109–10, 113–14, 118, 192, 197, 211; US embassy bombings (1998), 100, 109, 113, 115, 118; *Vanguards of Khorasan*, 198
al-Qa'ida in Iraq (AQI): 216; members of, 193
Qais: descendents of, 27
al-Qandahari, Abu Ja'far (Ayman Sabri Faraj): memoirs of, 75
Qatar: 124
al-Qurashi, Shirin Jamal: 87
Qutb, Sayyid: influence of, 39

Rabbani, Burhanuddin: 37, 44, 89; founder of JIA, 50, 53
Rabbani, Mullah: 106
al-Rahman, Abd: 207
ur Rahman, Mawlana Fazl: head of JUI-F, 38, 93

Rauf, Rashid: 191, 231
al-Razzaq, Mullah 'Abd: Taliban Interior Minister, 119
Reagan, Ronald: 111
Rohde, David: 207; kidnapping of (2009), 185, 224–5
Russian Empire: 26
Ruttig, Thomas: 15–16

al-Sa'idi, Abu-Hasan: al-Qa'ida commander in Afghanistan, 192
Salih, Ahmad (Abu Suhayl): 176; background of, 90
Salim, Mamduh Mahmud (Abu Hajar al-'Iraqi): co-founder of al-Qa'ida, 73
Sangari, Hamza: 216
Saqqao, Bacha: 31
Saudi Arabia: 48, 63, 68, 84, 88, 214, 231; financial aid provided for mujahidin by, 59, 68–9; funding government of, 88; provided to Haqqani network, 5; Mecca, 42, 211; Riyadh, 212
Saudi Red Crescent: personnel of, 72
Sawr Revolution (1978): 50, 59–60
Sayyaf, 'Abd al-Rabb Rasul: 37, 53, 61, 236; supporters of, 65, 84
Second Anglo-Afghan War (1878–80): 26
Shah, Hanif: 39
Shah, King Nadir: reign of, 30
Shah, King Zahir: 35; accession of (1933), 36; family of, 33; reform policies of, 36–7
Shah, Pir Zubayr: 15
Shahid, Sayyid Ahmad: 38
Shahkoor, Hamza: role in Indian embassy bombing (2008), 151
Shahzad, Faisal: attempted bombing of Times Square (2010), 167
Sharif, Nawaz: administration of, 110; electoral defeat of (1993), 102; Pakistani Prime Minister, 95; visit to UAE (1999), 111
al-Sharqi, Abu 'Ata: training support provided by, 95
Shinwari: 29
Shukrijumah, Adnan: 241
Shura-e-Murakeba: establishment of, 143
Shura Ittihad-ul-Mujahidin (SIM): 161; establishment of (2009), 143, 160; members of, 160
Siddiqi, Ahmed: capture of (2012), 232
Sikhism: 33, 38
al-Somali, Saleh: 191
Somalia: 89, 95, 99; Battle of Mogadishu (1993), 99–100; Mogadishu, 98
Soviet Union (USSR): 26, 35, 181; collapse of (1991), 91; Communist Party of Soviet Union (CPSU), 50, 71; Invasion of Afghanistan (1979–89), 4–7, 13, 17, 21, 31, 40, 53, 56, 59–61, 63–4, 67–8, 70–1, 76, 78, 83, 90, 96, 139, 153–4, 171–2, 176–7, 192, 196, 239; military of, 67; Moscow, 4, 33, 71
Stalin, Josef: writings of, 40
Sudan: Khartoum, 89; presence of al-Qa'ida in, 87, 95, 99
Sufism: 24, 26; *murids*, 25; *pirs*, 25
al-Suri, Abu Musab: 108, 113, 196, 216, 227; capture of (2004), 155

Tablighi Jama'at: 7

Tajikistan: 94, 240; borders of, 96; Civil War (1992–7), 80; Nahda Party, 95
Tajiks: 30, 50, 85, 105; territory inhabited by, 52
Taliban: 8, 17, 30, 83–4, 86, 102, 105, 110–11, 114, 119, 123, 125, 132–4, 154, 170–1, 192, 194, 197, 220; factions of, 116, 129–30; fall of (2001), 120, 156, 190, 208; ideology of, 13, 101, 105; insurgency activity of, 124, 136, 155, 175; land appropriation, 117–18; members of, 9, 31, 40, 101, 116–17, 119, 135–6, 138, 140, 156, 162, 167, 175–7, 190, 200, 203, 216–17, 222, 229, 242; Quetta Shura, 131, 135, 141, 160, 162, 176, 186–7, 196; Rahbari Shura, 137; relationship with ISI, 168, 172–3, 180; relationship with Osama Bin Laden, 107–8, 114, 116, 118; rise of (1994), 23–4, 57, 101–2; supporters of, 104, 131; territory controlled by, 102–3, 106–7, 118–19, 155, 165; use of Haqqani network support, 107–8, 135–6, 148
Taniwal, Hakim: Governor of Paktia, 216
Tanzania: Dar es Salaam, 100; US embassy bombing (1998), 100, 109, 113, 115, 118
Taraki, Nur Muhammad: 59, 63; President of Democratic Republic of Afghanistan, 50
Tayeb, Abu (Najibullah Naeem): kidnapping activities of, 138
Tehrik-e Taliban Pakistan (TTP): 9, 11, 126, 143, 147, 165, 167, 174–5, 206–7, 220–1, 240; ideology of, 224; Mehsud faction of, 130; members of, 108, 139–41, 146, 148–9, 159–60, 164, 191, 204, 225; relationship with Haqqani network, 126, 146–8, 205, 222–3, 233; sponsoring of suicide bombing activity, 139–40; suicide bombing of FOB Chapman (2009), 204, 222; supporters of, 224
Third Anglo-Afghan War (1919): 30
Tomsen, Peter: 44
Tufail, Mian Muhammad: leader of JI, 61
al-Turabi, Hassan: 90
Turangzai, Haji Sahib: 24
Turkestan Islamic Movement (ETIM): collapse of (1993), 112; reconstituted as TIP, 111, 207
Turkistan Islamic Party (TIP): 10, 112; formerly ETIM, 111, 207; media created by, 199; members of, 112, 210
al-Turkistani, 'Abd al-Haqq: 112; leader of TIP, 210

United Arab Emirates (UAE): 63, 81, 145, 211; Al-Ain, 212; Abu Dhabi, 62, 64, 111, 212; Bada Zayed, 212; Dubai, 196, 212; Al-Sharqa, 212
United Kingdom (UK): 232; London, 89; military of, 176; Parliament, 32
United Nations (UN): 89, 216–17; members of, 32
United States of America (USA): 11–12, 18, 28, 34–5, 44, 68, 71,

83–4, 91, 94, 106, 116, 122, 125, 149, 161, 166, 170–1, 176, 182, 184, 207, 218, 233, 238, 241–2; 9/11 attacks, 4, 17–18, 73, 79, 97–8, 102, 111, 113–14, 116–17, 120–1, 131, 170, 173, 179, 181, 184, 186, 200, 220, 228, 235, 237–9, 241; Central Intelligence Agency (CIA), 5–6, 51, 59, 68–9, 85, 92, 104, 140, 168, 204; Defense Intelligence Agency, 68; Department of Defense, 14; financial aid provided for mujahidin by, 59; former direct support for Haqqani network, 4–6, 104; government of, 178, 214; military of, 12, 16–17, 124, 152, 158, 160–1, 165, 176, 183–5, 241; Senate, 1–2; State Department, 84, 108–9; Treasury Department, 214; Washington DC, 1
al-Urduni, Abu'l-Harith: military forces led by, 82
al-Utaybi, Abu Sulayman: death of, 192; member of AQI, 193; sharia official for Mujahidin Shura Council, 193
Uthmanzai Wazir: 31
Uzbeks: 95, 97, 142, 190
Uzbekistan: 94, 97, 240; government of, 3

Vinas, Bryant Neal: 223; associates of, 202; background of, 231–2

War On Terror: 21
Waziri: 28, 146
Wikileaks: diplomatic cables leaked by, 15, 27
Wilson, Charlie: 68
World Islamic Front for Jihad Against Jews and Crusaders: formation of (1997), 70, 197; members of, 114, 197
Wyne, Khalil: background of, 226

al-Yazid, Mustafa Abu: 189–90, 197, 209, 231; al-Qa'ida commander in Afghanistan, 191; death of, 192
Yemen: 89, 99, 205, 239
Yousaf, Brigadier Muhammad: 177; *Bear Trap*, 175; forces led by, 72
Yuldashev, Tahir: 96–7

Zadran, Badshah Khan: 123–4
Zadrans: 27, 29, 108; prominent families of, 55–6; Sultankhel clan, 28; Uprising (1933), 30
Zaeef, Abdul Salam: memoirs of, 162
Zardari, Asif Ali: 161; President of Pakistan, 227; targeting of, 226–7
al-Zarqawi, Abu Mus'ab: 216
al-Zawahiri, Ayman: 184, 195, 204, 241; family of, 208